# Britain at the Polls 2010

# Britain at the Polls 2010

Nicholas Allen and John Bartle

Los Angeles | London | New Delhi
Singapore | Washington DC

SAGE Publications Ltd
1 Oliver's Yard
55 City Road
London EC1Y 1SP

SAGE Publications Inc.
2455 Teller Road
Thousand Oaks, California 91320

SAGE Publications India Pvt Ltd
B 1/I 1 Mohan Cooperative Industrial Area
Mathura Road
New Delhi 110 044

SAGE Publications Asia-Pacific Pte Ltd
33 Pekin Street #02-01
Far East Square
Singapore 048763

**Library of Congress Control Number available**

**British Library Cataloguing in Publication data**

A catalogue record for this book is available from
the British Library

ISBN 978-1-84920-845-1
ISBN 978-1-84920-846-8 (pbk)

Typeset by C&M Digitals (P) Ltd, Chennai, India
Printed by CPI Antony Rowe, Chippenham, Wiltshire
Printed on paper from sustainable resources

MIX
Paper from
responsible sources
FSC
www.fsc.org   FSC® C013604

# CONTENTS

# FIGURES AND TABLES

# CONTRIBUTORS

**Nicholas Allen** is Lecturer in Politics at Royal Holloway, University of London.

**Tim Bale** is Professor of Politics at the University of Sussex.

**Judith Bara** is Senior Lecturer in Politics at Queen Mary, University of London.

**John Bartle** is Senior Lecturer in Government at the University of Essex.

**Ben Clements** is Lecturer in Politics at the University of Leicester.

**Sebastian Dellepiane Avellaneda** is a Research Fellow at University College Dublin.

**Oliver Heath** is Senior Lecturer in Politics at Royal Holloway, University of London.

**Sukhdev Johal** is Reader in Strategy and Business Analysis at Royal Holloway, University of London.

**Ron Johnston** is Professor of Geography at the University of Bristol.

**Michael Moran** is W.J.M. MacKenzie Professor of Government at the University of Manchester.

**Philip Norton** is Professor of Government and Director of the Centre for Legislative Studies at the University of Hull. He sits in the House of Lords as Lord Norton of Louth.

**Charles Pattie** is Professor of Geography at the University of Sheffield.

**Thomas Quinn** is Lecturer in Government at the University of Essex.

**James A. Stimson** is Raymond Dawson Professor of Political Science at the University of North Carolina at Chapel Hill.

**Paul Webb** is Professor of Politics at the University of Sussex.

**Karel Williams** is Professor of Accounting and Political Economy and Director of the Centre for Research on Socio Cultural Change (CRESC) at the University of Manchester.

# FOREWORD

With masterful understatement, John Bartle, Sebastian Dellepiane Avellaneda and James A. Stimson include in the opening sentence of their chapter in this tome entitled 'The Policy Mood and the Moving Centre', the words: 'the 2010 general election was one of the most eventful and dramatic in British electoral history'. While there is much in this collection of essays that will (and indeed should) be a matter of debate and perhaps disagreement, that particular sentiment will surely not be disputed. Having been a candidate at every general election from 1987 onwards I can testify to its truth (and not merely because of the distinct peculiarities that arise from fighting a seat as 'The Speaker Seeking Re-Election').

This book is about the extraordinary story of this election and the no less striking saga of its epilogue. It is in many ways the most valuable of the wonderful Britain at the Polls series precisely because this was not a parliament, an election campaign or a set of results which can be dismissed as wholly predictable. There is an urgent need to discern not merely what happened on polling day but why it happened. A contest such as this one, though, is capable of multiple interpretations. The authority of this volume, nonetheless, means that it is destined to be the starting point for any serious discussion about British politics between 2005 and 2010 as well as what clues might be divined for the coming decade in politics.

The period examined here has a legitimate claim to be truly exceptional. A parliament which witnessed all three of the main parties changing their leaders (twice in the case of the Liberal Democrats) would be an unusual one. A society which experienced the sharpest economic downturn in seven decades would be worthy of close inspection. An election which saw the introduction of televised debates between the party leaders would surely be a matter of immense interest. For all three of these utterly seismic events to occur in the same timeframe is absolutely astonishing. There will not be many general elections over which historians a century hence choose to run the microscope but that of 2010 will achieve immortality.

All of this is lovingly covered in these pages. The main actors, a Labour party in transition from Tony Blair to Gordon Brown, a Conservative party destined to be recast by David Cameron and a Liberal Democrat party which in many senses endured the wildest rollercoaster ride of them all between 2005 and 2010, are examined in forensic detail. The principal external political shocks of the period – notably those covered in chapters on 'The Financial Crisis and its Consequences' and 'The Great Divide: Voters, Parties, MPs and Expenses' – are awarded their proper prominence. The analysis of the campaign itself (and those debates), the local contests and the outcome as well as the evolving policy mood of the electorate is fascinating. To cap it all, Lord Norton brings his insight to the ultimate result of the campaign, the first formal peacetime coalition since the 1930s, indeed the first official partnership of its kind since, arguably, that of the Conservative party and the Liberal Unionists in the last decade of the nineteenth century. This book is thus an intellectual feast for anyone with the slightest enthusiasm for the operation of British politics.

As a political practitioner, and as Speaker of the House of Commons, there are three aspects of what you are about to read that I would like to highlight.

The first, unavoidably, involves the debates. They are here to stay. Whether they will be as dominant a factor in future elections as this one as they become a more familiar aspect of the hustings is debatable but the notion that they might disappear is implausible. Many outsider observers, particularly from the United States, thought that they were a rather impressive exercise in civilised political cut-and-thrust by international standards, and I sympathise with that evaluation. They certainly showed that it is possible to have a lively partisan exchange without baying background noise from the crowd, an observation which I hope, as I said in a speech shortly after the new parliament assembled, is not lost on the House of Commons particularly when it comes on Wednesdays to questions to the prime minister.

The second element involves the local constituency campaigns. These manifestly mattered. It was not just the case that there was a national swing dictated by national themes which played itself out across the country. Results varied wildly often within areas and regions as well as across them. The calibre of those who wore the rosettes and who ran those campaigns was clearly important to the outcome. So too were the resources which could be mobilised by the contenders, but this is a complicated story and not merely the case of 'he who spends the most, wins the most' (mercifully so in my own example as I suspect I was outspent by both of my principal opponents in Buckingham!). We are some distance from former Speaker of the House of Representatives Tip O'Neill's dictum that 'all politics is local'. Yet on the other hand, the lazy assumption in Britain that 'all politics is national' is no longer a valid claim either.

Finally, there is the vexed matter of the scandal relating to MPs and expenses. This was a shameful episode and one which I devoted most of my first year as Speaker seeking to put an end to. It was undoubtedly a catalyst for the record level of retirements from the House in 2010. It explained some defeats for those whose indiscretions had created vast, hostile publicity, whose performance might otherwise be inexplicable. It was undoubtedly part of the DNA of the entire campaign. The expenses debacle did not, though, prevent incumbent MPs with a solid record of service from achieving a better result at the ballot box than might have been expected otherwise. To the extent that this demonstrates that parliament matters and being a good parliamentarian matters then it is a welcome development.

It is a pleasure to be associated with this book and series not least because of its connections to the University of Essex where I had such an enjoyable and stimulating time as a student. I am sure that those who read the words will have a similarly enjoyable and stimulating experience.

John Bercow MP
Speaker of the House of Commons.

# PREFACE

The 2010 general election was one of the most remarkable in recent history. Taking place against the backdrop of enormous economic and political turbulence, it offered, for the first time since 1997, when New Labour ousted the Conservatives, the real possibility of a change in government. As polling day approached, Gordon Brown's Labour party was generally expected to lose its parliamentary majority, and David Cameron's Conservatives were generally expected to make large gains. But beyond these vague expectations, there were mountains of doubt and uncertainty. A small number of optimistic Conservative supporters expected the party to win outright, but almost everyone else anticipated a hung parliament with no party winning an absolute majority of MPs. Such possibilities fuelled the uncertainty. If the Conservatives did sufficiently well, Cameron might try to form a minority government. Otherwise, Nick Clegg's Liberal Democrats might end up holding the balance of power, and Clegg would then have to choose between forming a coalition with Labour or the Conservatives. Labour was assumed to be the Liberal Democrats' obvious ideological bedfellow; but everything would depend on the results and the post-election parliamentary arithmetic.

The 2010 campaign began with the Conservatives enjoying a healthy lead over Labour and the prospect of the Tories consolidating their advantage. Then came the televised prime ministerial debates, the first such debates in British electoral history. To general amazement – and to the two major parties' consternation – the star of the first debate was Nick Clegg. His performance generated a terrific boost in support for the Liberal Democrats and turned the election on its head. Thereafter, the 2010 campaign appeared to become a genuine three-way contest, with the Liberal Democrats sometimes leapfrogging Labour into second place in the polls and very occasionally moving into first place. In the circumstances, there was general astonishment when the exit polls suggested that the Liberal Democrats would improve on their 2005 performance by just one point and actually lose around six seats.

The exit polls, however, proved correct, and Liberal Democrat hopes of progress were dashed. More importantly, the exit polls accurately predicted that the Conservatives would become the largest single party but fall short of a majority. For the first time since February 1974, a general election thus resulted in a hung parliament. Whatever the politicians had said before polling day, it was now up to them, not the voters, to thrash out a deal and decide who would govern. After five days of bargaining, first between the Conservatives and the Liberal Democrats and then, briefly, between Labour and the Liberal Democrats, the logic of numbers prevailed. The Liberal Democrats took five cabinet posts in a Conservative-dominated coalition. David Cameron became the new prime minister, Nick Clegg became the deputy prime minister. Almost immediately, the coalition set about reducing the burgeoning government deficit and making plans for significant political reforms.

This book tells the story of this remarkable and landmark election. *Britain at the Polls 2010* is the ninth book in a series that has described and analysed every election since February 1974 with the exception of the 1987 election. As with previous volumes, this book's principal aim is to provide general readers, students of British politics and professional political scientists, in North America and Europe as well as in the United Kingdom, with an analysis of the major social, economic and political developments during the 2005–10 period, and with an assessment of the impact of these developments on the election outcome.

General elections are not just stories in their own right, of course. They are also chapters in the unfolding story of British democracy. *Britain at the Polls 2010*, like previous volumes, therefore aims to provide readers with informed reflections on the election's long-term significance. Other books can be expected to provide a blow-by-blow account of the formal campaign, including: *The British General Election of 2010*, written by Dennis Kavanagh and Philip Cowley; *Britain Votes 2010*, edited by Andrew Geddes and Jonathan Tonge; and *Political Communications: The British General Election Campaign of 2010*, edited by Dominic Wring, Roger Mortimore and Simon Atkinson. As usual, *The Times Guide to the House of Commons* provides a definitive work of reference for the actual results, and the British Election Study, currently based at the University of Essex, will provide a detailed survey-based account of voting behaviour.

As with previous volumes in the series, *Britain at the Polls 2010* contains chapters on the chief protagonists and the actual result. Nicholas Allen in Chapter 1 provides a detailed overview of the major developments in British politics since 2005, with a particular focus on the trials and tribulations of the Labour government and its two prime ministers, Tony Blair and Gordon Brown. In Chapter 2, Tim Bale and Paul Webb examine the Conservatives' response to their third successive defeat in 2005 and analyse how David Cameron made his party electable. In Chapter 3, Thomas Quinn and Ben Clements analyse the fortunes of the Liberal Democrats, explaining why the party managed to get through three-and-a-half leaders after the 2005 election and why Nick Clegg was able to bring his party into a coalition with the Conservatives. And in Chapter 8, Ron Johnston and Charles Pattie explain why the Conservatives won the most seats in the new House of Commons but not an overall majority, with a particular emphasis on the impact of local campaigning and the workings of Britain's first-past-the-post voting system.

Other chapters cover distinctive features of the 2010 election and relevant long-term developments in British politics. In Chapter 4, Michael Moran, Sukhdev Johal and Karel Williams analyse the impact of the financial crisis on both the election and the structure of Britain's economy, the dominant issue in 2010. In Chapter 5, Oliver Heath examines the gulf between ordinary voters and the political class and how the 2009 parliamentary expenses scandal made this gulf a central concern at the election. In Chapter 6, John Bartle, Sebastian Dellepiane Avellaneda and James Stimson describe long-term changes in the British public's policy mood and the significance of popular preferences surrounding the size of government and its implications for the new coalition's deficit reduction plan. In Chapter 7, Nicholas Allen, Judith Bara and John Bartle describe how British politics finally came to embrace televised election debates and analyse the debates' impact on the campaign and outcome. In Chapter 9, Philip Norton charts the formation of Britain's first post-war coalition government and surveys the wider post-election landscape.

As editors, we would like to acknowledge and thank the support of several people in connection with this volume. John Bercow kindly gave his time and read through the manuscript before penning his foreword. David Mainwaring at Sage enthusiastically supported us throughout the production of this book. Graham Keilloh of Ipsos MORI, Caroline Lawes of Comres and Anthony Wells of YouGov all contributed their time and knowledge at a specially convened workshop in London, where many of the authors met and discussed their ideas. We are especially grateful to the Faculty of History and Social Sciences, Royal Holloway, University of London, for providing the funds to make that workshop possible. Finally, several colleagues read through draft chapters and provided helpful feedback. Some have preferred to remain anonymous, but we would like to single out Anthony King, Katja Mirwaldt, Thomas Quinn, Warren Ward and Steffen Weiss, who commented on our own chapters. Those familiar with the Britain at the Polls series will be aware that this is the first book not to contain a chapter by Tony King. As editor of the series since 1992, Tony set an exacting standard in scholarship and style. Although he was not formally involved in this volume, his example, advice and guidance were invaluable.

Nicholas Allen,
Royal Holloway, University of London
John Bartle,
University of Essex

# 1 LABOUR'S THIRD TERM: A TALE OF TWO PRIME MINISTERS

Nicholas Allen

In the early hours of Friday 6 May 2005, Tony Blair's Labour party won its third successive general election and another term in office. Blair was now indisputably his party's most successful election winner.[1] His modernisation of Labour's programme and organisation, encapsulated in the name 'New Labour', had delivered 43.2 per cent of the vote and a landslide win in 1997, and 40.7 per cent of the vote and another landslide in 2001. Now Blair and Labour had scored a hat trick. Yet, the win in 2005 was far from convincing. Labour's share of the vote dropped sharply to just 35.2 per cent, a consequence of mounting dissatisfaction with the government's record and with Blair's personal conduct and opposition to the Iraq war. A weak Conservative opposition and the vagaries of the 'first-past-the-post' electoral system still ensured a handsome parliamentary majority but Labour's win was only superficially impressive.

Labour had never won more than two consecutive elections, and historical precedents from earlier third-term governments offered little guidance about what to expect. Harold Macmillan's 1959 Conservative government faced economic difficulties and scandal and went on to lose in 1964. Margaret Thatcher's 1987 Conservative government faced economic difficulties and internal divisions but went on to win again in 1992. History would, however, be a certain guide to Labour's third-term prospects in one respect: neither Macmillan nor Thatcher had survived as prime minister to fight the next election, and nor would Blair.[2] Blair had already announced that he would not fight another election so as to placate Gordon Brown, his hugely respected chancellor of the exchequer. Virtually no one thought that Blair would last for very long after 2005, and virtually everyone expected Brown to succeed him. The only real doubt was over whether Brown would subsequently call a snap election to secure a personal mandate, whether he would bide his time, or whether he would hold out until the last possible moment permitted by law. After all, a change in prime minister would not automatically trigger an immediate election. Britain is a parliamentary system, and prime ministers are customarily the leader of the majority party in the House of Commons. When a prime minister steps down or is forced out in between elections, it is a matter for the party, not the voters, to choose a new leader and head of government.[3]

In 1997, Labour's campaign song had been called 'Things can only get better'. That title summed up the party's grounds for optimism in 2005. Memories of Iraq would fade, Blair would soon be gone. There was every reason to suppose that Labour under Brown might win a fourth term. But things did not get better. The economy deteriorated and the public turned against a government that seemed accident prone, directionless and haunted by earlier policy decisions. This chapter examines what went wrong during Labour's third term and how things got worse.[4]

## Change at the top

To the outside world Tony Blair appeared to dominate the Labour party after becoming its leader in 1994. He persuaded the party to change Clause IV of its constitution and end its commitment to public ownership, and he engendered a previously unknown sense of discipline and unity in the party. But there was always one impediment to Blair's dominance: Gordon Brown. Blair and Brown had both entered parliament in 1983, an election famous for Labour's lurch to the left and for being a contest in which Labour came close to coming third. This formative experience fostered in both men a shared determination to anchor the party firmly in the centre of British politics. In this enterprise they seemed closer than brothers. When John Smith, the then Labour leader, died in 1994, Blair and Brown reputedly made a pact: Brown would not contest the leadership and Blair, in return, would make way for Brown at some point in the future.[5] In the meantime, Brown as shadow chancellor was granted unprecedented autonomy to shape the party's economic policies and great swathes of its domestic policies. Between them, the two men drove forward New Labour's electoral strategy.

After the 1997 election, Blair and Brown worked together in an almost semi-presidential arrangement. Blair was like a French Fifth Republic president, Brown, ensconced in the Treasury, a Fifth Republic prime minister. Initially the relationship appeared to work well. During Labour's second term, however, it deteriorated markedly.[6] It began to resemble the French dual-executive during periods of cohabitation, but with Abel in the Élysée Palace and Cain in the Hôtel Matignon. It was no secret that Brown wanted Blair's job, nor was it a secret that Brown believed Blair had broken his promise to step aside.[7] Moreover, Brown's frustrated ambitions fuelled an intense and increasingly public feud that extended into the wider party. In the 1950s, Labour had been split between supporters of Aneurin Bevan on the left and supporters of Hugh Gaitskell on the right. In the 2000s, it was divided between loyal Blairites and die-hard Brownites. With each clan working hard to undermine the other, British government at times resembled a cross between a soap opera and a turf war.[8]

The feuding was truly remarkable. It undermined the sense of unity at the top of government. It affected the conduct of government. It affected the way voters viewed the government. It weakened Blair's authority as leader and prime minister. And it ultimately led to both Blair's departure and Brown's accession.

## Blair's long goodbye

Tony Blair had announced his intention to serve 'a full third term' if Labour was re-elected, but not to seek a fourth term, as far back as September 2004.[9] He had apparently calculated that his announcement would end speculation about his long-term plans and forestall any plot to remove him by an increasingly agitated Gordon Brown and his supporters. Making such an announcement was always risky, however. A prime minister's power depends, to some extent, upon others' judgements about his future prospects. As Richard Neustadt stressed in his classic study of the American presidency, any chief executive's capacity to influence others is affected by their public prestige – others' evaluations of how the public judges them, including their electoral prospects – and by their professional reputation – others' evaluations of their skills, tenacity and ruthlessness.[10] A prime minister who is not expected to lead his party into the next election will almost inevitably see his authority reduced, just as any president who is re-elected for a second term soon tends to become a lame duck. Any prime minister who sets a limit on his own tenure is likely to limit his own authority. And any prime minister who is perceived to have made himself a lame duck also diminishes his professional reputation.[11] For these reasons, few prime ministers talk publicly about their retirement plans. Margaret Thatcher famously talked of going 'on and on' after winning the 1987 general election. Not so Blair. No prime minister in the modern age had announced a limit to his ambitions so far in advance.

Blair's undermining of his own future prospects would have limited his standing in any event. Yet, his authority was also ebbing because of Labour's performance in the 2005 election. Many held Blair responsible for the party's reduced majority, which fell from 166 to 65.[12] Many ardently believed that the party's majority would have been much larger if Labour had been led by Brown. Immediately after the election, *The Sunday Times* contacted 100 Labour MPs, at least thirty of whom wanted to Blair to step down 'sooner rather than later'.[13] With the number of such 'friends' behind him on the backbenches likely to grow, the odds were always against Blair serving a full third term.

Blair's diminishing influence over Labour MPs was evident in their opposition to a number of key government measures. In the wake of the July 2005 London bombings, when four radicalised Muslims murdered fifty-two people, Blair pushed hard for new powers to allow the police to hold and question terrorist suspects for up to ninety days without charge. However, the government lost a vote on this measure in the House of Commons when forty-nine Labour MPs rebelled, and Blair had to settle for a twenty-eight-day detention measure. It was the first occasion on which his government had been defeated. Twelve weeks later, the government suffered two further Commons defeats when a number of Labour MPs rebelled over the contro-versial Racial and Religious Hatred Bill, which sought to extend race-hate laws to cover religious beliefs.

Blair's loss of authority also told in his failure to cement his domestic legacy and carry through his 'choice agenda'. Education was singled out for reform in Labour's third term. A 2006 education White Paper promised to give parents more rights and to establish new 'trust schools' that would have greater autonomy from local authorities in managing their affairs.[14] This policy touched a raw Labour nerve. Many in the party feared that the proposals could lead to a two-tier system, in which only the rich would go to the best schools. Amidst mounting opposition among ministers and MPs, Blair's education secretary Ruth Kelly was obliged to make a number of concessions, including sacrificing the name 'trust school'. When MPs debated the principle of the proposed changes in March 2006, a total of fifty-two Labour Members voted against the government. The bill passed but only because it had Conservative support.

Events compounded the sense that Blair's government was losing its way. In April 2006, it emerged that 1,023 foreign prisoners had been released without being considered for deportation, as the law demanded. There was further embarrassment when it emerged that the minister responsible, home secretary Charles Clarke, had been warned of the problem nearly a year before and that 288 prisoners had been released in the intervening period. Clarke was sacked a month later. It was left to his successor as home secre-tary, John Reid, to pass judgement on his own officials and his predecessors' legacies: 'not fit for purpose', was how Reid described his new department to a committee of MPs.[15]

By the summer of 2006, Blair's authority was stretched to breaking point. The prime minister seemed to acknowledge his political mortality when, in June, he began a series of valedictory lectures on domestic policy under the slogan 'Our Nation's Future'. Then, in July, he further antago-nised his party by refusing to criticise Israel for its invasion of Lebanon. Many Labour MPs were still outraged by Blair's consistent support for President George W. Bush's foreign policy, and this was, for them, the final straw. More importantly, supporters of Gordon Brown had also reached the limits of their patience with Blair's reluctance to stand aside and were now prepared to strike. In September, just before the party's annual conference, over a dozen Labour MPs signed a letter calling on Blair to step down. Brown was widely believed to be behind this move.[16] Meanwhile, and unbeknownst to the signatories, John Prescott, Labour's deputy leader and deputy prime minister, had already extracted from Blair a pledge to announce a timetable for his departure.[17] The letter now forced the prime minister to bring forward his announcement. Blair confirmed the following day that the coming party conference would be his last as leader. He would step down before the autumn of 2007.

Blair had never been loved by Labour but he had been tolerated because of his election-winning talents. Now, with Labour's popularity in the doldrums, as Figure 1.1 shows, Blair was finding that support within his party was not broad enough to sustain him in the bad times. Labour MPs and activists were all too aware of their party's diminished standing. They were also aware of Blair's diminished personal standing. Each month since he first came to office, Ipsos MORI had asked respondents whether they were satisfied or dissatisfied with the way Blair was doing his job as prime minister.[18] During his first term, between May 1997 and June 2001, 56 per cent of respondents were, on average, satisfied with Blair. During his second

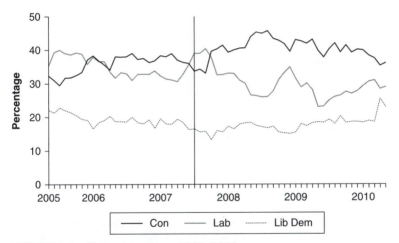

FIGURE 1.1   *Voting intentions, 2005–2010*

*Source*: UK Polling Report, 'Voting intention', available at http://ukpollingreport.co.uk/blog/voting-intention. Last accessed on 26 August 2010.

*Note*: The figure displays average findings by calendar month of all polls published by Angus Reid, BPIX, Communicate, ComRes, Harris, ICM, Ipsos-MORI, Marketing Sciences, Opinium, Populus, TNS BMRB and YouGov between June 2005 and March 2010. The May 2005 voting intentions are the results of the 2005 election. The vertical line indicates Tony Blair's departure.

term, between June 2001 and May 2005, this proportion fell to 39 per cent. Between May 2005 and his final departure from office, only 32 per cent of respondents were, on average, satisfied with Blair. Conscious that the prime minister was no longer an asset, most in the party were relieved at his going. In a YouGov survey that September, 82 per cent of Labour members agreed that Blair should be gone by the next conference, if not sooner.[19]

What Figure 1.1 does not show, but what Labour MPs and activists were fully aware of, was that the press was also becoming more intensely censorious of Labour. The party had been backed by fewer newspapers in 2005 than in 2001, and even those that had supported Labour, such as the left-wing *Guardian*, were increasingly critical. Other newspapers, notably the right-wing *Daily Mail*, were plain hostile. At the very end of his premiership, Blair took on his critics when he likened the media to a 'feral beast' in its political coverage.[20] His critics responded by pointing out that Blair had enthusiastically manipulated the media in the early years of New Labour and contributed to a culture of 'spin'. The important point, of course, was that a hostile press made life harder for Labour, and in this respect, Blair's going would probably make little difference. Indeed, in September 2009, *The Sun*, Rupert Murdoch's tabloid newspaper and political bellwether, would publicly shift its support from Labour to the Conservatives.

Blair soldiered on for another nine months after his final autumn conference. His government had already taken a few long-term and sometimes difficult decisions, including increasing the state retirement age to 68 and pressing ahead with building new nuclear power stations. Now it took another and in March 2007 the government won a parliamentary vote to renew Trident, Britain's nuclear deterrent. Yet, despite all this policy activity, all eyes were looking to the future. In May 2007, the prime minister confirmed that he would resign on 27 June. Blair then undertook an extended farewell tour, visiting Washington, DC, Iraq and even the Vatican.[21] His formal resignation followed one last prime minister's questions. After the usual exchanges, Blair told MPs simply: 'That is that. The end.'[22] MPs from all parties responded with a rare standing ovation.

## Great expectations

In 2005, many disillusioned supporters had held their nose and voted Labour, comfortable in the knowledge that they would 'vote Blair, get Brown'.[23] There was widespread hope in the party that Gordon Brown, when he became prime minister, would provide the government with a renewed and improved sense of direction. This hope rested on three foundations. The first was Brown's immense reputation as chancellor of the exchequer. Brown had presided over a booming economy since May 1997. Unusually for a Labour chancellor, Brown had also won the confidence of the City and the financial markets. But his reputation did not extend solely to macro-economic management. As chancellor, he had initially reined in public spending before rapidly increasing the money available to pay for schools and hospitals in the 2000 comprehensive spending review. He had also used his position in the Treasury to determine large measures of domestic policy, especially in the field of social security, through his tax-credit schemes. In a 2006 survey of British political scientists, Brown was judged to be the most successful post-war chancellor by a country mile.[24]

The second foundation of Labour's optimism was the expectation that Brown's leadership would be more in tune with the party's traditions and ethos than Blair's. Even though Brown had been Blair's co-architect in the creation of New Labour, and even though the policy differences between them were difficult to discern, Brown was thought to be closer to Labour's ideological heart. Labour party members tended to regard Blair as a centrist or even right-of-centre politician and Brown as a left-of-centre politician whose views were much closer to their own. Such perceptions were partly a consequence of many in the party wanting or needing to believe that this was the case. They were also a consequence of what Brown said and did. Unlike Blair, Brown was steeped in Labour history and his speeches were carefully crafted to project an image of him being the champion of 'True Labour'.[25] Many in the party, longing for reassurance as Blair took them to unfamiliar places, lapped it up. It probably helped that Brown spoke with an authentic Labour accent, a Scottish accent, whereas Blair spoke very un-Labour public-school English. Blair's electoral success had given him license to change the party. Now, with memories of that success fading, many in the party hoped that Brown would return Labour to its roots.

The third foundation of Labour's optimism was more mundane: there was simply no one other than Brown who seemed able to offer a clear sense of direction. In most governments, heavyweight figures emerge who wield an unusually large influence and who often come to be thought of as potential leaders. Clement Attlee's government had Ernest Bevin, Herbert Morrison and Sir Stafford Cripps. Harold Wilson's had George Brown, James Callaghan, Roy Jenkins and others. Callaghan's had Denis Healey. During Blair's premiership, there was only ever one prime minister in waiting: Gordon Brown. At various points, others were mooted as possible alternatives, including Charles Clarke, Alan Milburn, a former health secretary, and David Miliband, a youthful rising star of the party. But none managed to acquire a significant following. With the exception of Blair, Brown stood head, shoulders and torso above everyone else in the government.

Brown was unrivalled but he was still subject to criticism. Some colleagues were concerned about his operating style and his followers' tendency to brief against opponents. Clarke, never one of Brown's fans, labelled him a 'control freak' and 'totally uncollegiate'.[26] Others were concerned about his indecisiveness when big decisions had to be taken.[27] Yet others expressed concern about Brown's obsession with politics, his obsession with detail and his thin skin.[28] In a particularly withering attack, Frank Field, a former social security minister who had once crossed swords with the chancellor, warned that: 'Allowing Gordon Brown into No 10 would be like letting Mrs Rochester out of the attic. He has no empathy with people'.[29] Neutral insiders echoed such reservations. Just before Brown's last budget as chancellor, Lord Turnbull, a former cabinet secretary, Britain's most senior civil servant, accused Brown of acting with 'Stalinist ruthlessness' and treating cabinet colleagues with 'more or less complete contempt'.[30] Turnbull also accused Brown of possessing a 'Macavity quality'; like the cat in T.S. Eliott's poem, Brown was never there when things went wrong.

In the event, such warnings did not induce any fellow cabinet minister to oppose Brown, who inherited the leadership and premiership by acclamation. A challenge by John McDonnell, chairman of the left-wing Socialist Campaign Group of Labour MPs, failed to secure sufficient nominations. There was, however, a contested election for the post of deputy leader, which was triggered by John Prescott's decision to bow out along with Blair. Six MPs were nominated: Alan Johnson, Hilary Benn, Peter Hain and Hazel Blears, all cabinet ministers; Harriet Harman, a junior minister; and Jon Cruddas, a backbench MP. Through successive rounds of counting, the field was gradually whittled down. Blears, the most Blairite candidate, went out in the first round, followed by Hain, Benn and then Cruddas. In the final round, Harman surprised most people by narrowly defeating Johnson, 50.4 per cent to 49.6 per cent.[31]

## From Stalin to Mr Bean

The widespread hope that Gordon Brown would bring a new sense of direction to the government soon withered. In the space of a dramatic twelve months, Brown's authority evaporated, and the government's standing collapsed, never fully to recover.[32]

In contrast to his reputation as chancellor, and probably because of it, Brown sought to demonstrate a more inclusive style when he became head of government. He appointed some of Blair's supporters to top jobs, most notably David Miliband as foreign secretary. He also sought to involve a number of figures from other parties: two Conservative MPs, John Bercow and Patrick Mercer, and a Liberal Democrat MP, Matthew Taylor, agreed to act as advisers to the government. Brown's attempt to entice the former Liberal Democrat leader Paddy Ashdown into his cabinet was rebuffed, but he was gifted with the defection of Quentin Davies, a Conservative MP who crossed the floor to join Labour.[33] Brown also invited a number of political outsiders to join his 'government of all the talents', including Sir Alan West, a former head of the Royal Navy, Professor Sir Ara Darzi, a consultant surgeon, Sir Digby Jones, a leading businessman and former director general of the CBI, and Sir Mark Malloch Brown, a former UN deputy general secretary. These 'GOATS' had mixed success in office. Their real value was always symbolic.

Brown also sought to counter his reputation by projecting a more collegial style as prime minister. He pledged to restore collective decision making, thereby dissociating himself from the 'command' style of leadership that Blair had exercised as prime minister and he had exercised as chancellor. He also sought to distance himself from Blair's style of 'sofa government', with all its informality and ever-changing circle of ministers, advisers and confidantes.[34] Brown made much of the fact that his first full cabinet meeting had involved a lengthy discussion about constitutional reform with everyone taking part. 'This is not what some people have called "sofa government". It is Cabinet government.'[35]

Within days of taking office, Brown had an immediate opportunity to counter another perceived weakness: his indecision. He responded robustly to attempted terror attacks in London and Scotland, making very public use of the government's emergency committee 'Cobra' (which takes its name from the Cabinet Office Briefing Room where it meets), and he responded swiftly three weeks later when heavy rain caused extensive flooding to some parts of the country. Brown again convened Cobra and visited the worst-hit areas.

Brown's first few weeks as prime minister were generally praised, and there was a bounce in support for Labour, as a glance back to Figure 1.1 shows. Almost inevitably, speculation mounted of a snap election. The main argument for going to the country now was that Labour was ahead in the polls, and there was an opportunity for Brown to gain his own mandate. The main argument against was that Labour was only two years into a five-year term, and holding an election was risky. Brown was torn. He had waited years to become prime minister and had no wish to risk losing office so soon; yet he also coveted winning without Blair. He was also probably mindful of the fate of James Callaghan, who succeeded Harold Wilson as Labour prime minister in 1976. Callaghan decided against calling a snap election in the autumn of 1978, when he might have won, and went on to lose in 1979.

As Brown considered his options, Labour prepared. At the party's 2007 conference, some of Brown's aides and several cabinet ministers talked more or less openly about a snap election. A decision was also taken to bring forward the government's pre-budget report and comprehensive spending review, which would set out long-term spending plans. It seemed to everyone that Brown would go to the country. But then: the Conservatives had a good conference of their own, and Labour's standing in the polls dipped. Brown blinked and announced there would be no election. No one believed him when he suggested that he had never seriously entertained the prospect. Labour had invested thousands of hours' worth of work and spent £1.2 million in preparing for an election that never was.[36] Critics claimed that the prime minister had bottled it.

Brown and Labour might have recovered from this setback. But it suddenly seemed that everything that could go wrong did go wrong. In September, as speculation mounted about an election, there was a run on the Northern Rock bank, one of Britain's largest mortgage lenders. Thousands of jittery investors queued to withdraw their funds. The government was forced to pump more and more taxpayers' money into the institution until about £55 billion had been spent. It was all to no avail. In February 2008, the government reluctantly took the bank into public ownership.

It was difficult to blame the government directly for the run on Northern Rock but it was possible to blame the government for the loss in October 2007 of two data disks containing the personal and banking details of more than 20 million people. Although the episode was a low-level operational failing by Her Majesty's Revenue and Customs, it contributed to a growing sense of an inept government that was bungling from one failure to the next.

Things went from bad to worse when, days after the data discs were lost, the *Mail on Sunday* published allegations that a wealthy Labour donor, David Abrahams, had donated large sums of money to the party in other people's names. On becoming prime minister, Brown had pledge to provide a 'moral compass' to his government. Questions were now raised as to how much he had known. During an exchange in the House of Commons, the Liberal Democrat Vince Cable joked about Brown's 'remarkable transformation in the past few weeks from Stalin to Mr Bean creating chaos out of order, rather than order out of chaos.'[37] There were howls of laughter on both sides of the House.

The last major fiasco of Brown's first year was all the more damaging because it was entirely of his making. As chancellor back in March 2007, Brown had announced a surprise cut in the basic rate of income tax, from 22 pence in the pound to 20 pence. At the same time, he had abolished the 10 per cent starting rate for income tax. The announcement was a blatant ploy to appeal to aspirational middle-class voters; the move actually harmed the very lowest-paid workers, Labour's traditional constituency. Brown got away with it at the time because his prestige and reputation were such that few in the party dared challenge him. The situation was very different in March 2008 when the tax-rate changes were due to take effect. Many Labour MPs, led by Frank Field, now pressed the government to compensate those worst affected by the changes. A threatened rebellion by MPs was only averted after ministers promised a compensation package. It was an embarrassing climb-down and it challenged the assumption that Brown would be more Old Labour than Blair.

The cumulative impact of all the events of Brown's first year can be seen in his approval ratings, which plummeted after he took office. Figure 1.2 tracks responses to a YouGov question that asked respondents whether they thought Brown was doing well or badly as prime minister. In August 2007, two months after Brown's accession, 65 per cent of respondents said Brown was doing well, as opposed to 17 per cent who said he was doing badly, a net rating of 48 points. Twelve months later, a mere 16 per cent of

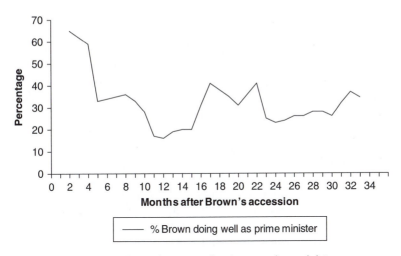

FIGURE 1.2    *Gordon Brown's approval rating as prime minister*

*Source*: YouGov, 'The Party Leaders', available at http://www.yougov.co.uk/extranets/ ygarchives/content/pdf/YG%20trackers%20-%20leaders.pdf. Last accessed on 26 August 2010.

*Note*: The figure reports the percentages of those who answered 'well' when asked: 'Is Gordon Brown doing well or badly as Prime Minister?'

respondents said Brown was doing a good job, and 78 per cent now said he was doing a bad job, a net rating of minus 62.

The sense of authority lost that pervaded Brown's first year in office was compounded by his failure to establish a distinctive agenda for his premiership. In fairness, that was never going to be easy. Labour's mandate to govern was based on its 2005 manifesto, and Brown had been Blair's virtual co-ruler for the last ten years. The new prime minister was unable to offer much that was new. The best he could offer was a programme of constitutional renewal, something that was never likely to resonate with the public or provide a clear sense of direction for the government as a whole. His apparent conversion to political reform also sat uneasily with his total lack of enthusiasm for constitutional change ten years earlier.

Brown may thus have been unlucky during his first year, but he was also the author of some of his own misfortunes. Many of the decisions he had made as chancellor returned to haunt him in his new job. More generally, Brown was the victim of a misplaced hope that he had cultivated. He could never provide the break with New Labour that many people craved because he had helped to create it. As a result, there was a structural expectations gap between what the party – and indeed the public – thought Brown would do and what he was actually capable of doing. That gap would magnify the political damage when things inevitably went wrong.

## It's the stupid economy

If clear leadership had been one ingredient in New Labour's past victories, a buoyant economy had been the crucial ingredient. During Labour's first decade in power, between 1997 and 2007, the economy had grown by an average of 2.7 per cent a year and inflation, unemployment and interest rates had all stayed low.[38] Most people were content with their finances. In March 2007, a newspaper poll found that 56 per cent of respondents thought that the last ten years had been prosperous for Britain as a whole, and 61 per cent thought the decade had been prosperous for them and their families.[39] The good times looked set to carry on when Brown became prime minister. As Table 1.1 shows, from the beginning of Labour's third term in 2005 to the end of the first quarter in 2008, the British economy continued to grow. Meanwhile, official unemployment remained low and inflation remained close to the government's 2 per cent target.

TABLE 1.1   *Objective economic indicators, 2005–2010*

|      |      | Growth of GDP (%) | Inflation (%) | Unemployment (%) | Interest rates (%) |
| ---- | ---- | ----------------- | ------------- | ---------------- | ------------------ |
| 2005 | Q2   | 0.7  | 2.0  | 4.8 | 4.8 |
|      | Q3   | 0.6  | 2.4  | 4.8 | 4.5 |
|      | Q4   | 0.7  | 2.1  | 5.2 | 4.5 |
| 2006 | Q1   | 1.1  | 1.9  | 5.2 | 4.5 |
|      | Q2   | 0.4  | 2.3  | 5.5 | 4.5 |
|      | Q3   | 0.5  | 2.4  | 5.5 | 4.8 |
|      | Q4   | 0.8  | 2.7  | 5.5 | 5.0 |
| 2007 | Q1   | 0.7  | 2.9  | 5.5 | 5.3 |
|      | Q2   | 0.6  | 2.6  | 5.4 | 5.5 |
|      | Q3   | 0.5  | 1.8  | 5.3 | 5.8 |
|      | Q4   | 0.5  | 2.1  | 5.2 | 5.5 |
| 2008 | Q1   | 0.7  | 2.4  | 5.2 | 5.3 |
|      | Q2   | −0.1 | 3.4  | 5.4 | 5.0 |
|      | Q3   | −0.9 | 4.8  | 5.9 | 5.0 |
|      | Q4   | −1.8 | 3.9  | 6.4 | 2.0 |
| 2009 | Q1   | −2.6 | 3.0  | 7.1 | 0.5 |
|      | Q2   | −0.7 | 2.1  | 7.8 | 0.5 |
|      | Q3   | −0.3 | 1.5  | 7.8 | 0.5 |
|      | Q4   | 0.4  | 2.1  | 7.8 | 0.5 |
| 2010 | Q1   | 0.2  | 3.3  | 8.0 | 0.5 |

*Sources*: Office for National Statistics and Bank of England.

*Note*: Growth is shown as the percentage increase in GDP at market prices compared with the previous quarter. The inflation measure is the Consumer Price Index annual percentage change. Unemployment is shown as the ILO rate, including all adults (16+) to retirement age. Interest rates refer to the Bank of England's official bank rate at the end of each quarter.

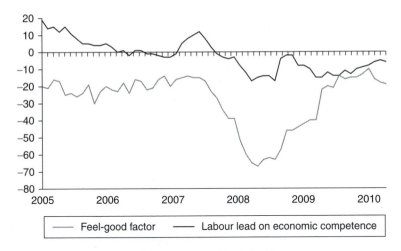

FIGURE 1.3  *Labour and the economy, 2005–2010*

*Sources*: YouGov, 'Daily Telegraph political trends', available at http://www.yougov.
co.uk/extranets/ygarchives/content/pdf/Political%20trends%20post%202005.pdf; and
'The Economy', available at http://www.yougov.co.uk/extranets/ygarchives/content/
pdf/YG%20trackers%20-%20economy.pdf. Last accessed 26 August 2010.

*Note*: The feel-good factor is calculated by subtracting the percentage of people who,
when asked: 'How do you think the financial situation of your household will change
over the next 12 months?', say 'get worse' from the percentage of people who say
'get better'. Labour's lead on economic competence is calculated by subtracting the
proportion of respondents who answered the Conservatives were more likely to run
Britain's economy well from the proportion who said Labour were more likely to.

Storm clouds were gathering, however. Figure 1.3 shows how the run on
Northern Rock in September 2007 triggered a sharp and extended fall in
the 'feel-good factor' (the proportion of people expecting their household
finances to improve minus the proportion expecting them to worsen). It
also triggered a drop in Labour's lead over the Conservatives as the party
best able to run the economy. Labour governments past had struggled to
maintain any reputation for economic competence, and since 1997, Brown
as chancellor had carefully nurtured it. Now that reputation was crumbling.
Brown resisted using the word 'recession', even when it was obvious that
that was where Britain was headed. Beginning in the second quarter of 2008,
the economy entered a recession, the worst since the 1950s, 1940s or 1930s,
depending on which newspaper you read. Inflation began to climb, so did
unemployment, and so too did levels of personal debt, which had stimulated
consumer spending. In August 2007, Britons' personal debt exceeded gross
domestic product (GDP) for the first time ever. Twelve months later, in
August 2008, the new chancellor Alistair Darling warned that the economic

circumstances were 'arguably the worst they've been in 60 years.'[40] His gloomy prognosis was borne out weeks later when the Wall Street giant Lehman Brothers went bankrupt, a consequence of the credit crunch strangling the American economy. British banks were soon in danger of going the same way as the financial crisis began to bite (see Chapter 4).

On one day in October 2008, share prices in London suffered a record fall, as nearly £100 billion was wiped off the value of the leading 100 companies, and the banks found themselves without money to lend. The government responded promptly by providing a £50 billion bailout, equivalent to £2,000 for every British taxpayer, and by making available a further £450 billion to fund short-term loans and inter-bank lending.[41] Over the crucial weekend of 11–12 October, the government further brokered a deal among G7 finance ministers to recapitalise the banks. As a result, the British government soon took major stakes – in some cases the majority stake – in several banks. Labour's unpalatably left-wing 1983 manifesto, mocked as 'the longest suicide note in history', had threatened to nationalise one or more of the major clearing banks. By 2009, Lloyds TSB and Royal Bank of Scotland, together with Northern Rock, were effectively in public hands.

With the economy contracting throughout the summer and autumn of 2008, Alistair Darling used his November pre-budget report to unveil a fiscal stimulus package, estimated to be worth about £20 billion. This package included a temporary cut in the rate of VAT, Britain's sales tax, which is levied on most goods and services. Darling also announced a plan to reduce the deficit by implementing spending cuts and by increasing national insurance contributions by half a point and raising the top rate of income tax to 45 per cent in 2011.[42] Raising income tax in this way was a gamble. It broke a long-standing manifesto pledge not to do so, and it risked alienating aspirational voters. However, in the straitened circumstances, Darling had little choice. The following spring he announced a further increase in the top rate to 50 pence in the pound, and the following autumn he announced a further half-point increase in national insurance, which the Conservatives criticised as a 'tax on jobs'. The logic behind the stimulus was obvious: deficit spend now, tax later. Keynes was back in vogue.

Another casualty of the stimulus measures was Brown's 'golden rule', a self-denying ordinance that pledged the state to borrow money only to finance investment. A further casualty was Brown's 'sustainable investment rule', which stipulated that the national debt be kept below 40 per cent of national income over the economic cycle. In the 2008–09 financial year, public debt, as a proportion of GDP, climbed to 43.8 per cent.[43] In his 2010 budget, Darling predicted that debt would rise to 54.1 per cent of GDP in 2009–10 and to around 75 per cent a few years thereafter.[44] To address this mounting debt, he pledged to halve public borrowing over four years from its expected peak in 2009–10.

The Bank of England also did what it could to stimulate economic activity by reducing interest rates repeatedly, until they fell to just 0.5 per cent, their lowest level in the Bank's 315-year history. When that proved insufficient to stimulate the economy, the Bank began to purchase financial assets as part of its policy of 'quantitative easing', the equivalent of printing more money. The inflationary risk was judged worth taking in order to stop unemployment rising out of control.

Overseeing all government responses to the economic downturn was Gordon Brown. Financial meltdown had finally given him a sense of purpose and a mission. Invoking all his prior experience as chancellor, he took it upon himself to save not only Britain's economy but the world's. There was an obvious irony to this new-found sense of direction. Labour's past success had been built on the foundations of a strong economy. The government now hoped to capitalise on the deteriorating economy and use it as a springboard for electoral recovery. There were some grounds for optimism amidst the pessimism. Margaret Thatcher's unpopular government had bounced back to win in 1983 thanks, in part, to a rise in the feel-good factor, as well as victory in the Falklands war.

Brown's stock rose in April 2009 when he presided over a special meeting of the G20 in London. He was instrumental in persuading world leaders to inject $1.1 trillion (£681 billion) into the global economy. The G20 also agreed to tighten financial regulation and to clamp down on tax havens. In marked contrast to domestic opinion, the prime minister was still a respected operator on the world stage. Unfortunately for him, he also still found it hard to shift domestic opinion. Gradually, Labour's reputation for economic management improved after the G20 success, but it was picking up from a low base. Much the same could be said of the economy, which emerged hesitantly from recession in September 2009.

## Policy hangovers

There was always the risk that a third-term government could appear to be running out of steam. All long-serving governments face similar problems, akin to what some economists call 'the cost of ruling'.[45] New policies seem jaded and rehashed, while the need for new policies is itself recognition that old policies have failed. More importantly, perhaps, long-serving governments find themselves unable to use the timeless excuse available to new governments: 'it was the other lot's fault!' After 1997, and to a lesser extent after 2001, Labour could plausibly blame the Conservatives for the country's problems. After 2005, they could blame only themselves, as their opponents liked to point out.

## Serving the public

Not surprisingly, as Table 1.2 shows, the economy was the dominant issue during Brown's premiership. But other issues mattered to voters throughout Labour's third term, just as they had always mattered. The public services, especially health and education, were of particular concern. Most Britons continued to rely entirely on the government for their healthcare and children's schooling. Labour therefore had a strong electoral incentive, as well as a long-standing ideological commitment, to fund and maintain these services. Striking the right balance between taxing and spending was as important as ever, but in the new economic circumstances, with levels of public debt rising, it was more difficult than ever.

TABLE 1.2    *Most important issue facing Britain today, 1997–2010*

| | First term | Second term | Third term Blair | Brown | Total | 1997–2010 |
|---|---|---|---|---|---|---|
| Crime | 20 | 26 | 32 | 36 | 35 | 27 |
| Immigration | 7 | 26 | 34 | 32 | 33 | 22 |
| Economy | 14 | 11 | 10 | 42 | 30 | 17 |
| Health | 44 | 44 | 34 | 21 | 26 | 38 |
| Defence/Foreign Affairs | 6 | 31 | 34 | 17 | 22 | 20 |
| Education | 34 | 29 | 23 | 14 | 17 | 27 |
| Unemployment | 25 | 8 | 7 | 14 | 12 | 15 |
| Inflation | 4 | 2 | 3 | 12 | 9 | 5 |
| Environment | 6 | 3 | 10 | 8 | 9 | 6 |
| Pensions/social security | 13 | 11 | 10 | 5 | 7 | 10 |
| Europe | 24 | 11 | 4 | 3 | 3 | 13 |

*Source*: Ipsos MORI, 'Issues Index: Trends since 1997', available at http://www.ipsos-mori.com/researchpublications/researcharchive/poll.aspx?oItemID=56&view=wide. Last accessed on 26 August 2010.

*Note*: Figures are the average percentage of respondents citing each issue in reply to the following questions: 'What would you say is the most important issue facing Britain today?', and 'What do you see as other important issues facing Britain today?' The answers combine responses and are unprompted. Only the most frequently cited and other selected issues are included.

Between 1996–97 and 2008–09, government spending on education as a proportion of national income increased from 4.6 per cent to 5.7 per cent. Spending on the National Health Service increased from 5.1 per cent to 7.8 per cent in the same period.[46] There were undoubted improvements in terms of NHS waiting lists and the education infrastructure, but Labour's largesse did not transform perceptions of these services or prompt universal praise. In March 2007, ICM asked the public: 'Overall would you say that the extra money the government has spent on public services such as health and education over the last decade has generally been spent well or spent badly?' Exactly a quarter of respondents said the money had been spent well. Nearly three-quarters, 71 per cent, said it had been spent badly.[47] Popular scepticism was doubtless fuelled by newspaper tales of badly negotiated GP contracts, which meant that doctors earned more for working less; of many hospitals ending their financial years in deficit; and of 'fat cat' senior public-sector managers, who earned more than the prime minister.

Vast sums were certainly being spent on salaries in parts of the public sector. There were tens of thousands more doctors, nurses, teachers and support staff as a result of Labour's increased spending. All these salaries contributed greatly to the structural deficit in the public finances. One obvious solution, reducing manpower, was always difficult. It was even more difficult amidst an economic downturn and before an election. The 2007 comprehensive spending review scaled down projected increases in health and education expenditure, but Labour took care to package the reductions as efficiency savings. Where it could, the government also sought to meet public concerns about the salaries of senior managers. In a 2009 speech on smarter government, Brown promised that overpaid public-sector workers would be 'named and shamed' and resources would be switched 'from the back office to the front line'.[48]

If people were sceptical of Labour's spending, it was also easy to be sceptical of yet more promised reforms. During its first term, Labour had introduced hundreds of binding targets in various public-sector agreements to improve the delivery of public services. During its second term, it had tried to decentralise education and healthcare provision. A key objective for Blair in Labour's third term was to inject a greater spirit of choice into Britain's public services and to make them, as its 2005 manifesto put it, 'free to all, personal to each'.[49] The 'choice agenda' was Blair's. It was ahead of mainstream Labour thinking, which favoured uniformity in public-service provision, and it was ahead of public opinion. Voters liked the idea of choice in accessing public services but did not necessarily want those services to be provided by the private or charitable sectors.[50] Moreover, even if the reforms were effective, there would be a considerable lag before voters perceived any marked improvements.

Contrary to the expectations of many in the Labour party, Brown had indicated his commitment to the choice agenda before he became prime minister. In March 2007, he enthused about public services that were 'personal to the citizen's needs, and to the citizen's wishes', and called for 'greater choice, greater competition, greater contestability' in their provision.[51] By 2008 commentators were noting the near-total conversion of Brown to Blairism.[52] The idea that Brown had undergone any kind of conversion was misleading, however. Brown had always had much more in common with his predecessor than some liked to admit. To be sure, Brown was more of a statist than Blair by inclination, but the difference between them was more one of degree, not of kind. Brown's conversion occurred largely in people's perceptions.

The essence of the choice agenda was simple: citizens should have greater choice among state-financed schools and hospitals and should even be able to access state-financed but privately-provided services, if appropriate. In healthcare in England, choice and diversity would be strengthened by allowing local providers to deliver more services. London experimented with 'polyclinics', and outside London there was a push to establish more GP-led health centres. Meanwhile, service users' rights were to be protected by a new NHS constitution; there would even be a legal entitlement for patients who had to wait longer than eighteen weeks for NHS treatment to receive free private healthcare. In education, Blair sought to entrench choice and diversity with his half-successful plan to create 'trust schools', and Brown's education secretary Ed Balls pressed ahead with plans to create legally enforceable rights for children and parents. The planned rights included one-to-one tuition in maths and writing for children who needed it, national report cards for primary and secondary schools and five-yearly check-ups on teachers' competence. The onset of the 2010 election meant that the measures did not enter onto the statute book, however.

## Protecting the public

Labour had come to power in 1997 promising to be 'tough on crime, tough on the causes of crime'. Successive home secretaries preferred to emphasise the former, particularly when courting favourable headlines in right-wing newspapers like the *Daily Mail*. Toughness on crime remained the central message of Labour's third term. This approach was both a consequence, and perhaps also a cause, of an increase in people's fear of crime. The authoritative British Crime Survey found a marked rise in the proportion of people who thought crime had increased nationally from 61 per cent in 2004–05 to 75 per cent in 2008–09.[53] Fears were stoked by a spate of knife attacks in London and elsewhere in 2007 and 2008. The reality was that the number of reported crimes had declined, and so too had the risk of being a victim of crime.[54]

Labour's tough approach extended to drugs policy. Here the government was torn between wanting to appear liberal and pragmatic – by making the possession of the widely-used drug cannabis a less serious offence – and wanting to appear tough – by making illegal previously legal substances and by backtracking on a more liberal cannabis policy. Toughness won out, but this brought the government into conflict with its own Advisory Council on the Misuse of Drugs. Professor David Nutt, its chairman, was sacked by home secretary Alan Johnson in November 2009 for stating that two currently illegal substances, LSD and ecstasy, were less dangerous than alcohol. Other members of the Council resigned in protest at the sacking. The incident was not as damaging to the government as it might have been; most voters broadly favoured a tougher anti-drugs line.[55]

Toughness also characterised Labour's approach to dealing with terrorism. Blair pushed to allow the police to hold and question terrorist suspects for up to ninety days without charge, which fuelled concerns that the government was trampling on civil liberties in the name of security. An especially tragic *cause célèbre* was the 2005 shooting of an innocent Brazilian, Jean Charles de Menezes, who police mistook for a suicide bomber. Campaigners like Shami Chakrabarti, the director of the campaign group Liberty, criticised Labour's authoritarianism. She and others also campaigned against the growing number of closed-circuit television cameras as well as government plans to introduce a national identity-card scheme. Concerns about the erosion of civil liberties also drew the Conservatives and Liberal Democrats closer together.

When Brown replaced Blair, the new prime minister proved just as keen to take a tough approach to dealing with terrorism. In June 2008, he reignited the controversy of detaining terrorist suspects without charge and pushed for an extension of the current twenty-eight-day limit to forty-two days. Like Blair, Brown met resistance, and his proposals were defeated in the House of Lords. Although Brown lost face among his colleagues, he did not do himself too much damage in the eyes of British voters, who tolerated such measures in the name of security.[56]

## Europe and immigration

Britain's membership of the European Union had the potential to derail the government in its third term thanks to a commitment made in its second. In 2004, Labour promised voters a referendum on the proposed EU Constitution, a referendum it was widely expected to lose.[57] However, thanks to the people of France and the Netherlands, who rejected the Constitution in referendums in 2005, Labour was spared the need to hold a vote and the potential embarrassment of losing it. The Constitution, with all its symbolism, was dead. It was no more. It was an ex-Constitution. In its place, EU leaders cobbled together at Lisbon in 2007 an 'amending treaty', which salvaged most but not all of the Constitution's provisions. This time, following the lead of the French and Dutch governments, Labour declined to hold a referendum on the new treaty, which it again probably would have lost, on the grounds that it was 'substantially' different to the abortive Constitution. On a strict legal interpretation, the two texts were clearly not identical.[58] But some took a different view, including a committee of MPs, who insisted that the Lisbon Treaty and the Constitution were 'substantially equivalent'.[59] For most voters, however, Europe was, by now, an unimportant issue. Calls for a new referendum never fired the public imagination.

Of all the government's third-term policy hangovers, immigration was one of the hardest for Labour to deal with. It might easily have become a race issue, especially after the London bombings in July 2005; it soon became an economic one, especially when figures released in 2007 suggested that half the new jobs created since 1997 had gone to foreign workers.[60] Labour had no wish to be seen supporting racist tendencies in British society, but it did wish to be seen supporting blue-collar workers who were fearful of foreign workers taking their jobs. Brown talked of 'British jobs for British workers', and in March 2008 the government unveiled a new points-based system to deter unskilled economic migrants from outside the EU from entering the UK. A majority of the public seemed to approve of Labour's approach to restricting immigration. In a 2009 ICM survey, 54 per cent said that the best policy of dealing with immigrants from outside the EU was to 'allow entry based on a points system' compared with 28 per cent who said the best policy was to 'set an annual limit on the numbers allowed into Britain', the solution proposed by the Tories.[61] Only 15 per cent said no more immigration at all should be allowed. Nevertheless, for those for whom the issue burned, the Conservative policy appeared more attractive.

In one curious episode, the government was actually criticised for its restrictive policies towards one group of foreign nationals, the Gurkhas. Gurkhas are Nepalese mercenaries recruited by the British army, and in 2004, the government had decided to allow those who had retired after 1997 – the year the regiment moved its base from Hong Kong to the UK – to live in Britain. A Gurkha Justice Campaign called for all former Gurkhas to have residency rights. Led by Joanna Lumley, the popular actress and star of *Absolutely Fabulous*, the campaign brought enormous pressure to bear on the government. At times, it seemed, the actress was dictating terms to ministers. A government defeat in the House of Commons on a Liberal Democrat motion only added to the pressure, and the government eventually decided to allow all Gurkha veterans who had served for at least four years to settle in Britain. It was an enormous loss of face for Brown's government, which had managed to appear on the wrong side of the argument even when it thought it had been following public opinion. Once the mood turns against a government, it can potentially get everything wrong.

## Iraq and Afghanistan

The most costly hangover for Labour in its third term – at least in human terms – lay in the field of foreign policy. After 9/11, Blair had been an active cheerleader of President Bush's war on terror. He had led Britain to war in Afghanistan to oust the Taliban regime, and he had also been an ardent supporter of the invasion of Iraq. The Iraq war was especially controversial. Hundreds of thousands if not millions of British citizens had taken to the streets in 2003 to march against it, and four ministers had resigned from the government in protest.

Iraq was still a running sore in British politics after 2005, but at least it was no longer an open wound for the government. In December 2007, Basra, the last Iraq province under British control, was returned to the Iraqis, and combat operations officially finished at the end of April 2009. By that time, 179 UK servicemen and women had been killed. The conflict had also claimed the lives of many Iraqis and cost the UK taxpayers about £8 billion.[62]

Ever since the invasion, there had been demands for a full inquiry into the UK's involvement in Iraq. Blair had conceded two very limited inquiries during his second term. The first, the Hutton Inquiry, had examined the circumstances surrounding the death of Dr David Kelly, a government adviser who may have briefed a journalist against the government. The second, the Butler Inquiry, had examined the government's intelligence relating to Iraq's alleged weapons of mass destruction. Brown went much further in June 2009 when he decided to establish an official committee of inquiry, chaired by Sir John Chilcot, a former civil servant, with wide-ranging terms of reference. There was no danger of Chilcot publishing a damaging report before the general election but his inquiry could still embarrass. There was particular anticipation ahead of Tony Blair's public appearance before the inquiry on 29 January 2010 and Gordon Brown's on 5 March. Blair gave little away and offered no regrets when he gave evidence. Brown did admit regret but he robustly defended the invasion and insisted it was 'the right decision, and it was [done] for the right reasons'.[63]

Brown's appearance was important, not because he was closely associated with the Iraq war, but because as chancellor he had had to find the money for it. He faced criticisms that he had failed to provide sufficient funds to equip the armed forces. This criticism carried greater weight because similar concerns were being expressed in respect of Britain's ongoing commitment in Afghanistan. In particular, a shortage of helicopters was exposing soldiers to improvised explosive devices on the ground. At one point, the head of the army, General Sir Richard Dannatt, voiced his concerns about the shortage of equipment, a rare venture into the political arena by a serving solider. Dannatt's intervention was condemned by fellow officers but his concerns resonated among the public. In July 2009, YouGov asked voters whether they thought Brown was doing his best to supply British troops with the equipment they needed, or was failing to provide adequate resources. Exactly three-fifths agreed that 'He is deliberately trying to fight the war "on the cheap"'.[64]

The growing body count in Afghanistan seemed to support such concerns. During Blair's second term just four British servicemen died in Afghanistan. The first fatality during Labour's third term came in October 2005. Thereafter, the death count climbed: thirty-nine in 2006, forty-two in 2007, fifty-one in 2008 and then 108 in 2009.[65] Many of the dead soldiers' bodies were driven through a small English market town, Wootton Bassett, after being repatriated to nearby RAF Lyneham. Played out in front of the television cameras, these journeys became something of a morbid ritual and were a stark reminder of the war's human cost.

Brown continued his predecessor's practice of writing letters of condolence to bereaved families. Somehow even this act of kindness became a stick with which to beat him after the mother of one fallen soldier accused him of careless handwriting and misspelling her name. *The Sun*'s attempts to make more of the incident – another instance of the press's hostility towards Labour – backfired after it was pointed out that Brown's handwriting was affected by his poor eyesight, the result of an old sporting injury.

Despite the growing body count, Afghanistan never provoked the passions aroused by Iraq, not least because this invasion had clear United Nations support. It was not as divisive among Labour MPs, nor was it as unpopular among the public. In an ICM survey conducted in July 2009, 46 per cent of respondents supported the British military operation in Afghanistan (as opposed to 47 per cent who opposed it), an increase on the 31 per cent who had supported the operation in September 2006.[66] Most people recognised that Brown had inherited Afghanistan. It was never *his* war, even if he was criticised for its funding.

# Scandal!

By virtue of their longevity, long-serving governments are more likely to have to contend with a greater number of fiascos, cock-ups and other assorted scandals. More than that, they face the disadvantage that mistakes tend to accumulate in the public consciousness and create an impression of systematic incompetence.

The Labour government during its first and second terms had survived its share of fiascos. None of those that occurred during its third term was fatal by itself, but each made it easier to characterise the government as being accident prone. Each knocked confidence in the government and damaged its morale.

## Labour sleaze

Labour's third term was blighted by a number of scandals that cast doubt on the government's integrity. In 1997, Blair had pledged that his government would be 'purer than pure'. After its first term and a series of financial scandals, one commentator described Labour as 'slightly soiled'.[67] By 2010, 'totally tarnished' was perhaps more appropriate.

The scandals came in various forms. The least consequential were those of a personal nature. In this category fell the November 2005 resignation of work and pensions secretary David Blunkett. Blind since birth, Blunkett was a senior figure in the government. He had already resigned once from the government – in December 2004, after allegedly abusing his position to speed up his lover's nanny's visa application – but had returned in May 2005. During the lull in his ministerial career, he had taken up a directorship with a DNA-testing company but had not sought official approval before doing so, as the rules required. Blair had no choice but to accept Blunkett's resignation a second time.

Much more significant were two party-funding scandals. One, the David Abrahams controversy, has already been referred to in the context of Gordon Brown's first-year woes. The other, the 2006 'loans for peerages' scandal, was even more damaging for Labour. In March that year, the newspapers printed allegations that Labour had received a large number of secret loans from benefactors who were subsequently nominated to the House of Lords. Whereas many upper houses, like the US Senate, are directly elected, the Lords is largely appointed. All parties have, at some point, rewarded benefactors by appointing them to the Lords. The practice is technically legal provided there is no explicit quid pro quo; but it has always been unsavoury. What was especially damning about this scandal, however, was that Labour was also breaching the spirit of its own legislation, the Political Parties, Elections and Referendums Act 2000. Labour appeared to be treating many of the loans as open-ended donations but had not registered them with the Electoral Commission, as it was required to do. Some £14 million had poured into Labour's coffers in this way. The party would have been unable to fund its 2005 election campaign without them.

Attention soon focused on the role of Lord Levy, Labour's principal fundraiser, who was sometimes known as 'Lord Cashpoint'. Levy was close to Blair. His ability to raise large sums of money from wealthy individuals was highly prized as Labour tried to reduce its financial reliance on the trade unions. Levy was one of several individuals close to the prime minister to be arrested over the scandal – Levy was actually arrested twice – and Blair himself suffered the ignominy of being interviewed twice by police. Following an investigation that lasted for the remainder of Blair's time in office, no one was charged. The damage to Labour, however, was considerable.

Other scandals involved parliamentarians and their relations with lobbyists. In 2009, two Labour peers, Lords Truscott and Taylor, were suspended from the House of Lords for telling undercover reporters of their willingness to amend legislation for money. In 2010 several MPs were secretly filmed boasting of their abilities to influence ministers. The former transport secretary Stephen Byers, described himself as 'sort of like a cab for hire'.

One of the most intriguing scandals – intriguing because it revealed something of the workings of the Brown government – occurred in April 2009. This affair centred on the activities of one of Brown's closest aides, Damian McBride.[68] McBride had sent emails from his official Downing

Street email account discussing the possibility of spreading false rumours about the private lives of Conservative politicians. Once the planned dirty-tricks campaign came to light, there was no option but for McBride to quit. Some people believed that Brown had sanctioned McBride's dirty tricks, others that he had simply tolerated them. Either way, the company he kept reflected badly on the prime minister. It also reminded people of New Labour's proclivity to 'spin'.

Thanks to such scandals, Labour's image after 2005 was distinctly grubby. Various opinion pollsters had occasionally asked the question: 'Do you agree or disagree with the following statement: "Labour these days gives the impression of being very sleazy and disreputable"?' In March 1997 the Gallup organisation reported that only 19 per cent of respondents agreed. By January 2001, when NOP asked the question, 49 per cent now agreed that Labour gave the impression of being sleazy and disreputable. Mid-way though Labour's third term, in November 2007, when YouGov asked the question, the proportion of respondents was 60 per cent.[69]

## The expenses scandal

The 2009 MPs' expenses controversy was in a league of its own. It was not a Labour scandal but a parliamentary one: every party had MPs' implicated in the widespread misuse and abuse of parliamentary expenses. It was also a scandal that revealed much about the growing divide between voters and all politicians, as Chapter 5 describes in greater detail. But Labour was the party of government and its MPs dominated the House of Commons. As such, it came to be held responsible for much of the wrongdoing.

As a foretaste of the drama to come, two Labour ministers, home secretary Jacqui Smith and employment minister Tony McNulty, were accused of taking advantage of parliament's second-home allowance scheme at the beginning of 2009. Smith had claimed money for the upkeep of her main family home, located in her Redditch constituency, by designating her sister's house in London as her main residence. McNulty had claimed money for a second home in Harrow just eight miles from his main home in Hammersmith. Both MPs were later found to have breached the Commons code of conduct.

The real drama came in May, when the *Daily Telegraph* newspaper began publishing the details of all MPs' expenses and allowances claims, information that MPs had previously kept secret. Day after day, the newspaper exposed a number of scandalous claims, ranging from the banal, such as bath plugs, biscuits and fluffy dusters, to the outlandish, such as duck houses and bags of manure. Rarely was it obvious how such objects were needed by MPs to perform their parliamentary duties. Even more scandalous was the fact that some MPs had 'flipped' or re-designated their main addresses in order to redecorate their house at public expense and, in a few cases, to avoid paying tax. Voters were incensed. A YouGov survey, published shortly after the expenses scandal first broke, found that 86 per cent of respondents felt there was 'a widespread problem involving a large number of MPs claiming money to which they are not entitled'.[70] The police agreed. In February 2010, it was announced that criminal charges would be brought against three Labour MPs, Elliot Morley, David Chaytor and Jim Devine, in relation to false accounting.[71]

Meanwhile, as the media whipped up the public's anger at 'the rotten parliament', politicians sought desperately to respond. Heads rolled, including that of the Speaker, Michael Martin, who became the first holder of that office to be forced out since 1695. Many of the worst transgressors announced their intention to stand down at the next election. Others were forced to by their local party associations. Yet others were punished by their national party organisations. Labour barred five MPs from standing as candidates in future elections, including Dr Ian Gibson, a popular local MP, who immediately quit in protest at his treatment by a 'kangaroo court' and triggered a by-election that Labour lost.[72]

MPs and the public looked to the government to provide leadership. Brown duly promised to overhaul the expenses regime in a disastrous YouTube video, made infamous by his awkward smiling. Parliament later established a new Independent Parliamentary Standards Authority that would take responsibility for paying MPs' salaries and for drawing up, reviewing and administering the system of parliamentary allowances. But there was little credit in shutting the stable doors.

Labour was unlucky that the expenses scandal exploded on its watch. It was, after all, an institutional scandal that affected all parties, and the parliamentary culture of treating allowances and expenses as a top-up to MP's wages pre-dated Labour's coming to power in 1997. But as the majority and governing party, Labour could expect a proportional share of public opprobrium, and a proportional share meant that its credibility would take the biggest hit. Labour may even have suffered more because it was traditionally the party of the working man and woman, yet its MPs seemed no less willing to profit from taxpayers' money. When an ICM poll asked which of the three main parties had been damaged most by the scandal, 2 per cent said the Liberal Democrats, 13 per cent said the Conservatives, 25 per cent said all parties equally and 53 per cent said Labour.[73]

## Opposition forces

Whenever slings and arrows had been thrown at the government during its first and second terms, Labour had taken comfort in being faced by a weak opposition. The Conservatives, once the natural party of government, were a broken force after 1997. As Labour leader, Blair had faced five Conservative leaders – John Major, William Hague, Iain Duncan Smith Michael Howard and David Cameron – and bested all but the last, who he never faced in a general election. The Conservatives' weakness allowed Labour to repeat their landslide win in 2001, and it had also been a major factor in allowing the government to win despite its unpopularity in 2005. The election of Cameron as Conservative leader signalled that Labour could no longer count on being so lucky. The Conservatives once more became a potential party of government.

A glance back at Figure 1.1 shows how, from 2006, Labour tended to trail in the opinion polls. Labour also haemorrhaged support in actual elections. During Labour's first term, the party avoided losing any by-elections, what Americans call special elections. In Labour's second term, six by-elections were held, all in seats previously held by Labour, and the party lost two, both to the Liberal Democrats. During Labour's third term, there were fourteen by-elections, and Labour lost four of the eight seats it was defending (see Table 1.3). Of these, perhaps the most significant was the Nantwich and Crewe by-election in 2008, which marked the first time that Labour had lost a by-election to the Conservatives since 1982. Labour again lost to the Conservatives in the Norwich North by-election caused by Ian Gibson's resignation in July 2009.

Labour also suffered setbacks in every set of second-order elections between the 2005 and 2010 general elections. Back in 1999, Labour had created a Scottish Parliament and National Assembly for Wales as part of its devolution programme, and the party dominated both institutions until 2007. Its results in that year's Scottish parliamentary and Welsh assembly elections were hugely disappointing. In Wales, Labour's share of the vote fell from 38.3 per cent to 30.9 per cent, and the party, which had governed alone since 2003, was forced to enter into a coalition with the Welsh nationalists, Plaid Cymru. In Scotland, Labour's share of the vote fell by less than two points, from 32 per cent to 30.6 per cent, but it lost the popular vote to Alex Salmond's Scottish National Party, which won 32 per cent of the vote and a plurality of MSPs. The SNP proceeded to form a minority government.

Labour also fared badly in the 2008 London authority elections. The maverick Labour politician Ken Livingstone had been London's directly elected mayor since the office was created in 2000, first as an independent, when Labour refused to make him their official candidate, and then as an official Labour man, after the party welcomed him back. By 2008, Livingstone's personal popularity had ebbed and was no longer sufficient to counter Labour's unpopularity. He was beaten by the blond-haired Conservative, Boris Johnson. The defeat was all the more galling for Labour activists who generally saw Boris as an upper-class buffoon.

TABLE 1.3 *By-election results, 2005–2010*

| Date | Constituency | Reason for by-election | Result |
|------|--------------|------------------------|--------|
| 14 July 2005 | Cheadle | Death of Patsy Calton (Lib Dem) | Lib Dem hold |
| 29 September 2005 | Livingston | Death of Robin Cook (Lab) | Lab hold |
| 9 February 2006 | Dunfermline West | Death of Rachel Squire (Lab) | Lib Dem gain |
| 29 June 2006 | Bromley and Chislehurst | Death of Eric Forth (Con) | Con hold |
| 29 June 2006 | Blaenau Gwent | Death of Peter Law (Ind) | Ind hold |
| 19 July 2007 | Ealing Southall | Death of Piara Khabra (Lab) | Lab hold |
| 19 July 2007 | Sedgefield | Resignation of Tony Blair (Lab) | Lab hold |
| 22 May 2008 | Crewe and Nantwich | Death of Gwyneth Dunwoody (Lab) | Con gain |
| 26 June 2008 | Henley | Resignation of Boris Johnson (Con) | Con hold |
| 10 July 2008 | Haltemprice and Howden | Resignation of David Davis (Con) | Con hold |
| 24 July 2008 | Glasgow East | Resignation of David Marshall (Lab) | SNP gain |
| 6 November 2008 | Glenrothes | Death of John MacDougall (Lab) | Lab hold |
| 23 July 2009 | Norwich North | Resignation of Dr Ian Gibson (Lab) | Con gain |
| 12 November 2009 | Glasgow North East | Resignation of Michael Martin (Speaker) | Lab win |

*Note*: Three further by-elections could have been held following the death in December 2009 of the Labour MP for North West Leicestershire, David Taylor, the resignation in January 2010 of the Democratic Unionist MP for Strangford, Iris Robinson, and the death in March 2010 of the Labour MP for Middlesbrough South and East Cleveland, Ashok Kumar. In the event, by-elections were not held before the general election.

Labour also lost ground in every set of annual local elections held after 2005. In 2006, Labour's estimated equivalent share of the national vote, based on their performance in that year's local elections, was just 26 per cent. This result put the party behind the Conservatives on 39 per cent but ahead of the Liberal Democrats on 25 per cent. In the May 2008 local elections, Labour's estimated share fell to just 24 per cent, and the party lost 334 local council seats and the control of nine councils. It was their worst showing in decades.[74] In the 2009 local elections in England, the last before the general election, Labour's 22 per cent of the vote meant the party slumped into third place, behind the Conservatives on 35 per cent and the Liberal Democrats on 25 per cent.[75]

The 2009 local elections were held on the same day as that year's European parliamentary elections. Labour again came third with 15.7 per cent, the worst performance by any governing party since direct elections were first held in 1979. This time, Labour was beaten by the Conservatives (27.7 per cent) and the United Kingdom Independence Party or UKIP (16.5 per cent), a party committed to withdrawal from the EU. There were also successes for the far-right British National Party (BNP). Worryingly for the government, the BNP tended to perform best in areas that were considered to be natural Labour territory, in the Midlands and the North. Here, many white working-class voters, hostile to immigration, felt let down and forgotten by Labour. In Barnsley, a former mining town in Yorkshire and the archetypal compact working-class community, the party's share of the vote dropped from 45 per cent to 25 per cent. The BNP's rose from 8 per cent to 17 per cent.

## Enemies within the gates

The Labour government also had to contend with internal opponents. One group who might have been expected to cause mischief were the trade unions. Both the party and the unions were part of a wider Labour movement; the unions had founded the party in 1900 and bankrolled it ever since. Together, the unions and Labour formed a mutually beneficial but sometimes 'contentious alliance'.[76] One of Blair's objectives as leader had been to end Labour's symbolic dependence on the industrial wing of the movement. He had promised them 'fairness not favours', a promise generally made good. Labour's second term witnessed an acrimonious strike by the Fire Brigades Union, but otherwise, and by historical standards, Labour faced no serious industrial unrest.[77] It was much the same during Labour's third term. The unions obtained concessions from the government over its plans to raise the public-sector retirement age to 65, and the Communication Workers Union inconvenienced the public with a series of strikes by postal workers in 2007 and 2009. But there was no hint of a repeat of the 'Winter of Discontent' and the breakdown in government-union relations that had hamstrung Callaghan's ministry in 1979.

Much more threatening for the government was its own parliamentary party. Historically, Labour MPs had been riven by factionalism and tribalism. Another of Blair's objectives as leader had been to introduce greater discipline. In this, he was initially too successful. Labour MPs were actually criticised for their servility in the government's first term. The unity began to fray during Labour's second term. Opposition to the Iraq war, discontent with the government's public-service reforms and dissatisfaction with Blair's style, coupled with a now solid core of refuseniks, fuelled a wider confidence among backbench Labour MPs that they could rebel and get away with it.[78]

The fraying of discipline continued in the third term, as Table 1.4 shows. Labour's third term was in fact the most rebellious in the whole of the postwar period, with 365 rebellions involving government MPs (28.3 per cent of all votes in the Commons). During Blair's final two years in office, the government was defeated four times, despite its healthy overall majority. The party proved no less rebellious under Brown, who suffered two defeats and 235 rebellions in three years.

TABLE 1.4    *The restless PLP, 1997–2010*

| | First term | Second term | Third term | | | 1997–2010 |
| --- | --- | --- | --- | --- | --- | --- |
| | | | Blair | Brown | Total | |
| Total number of rebellions | 96 | 259 | 130 | 235 | 365 | 720 |
| Rebellions as % of all divisions | 7.5% | 20.8% | 26.0% | 29.8% | 28.3% | 18.9% |
| Rebellions involving 20+ MPs | 28 | 63 | 23 | 23 | 46 | 137 |
| Number of individual Labour MPs who rebelled at least once | 133 | 218 | 109 | 142 | 174 | 292 |
| Government defeats | 0 | 0 | 4 | 2 | 6 | 6 |

*Source*: Philip Cowley and Mark Stuart, www.revolts.co.uk.

As ever, the most worrying internal opponents for both Blair and Brown were to be found at the very top of government. Brown was Blair's most dangerous rival, while Brown discovered that his closest colleagues were potential assassins. Labour's dire electoral performances, coupled with his own perceived shortcomings, contributed to a run on Brown's personal authority no less dramatic than the run on Northern Rock. Brown endured no fewer than three attempted putsches during his premiership. The first came in the late summer of 2008 when David Miliband, the foreign secretary, added his voice to the dissatisfaction being expressed by many MPs about Brown's leadership. Miliband soon backed down, conscious that there was no consensus in the cabinet to oust Brown and absolutely no consensus on who should replace him. The prime minister's hold on office was strengthened when he brought back Peter Mandelson into the government in an autumn reshuffle.[79] Mandelson was the third man of the New Labour project, and, with Blair and Brown, was one of its chief architects. His presence temporarily neutered Blairite opposition to Brown. Although a controversial character – he had twice resigned from Blair's cabinet because of scandal – Mandelson's stint as Britain's commissioner in the European Commission had given him additional stature. His authority bolstered Brown's.

The second putsch came in the summer of 2009 and was a much more serious affair. In the immediate wake of the expenses scandal, one cabinet minister, Hazel Blears, publicly criticised the government's failure to connect with the public and personally criticised the prime minister. Ministers who speak out in such ways rarely last long. Blears, aware that a reshuffle was imminent, quit the government. Then, on the day of the local and European parliamentary elections, an up-and-coming Blairite minister, the work and pensions secretary James Purnell, resigned. Purnell's letter to Brown was blunt: 'I now believe your continued leadership makes a Conservative victory more, not less likely.' Again, however, the putsch failed, partly because the party's own rules made it very difficult to mount a challenge, partly because other ministers were unsure whether having a new leader would actually help Labour's prospects or not, but largely because there was still no consensus on who should replace him.[80] A large number of Labour MPs and ministers wanted Brown gone, yet no one was prepared to wield the dagger. Mandelson, the man who might have tipped the balance, remained loyal.

The last Labour prime minister to be the object of such intense vilification in his own cabinet, Harold Wilson in the late 1960s, had been fortunate in that there were always at least two very obvious contenders for his crown, first George Brown and Jim Callaghan, then Callaghan and Roy Jenkins, who each checked the others' ambitions.[81] Gordon Brown was helped by the fact that there was no pretender to his throne. The political dominance that he had shared with Blair since 1997 was reaping dividends. This factor, coupled with his almost super-human doggedness, probably saved his skin.

The final attempted putsch came in January 2010 when two former cabinet ministers, Geoff Hoon and Patricia Hewitt, wrote an open letter calling for a vote of confidence in Brown's leadership. Despite garnering headlines, their call attracted little support among Labour MPs, not least because an election was now months away. Nevertheless, it was a good indication of how panicked many in the party were by fears of an impending electoral meltdown. The episode also confirmed what the public suspected. In April 2008, YouGov had asked voters: 'Do you think the Labour Party at the moment is united or divided?' In response, 76 per cent had answered 'divided'.[82] The attempts to unseat Brown only made the party seem more so.

## Conclusion

By the beginning of 2010, with an election looming, Labour's disunity in the face of political adversity was just one of many problems confronting the government. The once-buoyant economy, which had underpinned the government throughout its first and second terms, had punctured, and Brown, like Blair in his final months, seemed unable to give the government a clear sense of direction. Blair and Brown in tandem had been a powerful and dominant partnership. As their relationship disintegrated, so too did the New Labour project. By 2010, the party was Old and Tired Labour.

A lack of direction from the top was also evident in the party's preparations for the forthcoming election. Brown, the tribal politician, wanted to stress the dividing lines between Labour, the party of social justice and fairness, and the Conservatives, the party of privilege. Brown, the astute big-tent strategist, wanted to appeal to aspirational voters and perhaps reach out to the Liberal Democrats in the event of a hung parliament. And Brown, the former chancellor, wanted to emphasise that he above all had the know-how to rescue the faltering British economy in the wake of the financial crisis. It was difficult to be certain what Labour now stood for. In the event, Labour lost, though its defeat was far from catastrophic, and Brown resigned as leader. As the party prepared to choose a successor, its surviving MPs could lick their wounds and wonder whether they would have done better had they ditched Brown sooner.

## Endnotes

1   Clement Attlee, Labour's great post-war prime minister, had led the party to victory in 1945 and again in 1950. Harold Wilson had led the party to victory in 1964 and 1966 and again, after the Conservatives triumphed in 1970, in February and October 1974. But none of Wilson's victories matched those of Blair's in 1997 or 2001.

2   Macmillan quit because of ill health in 1963 and was succeeded by Sir Alec Douglas Home. Thatcher was forced out by colleagues in 1990 and replaced by John Major.

3   Gordon Brown became the sixth man since 1945 to become prime minister by accession: Sir Anthony Eden succeeded Sir Winston Churchill in 1955; Harold Macmillan succeeded Eden in 1957; Sir Alec Douglas Home succeeded Macmillan in 1963; James Callaghan succeeded Harold Wilson in 1976; and John Major succeeded Margaret Thatcher in 1990.

4   An enjoyable history of Labour in government after 2001 is Andrew Rawnsley, *The End of the Party: The Rise and Fall of New Labour* (London: Penguin, 2010). A number of

other books analyse Blair's final years in office, including: Anthony Seldon, ed., *Blair's Britain, 1997–2007* (Cambridge: Cambridge University Press, 2007); Matt Beech and Simon Lee, eds, *Ten Years of New Labour* (Basingstoke, Hants.: Palgrave Macmillan, 2008); and Terence Casey, ed., *The Blair Legacy: Politics, Policy, Governance, and Foreign Affairs* (Basingstoke, Hants.: Palgrave, 2009). Finally, two of New Labour's leading figures published memoirs within months of the party's defeat: *Tony Blair, A Journey* (London: Hutchinson, 2010); and Peter Mandelson, *The Third Man: Life at the Heart of New Labour* (London: HarperPress, 2010). This chapter draws on these books and also on contemporary newspaper reports.

5   The nature of that promise is discussed in James Naughtie, *The Rivals: The Intimate Story of a Political Marriage* (London: Fourth Estate, 2001), pp. 69–75.

6   For a concise oversight of Labour's second term, see Thomas Quinn, 'Tony Blair's second term', in John Bartle and Anthony King, eds, *Britain at the Polls 2005* (Washington, DC: CQ Press, 2006), pp. 1–30.

7   Brown's interpretation is corroborated to some extent by John Prescott, Blair's long-serving and loyal deputy, who insists that Blair told Brown in November 2003 that he would go by the next (2005) election. As Prescott writes, 'Tony maintained later that he hadn't said it. As far as I'm concerned, he did. Tony reneged on his promise.' See John Prescott, *Prezza: My Story: Pulling No Punches* (London: Headline Review, 2008), p. 315. Blair confirms his offer to Brown at this meeting but insists that it was conditional on the chancellor's 'full and unconditional support' for the prime minister's reform agenda. When that support was not forthcoming, Blair felt himself absolved from the deal. See Blair, *A Journey*, p. 497.

8   Polly Toynbee, 'After years of skirmishing, the civil war Labour dreaded has broken out', *Guardian*, 7 September 2006.

9   'Transcript: 'I wouldn't go on and on and on'', *Guardian*, 1 October 2004.

10  The most recent edition of this classic study is Richard E. Neustadt, *Presidential Power and the Modern Presidents: The Politics of Leadership from Roosevelt to Reagan* (New York: Free Press, 1990).

11  Reflecting on the weeks after the 2005 election, Blair recognised that 'talking about the transition to a new leader was … both a little humiliating and weakening' (Blair, *A Journey*, p. 553). In September 2006, a senior minister serving in Blair's government, home secretary John Reid, said publicly about the prime minister: 'I think he was stupid to himself and to our prospects by saying he was going to go – but he said it.' See Tania Branigan, 'Blair was stupid to announce departure, says home secretary', *Guardian*, 26 September 2006.

12  These figures are those reported in House of Commons Standard Note SN/PC/05650, *Twentieth Century Prime Ministers and their Governments*, available at: www.parliament.uk/documents/commons/lib/research/briefings/snpc-05650.pdf (last accessed 26 August 2010).

13  David Cracknell, 'Labour MPs tell Blair to quit Downing Street', *Sunday Times*, 8 May 2005.

14  Department for Education and Skills, *Higher Standards, Better Schools for All: More Choice for Parents and Pupils*, Cm 6677 (London: TSO, 2005).

15  Patrick Wintour, 'Reid vents fury at Home Office over prisoners fiasco', *Guardian*, 24 May 2006.

16  For his part, Blair 'never had any doubt' that Brown had organised the letter: Blair, *A Journey*, p. 620.

17  See Prescott, *Prezza*, pp. 324–5.

18  Ipsos MORI, 'Political monitor: satisfaction ratings 1997–present', available at: www. ipsos-mori.com/researchpublications/researcharchive/poll.aspx?oItemID=88&view=wide (last accessed 26 August 2010).

19  Some 22 per cent said Blair should go 'Between next May and next year's party conference', 23 per cent said 'Before next May's elections in Scotland, Wales and English local councils', and 37 per cent said 'This autumn'. See YouGov survey for Channel 4 News, September 2006, available at: www.yougov.co.uk/extranets/ygarchives/content/pdf/Labfinal060907.pdf (last accessed 26 August 2010).

20  'Tony Blair's "Media" speech: the prime minister's Reuters speech on public life', *The Political Quarterly*, 78 (2007): 476–87.

21  Soon after leaving Downing Street, Blair, a religious man and ostensibly an Anglican, made public his conversion to Catholicism.

22  *House of Commons Debates*, Vol. 462, Part 113, 27 June 2007, column 334.

23  Polly Toynbee, 'Hold your nose, vote Blair and Brown will be the victor', *Guardian*, 6 April 2005.

24  Ipsos MORI conducted the survey. One of the questions asked respondents how successful or unsuccessful they thought each chancellor was using a 0–10 scale, with 0 being highly unsuccessful and 10 being highly successful. Brown's average score of 7.9 was nearly two points greater than the 6.1 scored by his two nearest rivals, the former Conservative chancellor Kenneth Clarke and the former Labour chancellor Sir Stafford Cripps. See Ipsos MORI, 'Brown most successful chancellor, say british political scientists', available at: www.ipsos-mori.com/researchpublications/researcharchive/poll.aspx?oItemId=367  (last accessed 26 August 2010).

25  Rawnsley, *The End of the Party*, p. 223.

26  Rachel Sylvester, Alice Thomson and Toby Helm, 'Clarke attack on Brown "the deluded control freak"', *Daily Telegraph*, 9 September 2006.

27  See, for example, Peter Watt, *Inside Out: My Story of Betrayal and Cowardice at the Heart of New Labour* (London: Biteback, 2010), p. 174.

28  For a full – and critical – critique of Brown's personality and politics, see Tom Bower, *Gordon Brown: Prime Minister* (London: Harper Perennial, 2007).

29  Mrs Rochester was the mad woman in the attic in Charlotte Bronte's novel *Jane Eyre*. See Simon Walters, 'Brown at No. 10? It's like letting Mrs Rochester out of the attic', *Mail on Sunday*, 25 February 2007. Tony Blair was sympathetic to Field's appraisal. In his memoirs (p. 616), he describes Brown as lacking political feelings and emotional intelligence. For this reason, and others, Blair writes: 'I had a feeling that that my going and being succeeded by Gordon was also terminal for the government'. See Blair, *A Journey*, p. 617.

30  Philippe Naughton, 'Brown hit by "Stalinist" attack on Budget eve', *The Times*, 20 March 2007.

31  See Watt, *Inside Out*, p. 158. Brown appointed Harman to the position of Labour party chairwoman and charged her with the strengthening relations between the party leadership

and its activist base. This intermediary role was further augmented by her appointment to the post of leader of the House, which would mean her taking a more prominent role in liaising with Labour MPs.

32  An edited volume of articles first published in the *Guardian* and *Observer* newspapers tracks the unfolding drama. See Colin Hughes, ed., *What Went Wrong Gordon Brown? How the Dream Job Turned Sour* (London: Guardian Books, 2010).

33  To demonstrate his inclusive approach to politics, Brown even invited former prime minister Margaret Thatcher to tea at Downing Street in September 2007. The invitation was criticised by both the Conservative right, for whom Thatcher was a hero, and the Labour left, for whom Thatcher was a villain. But the visit served its purpose of making Brown seem inclusive, it ensured good publicity, and it also probably made an elderly lady happy.

34  Peter Hennessy, 'Rulers and servants of the State: the Blair style of Government 1997–2004', *Parliamentary Affairs*, 58 (2005): 6–16.

35  George Jones, 'Brown moves to restore power to Cabinet with dig at Blair', *Daily Telegraph*, 2 July 2007.

36  For an insider's account of just how prepared the party organisation was for an early election, see Watt, *Inside Out*, pp. 164–77.

37  *House of Commons Debates*, Vol. 468, Part 14, 28 November 2007, column 275.

38  For a brief overview of Labour's macro-economic performance during the period, see Peter Sinclair, 'The Treasury and economic policy', in Seldon, ed., *Blair's Britain*, pp. 186–90.

39  Tania Branigan, 'Labour – and Brown – slide further says ICM poll', *Guardian*, 20 March 2007.

40  Decca Aitkenhead, 'Storm Warning', *Guardian*, 29 August 2008.

41  Patrick Wintour, Jill Treanor and Ashley Seager, '£50bn bid to save UK banks', *Guardian*, 8 October 2008.

42  Chris Giles and George Parker, 'Tax hit to fund £20bn fiscal stimulus', *Financial Times*, 24 November 2008.

43  HM Treasury, *Budget 2010: Securing the Recovery*, HC 451 (London: TSO, 2010), p. 221.

44  HM Treasury, *Budget 2010*, p. 4.

45  The most famous exposition of this idea can be found in Martin Paldam, 'The distribution of election results and the two explanations of the cost of ruling', *European Journal of Political Economy*, 2 (1986): 5–24.

46  Rowena Crawford, Carl Emmerson and Gemma Tetlow, *A Survey of Public Spending in the UK* (London: Institute for Fiscal Studies, 2009), p. 17.

47  ICM poll for the *Guardian*, March 2007, available at: www.icmresearch.co.uk/pdfs/2007_march_guardian_poll.pdf (last accessed 26 August 2010).

48  Gordon Brown, 'Speech on smarter government', 7 December 2009.

49  *Labour Party, Britain Forward Not Back* (Sutton, Surrey: The Labour Party, 2005), p. 6.

50  John Curtice and Oliver Heath, 'Do people want choice and diversity of provision in public services?', in Alison Park, John Curtice, Katarina Thomson, Miranda Phillips, Elizabeth Clary and Sarah Butt, eds, *British Social Attitudes: The 26th Report* (London: Sage, 2010), pp. 55–78.

51  Gordon Brown, 'Speech to Public Service Reform Conference: 21st century public services – Learning from front line', 27 March 2009.

52  Matthew Taylor, 'Blair is dead, long live Blair', *New Statesman*, 31 January 2008; Andrew Rawnsley, 'The latest version of the PM – Brown with added Blair', *Observer*, 10 February 2008.

53  Alison Walker, John Flatley, Chris Kershaw and Debbie Moon, eds, *Crime in England and Wales 2008/09 Volume 1: Findings from the British Crime Survey and Police Recorded Crime* (London: Home Office, 2009), p. 97.

54  Walker et al. *Crime in England and Wales 2008/09 Volume 1*, pp. 20–3.

55  Ross Bailey, Elizabeth Fuller and Rachel Ormston, 'Smoking, drinking and drugs: reactions to reform', in Park et al., eds, *British Social Attitudes*, pp. 243–68, at p. 260.

56  Andrew Porter, 'British public wants 42-day terror detention', *Daily Telegraph*, 10 June 2008.

57  For example, just after the 2005 election, YouGov presented respondents with the proposed referendum question: 'Should the United Kingdom approve the treaty establishing a constitution for the European Union?' In response, 21 per cent said they would vote yes, compared with 46 per cent who said they would vote no. See YouGov survey for the *Daily Telegraph*, May 2005, available at: www.yougov.co.uk/extranets/ygarchives/content/pdf/TEL050101004_2.pdf (last accessed 26 August 2010).

58  For a scholarly assessment of the documents, see Steve Peers, 'Analysis of the amended text of the draft Reform Treaty', *Statewatch Analysis 5: EU Reform Treaty*, available at: www.statewatch.org/news/2007/oct/analysis-5-reform-treaty-oct-2007.pdf (last accessed 26 August 2010.

59  European Scrutiny Select Committee, *European Union Intergovernmental Conference, Thirty-fifth Report of Session 2006–07*, HC 1014 (London: TSO, 2007), p. 16.

60  Richard Ford, 'More than half of new jobs go to migrants', *The Times*, 31 October 2007.

61  ICM poll for the *Sunday Telegraph*, available at: www.icmresearch.co.uk/pdfs/2009_oct_sunday_telegraph_political_poll.pdf (last accessed 26 August 2010).

62  The precise human cost of the Iraq war will almost certainly never be known. The Iraq Body Count, which records reported violent deaths, report a number in the region of 100,000. The figure of £8 billion was offered up by Gordon Brown in evidence to the Chilcot Inquiry. See Patrick Wintour, 'Right war, right reasons: day Gordon Brown came clean on Iraq', *Guardian*, 6 March 2010.

63  David Brown, Michael Evans and Deborah Haynes, 'Ex-defence chief attacks Brown's evidence to Iraq inquiry', *The Times*, 6 March 2010.

64  YouGov survey for the *Sunday Times*, July 2009, available at: www.yougov.co.uk/archives/pdf/ST-toplines_JULY09.pdf (last accessed 26 August 2010).

65  The numbers include all deaths occurring as a result of accidental and violent causes while deployed, as well as deaths due to disease related causes during the deployment. See Ministry of Defence, 'Operations in Afghanistan: British casualties', available at: www.mod.uk/DefenceInternet/FactSheets/OperationsFactsheets/OperationsInAfghanistanBritishCasualties.htm (last accessed on 26 August 2010).

66  Richard Norton-Taylor, Julian Glover and Nicholas Watt , 'Public support for war in Afghanistan is firm, despite deaths', *Guardian*, 13 July 2009.

67  Slightly Soiled was a character in J. M. Barrie's *Peter Pan*. Anthony King, 'Tony Blair's first term', in Anthony King, ed., *Britain at the Polls, 2001* (Chatham, NJ: Chatham House, 2002), pp. 1–44, at p. 29.

68  Lance Price, *Where Power Lies: Prime Ministers v the Media* (London: Simon & Schuster, 2010), pp. 424–8.

69  Anthony King, 'Poll shows Labour in freefall', *Daily Telegraph*, 30 November 2007.

70  Andrew Porter, 'MPs expenses row hurts major parties, Telegraph poll suggests', *Daily Telegraph*, 18 May 2009.

71  A Conservative peer, Lord Hanningfield, was also charged for similar offences in respect of House of Lords allowances. After the election, another Labour MP, Eric Illsley, was charged with false accounting.

72  The other MPs to be barred were Margaret Moran, Elliot Morley, David Chaytor and Jim Devine. It was Dr Gibson's supportive local constituency chairman who described the process as a 'kangaroo court'. See Allegra Stratton, 'Labour accused of operating 'kangaroo court' in expenses row', *Guardian*, 3 June 2009.

73  ICM poll for the *Sunday Telegraph*, available at: www.icmresearch.co.uk/pdfs/2009_may_suntele_euro_poll.pdf (last accessed 26 August 2010).

74  See House of Commons Research Paper 08/48, *Local elections 2008*, available at: www.parliament.uk/commons/lib/research/rp2008/RP08-048.pdf (last accessed 26 August 2010).

75  See House of Commons Research Paper 09/54, *Local elections 2009*, available at: www.parliament.uk/commons/lib/research/rp2009/rp09-054.pdf (last accessed 26 August 2010).

76  The fullest historical account of Labour's relations with the trade unions is provided in Lewis Minkin, *The Contentious Alliance: Trade Unions and the Labour Party* (Edinburgh: Edinburgh University Press, 1991).

77  See Thomas Quinn, 'New Labour and the trade unions in Britain', *Journal of Elections, Public Opinion and Parties*, 20 (2010): 357–80.

78  Philip Cowley and Mark Stuart, 'A rebellious decade: backbench rebellions under Tony Blair, 1997–2007', in Beech and Lee, eds, *Ten Years of New Labour*, pp. 103–19, at p. 109.

79  See Mandelson, *The Third Man*, pp. 1–39.

80  Under the rules, seventy MPs had to nominate a challenger to an incumbent leader and a special vote of the party conference, Labour's sovereign body, was required. See Thomas Quinn, 'Leasehold or freehold? Leader-eviction rules in the British Conservative and Labour Parties', *Political Studies*, 53 (2005): 793–815.

81  To protect his crown, Wilson always sought to increase the number of crown princes. For a brief overview of this strategy and how it helped to save his job, see Ben Pimlott, *Harold Wilson* (London: HarperCollins, 1992), pp. 489, 534–6.

82  YouGov, survey for the *Daily Telegraph*, April 2008, available at: www.yougov.co.uk/extranets/ygarchives/content/pdf/DT%2008%2004%2023%20topline.pdf (last accessed 26 August 2010).

# 2 THE CONSERVATIVE PARTY

Tim Bale and Paul Webb

For eight years after its disastrous defeat at the general election of 1997, the Conservative party found it difficult, if not impossible, to accept that the Thatcherite strategy for electoral success just was not working any more.[1] Populist policies that promised to be tough on law and order, limit immigration and resist European interference in British affairs, together with neo-liberal policies of low taxation, deregulation and a generally smaller state simply did not attract enough voters. Attempts by Conservative leaders to depart from that orthodoxy and steer a more pragmatic, moderate course were inconsistent, incoherent and uncommitted. Neither William Hague (who led the party between 1997 and 2001) nor Iain Duncan Smith (2001–03) were taken seriously by the electorate and both spent much of their time worrying about how they were going to retain the leadership.[2] This continual threat of replacement limited their ability to formulate an electoral strategy. Michael Howard became the unopposed leader after Duncan Smith was defeated on a vote of confidence by his fellow Tory MPs in October 2003. Howard had no need to worry about challenges to his leadership because, by the time he was drafted in to pick the party up off the floor, there was no one else willing to do the job. But he, too, was a convinced Thatcherite. None of these three leaders, therefore, really believed in an alternative approach to what they knew best. Nor did they have any confidence in their ability to sell one to voters. Instead they chose to fight elections on those issues – crime, tax, immigration, and Europe – where they believed that they had at least some small advantage over Labour. The results in 1997, 2001 and 2005, as some of their own advisors and most pollsters had predicted, were awful.

## The Conservatives smell the coffee

Surveys of public opinion regularly showed that the Conservative party had serious problems. Post-election surveys suggested that the party was not trusted to manage the economy or to run the public services. Historically, the Labour party – the Conservatives' main competitor – was thought to be more caring than the Conservatives but less competent, while the Conservatives were less caring but a good deal more competent.[3] The Conservative party's reputation for competence was shattered after Britain had been forced out of the Exchange Rate Mechanism (ERM) in 1992, however, and the party became increasingly and bitterly divided over the issue of Europe, which had contributed to Margaret Thatcher's downfall as leader in 1990.[4] To add to their problems, Tony Blair's government had governed with a degree of competence that surprised many Tories. By 2005 there was no assurance that the Conservatives could simply wait for Labour to fail, as it had done so often in the past.

Lord Ashcroft, the Conservative donor, commissioned detailed research on the public's attitudes towards the Conservative party in the wake of the defeat in 2005, and it was published under the provocative title of *Smell the Coffee*. The findings, such as those displayed in Table 2.1, provided a wake-up call to the party. Labour enjoyed a net lead of 40 points over the Conservatives on competence and of 29 points on being caring. Other evidence, displayed in Table 2.2, suggested that voters thought the Tory party was stuck in the past, had not learned from its mistakes, cared more about the well-off than the have nots and did not offer opportunity. Even those Tory policies that appeared to resonate with the electorate proved less popular once they had the party's label attached to them. As Table 2.3 shows, a proposal to restrict immigration gathered net support of +55 but this fell to +43 when it was presented as Conservative policy. Ashcroft's evidence invited the party to consider why their 'brand' had become contaminated.

The party's electoral strategy up to 2005 had failed even to mobilise many of its own partisans. Party membership and identification with the party continued to fall. William Hague's wholesale reorganisation of the party in his *Fresh Future* administrative reforms did nothing to halt the decline.

TABLE 2.1    *The Conservative and Labour brands, spring 2005: the nationwide view*

| | Labour | | | Conservative | | | |
| --- | --- | --- | --- | --- | --- | --- | --- |
| | Agree % | Disagree % | Net | Agree % | Disagree % | Net | Total Net |
| Competent and capable | 59 | 38 | 21 | 38 | 57 | −19 | 40 |
| Cares about ordinary people's problems | 53 | 43 | 10 | 38 | 57 | −19 | 29 |
| Shares my values | 49 | n/a | n/a | 36 | 60 | −24 | n/a |

*Source*: Adapted from Michael Ashcroft, *Smell the Coffee: A Wake-Up Call for the Conservative Party* (London: n.p., 2009), pp. 94–7.

TABLE 2.2  *The Conservative brand, spring 2005: the view from swing seats*

|  | Agree – disagree |
|---|---|
| Stuck in the past | 13 |
| Learned from past mistakes and more likely to deliver promises than Labour | −9 |
| Offers opportunity for all whatever their background | −17 |
| Cares more about the well-off than the have-nots | 10 |

*Source*: Adapted from Ashcroft, *Smell the Coffee*, pp. 49–50.

*Note*: The figures show the differences between the percentage of respondents who agreed with each statement and the percentage who disagreed.

TABLE 2.3  *The Conservative brand, spring 2005: putting people off their policies?*

|  | Agree % | Disagree % | Net |
|---|---|---|---|
| Immigration policy not attributed to the Conservatives | 73 | 18 | +55 |
| Same immigration policy attributed to the Conservatives | 70 | 27 | +43 |
| Difference | −3 | +9 | −12 |

*Source*: Adapted from Ashcroft, *Smell the Coffee*, pp. 51–2.

The Tories defeat in 2005, therefore, came as no surprise. Only Labour's poor performance allowed the Conservatives to win back some seats. Nevertheless, the election still represented, as one respected Conservative commentator reminded his party, its third worst result for over a century.[5]

# Responding to defeat in 2005: the long leadership contest

At first glance, the Conservative party's immediate response to their loss in the 2005 election was par for the course: like John Major in 1997 and William Hague in 2001, Michael Howard announced his resignation on the morning after the election. There was, however, a twist. Privately, Howard blamed himself for the Tories' failure to win back more seats from Labour and believed that he had effectively tested the right-wing or Thatcherite strategy to destruction. Indeed, behind the scenes he encouraged pollsters to tell his MPs as much when they returned to parliament. It was time, he concluded, for the party to be led in a different direction, preferably by one or other of two of his younger colleagues, George Osborne, the shadow chancellor of the exchequer, or David Cameron, the shadow education spokesman. In order to ensure that they would have enough time to decide who would stand for the leadership and then win over doubters, Howard announced that the contest to replace him would not take place until the party had had a chance to vote on some significant rule changes. The most important proposal was to alter the method of selecting the leader. Under existing rules introduced in 1998 and first used to elect Duncan Smith in 2001, the Tory leader was chosen by a two-stage process: first, there was a series of ballots among MPs that reduced the field to two candidates; and second, there was a ballot of the national membership that chose between these two. Howard's reform would have given MPs the final say on who should be leader and removed the need for a ballot of the membership. This was coupled with proposals to give the party's governing board new powers to reorganise dysfunctional or underperforming local constituency associations and dilute their influence on the party's national convention.

The plan to alter the leadership selection rules was controversial. It was partly responsible for the success of the website, ConservativeHome, which became *the* aggregator of media stories and blogs on the Tories, as well as a source for those wanting juicy gossip and indicators of what activists thought. But the plan also had one very big plus point: it would make it very difficult for anyone to become leader who did not enjoy the confidence of a majority of his fellow MPs. This would effectively block the ambition of one of the obvious contenders, David Davis. Moreover, even if the plan were rejected (which was in fact what happened), the time taken to put it to the vote would allow candidates other than Davis, some of whom – notably Cameron – were less well known outside Westminster, to set out their stall.

David Cameron had a traditional Tory background. He was born into a wealthy family and went to Eton, Britain's most famous and prestigious public (that is, private) school. He subsequently went to Oxford, where – together with George Osborne and Boris Johnson, another Conservative MP and future London mayor – he was a member of the infamous Bullingdon Club, an elitist dining club, where membership is by invitation only. From Oxford he went straight into the Conservative party's research department. He then served as a special advisor to Norman Lamont, the chancellor of the exchequer, between 1990 and 1993. Cameron was working for Lamont when Britain crashed out of the ERM in September 1992.[6] He later worked as an advisor to Michael Howard, then home secretary. After the Conservatives lost power in 1997 he worked in public relations for Carlton Television, before securing election as MP for Witney, a very middle-England Oxfordshire seat in 2001.

Cameron was seen by many at Westminster as someone with a bright future. He quickly rose to the shadow cabinet and helped to write the 2005 manifesto. He was, however, regarded as much more of a moderate and a moderniser than Howard. Cameron not only read the findings from opinion polls and focus groups but, like his close political friends George Osborne and Steve Hilton, a Tory strategist, he was determined to act on them. These three men, together with a wider circle of friends, were quickly dubbed 'the Notting Hill Set' because of their supposedly privileged lifestyles. While all admired Margaret Thatcher, they realised that her strategy would not necessarily work two decades after her downfall. They believed that the Tories must do all those things that Tory oppositions, including Thatcher's between 1975 and 1979, had done to put the party back in contention. Instead of 'banging on' about issues that whipped up the party faithful but alienated large numbers of voters – especially many liberal middle-class voters who ought otherwise to be Tory supporters – the party should concentrate on bringing in fresh faces and emphasising unity of purpose and personnel. It should also start talking about a new agenda that distinguished the party from its past, improve its research and campaigning capacity, and prioritise pragmatism over ideology.[7]

The big question was whether the Conservative party was ready – at last – to be told it had to change. The prospects did not appear wholly encouraging. Four years earlier, Michael Portillo, the former defence secretary, had stood for the leadership offering the same message that Cameron was now delivering and was defeated. Portillo's narrow failure to get though the parliamentary round of voting, however, had as much to do with revelations about his sexuality and Spanish origins as his policy platform.[8] Cameron, in contrast, was as English as they come (despite his Scots surname) and was happy to stress that his tolerance and inclusivity did not preclude a strong commitment to the 'family values' supported by traditional Tories. As such, he was Portillo without the problems. Rather than campaigning simply as Howard's anointed successor, Cameron decided to ask for nothing less than a mandate for change against opponents who, it became clear, had little or nothing new to offer.

Only one of Cameron's opponents, Ken Clarke, a former chancellor of the exchequer, could claim to want to return the party to the centre ground. But he was a Europhile in a thoroughly Eurosceptic party and had great difficulty attracting support for that reason. He had, moreover, withdrawn from front-line politics since losing two previous leadership contests in 1997 and 2001. Clarke stood no more chance – in fact probably less chance – in 2005.[9]

Another contender, Dr Liam Fox, had, like Cameron, youth and Euroscepticism on his side. He was a neo-liberal committed to low taxation and deregulation but also appealed to the instincts of many Conservatives by claiming that Britain was a 'broken society' that needed to re-emphasise traditional values and welfare reform (themes associated with the 'neo-conservatives' in the US). Such policies suggested that he might be to the right of even those leaders who had lost the Tories the last three elections. The same, some argued, could be said of the supposed favourite, David Davis, the man whose ambition the proposed reforms to the leadership-election process looked designed to thwart. Davis had something of a rags-to-riches story since he was brought up on a South London housing estate by his single mother. He was a self-made man, a successful business-man and a former member of the territorial (that is, part-time) Special Air Service (SAS), Britain's elite army unit. He had been an MP since 1987 and was minister for Europe in the Major government. In opposition he became chairman of the House of Commons Public Accounts Committee. He had contested the Conservative leadership in 2001 but came a poor fourth and was made party chairman by Duncan Smith. His sacking from that role in 2002 created some sympathy and helped to cement his standing in the party at large. To the irritation of some of his fellow MPs he acted as if he believed that he was the Tory leader in waiting. He was, however, thought to have a following among older party members, Eurosceptics, Thatcherites and those ordinary party members for whom the military association mattered a great deal.

Unfortunately for Davis, his innate conservatism meant that he failed either to appreciate or to communicate the extent to which the party had to change, thereby labelling himself as the 'one more heave' candidate (a posi-tion that had characterised the most cautious reformers in the Labour party after its fourth successive defeat in 1992). Davis had also had time to make enemies. Indeed, so great was the dislike and distrust of Davis among his fellow Tory MPs that, despite his frontrunner status, he was very unlikely to emerge in first place in the final parliamentary ballot.

Cameron, therefore, had a much better chance than many realised. He was likely to get votes from those right-wingers impressed by his fluency and his willingness to commit to some of their pet projects, such as pro-moting marriage in the tax system and withdrawing Tory MEPs from the European People's Party (EPP-ED), a grouping in the European Parliament that was committed to a federal future for Europe. He also did his chances a power of good by producing a fantastic, no-notes pitch to his party at the Conservatives' annual conference in Blackpool at the end of September. Just as importantly, it introduced the fresh-faced, highly personable old Etonian to party members and the general public. It also allowed him to present himself as a modern family man with Samantha, his 'yummy mummy' wife, and his young children, including his severely disabled son, Ivan.[10] Focus groups conducted for the BBC by US Republican consultant Frank Luntz recorded a highly favourable response to Cameron. Davis's conference performance, in marked contrast, was distinctly underwhelm-ing and the focus groups were not impressed. When it finally came to the parliamentary ballot, Davis actually lost supporters between the first and second ballot of MPs (Table 2.4). It was clear that his campaign had lost momentum.

The generally favourable reaction to Cameron was evident in an imme-diate boost in his opinion-poll ratings and recognition. Once he made it through to the final two, which he did with ease, this reaction helped him

TABLE 2.4   *The results of the 2005 Conservative party leadership contest*

| Candidate | Parliamentary stage | | National ballot | |
|---|---|---|---|---|
| | **First ballot of MPs** | **Second ballot of MPs** | **Votes of members** | **%** |
| David Cameron | 56 | 90 | 134,446 | 67.6 |
| David Davis | 62 | 57 | 64,398 | 32.4 |
| Liam Fox | 42 | 51 (eliminated) | | |
| Kenneth Clarke | 38 (eliminated) | | | |
| Total | 198 | 198 | 198,884 | 100 |

*Source*: House of Commons Standard Note SN/PC/1366, *Leadership Elections: Conservative Party*, available at http://www.parliament.uk/documents/commons/lib/research/briefings/snpc-01366.pdf. Last accessed 26 August 2010.

beat Davis in the ballot of party members announced at the beginning of December 2005 (Table 2.4).

After three successive defeats, and polling presentations organised by Howard that reinforced the same depressing message, many Conservative MPs and members had come to realise that, whether they liked it or not, the party could no longer sit tight, stand pat, and simply wait for Labour to lose. Moreover, even those who thought it could and should were prepared to try a new type of salesman. Surveys of Tory members showed Cameron winning comprehensively among those who believed that the party should move towards the political centre with more moderate 'One Nation' policies. That was no surprise. More interestingly, he gained about the same share of support as Davis among those who thought the party 'should remain firmly on the right of politics and put clear blue water between the Conservatives and the Labour party'.[11]

Cameron's victory did not mean that everybody in the party had bought wholesale into his 'modernisation' project. Nevertheless, the new leader was at the very least being given a chance to show what he could do – a task made easier by two related developments. First, Cameron, simply in the act of taking over, it appeared, had moved his party into a narrow lead in the opinion polls. The confidence this gave him, combined with his formidable communication skills, helped Cameron put in a series of impressive early appearances in the House of Commons. Second, and a few months later, behind-the-scenes machinations by Gordon Brown's supporters helped persuade Labour MPs that it was about time that Tony Blair stepped aside in favour of his chancellor. In the minds of many Tories, especially those closest to Cameron, who greatly admired the way the Labour leader had taught his party how to win again, Blair's resignation would remove the biggest obstacle to a Tory victory. And many believed that Brown would prove to be a far easier opponent.

## The Cameron project I: 'brand decontamination'

It was fairly clear after Blackpool that Cameron would win the leadership, especially once he had seen off a rather half-hearted attempt to smear him with past stories of teenage and twenty-something drug-taking.[12] The new leader was therefore lucky enough to have more time than his predecessors to plan what he wanted to do. Cameron gathered around him old friends who had worked for the party as advisors and researchers after graduating from university: Steve Hilton and George Bridges, Kate Fall and Ed Llewellyn (a former diplomat who became Cameron's chief of staff), along with Osborne and, later on, the rather older Andrew Mackay MP. In July 2007 they were also joined by Andy Coulson, the former editor of the best-selling Sunday newspaper the *News of the World*, who became the party's director of communications. This group was increasingly referred to in the media as 'Team Cameron'. All of them were determined that the new leader should hit the ground not so much running as sprinting. Symbols and substance, structures as well as specific policies – anything that prevented the party from 'cutting through' to and reconnecting with the electorate – should seem to be open to question and renewal.

The strategy developed for Cameron's first few months in the job required him to do everything he could to personally embody change, modernisation, and, most vitally of all, move onto the centre ground where – in a first-past-the-post system and in a country whose voters are notoriously moderate – elections are most often won and lost. In so doing, Cameron made much of his party's Disraelian commitment to so-called 'One Nation' politics that would unite the country rather than Thatcherite policies that had so divided the country in the 1980s. This did not, for him at least, mean the sort of compromise with social democracy so despised by Thatcherites. It did mean, however, an attempt to come to terms with Britain as it was, post-Blair, rather than with an imagined country (white, middle-class, middlebrow and middle-England) that some fellow Conservatives still believed could and should be reconstituted.[13] It also meant that, at least until the latter half of 2007, Cameron would pursue a modernising strategy with a consistency, coherence and commitment that none of his predecessors since 1997 had come close to achieving.

The New Year of 2006 saw a series of initiatives and announcements on the environment, on big business and on protecting and promoting the country's popular health service, the NHS, that were designed to challenge voters' preconceived views of the Conservative party. Thatcherite policies on health and education – most obviously the patients' and pupils 'passports' that had appeared more geared toward subsidising access to private provision than improving the quality of public services – were unceremoniously dropped. In addition, Cameron took every opportunity to stress his own personal experience and commitment to state provision – realising, as the pollsters had been telling them for years, that, however much it preferred market solutions, the party stood little chance of winning unless it could persuade the public that their schools and hospitals were safe in Tory hands. Cameron and Osborne believed that it was crucial that they tell their party from the very beginning that they could not promise 'up-front, un-funded' tax cuts. They maintained that New Labour had altered the terms of the political debate. In the past, the Tory party had managed to persuade voters that Labour's proposed increases in public spending could only be achieved through a 'double whammy' of higher taxes and higher inflation. New Labour had, however, turned the tables and managed to convince the public that tax cuts would lead to reductions in public services. The Conservatives might one day be able to persuade people that this was not the case, but, as the last two elections had clearly shown, it was not something they should risk trying to do until they were in power.

Team Cameron decided early on that the Conservatives simply had to win back the relatively well-heeled and increasingly well-educated voters (a sizable minority of whom worked in the public sector). This group had deserted the Conservative party at recent elections, partly because of the Tories' reputation as the 'nasty party': obsessive, selfish, moralistic and intolerant. While many of these voters had gone over to Labour, quite a few of them had also voted for the Liberal Democrats. The Conservatives accordingly began a so-called 'love bombing' of Liberal Democrats by stressing the importance of civil liberties. The party's decision to oppose ID cards and draconian anti-terror legislation was also regarded as an important appeal to former Liberal Democrats and no less important than wooing those disillusioned with Labour. The Tory leader proclaimed himself to be a 'liberal conservative' and interested in forging a 'progressive alliance'. He stressed that although civil society often provided better solutions than the top-down, bureaucratic state, he rejected a simplistic 'private good, public bad' mentality associated with his predecessors.

Cameron also sought to blot out the old images with new, more arresting visuals. Some of the most striking of these were photographs taken of him on a husky-drawn sled at the Arctic Circle that were designed to reinforce the party's new-found commitment to the environment (an issue, again, traditionally associated with the Liberal Democrats). This change was captured in the slogan 'Vote blue, go green' that was used in the 2006 local elections. Equally striking – rhetorically if not visually – were the criticisms Cameron made about some of the supposed excesses of big business, particularly its tendency to exploit children by displaying confectionary at the supermarket checkout. Likewise, he criticised chain stores for stocking age-inappropriate clothing for young girls.

Cameron tried to put some distance between the old and new Conservative party. In 2006 he issued an apology for his party's approach to the African National Congress during the apartheid era in South Africa.[14] He also made it clear once again in his first conference speech as leader in the autumn of 2006 that his enthusiasm for supporting marriage and the family did not mean the party had no time for people for whom the meaning of 'family' went beyond the definitions subscribed to by many Conservatives: the term meant something, he insisted, 'whether you're a man and a woman, a woman and a woman, or a man and another man.'[15] Cameron later issued a formal apology for his party's introduction of section 28 of the Local Government Act 1988, which made it illegal for local authorities to 'promote' homosexuality. He told those attending a Gay Pride event: 'I am sorry for section 28. We got it wrong. It was an emotional issue. I hope you can forgive us'.[16]

A similar 'in touch with the twenty-first century' message was sent by the action that Cameron announced would be taken to broaden the party's list of candidates in order to make the Conservatives look more like the electorate whose votes they were seeking. Local constituencies would henceforth be encouraged, although ultimately never absolutely obliged, to select from a 'priority' or 'A List' of candidates, a large proportion of whom were women, deemed especially eligible by the leadership. The list included: Adam Rickitt (a former star of *Coronation Street*, one of Britain's most popular soap operas), Louise Bagshawe, a prominent 'chick-lit' novelist, Zac Goldsmith (an environmentalist and son of the financier James Goldsmith, who had founded the Eurosceptic Referendum Party), Margot James (one of the few openly gay Tories) and Shaun Bailey and Priti Patel (both high-profile ethnic minority candidates).

Cameron's mantra was change. Ideology was out and pragmatism very much in. Thatcherism was not so much apologised for as simply turned into history.[17] The harsh medicine applied by the Conservatives in the 1980s was said to be just what was needed to mend a broken economy, but now the challenges had changed and required different solutions. Cameron picked up on the theme of Liam Fox's leadership campaign and the work of Iain Duncan Smith's think tank, the Centre for Social Justice, by declaring that it was now society that was 'broken'. Moreover, he would say little about Europe, crime, tax and immigration – until the Tory 'brand' had been 'decontaminated' and the party had earned 'permission to be heard'. Cameron-friendly commentators spoke of the so-called 'dinner-party test', whether well-educated, middle-class voters who had hitherto dismissed the Conservatives as too 'nasty' would talk about voting for it when in polite company. Once this reassurance was provided, Cameron and his team hoped that the party could then re-introduce, albeit in more measured language, some of the populist and neo-liberal policies that they still believed in and which, if carefully combined with the modernising and moderate policies, would appeal to a significant numbers of voters. This combination – the assertion that there was no necessary contradiction between the tough and the tender – was 'the politics of *and*' rather than the 'politics of *either or*'.

## The Cameron project II: resistance, rebalancing and recovery

Not everything that was tried in the decontamination phase worked. Some stunts either immediately or eventually backfired. It was revealed, for example, that Cameron was followed on his much publicised (and environmentally friendly) cycle-ride to work by a chauffeur-driven limo carrying his shoes, papers and spare shirts. Others simply fell flat. The document that summarised the new party called *Built to Last* was put to the membership and some 93 per cent voted in its favour. It was subsequently revealed that only 27 per cent of the party's members actually bothered voting at all and that the membership as a whole had shrunk under the new leader.[18] Still, most of the opinion polls that coincided with Cameron's first anniversary as leader in December 2006 brought positive news. Not only was the party maintaining its lead over Labour but Cameron appeared to be shifting perceptions. Some 52 per cent of respondents to YouGov's regular poll agreed that he was 'improving the Conservatives' image' against only 27 per cent who disagreed and 45 per cent agreed he was 'moving the party in the right direction' compared to just 19 per cent who did not.[19]

The battle, however, was by no means won. In early February 2007, some 56 per cent of voters in the South East of England told Populus that they saw the Conservatives as 'mainly the voice of people who are already quite well-off, rather than ordinary working people'.[20] This figure rose to 67 per cent in the North of England and 72 per cent in Scotland. Clearly the party, which was trying to divert more of its resources into reviving its ailing or non-existent infrastructure in the North and Scotland, still had an image problem, as well as a regional problem. Looking on the bright side, however, there was still some time to turn perceptions around and people – even people in the North – were no longer as automatically hostile as they had been. The proportion of people telling YouGov that they would be 'dismayed' by the election of a Tory government had dropped from 46 to 31 per cent between 2005 and March 2007, while the proportion saying they would 'not mind either way' rose from 25 to 36 per cent.[21] The local elections in May 2007 gave the Conservatives a notional share of the vote of around 40 per cent and delivered the party an additional 900 councillors to go out and spread the party's message. Just as importantly, it appeared that Cameron's efforts to win over converts were not, as some traditionalists feared, alienating the faithful. Most dyed-in-the-wool supporters, polls suggested, were content for the moment to give him his head rather than demand he come out with some 'real' Conservative policies. Cameron effectively headed off such calls early on by establishing policy 'review groups' that would come up with suggestions (none of them binding) for the manifesto.[22]

The survey findings and election results matched the mood of the majority of Conservative MPs, especially those thirty- and forty-somethings who had entered parliament in 2001 and 2005. This group either bought into or could at least live with what Cameron was trying to do, especially if it looked like delivering victory. While not necessarily less right-wing than the Conservative MPs they replaced, they were different, regarding Euroscepticism as a given rather than a *casus belli* and admiring Thatcher without actively worshipping her. They – and some of the younger members of the party in the country – were also more comfortable with the UK as it was now rather than how it used to be. And, while no doubt deprecating the idea that a party should form its policies solely on the basis of survey research or focus groups, they did understand that, at least when in opposition, the party had to move towards the voters rather than heroically assuming it could pull those voters towards its own cherished positions. This represented a marked contrast with the attitudes of many of their predecessors.

Despite such support Cameron had to be careful not to alienate some of his more suspicious supporters. His refusal to promise up-front tax and spending cuts created some discontent on the right.[23] But Cameron effectively soothed the latter by emphasising his personal commitment to marriage, the family, and mending 'broken Britain' via the voluntarism and charity of civil society rather than the supposedly failed solutions often favoured by the state. The goodwill thus created overrode not only Cameron's failure to deliver on his promise to pull Conservative MEPs out of the EPP–ED in Brussels and Strasbourg (a pledge fulfilled only after the 2009 European elections) but also his insistence on according due respect to women, homosexuals and ethnic minorities.[24]

Cameron could, not, however, please everyone on the right of his party. And in the spring of 2007 he ran into real trouble. Cameron's stress on targeting the centre-ground and modernisation had from the outset attracted criticism from significant sections of 'the party in the media' – the right-wing commentators and leader-writers whose hysterically negative reaction to any talk of moderation had done nothing to encourage the party's leaders to move it back into the mainstream between 1997 and 2005. Such figures included Peter Hitchens of the *Daily Mail* and Simon Heffer and Janet Daly of the *Daily Telegraph*. Their dire warnings, that it would all end in tears, always resonated with some on the right but only really found an echo when, in early 2007, David Willetts, the education spokesman, called on the party to shift the focus of its education policy from promoting selective grammar schools and instead concentrate on improving the vast majority of state schools that did not select according to ability at age eleven.[25] Cameron was quickly portrayed by members of his own party as a privately-educated elitist who neither knew nor cared about meritocracy. It was also said that he was prepared to ride roughshod over the feelings of a party that still did. Faced with this onslaught Cameron ultimately executed a tactical retreat. He argued that while he had no intention of creating new grammar schools, those already in existence had nothing to fear from a Tory government. He also said that he would look sympathetically on requests from local authorities running such schools to be allowed to build new ones in order to cope with population growth. Discretion probably proved the better part of valour, since Cameron soon came under further pressure as a result of the party's poor performance in the Ealing Southall by-election in July 2007, where its ethnic minority candidate ended up embarrassing the leadership and coming third behind the Liberal Democrats. Even worse, there was increasing evidence of a 'Brown bounce' for Labour in the opinion polls – a development that might, some suggested, lead the new prime minister to call a snap election and defeat the Tories for an unprecedented fourth time in a row.[26]

Cameron, who had looked as if he might be able to coast to victory against Tony Blair's dying Labour government, was suddenly in a tight spot. Despite his best efforts to decontaminate the Tory brand, it was clear that although the public might have warmed to him much more than his immediate predecessors, they were not yet completely convinced about the Conservative party as a whole. YouGov, for instance, found in the summer of 2007 that the average voter located him or herself at –3 on a left-right scale running from –100 to +100, and put Labour at –22. While Cameron was placed at +28, the Conservatives in general were still stranded well out to the right on + 46, only 6 points nearer the centre than they had been when the question had been asked during Michael Howard's tenure as leader.[27] Moreover, as if to emphasise quite how sticky party images are, Labour still enjoyed substantial leads on health, education and the economy, while the Conservatives' only real strong points were – as always – law and order and asylum and immigration.[28] The message from the right-wing media, however, as well as from some of his backbenchers, was a crushingly familiar one, namely that Cameron should forget 'the touchy-feely stuff' and get back onto traditional Tory territory – precisely the ground on which the Conservatives had fought and lost the last two elections.

Cameron and his team had always intended, when the time was right, to begin to talk once again about crime, immigration and tax: after all, as believers in 'the politics of *and*', they did not accept that traditional themes and modernising messages were mutually exclusive.[29] That said, as Cameron's much criticised refusal earlier in the summer to abandon a visit to Rwanda in order to be seen to be responding to large-scale flooding in Britain had symbolised, they were determined not to be panicked back into the Conservative 'comfort zone'. On the other hand, they knew they had at all costs to dissuade Brown from calling an election before, as they saw it, voters woke up to just how poor a prime minister he would really make. As a result, they decided it was worth temporarily risking the allegations of a lurch to the right and bringing forward the 'rebalancing' of the Tory offer. While the party would continue to reassure voters on the NHS and show them that the party looked and sounded more like the twenty-first century country it was hoping to govern, it would also feature plans for more policing and prisons and tighter border controls. Cameron confessed that he too was concerned about immigration. And, in response to concerns that many families would not be able to pass on their fortunes to their children, George Osborne promised to raise the inheritance tax threshold so that no estates under £1 million would pay the tax in future.

These changes put the grassroots, as well as the backbenches and the party in the media, in good heart. The announcement on inheritance tax was particularly well received and had much the same effect as a conjuror pulling a rabbit from a hat. It was also associated with a sudden and unexpected rise in the Conservatives' poll ratings, which was enough to scare Brown off of calling an early election – a mistake the prime minister then compounded by (a) trying to pretend he simply wanted more time to unveil his vision to the electorate and (b) presiding over a chapter of administrative accidents. The events allowed Cameron (now mightily relieved and once again on a roll) to portray his opposite number as a hapless and dithering 'bottler' who nevertheless thought he could treat voters like idiots and get away with it. Just before the Tory conference at the end of September 2007, YouGov had found that only 21 per cent of respondents thought Cameron was doing a good job, as against 48 per cent who did not and only 32 per cent intended to vote Conservative. Polling soon after the conference, the same company found 54 per cent of people thought Cameron was doing well, as against 34 per cent thinking he was doing badly, with some 41 per cent saying they intended to vote Tory. This, observers noted, constituted the biggest and swiftest turnaround in political fortunes since victory in the Falklands war had helped Margaret Thatcher out of the doldrums in the early part of 1982.[30]

From that point on, the Tory press recognised that, even if they themselves were not wholly convinced by the Cameron project, Cameron himself was the only game in town, then and for the foreseeable future. This was partly because Cameron was happy to provide journalists with iconic and intimate visuals and to talk about his family life. But it was also because the party in the media, like the party in parliament and in the country, could read the opinion polls, and because real election results began to confirm their message of a swing back to the Conservatives. A YouGov poll in December 2007 gave the Conservatives a 13-point lead, their biggest in fifteen years, and research published around the same time by ICM suggested the Tories were at last beginning to attract support in the North.[31] This finding seemed to be borne out when, in May 2008 they made their first by-election gain in twenty-five years at Crewe and Nantwich, on a swing of nearly 17 per cent from Labour. This victory was all the sweeter because Labour's crass attempt to cultivate popular resentment towards both the Tory candidate's and Cameron's privileged upbringings fell flat. Following close on from the victory of Boris Johnson, the flamboyant former Etonian and Bullingdon Club member, in the London mayoral election, Crewe and Nantwich gave the Conservatives renewed hope. Their success at the Norwich North by-election in 2009 confirmed the trend in their favour.

Real electoral successes such as these made it all the more difficult for Cameron's critics to complain that what he was doing was misguided electorally. Admittedly, the reassuring results could do little to assuage the irritation (now mostly whispered in private) felt by more than a few Tories at Westminster about what they saw as a closed-door, cliquey side to his leadership. Team Cameron often forgot that both front- and backbenchers' egos needed massaging now and then. Moreover, beneath the healthy headline numbers, there was still cause for concern: surveys suggested that, even if they saw him as an asset to the party, many voters thought there was more spin than substance to Cameron.[32] The sudden reversal of Labour's leads on key issues seemed to owe more to a drop in people's estimation of the government than it did to rising confidence in the Conservatives – something that would continue to dog the party up to and indeed during the coming election. Even party members, though broadly supportive of the party's general strategy, were uncertain about what he really stood for, and were less than enamoured by the new emphasis on things like environmentalism (some were climate-change sceptics).[33] A survey of the membership in July 2009 suggested grassroots Tories saw a difference between themselves and the leadership in terms of left-right ideology: on a seven-point scale, where one represented a very left-wing position and seven a very right-wing position, the mean score of members was 5.32 while their mean perception of Cameron's location was 4.85.[34]

## The long campaign

The Cameron project had been based on the assumption that the solid if not spectacular economic growth the country had experienced under Labour would continue. Not surprisingly, the increasingly serious economic downturn that followed the near collapse of the banking system in 2008 presented the Tories with a strategic dilemma. Cameron's previous statements about the economy included woolly talk of how Britain needed to concentrate on quality of life rather than simply on standard of living, to focus on GWB (or general well-being) rather than GDP and to 'share the proceeds of growth'. That was now abandoned. But it was not immediately obvious what the party's response should be to the 2007–08 financial crisis, especially after the leadership was widely regarded as having made the wrong call about the need for emergency government assistance for the banks and the need for some kind of fiscal stimulus to prevent recession from turning into full-blown depression. It was particularly difficult to know what the party should do about Osborne's promise, made in the late summer of 2007, to match Labour's spending plans until 2010–11. This promise was made when the shadow chancellor was concerned Labour might call a snap election and offer voters, once again, an apparent choice between 'Tory cuts' and Labour 'investment'. It now appeared extravagant.

Cameron and Osborne's eventual decision in late 2008 not only to ditch this spending pledge, but also to refuse to support a temporary reduction in VAT and to go even further than the government in promising to cut public expenditure in order to reduce Britain's growing budget deficit was a brave one. It was based on the belief that the next election would be about (or could, by a concerted effort on the party's part, be made to be about) the deficit rather than public services and the economy. But it was not merely a matter of political strategy; it was also ideological. The financial and fiscal crisis had exposed the limits of the party's rhetorical commitment to the centre ground. When it came to the crunch, it was clear that Conservatives still believed, as they did in the 1980s and 1990s, that public services and welfare spending, rather than corporate and income tax, would have to bear the burden of adjustment, even if they were not prepared to spell out the extent of any cuts before the election. The subsequent decision to start softening up the public for what was to come and to make a virtue of the party's more forthright approach by talking about the need for 'an age of austerity' was, however, a risky one.[35] Indeed, for a party which, according to polls, had yet to convince voters that it really understood and represented ordinary people, it may well have been a soundbite too far.

Although the Tory leader calculated that the party would win respect for its honesty, he also was careful to try to reassure voters by promising that 'paying down our debt must not mean pushing down the poor' and that he was all about 'fiscal responsibility with a social conscience'.[36] Likewise, Osborne decided it would be politically prudent not to heed backbench calls to reverse the government's decision to raise the top rate of income tax to 50 per cent and stressed in his speech to the party's 2009 annual conference in Manchester that, while it would cut the deficit further and faster than Labour, 'We are all in this together'.[37] Whether warm words like these would be capable of carrying the Conservatives unscathed through the heat of an election – one which would require a massive swing and a double-digit lead in order to see them win with a workable majority – remained to be seen. The electorate might be persuaded that the country needed a little honesty and possibly even some 'tough love'. But would they trust the Conservatives not to take the latter too far?

The signs, by early 2010, suggested that they might not. Even before then, there were hints that the party might be slipping a little. Labour's woeful performance in the local and European elections in May 2009 had disguised the fact that Conservatives did not do as well as they might have hoped: the party's notional share of the vote extrapolated from the local results slipped below 40 per cent, while it polled just 28 per cent in the European elections. This decline was initially attributed to the parliamentary expenses scandal, which provided evidence of Tory MPs claiming public money for cleaning out moats and repairing tennis courts. The scandal risked giving the lie to the rather more modern and ordinary image the leadership had spent so long projecting. Cameron handled the fall-out more deftly and authoritatively than Brown, although he risked infuriating some of his own backbenchers by his high-handed treatment of them that contrasted with the way he dealt with his friends in the shadow cabinet. By early 2010, however, things looked rather less rosy. Labour was still in deep trouble and unable to summon up the courage to replace Brown at the last minute. But the Tories' opinion-poll lead nevertheless narrowed. Until January they held around a 10-point lead, but by early March this had been substantially eroded: one YouGov survey even placed the Conservatives on 37 per cent and Labour on 35 per cent, which was the closest gap since the 'bottled' election in the autumn of 2007.[38]

The same survey also revealed voters' concerns about Cameron's 'posh' background and possible lack of empathy with ordinary families, as well as a loss of confidence in the ability of Cameron and Osborne to manage the faltering economy. This forced Cameron to suddenly rule out 'swingeing cuts' and reaffirm his admiration for public servants. The media talk of backtracking, muddle and confusion that inevitably followed was exacerbated by the party's ongoing difficulty in spelling out how exactly it was going to support marriage through the tax system. It was, however, considered a price worth paying in order to avoid Labour and Liberal Democrat accusations that the Tories were about to kill off a recovery that had barely started. But it was not exactly the ideal way to begin the battle for Downing Street.

It was not, however, all doom and gloom. The press (apart from the *Mirror*, the *Guardian* and the *Independent*) was pretty much onside: most gratifyingly Britain's top-selling tabloid, *The Sun*, owned by Rupert Murdoch, had at last come out for the Conservatives in September 2009 after over a decade of not always enthusiastic support for Labour.[39] The *Daily Mail* under the editorship of Paul Dacre similarly returned to the Tory fold, though its tone was often critical of Cameron's 'touchy feely' style of politics. Cameron's risky decision not to promise a referendum on the EU Lisbon Treaty once it had been ratified by all member states, was also greeted with resignation rather than widespread indignation, both in the country and in the party. The Conservative campaign to put Cameron into Number 10 Downing Street, moreover, looked like being the best-prepared, best-funded and most technically-advanced campaign ever launched by a British party. The party's financial position improved greatly with its overall debt shrinking from £20 million to £3 million. Yet when it was all over – and in spite of the fact that David Cameron ended up in Downing Street – a YouGov poll found that nearly twice as many voters thought the Liberal Democrats had run a better campaign than the Conservatives (37 to 19 per cent).[40]

The Tories' core election team comprised shadow chancellor and election coordinator George Osborne, director of strategy Steve Hilton, Andy Coulson and Osborne's deputy, George Bridges. Osborne, Bridges and Coulson ran much of the day-to-day campaign, though in the run-up to the election there had also been weekly meetings of an 'electoral board' that was attended by Stephen Gilbert, a strategist who worked closely with Lord Ashcroft, the party deputy chairman, and Ed Llewellyn, Cameron's chief of staff. Ashcroft was an extremely important player in the campaign planning, since he was the force behind a long-term 'target seats' campaign and provided much of the money himself or via his companies. This campaign initially focused on about 100 seats but this rose when the party was prospering in the polls before Christmas 2009. Within these areas, the key demographic was identified as relatively affluent blue-collar families – the critically important 'C2s' who had swung to Thatcher in 1979 and Blair in 1997. With these voters in mind, the Tories focused their campaign messages on protecting the NHS and reducing the deficit. 'I'll cut the deficit, not the NHS', Cameron declared. But he also belatedly promised to cut immigration. Cameron tried to style his party, quite simply, as the party of 'change' but not the sort of change that would scare voters back to Labour.

The challenges that confronted the campaign team generated internal friction, some personal, some strategic. Whatever the explanation, media leaks concerning these tensions did little to calm growing nervousness within a party, which had put up with the fact that Team Cameron seemed to be a small, tight-knit group of people determined to drive through change in a top-down fashion as long as that change seemed to be doing the trick and the team worked well together. Now that looked less certain and grumbling started once again. And just when even loyal backbenchers and activists were struggling to understand why the start of the year had been so ragged, the longstanding issue of Lord Ashcroft's tax status erupted again.[41] The affair threatened to revive the Tories' image as a wealthy, self-serving tribe and calling into question Cameron's judgement. Surely, some argued, the leadership must have known that Ashcroft was 'non-domiciled' for tax purposes and contravening the spirit if not the letter of assurances given about his moving back to the UK when he was nominated for a peerage by William Hague? So why, notwithstanding his huge and controversial donations to the party, did no one take steps to sort the matter out long before the election?

Despite these doubts, and despite the first opinion polls of the campaign pointing to a hung parliament, most observers felt that the Conservatives still stood a chance of squeaking an overall majority – a feeling strengthened by what was widely regarded as the party's relatively strong start in the first few days of the campaign. The all-out attack on Labour's decision to raise national insurance contributions in order to cut the deficit – labelled by the Tories as a 'tax on jobs' and condemned by businessmen – seemed to cut through to the electorate. The party's manifesto, launched against the dramatic backdrop provided by London's Battersea power station, was also well received.[42] Even some of those who were well-disposed to the Tories, however, had their doubts about the manifesto's key theme – the 'big society'. It seemed that the public would be encouraged to take the initiative on many social problems rather than simply leave them to the state to sort out. While the idea was welcome, some argued that the party should have prepared the public for this new key theme rather than launch it at the start of the election campaign proper. This concern was reinforced by polling that showed that even those voters who did not think it was simply a code for shrinking the welfare state were not sure what it meant.[43]

The low point of the Tory campaign came after the first televised leaders' debate. Clegg's impressive performance allowed him temporarily to wrest the mantle of 'the change candidate' from Cameron and provided a boost to the Liberal Democrats' poll ratings (see Figure 7.1). This caused some recrimination in the party. Team Cameron was criticised for agreeing to take part in the debates at all. In the end, however, Cameron's performance picked up markedly in the later debates, while Brown's 'Bigotgate' disaster – when he was overheard calling a traditional Labour voter a bigot simply for raising the immigration issue – came as a heaven-sent opportunity. It helped immigration and asylum rise up the news agenda without the party having to do a thing and freed it from the charge of 'playing the race card'. Partly as a result, the Conservatives may have benefited from a late swing in their favour or at least away from the Liberal Democrats, whose own amnesty for illegal immigrants was savagely attacked in the media and was highly unpopular.

## Close, but no cigar: explaining the outcome

The underlying explanation for the Conservatives emerging as the largest party but without an overall majority inevitably involves more than the events of the campaign. Despite Conservative and Liberal Democrat gains in 2010, Labour still appeared to have a larger pool of loyalists. The authoritative British Election Study suggested that fully 31 per cent of voters reported 'thinking of themselves' as Labour (down from 38 per cent in 2005) compared to 27 per cent for the Conservatives (up from 24 per cent), and 16 per cent for the Liberal Democrats (compared with 13 per cent in 2005).[44] Indeed, the same survey shows that the Conservative party was actually the least liked of the three main parties at the election, with an average score of just 4.34 on a scale running from 0 ('dislike') to 10 ('like'), compared to 4.44 for Labour and 5.40 for the Liberal Democrats. Moreover, it also suggests that on the question of taxation and spending – a classic synoptic indicator of left-right ideology in Britain and undoubtedly the major political fault-line in the 2010 election – voters certainly did not regard the Conservatives as the party closest to them overall. They were perceived to be more distant from the electorate than either Labour or the Liberal Democrats. However, since the average elector had moved towards reducing tax and spending by 2010, the Conservatives were closer to the centre than in 2005.[45]

As described more fully in Chapter 6 the public mood had shifted away from 'bigger government' in the thirteen years of New Labour. But as Table 2.5 shows, public opinion was still by no means Thatcherite in 2010. The electorate was deeply ambivalent about the issue of the deficit. It was split right down the middle on whether to start cutting the deficit straight away or postpone cuts. And more people were concerned that government would go too far and cut spending than would not go far enough and reduce the debt. There was, moreover, broad agreement that the time was not right to cut taxes. More generally, the public were broadly in favour of government intervention in the economy and of tighter regulation of the banks. Indeed, there was little evidence of the deep ideological hostility to the state that characterises right-wing sentiment. Even on the issue of immigration, a sizeable group appeared to recognise that this development could strengthen – rather than threaten – the country. The evidence contained in Table 2.5 suggests that Cameron was clearly well-advised when he rejected siren calls to put 'clear blue water' between the Tories and the Labour party by endorsing immediate savage cuts before the election. Public opinion appeared more supportive of the Conservative party on the issue of Europe but that was simply not a major issue in 2010. The poll also showed, moreover, that the electorate was split down the middle when it came to the question of whether David Cameron had really changed the party. It seems that the party had only partially succeeded in throwing off old reputations.

More detailed research suggests that there were few surprises when it came to the social and attitudinal basis of support for the Conservatives and that the latter's emergence as the largest party in parliament had more to do with the instrumental evaluations, associated with 'valence politics', namely relative judgements about leadership, credibility and competence.[46] Compared to manual workers, all other occupational grades (especially senior white-collar and small-business owners) were more likely to vote Conservative. Private-sector employees were more likely to do so than voluntary-sector employees, but public-sector workers were less likely to do so. And men were significantly less likely to vote Conservative than

TABLE 2.5   *Voters' positions on key themes and policies, May 2010*

| | % agreeing with statement | Gap between statements |
|---|---|---|
| David Cameron changed the Conservative Party | 46 | −4 |
| The Conservative Party has not changed very much | 50 | |
| I'm more worried that we will go too far in cutting social spending and public services | 57 | 17 |
| I'm more worried that we won't go far enough to cut spending and reduce the debt | 40 | |
| To reduce the debt, we will need to make major cuts in spending and public services | 45 | −1 |
| To reduce the debt, we must raise taxes broadly and do less cutting of spending and services | 46 | |
| It is time to cut taxes | 30 | −36 |
| It is not the time to cut taxes | 66 | |
| We must start cutting the national debt right away | 49 | 1 |
| We must wait to cut the debt until the economic recovery is underway | 48 | |
| I'm more worried that we will do too little to regulate the financial community and allow for another era of speculative booms and busts | 58 | 20 |
| I'm more worried that we will go too far in regulating the financial community, which will harm the British economy | 38 | |
| This is a time for government to get more involved | 71 | 49 |
| This is a time to depend more on markets | 22 | |
| We need policies to create greater opportunity | 48 | 0 |
| We need policies to bring less inequality and more fairness | 48 | |
| To get future economic growth, the British government will need to encourage investment in new industries and sectors | 65 | 35 |
| To get future economic growth, Britain will have to create an environment with less regulation and more freedom of enterprise | 30 | |
| If government gets the right policies, Britain can do well | 57 | 18 |
| If society is strong, Britain can do well | 39 | |
| Britain will need new immigration, which can strengthen Britain | 51 | 9 |
| Immigration undermines Britain | 42 | |
| Britain needs to be more involved in the EU | 32 | -32 |
| Britain needs to be less involved in the EU | 64 | |
| Britain should be more independent of the United States | 54 | 11 |
| Britain should be a strong ally of the United States | 43 | |

*Source*: Greenberg Quinlan Rosner, 'The change election – what the voters were really saying', available at http://gqrr.com/articles/2445/5678_ukeu05182010charts.pdf. Last accessed 9 June 2010.

*Note*: Responses are to the following question: 'Now I'm going to read you some pairs of statements about what should happen in Britain. As I read each pair, please tell me whether the FIRST statement or the SECOND statement comes closer to your views, even if neither is exactly right.'

women, suggesting that the long-standing gender gap has begun to reassert itself.[47] The more socially liberal an individual was and the keener they were on taxing and spending and Europe, the less likely they were to support the Conservatives. But what is also clear is that those who thought the Tories were the best party to handle economic difficulties, and those who thought that David Cameron was the best leader to manage the economy, were significantly more likely to support the party. Similarly, the more voters regarded Cameron as generally competent, the more likely they were to vote for the Conservatives. In the end, then, the Conservatives appear to have emerged from the election as the largest party because the electorate could no longer stomach an exhausted Labour government and found Gordon Brown unpalatable. David Cameron was perceived as a better bet but, despite his efforts to decontaminate his party's brand and rebalance its offer, and perhaps because of his decision to focus on dealing with the deficit, the Conservatives were not widely admired or trusted. Those doubts ensured that what the polls had been predicting for months – a hung parliament – was indeed the eventual outcome of the election.

## Aftermath

For the world's oldest and most successful political party, the thirteen years it had spent out of office between 1997 and 2010 seemed like an eternity. To have added another five to the total was simply unconscionable. Accordingly, David Cameron made an immediate 'big, open, comprehensive', and ultimately successful, offer to the Liberal Democrats of a coalition government. That offer was not a premeditated strategy. It was simply the only thing to do in the circumstances. The option of a minority Tory government was problematic, as Philip Norton describes in Chapter 9, and the Liberal Democrats were uninterested in a 'confidence and supply' arrangement that fell short of a full coalition. There was in any case little appetite (or money available) for another election and not much confidence it could have been easily won after imposing an unpopular deficit-reduction programme, especially if Labour was able to make a convincing appeal to disillusioned Liberal Democrat voters. Some Conservative backbenchers chafed at the idea of sharing the spoils of office. But most were prepared to acknowledge the reality of the situation and even to accept (in private at least) that Cameron got a good deal out of the negotiations.

The coalition was clearly facilitated by the advent of the Liberal Democrat *Orange Book* generation, which drew the two parties closer together than many observers had realised. The ideological affinity, indeed, was such that some were soon suggesting that Clegg and Cameron might try to fight the next election as some kind of package deal, effectively marginalising the

Tory right and pitching for the centre ground. Cameron's ability and willingness to do that, however, will ultimately depend on the extent to which his administration marks a departure from the kind of policies practised by the Tory governments of the 1980s and 1990s. The early signs suggested, especially to critics on the left, that the Cameron government would simply revert to type and pick up where its predecessors left off, using the need to balance the books and the presence of the Liberal Democrats as a cover for making the United Kingdom as much like the United States as possible, with a shrunken state, a welfare system that is little more than a safety net for the destitute, a labour market in which the employer's right to hire and fire is absolute, and a tax regime that encourages enterprise by letting corporations off lightly and widening the gap between rich and poor. Should this happen, it will arguably represent a negation of much of what David Cameron said and did after his election as leader in December 2005 to make his party competitive. On the other hand, as Margaret Thatcher and other Conservative leaders before her discovered, one can do all sorts of things in government that were no more than hinted at when in opposition and still win re-election, particularly if the new opposition is weak.[48]

## Endnotes

1 Much of the following account is informed by Tim Bale, *The Conservative Party from Thatcher to Cameron* (London: Polity, 2010). See also Peter Snowdon, *Back from the Brink: The Inside Story of the Tory Resurrection* (London: Harper Press, 2010).

2 Philip Norton, 'The Conservative Party from Thatcher to Major', in Anthony King, ed., *Britain at the Polls, 2001* (Chatham, NJ: Chatham House, 2002), pp. 29–69.

3 Ken Newton, 'Caring and competence: the long, long campaign', in Anthony King, ed., *Britain at the Polls 1992* (Chatham, NJ: Chatham House, 1992), pp. 129–70; John Bartle, 'Why Labour won – again', in King, ed., *Britain at the Polls, 2001*, pp. 164–206.

4 Ivor Crewe, 'The Thatcher legacy', in King, ed., *Britain at the Polls 1992*, pp. 1–28.

5 Philip Norton, 'The Conservative Party: the politics of panic', in John Bartle and Anthony King, eds, *Britain at the Polls 2005* (Washington, DC: CQ Press), pp. 31–53.

6 Francis Elliott and James Hanning, *Cameron: The Rise of the New Conservative* (London: Harper Perennial, 2009).

7 Stuart Ball, 'Factors in opposition performance: the Conservative experience since 1867', in Stuart Ball and Anthony Seldon, eds, *Recovering Power: The Conservatives in Opposition* (Basingstoke, Hants.: Palgrave, 2005), pp. 1–27, at pp. 4–5.

8 Norton, 'The Conservative Party: the politics of panic', pp. 36–7.

9 Andrew Denham and Kieron O'Hara, *Democratising Conservative Leadership Selection: From Grey Suits to Grass Roots* (Manchester: Manchester University Press, 2008); and Timothy Heppell, *Choosing the Tory Leader: Conservative Party Leadership Elections from Heath to Cameron* (London: IB Tauris, 2007).

10   Ivan died in February 2009. See David Thompson, 'How son shaped Cameron's politics', *BBC News* website, 25 February 2009, available at: news.bbc.co.uk/1/hi/uk_politics/7910121. stm (last accessed 26 August 2010).

11   John Garry, *The Political Attitudes of Conservative Party Members*, unpublished manuscript, (Belfast: Queen's University, 2006).

12   Benedict Brogan and Jane Merrick, 'Cocaine and me, by David Cameron', *Daily Mail*, 21 October 2005.

13   See Kieron O'Hara, *After Blair: David Cameron and the Conservative Tradition* (Cambridge: Icon, 2007); David Seawright, *The British Conservative Party and One Nation Politics* (New York: Continuum, 2009); Simon Griffiths and Kevin Hickson, eds, *British Party Politics and Ideology after New Labour* (Basingstoke, Hants: Palgrave Macmillan, 2009).

14   Ned Temko, 'Cameron: we got it wrong on apartheid', *Observer*, 27 August 2006.

15   See the full text of David Cameron's speech, 4 October 2006, available at: www.guardian. co.uk/politics/2006/oct/04/conservatives2006.conservatives (last accessed 26 August 2010).

16   Andrew Pierce, 'Cameron says sorry over section 28 gay law', *Daily Telegraph*, 1 July 2009.

17   Stephen Evans, 'Consigning its past to history? David Cameron and the Conservative Party', *Parliamentary Affairs*, 61 (2008): 291–314.

18   Benedict Brogan, 'Cameron party reforms meet lukewarm response', *Mail Online*, 19 September 2006.

19   YouGov survey for the *Daily Telegraph*, November 2006, available at: today.yougov. co.uk/sites/today.yougov.co.uk/files/YG-Archives-pol-dTel-NovPolTrackers-061201.pdf (last accessed 26 August 2010).

20   Populus poll for *The Times*, February 2007, available at: populuslimited.com/uploads/ download_pdf-040207-The-Times-Political-Attitudes.pdf (last accessed 26 August 2010).

21   Anthony King, 'Voters warm to the idea of Cameron', *Daily Telegraph*, 30 March 2007.

22   Simon Lee and Matt Beech, eds, *The Conservatives under David Cameron: Built to Last?* (Basingstoke, Hants: Palgrave Macmillan, 2009).

23   Philippe Naughton, 'Osborne invokes Thatcher to ram home tax message', *The Times*, 3 October 2006.

24   Philip Lynch and Richard Whitaker, 'A loveless marriage: the Conservatives and the European People's Party', *Parliamentary Affairs*, 61 (2008) 31–51; and Tim Bale, Sean Hanley and Aleks Szczerbiak, '"May contain nuts"? The reality behind the rhetoric surrounding the British Conservatives' new group in the European Parliament', *The Political Quarterly*, 81 (2010): 85–98.

25   Stephen Pollard, 'Scandal of the Tory grammar school u-turn', *Daily Mail*, 17 May 2007.

26   James Porter, 'Tories defiant despite new poll set-back', *Daily Telegraph*, 29 September 2007.

27   See the YouGov poll for Channel 4, July 2007, available at: today.yougov.co.uk/sites/ today.yougov.co.uk/files/YG-Archives-pol-ch4news-PoliticalSpectrum-070727.pdf (last accessed 26 August 2010).

28   Tim Bale, '"A bit less bunny-hugging and a bit more bunny-boiling"? Qualifying Conservative Party change under David Cameron', *British Politics*, 3 (2008): 270–99.

29  See the interview with George Osborne in Fraser Nelson, 'Inside George Osborne's war room', *Spectator*, 26 September 2007. See also the interview with Greg Barker MP, in Bale, *The Conservative Party from Thatcher to Cameron*, p. 343.

30  Andrew Porter, 'Tories 3 points ahead of Labour', *Daily Telegraph*, 26 October 2007.

31  YouGov survey for the *Sunday Times*, December 2007, available at: www.yougov.co.uk/ extranets/ygarchives/content/pdf/2007%2012%2017%20ST%20toplines.pdf (last accessed 26 August 2010).

32  Benedict Brogan, 'Our major poll reveals David Cameron still has a mountain to climb', *Daily Telegraph*, 6 September 2009.

33  Sarah Childs, Paul Webb and Sally Marthaler, 'The feminization of the Conservative Party: party members' attitudes', *The Political Quarterly*, 80 (2009): 204–13.

34  Sarah Childs and Paul Webb, *From Iron Ladies to Kitten Heels: Gender and the Conservative Party* (Basingstoke, Hants: Palgrave, forthcoming).

35  George Osborne, 'Delivery in an age of austerity', *Guardian*, 7 May 2009.

36  See David Cameron's speech, 'Fiscal responsibility with a social conscience', 19 March 2009, available at: www.conservatives.com/News/Speeches/2009/03/David_Cameron_ Fiscal_Responsibility_with_a_Social_Conscience.aspx (last accessed 26 August 2010).

37  George Osborne, 'We will lead the economy out of crisis', speech to Conservative party conference, 6 October 2009, available at: www.conservatives.com/News/Speeches/2009/ 10/George_Osborne_We_will_lead_the_economy_out_of_crisis.aspx (last accessed 26 August 2010).

38  David Smith and Jonathan Oliver, 'Brown on course to win election', *Sunday Times*, 28 February 2010.

39  John Bartle, 'New Labour and the media' in Bartle and King, eds, *Britain at the Polls 2005*, pp. 124–50.

40  A ConservativeHome survey of more than 3,000 Tory members found 62 per cent judged the overall campaign to have been 'poor'; a majority of the party's successful parliamentary candidates agreed. In a generally critical review of the campaign, moreover, the editors of ConservativeHome claimed that the 16,000 more votes across nineteen seats needed for Cameron to have become prime minister at the head of a single party majority government could have been won if CCHQ (Conservative Campaign Headquarters) had really got its act together.

41  Joe Churcher, 'Lord Ashcroft confirms non-dom status', *Independent*, 1 March 2010.

42  Richard Chidwick, 'Conservative manifesto launch: what the papers say', *BBC News* website, 14 April 2010, available at: www.politics.co.uk/features/general-election-2010/ conservative-manifesto-2010-what-the-papers-say-$1371176.htm (last accessed 26 August 2010).

43  Ipsos MORI, 'Do the public really want to join the government of Britain?', 21 April, 2010, available at: www.ipsos-mori.com/Assets/Docs/News/Do%20the%20public%20 want%20to%20join%20government%20of%20Britain.PDF (last accessed 26 August 2010).

44  British Election Study weighted post-election panel survey.

45  The self-locations of the average voter and perceptions of the party are set out in Table 2.N1

TABLE 2.N1   *Perceptions of left-right distance between parties and the average voter in 2005 and 2010*

|  | 2005 | 2010 | Difference |
|---|---|---|---|
| Average voter | 6.2 | 5.8 | −0.4 |
| Labour | 6.4 | 5.9 | −0.5 |
| Conservative | 5.3 | 5.2 | −0.1 |
| Liberal Democrat | 6.0 | 5.4 | −0.6 |
| Distance between average voter and Conservative party | 0.9 | 0.6 | |

*Source*: British Election Study, pre-election, face-to-face survey

*Note*: The BES asked respondents to locate themselves and the parties on a scale from 0 (most left-wing position) to 10 (most right position) in both 2005 and 2010. The table suggests that Labour was nearer to the average voter in both years. The Conservative party was closer to the average voter in 2010 than 2005. This was almost entirely due to the fact that the average voter had moved rightwards. The Conservative party was perceived to have moved very slightly to the centre.

46   Paul Webb and Tim Bale, *The Conservative Vote in 2010*, submission to the Conservative Party 1922 Committee.

47   Rosie Campbell, *Gender and the Vote in Britain: Beyond the Gender Gap* (London: Routledge, 2006).

48   The key example is privatisation, which did not feature much in the 1979 Conservative manifesto and yet – together with trade-union reform – came to characterise 'Thatcherism'.

# 3 REALIGNMENT IN THE CENTRE: THE LIBERAL DEMOCRATS

Thomas Quinn and Ben Clements

On 12 May 2010, Nick Clegg, leader of the Liberal Democrats and newly-appointed deputy prime minister, stood alongside the Conservative prime minister, David Cameron, at a joint news conference in the gardens of 10 Downing Street.[1] It was the culmination of five days of post-election bargaining after an inconclusive poll had resulted in a hung parliament with the Tories as the largest party. In a decisive break with Britain's post-war tradition of single-party government, the centre-right Conservatives reached out to the supposedly centre-left Liberal Democrats and the two parties thrashed out a deal that paved the way for Britain's first peace-time coalition government since the 1930s. These two parties had seemed politically far apart for so long that few people had ever seriously thought that they would, or even could, cooperate at the national level. Indeed, one of Clegg's predecessors as Liberal Democrat leader, Charles Kennedy, had called on his party to replace the Conservatives as the main opposition to the governing Labour party in 2002.[2] At the 2005 general election, the Liberal Democrats tried – and failed – to 'decapitate' the Tories, by aggressively targeting the constituencies of key members of the Conservative shadow cabinet. Clegg himself had sometimes appeared to dismiss the idea of cooperation. In large parts of Britain the two parties competed fiercely for votes. There was little love lost between the two parties' members, all of whom could tell stories of the other's duplicity. Yet Clegg was joined in the new coalition cabinet by four colleagues, while another eighteen Liberal Democrat MPs and peers took junior frontbench roles. Political commentators were virtually unanimous in expressing their astonishment at this outcome. It was at one and the same time an *un*British spectacle and a 'very British revolution'.[3]

This chapter explores how and why the Liberal Democrats made their journey from the wilderness to government. A combination of strategic adjustments, ideological shifts, leadership changes and economic circumstances left the Liberal Democrats looking a different party from the one that Kennedy had led just five years earlier. These changes, however, were contested and the fissures within the party will continue to produce tensions, as the Liberal Democrats make the compromises that are necessary to sustain the coalition.

## The Liberal Democrats and the UK party system

The Liberal Democrats are Britain's third major party. They are generally considered to occupy a middle position between Labour on the centre-left and the Conservatives on the centre-right. The party is the descendent of the old Liberal party and the Social Democratic Party (formed by a breakaway group of moderate Labour MPs in 1981).[4] These two parties agreed an electoral pact and fought the 1983 and 1987 general elections as the SDP-Liberal Alliance, subsequently merging in 1988 to form the Liberal Democrats. The successor party has tried to resolve the tensions both within and between liberalism and social democracy, with their respective emphases on individual freedom and equality.

Since the merger, the Liberal Democrats have won 17–23 per cent of the vote in general elections and roughly trebled their parliamentary representation. Britain's plurality ('first-past-the-post') electoral system, however, has constrained the party's growth: the 23 per cent of the vote that the Liberal Democrats won in 2010, for example, translated into fifty-seven seats at Westminster, just 9 per cent of the total. Certainly, this ratio of seats to votes represented a considerable improvement on past elections. In 1983 the Alliance's 25 per cent of the vote translated into just 23 seats (3.5 per cent). Yet the electoral system continued to punish the centre party. In 2010 the Conservatives' 36 per cent of the vote won them 47 per cent of the seats in the House of Commons, while Labour's 29 per cent of the vote translated into 40 per cent of the seats. The Liberal Democrats' only realistic hope of gaining power in the short term was in a hung parliament. If they held the balance of power, they hoped to be in a position to demand a more proportional electoral system in return for their support. However, between 1945 and 2005, just one general election produced a hung parliament, in February 1974, and in this case there were insufficient Liberal MPs to provide either of the main parties with a parliamentary majority. Labour governed as a minority before calling another election and securing a slim majority in October that year. After by-election defeats robbed Labour of its majority, it formed a parliamentary agreement with the Liberals ('the Lib–Lab pact') that fell short of a full coalition and which lasted between 1977 and 1978.[5]

TABLE 3.1  *Location of Liberal/SDP/Liberal Democrat parliamentary seats, 1945–2010*

| | 1945 | 1950 | 1951 | 1955 | 1959 | 1964 | 1966 | 1970 | 1974 Feb | 1974 Oct | 1979 | 1983 | 1987 | 1992 | 1997 | 2001 | 2005 | 2010 |
|---|---|---|---|---|---|---|---|---|---|---|---|---|---|---|---|---|---|---|
| Seats won in Celtic fringe | 8 | 7 | 4 | 4 | 4 | 8 | 9 | 6 | 8 | 8 | 5 | 12 | 14 | 13 | 19 | 20 | 23 | 19 |
| Seats won outside Celtic fringe | 4 | 2 | 2 | 2 | 2 | 1 | 3 | 0 | 6 | 5 | 6 | 11 | 8 | 7 | 27 | 32 | 39 | 38 |
| Total seats | 12 | 9 | 6 | 6 | 6 | 9 | 12 | 6 | 14 | 13 | 11 | 23 | 22 | 20 | 46 | 52 | 62 | 57 |
| Celtic fringe seats as % of total | 67 | 78 | 67 | 67 | 67 | 89 | 75 | 100 | 57 | 62 | 45 | 52 | 64 | 65 | 41 | 38 | 37 | 33 |

*Note:* 'Celtic fringe' defined as Scotland, Wales and Cornwall & Devon. Table covers Liberal Party 1945–79; SDP-Liberal Alliance 1983–87; Liberal Democrats 1992–2010. In 1983, eight of Liberals' 17 seats and four of SDP's six seats in Celtic fringe. In 1987, 11 of Liberals' 17 seats and three of SDP's five seats in Celtic fringe.

The Liberal Democrats have been penalised by first-past-the-post because what matters under this system is not simply obtaining a significant share of the vote but winning votes in the right locations. Geographically-concentrated support is vital in single-member districts conducted under plurality rule.[6] The two major parties have usually enjoyed such concentrated support. In contrast, for most of the post-war era, the old Liberal party had few areas of strength, other than rural and affluent parts of the 'Celtic fringe' – the Scottish borders and highlands, northern Wales, and Cornwall and Devon, which together accounted for just 7 per cent of parliamentary constituencies. These areas were historically suspicious of the English centre and the established church, associated with the Conservatives, and the urban industrialism of the Labour party.[7] In the fourteen general elections between 1945 and 1992, the Liberal, SDP and Liberal Democrat parties won a combined total of 169 seats. No fewer than 110, or 65 per cent, of these were in the Celtic fringe, almost entirely in rural areas.[8] More recently, the geographical profile of Liberal Democrat seats has changed to the party's advantage. In the four general elections between 1997 and 2010 the Liberal Democrats won a combined total of 217 seats, of which eighty-one, or only 37 per cent, were in the Celtic fringe (see Table 3.1). The Liberal Democrats extended their presence in the wider South West of England, London and parts of the South East of England, as the party benefited from the Conservatives' intense unpopularity between 1992 and 2005. This change was partly the result of seat targeting and the careful deployment of campaigning resources. There was a notable 'contagion' effect: Liberal Democrat success in one constituency invariably led to success nearby. Furthermore, the Conservatives' unpopularity prompted tactical voting by Labour voters in Conservative–Liberal Democrat marginal constituencies in 1997 and 2001.[9] These factors collectively ensured that the Liberal Democrat vote was spread more efficiently in 1997–2010 so that the party won more seats for any given vote.[10]

## Realignment on the left

After the Liberal Democrats' formation, the party's overall electoral strategy was one of 'equidistance', in which it professed to be equally distant from Labour and the Conservatives. Accordingly, it would be willing to enter into negotiations with either party in the event of a hung parliament.[11] The unpopularity of the Conservative government in the 1990s and Labour's shift to the centre ground under Tony Blair, however, prompted a reassessment of this presumption. It also reignited interest in a strategy that Jo Grimond, the Liberal leader from 1956 to 1967, had called 'realignment on the left'. Grimond hoped that the Labour party might split and the moderate elements would cooperate with his party.[12] That did indeed happen in the 1980s, with the formation of the SDP, but the Alliance was ultimately unable to supplant Labour. The emergence of New Labour and its abandonment of socialist goals encouraged the Liberal Democrats under Paddy Ashdown formally to abandon equidistance in 1995 and revive the strategy of realignment on the left.[13] This change did not lead to a formal electoral or parliamentary pact but there was a great deal of cooperation at the elite level, with the two parties working particularly closely on constitutional reform. In 1997, the parties published the *Report of the Joint Consultative Committee on Constitutional Reform* (the 'Cook-Maclennan agreement', named after Robin Cook and Robert Maclennan, the Labour and Liberal Democrat co-chairs) that provided the basis for cooperation on Labour's governmental programme of constitutional changes. A joint cabinet committee of senior Labour and Liberal Democrat politicians was formed when Labour came to power in 1997 to discuss such issues. It was even suggested that Blair was prepared to form a Lib–Lab coalition. Only the scale of Labour's landslide victory made this move unfeasible.[14] The prospect of realignment was maintained, however, when Labour commissioned a committee on electoral reform chaired by Lord Jenkins, one of the founders of the SDP and the Liberal Democrats' elder statesman. The committee recommended the semi-proportional 'Alternative Vote Plus' system in October 1998. Labour then failed to hold the referendum on electoral reform promised in its 1997 manifesto, causing deep disappointment and embarrassment to Ashdown. Nevertheless, relations between the two parties remained generally close and the period 1997–99 would be described by Ashdown as one of 'constructive opposition'.[15]

The party's closeness to Labour created disquiet among Liberal Democrat MPs and activists. The unease was understandable. The Liberals had split twice in the twentieth century over their participation in coalition governments, fatally weakening the party and leading to its displacement by Labour as Britain's second major party.[16] Ashdown stood down as leader in 1999 amid rumours that his position had been undermined by growing hostility to constructive opposition within the party.

Ashdown's successor, Charles Kennedy, abandoned constructive opposition in favour of what he called 'effective opposition', which he contrasted with the ineffective opposition of William Hague's Conservative party. With most of the constitutional reforms implemented and electoral reform off the agenda, the Liberal Democrats felt able to be much more critical of Labour's record. Relations between the parties slowly deteriorated as a result of the Iraq war in 2003 and Labour's illiberal approach to civil liberties.[17]

The 2005 general election left the Liberal Democrats at a strategic crossroads. Realignment on the left had failed. This strategy, moreover, sat awkwardly with the fact that the Liberal Democrats were more often in contention in middle-class Conservative areas than in working-class Labour ones.[18] The perception that the Liberal Democrats were closer to Labour than the Conservatives was less of a problem under Blair because the Tory voters that they needed to win were less concerned about letting Labour in. However, with Labour's growing unpopularity after 2005, that could no longer be taken for granted.

The failure of the realignment strategy shifted attention back to two traditional and complementary strategies: the 'long-march' and 'quick-fix'.[19] The first focussed on building up support in council elections as a prelude to success in Westminster elections. The second prepared the party's position in the event of a hung parliament when it might be pivotal and well-placed to press its demands for proportional representation. The long march was a necessary strategy for the Liberal Democrats because of the rarity of hung parliaments. The quick fix required the party to maintain equidistance and appear as if it could cooperate with either of the two main parties in order to maximise its bargaining power. Developments both within and without the party pushed it back towards equidistance, though most Liberal Democrats did not take the idea of cooperating with the Tories very seriously.

# The political context in 2005

The Liberal Democrats rethought their policies, strategy and leadership between 2005 and 2010. This reappraisal was needed because politics had moved on from 1997: the Labour government had shifted the status quo and the Conservatives began 'modernising' under a new leader.

## Intra-party context: factional divisions

One of the most intriguing – but also least well-documented – developments in the Liberal Democrats in recent years has been the re-emergence of an ideological fissure, not seen since the days of the old Liberal party, over the role and size of the state. On one side stood a group who generally referred to themselves as 'social liberals'. They included former leaders Charles Kennedy, Sir Menzies Campbell, Paddy Ashdown and David Steel, as well as more leftist figures such as Simon Hughes. They were also heavily represented in the party outside of parliament, both on central-party bodies and in grassroots organisations such as the Social Liberal Forum. The social liberals included social democrats from the pre-merger SDP and left-leaning former members of the Liberal party. They constituted the centre-left mainstream that was in the ascendant in the post-merger years. They argued that state intervention was necessary to combat inequality and social injustice, and that redistribution from rich to poor and high-quality public services were needed to provide individuals with *freedom to* achieve fulfilling lives ('positive liberty').[20] Social liberals enthusiastically supported an increase in the top rate of income tax to 50 per cent and the abolition of university tuition fees, and opposed the Iraq war. These totemic policies reinforced the party's centre-left reputation.[21]

Standing aside from the social-liberal mainstream was another, much smaller, group of classical or 'economic liberals' that found itself increasingly uneasy with some of the party's policies. Members of this group were suspicious of state power and more concerned with the liberty of individuals in terms of *freedom from* the state ('negative liberty'). They strongly supported markets as a means of allocating resources, believing that this dispersed power throughout society. Economic liberals had dominated the old Liberal party for much of the nineteenth century but were overshadowed by 'new liberals' such as Leonard Hobhouse, T.H. Green and John Maynard Keynes in the first half of the twentieth century. Economic liberalism later became associated with the Conservative party of Margaret Thatcher, though her social policies were not liberal.[22] Yet as the state grew under Labour, more liberals expressed concern about the 'nanny state'. Classical liberal arguments appeared more relevant.

Personnel changes also influenced the direction of the Liberal Democrats. The growth of their parliamentary party between 1997 and 2005 resulted in an influx of ambitious MPs, including several with backgrounds in economics or finance. These included David Laws, an investment banker; Vince Cable, a chief economist for Shell; Ed Davey, a management consultant; Chris Huhne, a city economist and journalist; Mark Oaten, a lobbyist; and Nick Clegg, a political consultant. Most of these were young and had entered politics in the expectation of achieving power.[23] They were, on the whole, receptive to economic-liberal arguments about the balance between the market and the state.

On the eve of the Liberal Democrats' 2004 autumn conference, a group of MPs and parliamentary candidates – including all those named above – published a book of essays that called on the party to 'reclaim' its classical-liberal roots. *The Orange Book* covered topics such as the economy, public services and the environment, and argued for the greater use of market forces to bring about social justice.[24] The contributors criticised the 'statism' that they claimed characterised party policy. Their intention was to show that the party had credible thinkers, wanted power and had moved beyond its image as a fringe party that operated outside of the political mainstream.[25] (Liberal Democrat activists had helped seal the party's slightly odd-ball reputation by debating issues such as the legalisation of drugs and electing the head of state.) The book evoked much media interest and the authors were quickly labelled 'modernisers'.

Classical-liberal arguments in the party were given a boost by the growth of the state under Labour and the illiberal policies of the Blair government. The party was united in its opposition to Labour's anti-terror laws, identity cards and the Iraq war. The turn towards the left had itself been a response to the Thatcherite policies of Conservative governments in the 1980s and

1990s. The increasing emphasis on individual liberties was similarly a reaction to Labour's authoritarian policies after 1997.[26] Nevertheless, *The Orange Book* was met with suspicion by the party's mainstream.

The 'modernisers' in the Liberal Democrats were a fairly small group – perhaps a dozen MPs could be categorised as economic liberals in 2005.[27] The extra-parliamentary organisation was dominated by social liberals. Nevertheless, head counts are an imperfect indicator of the balance of power in parties. The Blairites were never a majority in the Labour party. They were dominant for more than a decade because their approach was in tune with 'middle England' and won elections. Liberal Democrat modernisers hoped to shape policy in exactly the same way.

## Electoral context: the Conservative resurgence

Intra-party developments are only one part of the story. The Liberal Democrats also needed to respond to a changed electoral context after 2005. The most obvious change was a resurgent Conservative party under David Cameron and that too pushed the party to adopt classical-liberal ideas.

Liberal Democrat electoral support has always increased as a result of the shifting fortunes of the major parties. Conversely, they have been vulnerable to any upturn in major-party fortunes. After 1992, the party benefited from anti-Conservative sentiment in the electorate. Tactical voting helped the Liberal Democrats double their parliamentary representation and the party remained close to Labour in its first term. During Blair's second term, however, the Liberal Democrats increasingly made inroads into Labour support, exploiting opposition to the Iraq war and student opposition to top-up fees.[28] The continuing weakness of the Conservatives ensured that the Liberal Democrats retained most of the seats they gained in 1997 and 2001. Of the twelve seats that the Liberal Democrats won from Labour in 2005, seven had been Conservative seats and one had been a Liberal Democrat seat until the 1990s. They were hardly Labour heartlands.[29]

By 2005, the Liberal Democrats' electoral advance against the Conservatives had stalled. Although the party won three seats from the Tories that year, it lost another five to them. That raised questions about the Liberal Democrats' strategic position after the election. The election of David Cameron as Conservative leader presented a clear threat to the Liberal Democrats. Those seats gained from the Tories in southern England suddenly looked vulnerable. That danger was heightened by the perception that the Liberal Democrats had shifted left under Kennedy and had become a tax-and-spend party.[30] Some feared that voters who had defected from the Tories could return to the fold.

The Conservative resurgence was a particular danger to the Liberal Democrats because of the pattern of party competition in the UK. Since 1945, the third party has usually competed with the Conservatives, rather than with Labour, in rural parts of the Celtic fringe or the South East of England.[31] Liberal Democrat voters have typically been similar to Conservative voters in terms of social class but closer in attitudes to Labour voters.[32] Of the sixty-two seats the Liberal Democrats won in 2005, the Conservatives finished second in forty-three, of which seventeen were marginal constituencies (defined as a majority of less than 10 points) and a further nineteen had majorities between 10 and 20 points. Labour was second in just eighteen Liberal Democrat seats and Plaid Cymru in one. Similarly, the Conservatives won forty-five marginal seats in 2005, with the Liberal Democrats second in fifteen. Labour, on the other hand, won eighty-eight marginal constituencies but the Liberal Democrats were second in only ten.[33]

The Liberal Democrats' response to Cameron assumed a central place in the party's strategic thinking after 2005. There was a genuine risk that a Tory revival could reverse the gains made since 1997. This threat strengthened the modernisers' hand in their battles with the social liberals.


## Three-and-a-half leaders

The Liberal Democrats' variable performance at the 2005 general election and the growing Conservative threat raised questions about Charles Kennedy's leadership. Kennedy was personally very popular. He had developed a friendly image and a penchant for the limelight, earning him the nickname 'chat-show Charlie'. The modernisers believed Kennedy was too laid back, too ready to play down differences between economic and social liberals and failing to provide direction.[34] Others criticised Kennedy's faltering public performances, notably at the launch of the party's 2005 general-election manifesto when he struggled to answer a question on his party's proposals for a local income tax. At the time he put it down to lack of sleep after the birth of his child. After the election, however, he gave several poorly-delivered public speeches and cancelled or was late for meetings. Unknown to most people, including most Liberal Democrat MPs, Kennedy was suffering from a serious alcohol problem.[35]

In December 2005 there was a revolt in the Liberal Democrat shadow cabinet, with many members voicing concerns about Kennedy's leadership. Later, eleven MPs, mainly economic-liberal shadow-cabinet members, signed a letter urging Kennedy to consider his position. The letter's existence was revealed to Kennedy but it was not handed to him. The authors' intention was to give him the Christmas break to reflect on his position. In January 2006 the issue was forced when the news broadcaster ITN informed Kennedy it would run a story alleging he had received treatment for alcohol abuse. He pre-empted the story by confirming the allegations to the media. Kennedy announced a leadership election and said he would contest it. This move caused consternation because the main rivals for his post – Sir Menzies (Ming) Campbell, Simon Hughes and Mark Oaten – had already signalled that they would not stand against him. Events, however, came to a head. Jenny Tonge, a Liberal Democrat peer, declared, 'the boil has to be lanced'.[36] Others agreed. Kennedy was forced to resign when twenty-five Liberal Democrat MPs declared they would not serve under him.[37]

Campbell became interim leader and quickly established himself as the frontrunner in the contest. He was one of the Liberal Democrats' elder statesmen and had developed a high profile in leading the party's opposition to the Iraq war. Many Liberal Democrats looked to Campbell as someone who could hold together the ideological wings of the party.[38] He was also endorsed by Lord Ashdown, a former leader, and gained support from the 'modernisers'.[39] Many saw Campbell as a stop-gap leader, who would take the party through to the next election.[40] Campbell signalled his willingness to end the party's commitment to raise the top rate of income tax to 50 per cent.[41] To head-off criticism from the left-leaning membership, he insisted that he would position the party to the left of Labour, emphasising poverty and green issues.[42]

Some of Campbell's opponents hinted that, at 64, he was too old to lead the party, and they looked elsewhere.[43] Early media speculation focused on Simon Hughes, the Liberal Democrats' president, and Mark Oaten, the home-affairs spokesman. Hughes was a social liberal, while Oaten was a contributor to *The Orange Book*. In the event Oaten folded his campaign before nominations closed, citing a lack of support. Days later a tabloid newspaper published lurid details about his private life. Hughes also became embroiled in media controversy over his sexuality. After the revelations about Kennedy's alcoholism, these developments lent an air of farce to the contest.

The one other serious candidate to emerge was Chris Huhne. His candidacy was surprising because he was associated with *The Orange Book* modernisers who largely backed Campbell. Indeed, there were rumours of an agreement between the modernisers that none would challenge Ming, although Huhne denied that there was a deal.[44] At the time, Huhne was considered to be on the right of the party. He wanted to abandon the policy on raising the top rate of income tax, although he sought a shift to green taxes, emphasising his environmental credentials.[45] He adopted a strong position on Iraq, an issue that burned for most Liberal Democrats, calling for British troops to be withdrawn by the end of 2006. Campbell, on the other hand, preferred not to set a timetable.[46]

When nominations closed, Campbell, Huhne and Hughes secured places in the membership ballot. Campbell enjoyed the greatest support among MPs – ending up with thirty-five declared supporters, including most leading frontbenchers.[47] Hughes and Huhne lagged far behind. The membership ballot, however, provided no guarantee that the members would elect

TABLE 3.2   *Liberal Democrat 2006 leadership election result*

| | First Count | | Second Count | |
|---|---|---|---|---|
| | **Votes** | **%** | **Votes** | **%** |
| Sir Menzies Campbell | 23,264 | 44.7 | 29,697 | 57.9 |
| Chris Huhne | 16,691 | 32.1 | 21,628 | 42.1 |
| Simon Hughes | 12,081 | 23.2 | – | – |
| *Total* | 52,036 | 100 | 51,325 | 100 |

Note: Alternative-vote electoral system. After no candidate achieved over 50 per cent on the first count, Hughes was eliminated and his votes reallocated on second preferences. There were 711 non-transferable votes in the second count. Turnout: 72.2 per cent.

the MPs' preferred candidate. Media commentators initially assumed that the contest would be a two-horse race between Campbell and Hughes. That changed with the revelations about Hughes's private life and Huhne became Campbell's main rival. In the event, Campbell won through, taking 44.7 per cent of votes on the first count, with Huhne in second place. Under the alternative-vote system, Hughes was eliminated and his supporters' second preferences transferred to the other candidates, giving Campbell a clear victory (Table 3.2).[48]

Campbell won largely because the party needed a unifying figure and a safe pair of hands after the trauma of Kennedy's brutal ejection from office. The long-term strategic argument between social and economic liberals was put on hold and Campbell was the beneficiary. The modernisers, however, had demonstrated their willingness to act decisively to improve the party's standing by playing the central role in forcing Kennedy out. They hoped to take over from Campbell after the general election, but they would get their chance sooner than expected.

Campbell's tenure as leader was brief and unsuccessful. He suffered from unfavourable media and public perceptions and unflattering comparisons with David Cameron that invariably centred on his age. His parliamentary performances as leader contrasted sharply with his assured performances as foreign-affairs spokesperson. He suddenly appeared nervous and uncertain in the Commons, leaving him vulnerable to critics in his own party.[49] He was also unlucky. Previous Liberal Democrat leaders had enjoyed the boost of a high-profile by-election victory. In the Bromley and Chislehurst by-election of June 2006, the party came within 600 votes of taking a safe Tory seat, a narrow defeat but one that denied Campbell early momentum.[50] Under his leadership, the Liberal Democrats' poll ratings declined from about 20 per cent to 15 per cent. Although Campbell still had his admirers, few believed that he was an electoral asset.

Campbell became leader just as the Liberal Democrats were being squeezed by the Conservatives and, from June 2007, by a temporarily rejuvenated Labour under Gordon Brown. The revival in Labour's fortunes prompted speculation that the prime minister would call a snap election in the autumn. However, after a surge in support for the Conservatives (which also pushed the Liberal Democrats down to just 11 per cent in the polls), Brown changed his mind. The 'election that never was' allowed the Liberal Democrats to reassess the leadership. Pressure had been building on Campbell over the summer and, with an early election off the table, it burst out into the open. Huhne's allies were suspected of briefing anonymously against the leader.[51] Party stalwarts such as Hughes said openly that Campbell had to raise his game.[52] It was the prelude to a putsch. MPs briefed the press that he should go quietly or face a rebellion. On 15 October 2007 Campbell announced he was standing down with immediate effect. His deputy, Vince Cable, took over as interim leader. Such was the strength of Cable's public and parliamentary performances that some Liberal Democrats lamented the fact that he would not enter the subsequent leadership contest. Cable ruled out a bid because, at 64, he thought that the 'irrational prejudice' shown towards Campbell because of his age would affect his chances.[53]

Several other key figures, including Kennedy and Hughes, also ruled themselves out of the leadership contest following Campbell's resignation. Ultimately, only two candidates secured the required seven nominations from MPs: Huhne and Nick Clegg. They differed in age – Huhne was 52 and Clegg was 39 – but otherwise shared much in common. Both had been MPs since 2005 and MEPs before that. Both were from the 'modernising' wing of the party and largely agreed on policy. In marked contrast to 2006 Huhne was quickly labelled the more left-leaning of the two candidates. His interest in green issues encouraged this shift in perceptions, as did his focus on fairness. But the main reason for the shift seems to have been the contrasting views (or tone) of his opponent. Where Clegg emphasised social mobility, Huhne spoke of the need to achieve equality and end child poverty. On public services, Clegg was open to market reforms, whereas Huhne was more sceptical. His supporters accused Clegg of being a 'Cameron clone', a comparison not intended as a compliment.[54]

Clegg quickly became the front-runner and attracted the support of thirty-nine MPs. Huhne was endorsed by eleven.[55] Some left-leaning MPs, including Hughes and Steve Webb, supported Clegg. Huhne's lack of parliamentary support appears to have been partly due to perceptions that he and his allies had undermined Campbell's leadership.[56] He was, however, thought to have a stronger following among party members.

The result was much closer than anticipated (Table 3.3). Clegg won 50.6 per cent of the members' votes to Huhne's 49.4 per cent, a margin of just 511 votes. The outcome was partly down to Huhne's effective campaigning and policies designed to appeal to the activist left. Clegg's campaign was, moreover, widely seen as lacklustre.[57] His victory was largely down to the perception that he would be better able to improve the party's electoral

TABLE 3.3    *Liberal Democrat 2007 leadership election result*

|  | Votes | % |
|---|---|---|
| Nick Clegg | 20,988 | 50.6 |
| Chris Huhne | 20,477 | 49.4 |
| *Total* | 41,465 | 100 |

*Note*: Turnout: 64.1 per cent

fortunes. The party had fallen in the polls under Campbell and dealing with the renewed Tory threat was a key issue in the contest. A YouGov poll of members found the candidates evenly matched on competence and ability to oppose Gordon Brown. However, Clegg beat Huhne easily (by 53 per cent to 9 per cent) as the candidate with the most 'voter-appeal'. He was also seen as better able to oppose Cameron by 40 per cent to 26 per cent.[58]

The two leadership contests followed growing dissatisfaction with the performances of Kennedy and Campbell. Ideological considerations scarcely figured in public accounts of both putsches. However, the consequence of

TABLE 3.4    Orange Book *contributors' jobs before and after election to parliament*

| Contributor | Job before entering elected politics | Job in 2005 | Job before 2010 election |
|---|---|---|---|
| Vince Cable | Chief economist at Shell | Shadow chancellor of the exchequer | Deputy party leader & shadow chancellor of the exchequer |
| Nick Clegg | Political advisor | MEP (until 2004) | Party leader |
| Ed Davey | Economist and management consultant | Shadow minister for Office of the Deputy Prime Minister | Shadow foreign secretary |
| Chris Huhne | Economist and journalist | MEP | Shadow home secretary |
| Susan Kramer | Financier | No political position | Backbencher |
| David Laws | Investment banker | Shadow chief secretary to the Treasury | Shadow children, schools & families secretary |
| Mark Oaten | Lobbyist | Shadow home secretary | Backbencher |
| Steve Webb | Researcher and academic | Shadow work & pensions secretary | Shadow work & pensions secretary |

*Note*: Two other *Orange Book* contributors are not included in the table: Paul Marshall, a hedge-fund manager not directly involved in Westminster politics; and Jo Holland, Webb's researcher and co-author.

these changes, in outcome if not by intent, was a small but significant ideological shift at the top of the party. With Clegg as leader, *The Orange Book* contributors held most of the senior positions in the parliamentary party (see Table 3.4). As the party approached the 2010 general election, the modernisers were in a strong position.

## Policy changes, 2005-10

One of the strengths of the Liberal Democrats' general-election campaign in 2005 was that it was based on a number of policies that clearly defined what the party represented. Such policies included opposition to the Iraq war and university tuition fees, and the proposal to raise the top rate of income tax from 40 to 50 per cent.[59] Each of these policies located the Liberal Democrats as a party firmly on the centre-left, helping them to win seats from Labour in university towns and increase their vote among Muslims.[60] But economic liberals in the party were worried that the proposed increase in the top rate of tax would deter former Tory voters in key marginal seats.[61] There were also concerns that some policies, such as abolishing tuition fees, might not be affordable. Abandoning cherished policies was not easy, however.

The Liberal Democrats have a rigorously democratic system of intra-party policy making (see Figure 3.1). Most major policy proposals emerge from the federal policy committee (FPC), a body that includes the leader, MPs, federal, state and regional officials, councillors and party activists. The FPC can set up policy working groups to produce detailed documents, which are circulated among local parties, English regional parties, state parties (English, Scottish and Welsh), and among specified associated organisations (SAOs), such as Liberal Youth and the Association of Liberal Democrat Councillors. After consultation, policy documents are submitted to the federal conference for debate. The various local, regional and state parties and SAOs can also submit resolutions and amendments to the conference, via the federal conference committee, which manages the agenda. The conference is sovereign on policy and passed resolutions acquire an official imprimatur. The FPC draws on these policies to compose the election manifesto, in consultation with MPs.

One noteworthy feature of this policy-making structure is the limited role of the parliamentary party. The leadership is represented on the FPC but does not control policy making. In the past it has had to endure debates at the conference it would have preferred to avoid.[62] The system makes it difficult for the leadership to undertake brisk changes of policy because an intra-party consensus must be constructed first.

Campbell and Clegg had to move carefully and prepare the ground for policy changes. During his leadership-election campaign, Campbell had indicated that he was prepared to challenge totemic policies, such as the

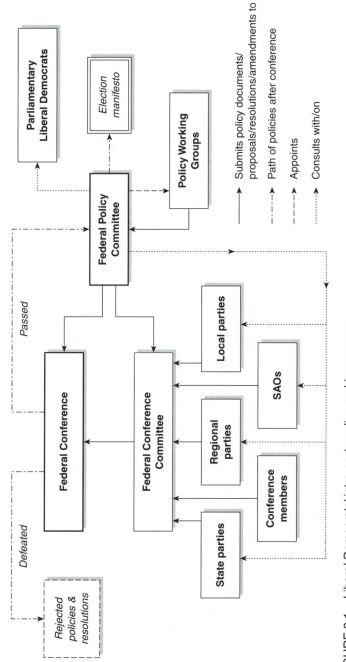

FIGURE 3.1  *Liberal Democrats' intra-party policy-making process*

*Source:* Derived from *The Constitutions of the Liberal Democrats: The Constitution of the Federal Party* (2004), Articles 5, 6 and 7.

pledge to raise the top rate of income tax. While many members viewed the existing policy as redistributive, economic liberals were concerned that the policy signalled hostility to aspiration. At Campbell's first autumn conference as leader in 2006 Cable unveiled a package of tax reforms that included dropping the proposed 50 per cent top rate. The overall tax burden would remain the same by switching to green taxes and reforming capital-gains tax. The leadership argued that it wanted 'fairer', not higher taxes and that the new proposals were more redistributive than those they replaced. The leadership mobilised leading party figures in support and won a convincing victory at the conference. However, a left-leaning MP, Phil Willis, complained, 'The proposals are essentially a massive tax benefit to the middle class and Vince Cable has got to prove that [this] isn't a slippery slope towards more right-wing draconian policies'.[63]

The financial crisis of 2007–08 and the subsequent recession forced the Liberal Democrats to rethink their policies and consider spending cuts to deal with the structural deficit. The launch of a draft manifesto at the 2009 party conference exposed tensions between economic and social liberals. Clegg told a newspaper interviewer that it was necessary to 'be quite bold or even savage on current spending, precisely to be able to retain spending where you need it in areas where the economy is weak in infrastructure'.[64] He indicated that the policy of abolishing tuition fees might have to be downgraded to an aspiration because it was not immediately affordable. His comments caused consternation among social liberals and earned him a rebuke from Charles Kennedy who declared that such policies were 'defining features ... of a Liberal Democrat society'. Evan Harris, a left-wing MP, warned that '[l]eaders of the Liberal Democrats don't always get their way' because it was the FPC and the conference that determined party policy.[65] Harris later added, 'I think Nick is a really great guy and a good leader. But good Liberal Democrat leaders only become great leaders when they recognise it's the party that makes the policy.' The previous year, social liberals had organised a slate of candidates for election to the FPC in order to defend policies such as the commitment to abolish tuition fees.[66] In December 2009, they used their power on the FPC to ensure that the pledge to abolish tuition fees was maintained, although it was agreed that fees would be phased out over six years.[67]

Going into the 2010 general election, the Liberal Democrats appeared to have altered their policy stance since 2005. They had sought to abandon their tax-and-spend image and now talked about the need for public-spending cuts. Their manifesto promised 'change that works for you' by 'building a fairer Britain'.[68] It contained four main themes. First, 'fair taxes' would involve raising the threshold for paying income tax to £10,000, giving taxpayers an extra £700 per year. This pledge would be paid for by closing tax loopholes for the rich, as well as cancelling projects such as ID cards. There would also be a 'mansion tax' of 1 per cent on properties valued over

£2 million. Second, 'a fair future' entailed breaking up the banks and shifting from a finance-dominated to a green economy through a 'green stimulus plan' to create 100,000 jobs. Third, 'a fair chance' for children would be secured by investing £2.5 billion in a 'pupil premium', targeting money at schools in poorer areas. The manifesto also maintained the pledge to phase out tuition fees within six years. Finally, 'a fair deal' for voters required 'cleaning up politics'. Corrupt MPs would be subject to recall elections to strengthen democratic control. However, the centre-piece of political reform would be a change in the voting system to proportional representation. Other important proposals in the manifesto included: saving money by not replacing the Trident nuclear missile system on a like-for-like basis; offering an amnesty to illegal immigrants who had been in Britain for ten years, could speak English and had clean records; and making £15 billion of efficiency savings to reduce the deficit.

The party leadership was ultimately able to get its way with its new talk of future spending cuts and tax cuts. That partly reflected loyalty towards Clegg at the start of his leadership.[69] It also reflected the greater authority acquired by the parliamentary party since its growth in size.[70] Activists supported the policy on raising the income-tax threshold because it would mainly benefit low- and middle-income families. However, social liberals were suspicious that such tax cuts indicated that the leadership wanted a smaller state. There was some truth to that: while the entire party wanted a larger state than existed in 1997, the leadership wanted a smaller state than Labour had created by 2010.[71]

## The return to 'equidistance'

The Ashdown strategy of 'realignment on the left' had either been abandoned or put on ice. Kennedy had seemingly returned to equidistance but had not appeared to take the prospect of working with the Conservatives seriously. Yet Clegg was keenly aware that whenever the party advanced in the polls the media would focus on what the Liberal Democrats would do in a hung parliament. He therefore sought to defuse the issue. In his first leader's speech to a party conference, in March 2008, Clegg hinted that he was prepared to support either Labour or the Conservatives in a hung parliament.[72] In November 2009, he stated that 'the party which has got the strongest mandate from the British people will have the first right to seek to govern'. It was unclear whether 'strongest mandate' meant most votes or seats. The point mattered to those who were aware that the biases in the electoral system might make Labour the largest party in the Commons even if it lagged behind the Tories in vote share. At the time, the polls indicated that the Conservatives were either likely to win a majority or be the largest party, and it was interpreted as a clear suggestion that the Liberal Democrats might support a minority Conservative administration.[73] It is clear, however, that 'first right to seek to govern' did not mean unchallenged right to form the government. Negotiations between possible coalition partners could fail. If that happened, the Liberal Democrats could enter into negotiations with the party with the next strongest mandate.

The narrowing of the polls and increasing predictions of a hung parliament put Clegg in a difficult position. He insisted that he would not be a 'king-maker', since that role was assigned to the electorate.[74] Being too close to Labour would leave Clegg open to the charge that he would prop up a fourth-term Labour government and an unpopular prime minister. It could also damage his party in those marginal seats where they competed with the Conservatives. Tilting towards the Tories, however, risked splitting the Liberal Democrats. The party as a whole, including its MPs and members, thought of themselves as centre-left, especially on equality, redistribution, the environment and European integration.[75] In 2007, a YouGov poll asked members where the party should position itself on the left-right spectrum. Fully 73 per cent opted for left-leaning positions, 19 per cent wanted the party in the centre and just 8 per cent wanted it on the right (see Figure 3.2). The same poll showed that, in the event of a hung parliament, 58 per cent thought a coalition with Labour would be a good idea (compared with 40 per cent for the Conservatives), while 26 per cent thought it a bad idea

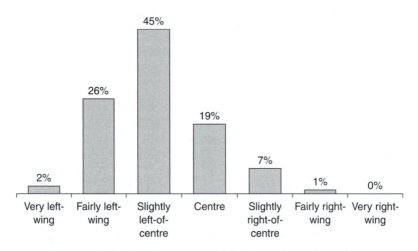

FIGURE 3.2    *Liberal Democrat party members' preferences on party's ideological position, 2007*

*Source*: YouGov survey for Sky News, November 2007, available at http://today. yougov.co.uk/sites/today.yougov.co.uk/files/YG-Archives-pol-skynews-LibDemLead Cntest-071203.pdf. Last accessed 7 July 2010.

*Note*: Responses to the following question: 'Where on the political spectrum would you like the Liberal Democrat party to be?' Don't knows excluded. N = 678

(44 per cent for the Tories). The net support figures were, thus, +32 for a Labour coalition and −4 for a Conservative coalition.

The views of the members and activists were important because Clegg faced an institutional constraint on his negotiating position: a 'triple lock' mechanism to ensure broad consensus for 'any important proposal which could affect the party's independence of political action'. The rule, passed at the party's 1998 conference by activists suspicious of Ashdown's closeness to Blair, stated that any such proposal required the consent of three-quarters of MPs and three-quarters of the party's federal executive. Failing that, a special conference of activists would be called. If that did not provide two-thirds majority support there would then be an all-member ballot, which would require a simple majority.[76]

Clegg may also have taken note of public opinion. In February 2010, a YouGov poll for the *Sunday Times* found that, in the event of a hung parliament, a small plurality wanted the Liberal Democrats to form a coalition with Labour (30 per cent). A coalition with the Tories was preferred by 26 per cent, while 26 per cent thought the party should remain in opposition. Among Liberal Democrat voters, 34 per cent wanted a coalition with Labour and only 22 per cent supported a coalition with the Conservatives, with 33 per cent wanting the party to remain in opposition.[77]

There were considerable tensions in the revived strategy of equidistance. Modernisers, including the leader, saw it as a fundamental repositioning of the party. To their mind, the Conservatives under Cameron had moved closer to the Liberal Democrats on civil liberties. The constitutional-reform and public-services agendas that had drawn Labour and the Liberal Democrats closer during 1997–99 were now less important.[78] Besides, there was little money for more public spending: all parties realised there had to be spending cuts and/or tax rises.

A shift towards the Conservatives was evident in the voting behaviour of MPs in parliament. In the 1997–2001 parliament, the Liberal Democrats supported the Labour government in 50 per cent of parliamentary votes and opposed it in 50 per cent. In the 2001–05 parliament, support fell to 25 per cent of votes, while the party opposed the government in 75 per cent of votes. In the first two years of the last parliament, support fell to 18 per cent of votes and opposition increased to 82 per cent of votes. The Liberal Democrats increasingly voted with the Conservatives, rising from 27 per cent of votes in 1997–98 to 71 per cent in 2006–07.[79]

Perhaps the most high-profile occasion on which the Liberal Democrats and the Conservatives joined forces was to defeat the government over residency rights for retired Gurkha soldiers in 2009. The government had introduced strict rules on the rights of Gurkhas, who are from Nepal, to settle in Britain. A campaign to give all Gurkhas this right (only those who served after 1997 enjoyed it), led by the actress Joanna Lumley, generated considerable public sympathy. A Liberal Democrat motion to give all Gurkhas the right to settle won the support of the Tories and twenty-seven Labour rebels, handing Gordon Brown his first parliamentary defeat as prime minister. A victory photo-call of Lumley, Nick Clegg and David Cameron, flanked by Gurkhas, symbolised the warmer relations between the Conservatives and the Liberal Democrats, and their opposition to Labour's perceived illiberal policies.[80]

Not everyone, however, thought the Liberal Democrats were now closer to the Tories. Richard Grayson, vice-chair of the FPC and formerly Charles Kennedy's director of policy, described equidistance as a 'short-term political tactic' rather than a long-term strategy. It might be helpful in the 2010 general election but in the longer term, the party should be closer to Labour, with whom it shared a 'progressive agenda', rather than the Conservatives.[81] Some Liberal Democrats rejected this stance because it left the party – mistakenly in their view – defining itself primarily by its relationship to other parties.[82] Furthermore, it ignored the fact that no one could foresee where the other two parties would be positioned ideologically in the future.[83] Nevertheless, the danger for Clegg was that if he moved too far away from the Liberal Democrats' socially liberal, anti-Conservative centre of gravity, he risked splitting the party.

Splits have a particular resonance for the third party. The Liberal party split in 1886 when the Liberal Unionists seceded because of their opposition to home rule for Ireland. They went into coalition with the Conservatives in 1895 and eventually the two parties merged. During the First World War, Lloyd George replaced Asquith as Liberal prime minister and led a Conservative-dominated coalition, while Asquith and his followers went into opposition. The split between Asquith's official Liberals and Lloyd George's Coalition Liberals, later renamed the National Liberals, deepened after the war, although the two branches were briefly reunited under Lloyd George's leadership in 1926. In the 1930s, the party split again when a new group calling itself the Liberal Nationals seceded because it supported the Conservative-dominated National government, formed in the midst of the Great Depression.[84] The Liberal Nationals became effectively an appendage to the Conservative party before being fully assimilated in 1968. These splits provide a cautionary tale for the Liberal Democrats, particularly to those within its leadership prepared to risk the party's independence in the quest for power.[85]

## The 2010 general election campaign

The election campaign was remarkable. It was shaped by three televised debates between the three main parties' leaders, the first ever to be held in Britain. In the first debate, Clegg seized the opportunity to introduce himself to voters and present his party as a viable alternative to what he called 'the old parties'. The impact was dramatic. The Liberal Democrats enjoyed a surge of 10 points in the polls, overtaking Labour to move into second place. As 'Cleggmania' gripped the nation, the buoyant leader claimed that the election was now a two-horse race between the Tories and the Liberal Democrats. However, the surge brought increased scrutiny. The party's proposal to offer an amnesty to some illegal immigrants was fiercely attacked by the other parties and the tabloid press. Other policies, such as the rejection of a replacement for the Trident nuclear-missile system, were also targeted by opponents.[86] Ultimately, the Liberal Democrat surge petered out on polling day and despite increasing its vote share by 1 point, the party made a net loss of five seats. It was a disappointing end to a campaign that had fostered so much optimism.

## Conclusion: coalition and beyond

The 2010 general election saw the Liberal Democrats lose seats but gain power. The hung parliament put them in a pivotal position and left Clegg in the king-maker role he had decried before the election. Five days of negotiations saw the agreement of a full coalition government between the Conservatives and the Liberal Democrats, an event that would have been unimaginable under previous leaders. It marked the ultimate triumph of *The Orange Book* MPs, as four of their number took up seats in the cabinet.[87]

The deal caused unease within the Liberal Democrats. Although activists endorsed the deal at a special conference, in a warning shot to the leadership they voted to reaffirm their backing for manifesto policies on tuition fees and proportional representation.[88] Ashdown, Kennedy and Campbell were all reportedly uncomfortable with the apparent abandonment of realignment on the left.[89] Kennedy abstained in the vote at the special conference, although Campbell and Ashdown backed it. Earlier, Ashdown had said: 'the British electorate [have] invented a deliciously painful torture mechanism for the Liberal Democrats because our instincts go one way but the mathematics go the other and we have to make our decision.' He doubted whether a 'rainbow coalition' of Labour, the Liberal Democrats and Celtic nationalists would be stable or strong enough to make the hard choices demanded by the country's fiscal crisis.[90] If the Liberal Democrats rejected the only feasible coalition available, they also risked undermining their case for proportional representation, which would inevitably entail regular hung parliaments.

One prospect for the Liberal Democrats would be to assume the pivotal position adopted by the Free Democrats (FDP) in the Federal Republic of Germany from the 1960s to the 1990s and again since 2009. As a small liberal party, the FDP played king-maker, alternating between centre-right and centre-left coalitions. However, the danger for the Liberal Democrats is that the coalition with the Conservatives will undermine the equidistance strategy. It will be difficult for the party to present itself as halfway between Labour and the Conservatives when they are sharing office with the latter.

In 2010, the Liberal Democrats were a centre-left party led by a centre-right leadership team. That the centre-right leadership is the most left-leaning (minority) component of the coalition government indicates the difficulties Clegg will face in holding his party together. Without careful party management, there is a risk that the Liberal Democrats will split. Much could depend on whether the coalition delivers on reform to the electoral system in the promised referendum on replacing first-past-the-post with the alternative-vote (AV) system. This promise alone persuaded many MPs and activists to hold their noses and support the coalition. The importance of electoral reform cannot be over-estimated: it was the failure of the Blair government to deliver on it in 1998 that effectively killed off any immediate prospects of realignment on the left. A defeat in the referendum could destabilise Clegg's leadership and leave left-leaning Liberal Democrats questioning the wisdom of remaining in the coalition.

The history of Liberal involvement in Conservative-dominated governments is not auspicious. The party has usually split with one part eventually being absorbed by the Tories. The risk for the Liberal Democrats is that something similar could happen in the coming parliament. They tried to minimise the chances of a split by securing the AV referendum, as well as fixed-term parliaments to stop the Conservatives from going to the polls early to capitalise on increased popularity. Even if the government survives, the Liberal Democrats face a dilemma at the next election. The Conservatives remain the major electoral threat in Liberal Democrat seats.[91] Since 1997, the Liberal Democrats have relied on tactical voting by Labour supporters in southern England to keep out the Tories. Appealing to them to continue voting tactically will be much harder now that the party has put the Conservatives in government. It is impossible to say whether the coalition deal is the precursor to realignment on the right. However, unless electoral reform is delivered, it will severely test the viability of the Liberal Democrats as a cohesive and independent party.

## Endnotes

1   We thank Emma Sanderson-Nash (University of Sussex) for her helpful comments on an earlier draft of this chapter.

2   Ivor Crewe, 'New Labour's hegemony: erosion or extension?', in John Bartle and Anthony King, eds, *Britain at the Polls 2005* (Washington, DC: CQ Press, 2006), pp. 200–20, at pp. 216–17.

3   Roland Watson, 'David Cameron and Nick Clegg introduce a very British revolution', *The Times*, 13 May 2010.

4  See David Dutton, *A History of the Liberal Party in the Twentieth Century* (Basingstoke, Hants: Palgrave Macmillan, 2004), pp. 235–93.

5  Dutton, *A History of the Liberal Party in the Twentieth Century*, pp. 229–31.

6  See David Farrell, *Electoral Systems: A Comparative Introduction* (Basingstoke, Hants: Palgrave, 2001), pp. 19–48.

7  Jack H. Nagel and Christopher Wlezien, 'Centre-party strength and major-party divergence in Britain, 1945–2005', *British Journal of Political Science*, 40 (2010): 279–304, p. 298; Michael Steed, 'The Liberal tradition', in Don MacIver, ed., *The Liberal Democrats* (Hemel Hempstead: Prentice Hall/Harvester Wheatsheaf, 1996), pp. 41–61, at pp. 57–8.

8  Only three candidacies, all SDP, were successful in urban seats in the Celtic fringe between 1945 and 1992: Roy Jenkins in Glasgow Hillhead in 1983; and David Owen in Plymouth Devonport in 1983, and again in 1987.

9  John Curtice and Michael Steed, 'An analysis of the results', in David Butler and Dennis Kavanagh, *The British General Election of 2001* (Basingstoke, Hants: Palgrave, 2002), pp. 304–38, at p. 321.

10  Paul Whiteley, Patrick Seyd and Antony Billinghurst, *Third Force Politics: Liberal Democrats at the Grassroots* (Oxford: Oxford University Press, 2006), pp. 140–1.

11  Don MacIver, 'Political strategy', in MacIver, ed., *The Liberal Democrats*, pp. 173–90, at p. 181. For differing perspectives on the effect of the Liberal Democrats on party competition in the UK, see James Adams and Samuel Merrill III, 'Why small, centrist third parties motivate policy divergence by major parties', *American Political Science Review*, 100 (2006): 403–17; Nagel and Wlezien, 'Centre-party strength and major-party divergence in Britain'.

12  MacIver, 'Political strategy', p. 174.

13  Andrew Russell and Edward Fieldhouse, *Neither Left Nor Right? The Liberal Democrats and the Electorate* (Manchester: Manchester University Press, 2005), p. 40.

14  Russell and Fieldhouse, *Neither Left Nor Right?*, p. 41.

15  David Denver, 'The Liberal Democrats in "Constructive opposition"', in Anthony King, ed., *Britain at the Polls, 2001* (Chatham, NJ: Chatham House, 2002), pp. 143–63.

16  Vernon Bogdanor, 'The Liberal Democrat dilemma in historical perspective', *The Political Quarterly*, 78 (2007): 11–20.

17  Andrew Russell, David Cutts and Ed Fieldhouse, 'National-regional-local: the electoral and political health of the Liberal Democrats in Britain', *British Politics*, 2 (2007): 191–214, pp. 193–4.

18  Bogdanor, 'The Liberal Democrat dilemma in historical perspective', p. 19.

19  MacIver, 'Political Strategy', pp. 176–7.

20  Andrew Heywood, *Political Ideologies: An Introduction*, 4th edn (Basingstoke, Hants: Palgrave Macmillan, 2007), pp. 23–63.

21  Richard Grayson, 'Social democracy or social liberalism? Ideological sources of Liberal Democrat policy', *The Political Quarterly*, 78 (2007): 32–9.

22  David Laws, 'Reclaiming Liberalism: A liberal agenda for the Liberal Democrats', in Paul Marshall and David Laws, eds, *The Orange Book: Reclaiming Liberalism* (London: Profile Books, 2004), pp. 18–42.

23  Greg Hurst, *Charles Kennedy: A Tragic Flaw* (London: Politico's, 2006), p. 226.

24  Marshall and Laws, eds., *The Orange Book*.

25  Mark Oaten, private interview, Westminster, 22 March 2010.

26  Grayson, 'Social democracy or social liberalism?' p. 37.

27  Oaten, private interview.

28  Edward Fieldhouse and David Cutts, 'The Liberal Democrats: steady progress or failure to seize the moment?', in Andrew Geddes and Jonathan Tonge, eds, *Britain Decides: The UK General Election 2005* (Basingstoke, Hants.: Palgrave Macmillan, 2005), pp. 70–88.

29  See Russell et al., 'National-regional-local', pp. 203–4.

30  Crewe, 'New Labour's hegemony', p. 216.

31  Whiteley et al., *Third Force Politics*, pp. 139–40.

32  Russell and Fieldhouse, *Neither Left Nor Right?*, p. 99.

33  See House of Commons Research Paper 05/33, *General Election 2005*, pp. 105–16. Available at: www.parliament.uk/documents/commons/lib/research/rp2005/rp05-033.pdf (last accessed 7 July 2010).

34  Hurst, *Charles Kennedy*, pp. 232–3.

35  Hurst, *Charles Kennedy*, pp. 170–91.

36  Menzies Campbell, 'How drink destroyed Charles Kennedy', *Daily Mail*, 24 February 2008.

37  Brendan Carlin and George Jones, 'Long day's journey into political oblivion', *Daily Telegraph*, 7 January 2006.

38  Andrew Denham and Peter Dorey, 'The "caretaker" cleans up: the Liberal Democrat leadership election of 2006', *Parliamentary Affairs*, 60 (2007): 26–45, p. 35.

39  Nick Clegg, 'We need a leader with experience, not youth', *Independent*, 10 January 2006.

40  Alice Miles, 'What deal? Obscure Lib Dem fends off unwelcome attention', *The Times*, 2 February 2006.

41  Andrew Grice, 'Campbell plans to ditch 50p tax on £100,000 plus', *Independent*, 19 January 2006.

42  Tania Branigan and Michael White, 'Menzies Campbell: I will take Lib Dems to the left of Labour', *Guardian*, 13 January 2006.

43  Brendan Carlin, 'Campbell would be a stop-gap leader, hints his leadership rival', *Daily Telegraph*, 11 January 2006.

44  Miles, 'What deal?'

45  Rachel Sylvester and Alice Thompson, 'Lib Dem new boy aims straight for top', *Daily Telegraph*, 21 January 2006.

46  Patrick Wintour, 'Huhne tries to outflank Campbell on Iraq withdrawal', *Guardian*, 31 January 2006.

47  Denham and Dorey, 'The "caretaker" cleans up', p. 43.

48  Thomas Quinn, 'Membership ballots in party leadership elections in Britain', *Representation*, 46 (2010): 101–17, pp. 103–6.

49  Andrew Pierce, 'Knives are out for Sir Ming as Lib Dems look for poll boost', *Daily Telegraph*, 12 October 2007.

50  Lord Rennard of Wavertree, private interview, Westminster, 15 June 2010.

51  Greg Hurst, 'Rapid exit of conference hero who defied his critics but not the polls', *The Times*, 16 October 2007.

52  Andrew Pierce, 'Hughes: Ming must do better', *Daily Telegraph*, 13 October 2007.

53  Patrick Wintour and Tania Branigan, 'Huhne points to his economic expertise in leadership fight', *Guardian*, 18 October 2007.

54  Colin Brown, 'Clegg rejects Huhne supporters' claim that he is a "Cameron clone"', *Independent*, 20 October 2007.

55  Tania Branigan, 'All still to play for in Liberal Democrats' leadership race', *Guardian*, 23 November 2007.

56  Daniel Foggo and Roger Waite, 'LSD article plays tricks on Huhne's mind', *Sunday Times*, 21 October 2007.

57  Tania Branigan, 'Clegg seeks new dawn for his party, and for politics', *Guardian*, 19 December 2007.

58  YouGov survey for Sky News, December 2007, available at: today.yougov.co.uk/sites/today.yougov.co.uk/files/YG-Archives-pol-skynews-LibDemLeadCntest-071203.pdf (last accessed 7 July 2010). See also Quinn, 'Membership ballots in party leadership elections in Britain', pp. 106–8.

59  See Andrew Russell, 'The Liberal Democrat campaign', in Pippa Norris and Christopher Wlezien, eds, *Britain Votes 2005* (Oxford: Oxford University Press, 2005), pp. 87–100.

60  Fieldhouse and Cutts, 'The Liberal Democrats', pp. 82–5.

61  Patrick Wintour and Tania Branigan, 'Campbell confronts prospect of defeat on green tax switch', *Guardian*, 19 September 2006.

62  Duncan Brack, 'Liberal Democrat policy', in MacIver, ed., *The Liberal Democrats*, pp. 85–110.

63  Tania Branigan, 'Row as 50p tax for high earners goes', *Guardian*, 20 September 2006.

64  Patrick Wintour and Allegra Stratton, 'Britain needs "savage" cuts, says Clegg', *Guardian*, 19 September 2009.

65  James Kirkup, 'Backlash over end of free tuition pledge', *Daily Telegraph*, 21 September 2009.

66  Dr Richard Grayson, private interview, Goldsmiths College, 1 March 2010.

67  'Liberal Democrats to keep pledge to scrap tuition fees', *BBC News* website, 18 December 2009, available at: news.bbc.co.uk/1/hi/uk_politics/8421092.stm (last accessed 7 July 2010).

68  *Liberal Democrat Manifesto 2010* (London: Liberal Democrats, 2010).

69  Grayson, private interview.

70  Andrew Russell, Edward Fieldhouse and David Cutts, '*De facto* veto? The Parliamentary Liberal Democrats', *The Political Quarterly*, 78 (2007): 89–98.

71  Lord Rennard of Wavertree, private interview, Westminster, 9 June 2010.

72  Sam Coates, 'Renegade Clegg promises he will shake things up at Westminster', *The Times*, 10 March 2008.

73  Sam Coates, 'Lib Dems set to steer Cameron into No 10 if election ends in a hung Parliament', *The Times*, 23 November 2009.

74  Sam Coates, 'Voters will be kingmaker, not me, Clegg tells party', *The Times*, 15 March 2010.

75  Whiteley et al., *Third Force Politics*, pp. 48–67.

76  The full text available at: blogs.ft.com/westminster/files/2010/03/the-lib-dem-triple-lock.pdf (last accessed 7 July 2010).

77  YouGov survey for the *Sunday Times*, February 2010, available at: today.yougov.co.uk/sites/today.yougov.co.uk/files/YG-Archives-Pol-STResults-100219.pdf (last accessed 7 July 2010).

78  Oaten, private interview.

79  Philip Cowley and Mark Stuart, 'A long way from equidistance: Lib Dem voting in Parliament, 1997–2007', unpublished mimeo, available at: www.revolts.co.uk (last accessed 7 July 2010).

80  Andrew Grice and Michael Savage, 'Gurkhas force Brown into yet another retreat', *Independent*, 30 April 2009.

81  Grayson, private interview.

82  Rennard, private interview, 9 June 2010.

83  Rt Hon David Laws MP, private interview, Westminster, 15 June 2010.

84  See Dutton, *A History of the Liberal Party in the Twentieth Century*, pp. 68–136.

85  Bogdanor, 'The Liberal Democrat dilemma in historical perspective'.

86  Ben Padley, 'Ainsworth condemns "ridiculous" Lib Dem Trident policy', *Independent*, 17 April 2010.

87  The four *Orange Bookers* were Clegg, Cable, Huhne and Laws, although Laws quickly departed after criticisms of his claims for parliamentary expenses. Two other *Orange Bookers*, Webb and Davey, became junior ministers.

88  Polly Curtis, 'Liberal Democrats approve coalition deal – but with provisos', *Guardian*, 17 May 2010.

89  Toby Helm and Anushka Asthana, 'Top Liberal Democrats open rift over coalition with Conservatives', *Observer*, 16 May 2010.

90  Lord Ashdown, interviewed on *The Andrew Marr Show*, BBC One, 9 May 2010.

91  At the 2010 election, the Conservatives came second in thirty-eight of the Liberal Democrats' fifty-seven seats, of which nineteen were marginals (majorities of less than 10 points), eight were safe (majorities of at least 20 points ) and eleven were intermediate, with majorities between 10 and 19.9 per cent. Labour were second in seventeen Liberal Democrat seats, of which eight were marginals, three were safe and six were 'intermediate'. Plaid Cymru came second in one safe Liberal Democrat seat and the SNP were second in one 'intermediate' seat.

# 4 THE FINANCIAL CRISIS AND ITS CONSEQUENCES

Michael Moran, Sukhdev Johal and Karel Williams[1]

The 'credit crunch' and the 'financial crisis' conventionally define a searing experience in the life of the Brown government, but they actually only catch a part of that experience. The 'crunch' specifically refers to the virtual cessation of the banking system's provision of credit for the wider economy in the great banking crisis of October–November 2008. Indeed, it was the most difficult economic event confronting any government since Britain was evicted from the European Exchange Rate Mechanism on 'Black Wednesday' in September 1992. Yet, the great banking crisis was just one part of a bigger story involving the discrediting of New Labour's economic and regulatory policies and the end of fifteen years of sustained economic growth, low unemployment and low inflation. The crash which ended all that also raised fundamental questions about the success of a thirty-year experiment in economic management that can be traced back to Margaret Thatcher's first administration in 1979. This chapter is therefore about the crisis, but it is also about much more. It is about how New Labour's policy response of bailing out the banks and markets terminated New Labour and opened the way for the new coalition government's subsequent attack on the public sector. This chapter traces the origins of the thirty-year economic experiment, shows how it ended, and concludes by arguing that it has left economic policy makers without a convincing solution to the problem that the experiment was supposed to solve – how to create an economy capable of generating sustainable employment, especially in the private sector.

The symbolic beginning of the Brown government's financial woes occurred on 14 September 2007 when depositors queued to withdraw funds from Northern Rock, a bank founded and still based in Labour's North East heartland. It was the first occasion since the Overend Gurney crisis of 1866 when a British bank had failed as a result of a public run by depositors. Seemingly taken by surprise, the government was forced to save Northern Rock from imminent collapse, eventually taking the bank into public ownership. It was a hugely traumatic event for Labour. But though traumatic, it was just the beginning of a long calvary for the economy and for everyone whose lives – and political fortunes – depended on it. In his last budget statement as chancellor of the exchequer in March 2007, Gordon Brown claimed to have abolished 'the old boom and bust'.[2] Within months, however, the British economy was engulfed by the greatest bust for over seventy years. The 2008 banking crisis destroyed reputations and institutions and, over the course of one critical October weekend, threatened the very functioning of the banking system itself. Despite (or because of) the best efforts of the Bank of England and the huge amounts of liquidity pumped into the system – in what was the most radical rescue measure since before the First World War – the crash had prolonged, damaging consequences. Household names, most famously the retailer Woolworths, were bankrupted as credit lines were closed. Gaps appeared in high streets up and down the country as traders went out of business. Less visibly, countless town centre development sites were mothballed as credit for developers dried up. Tens of thousands of potential buyers were frozen out of the housing market by suddenly prohibitive mortgage terms. And the resulting recession left a large hole in the public finances, forcing all the political parties to consider raising taxes and cutting public spending.

The scale and prolonged effects of the crisis meant that the general election of 2010 was fought in the most difficult and threatening economic conditions since 1979 or possibly February 1974. In the international recession of the 1970s that had been precipitated by a huge rise in oil prices, Britain was exposed as the most fragile of the larger capitalist economies. In 1979, voters had turned from Labour to Margaret Thatcher's Conservative party, heralding the start of its eighteen years in office. The Thatcher government's economic revolution, which New Labour consolidated after 1997, was a radical response to the country's perceived economic fragility and decline. It was designed to transform Britain from a sick to a healthy capitalist economy, capable of weathering future international storms. Until 2008, the transformation seemed successful. Establishment commentators, politicians and economists all bought into the proposition that the British economy was strong. The experience since 2008 shows this to have been a delusion. Far from being uniquely prepared to withstand the global crisis, Britain was once again especially vulnerable. The country had uniquely inflated housing- and financial-market bubbles, and it had a state with among the very highest levels of indebtedness. Britain soon reverted to being among the sickest of the big capitalist economies. Its economy was among the first to enter recession and among the last to exit, and even when economic growth resumed, the resumption was hesitant and fragile.

The banking crash, therefore, signified many things. It destroyed the proposition that Labour's post-1997 economic management had eliminated 'boom and bust'. It brought an end to a sustained period of growth, low inflation and full employment. And, most importantly, it ended a thirty-year experiment, started in 1979 and continued under New Labour, which presumed that private enterprise would create jobs, and which relied on light-touch financial regulation to promote the growth of the City. Not surprisingly, the financial crisis provided the central backdrop to the 2010 election. Labour could no longer tell a story about uninterrupted economic progress, as it had in 2001 and 2005. Instead, it now had to compete with the Conservatives over who could tell the most convincing story about managing the economy in hard times and who could most credibly reduce the deficit without retarding economic recovery. And the Liberal Democrats could justly accuse both major parties of being complicit in creating the conditions for the crisis.

# The origins of New Labour's economic programme

The seeds of the great banking crisis lay in decisions taken after 1979 by Margaret Thatcher's Conservative government. By the time New Labour won its first landslide election in 1997, much had changed. The financial world was different, and Labour under Tony Blair and Gordon Brown had come to view that world very differently compared to how it once did.

## Regulation in the City

The first fateful change that occurred between 1979 and 1997 was in the character of the financial markets, especially their centrality in the wider economy and the nature of regulation in the City of London. The City is the oldest, and the most distinctive, part of Britain's business community. It comprises various markets and institutions – including such famous names as the Bank of England, the London Stock Exchange and Lloyd's of London – and dates back to the creation of the 'military fiscal state' at the end of the seventeenth century.[3] The City was deeply involved in the military and colonial expansion of the British state, in slave trading and in the creation of a global financial system. In the process, the various City markets established their claim to self-government. That claim developed its own legitimising ideology: that there was a kind of unique English genius for self-regulation and that the City prospered in the absence of legal controls. This ideology was well established by the end of the nineteenth century and was given renewed impetus after the First World War. The combination of an increasingly interventionist and democratic state and the replacement of the Liberals by Labour as the Conservatives' main opponents, created a new political environment that threatened the City's autonomy. The City responded by developing protective strategies. It elaborated on and sought to justify its ideology of self-regulation. It reorganised the Bank of England so that it became the City's voice in government. And it reorganised various markets, mostly into cartels, which could now regulate the activities of participants under the eye of the Bank.[4]

The resulting regulatory system survived subsequent war and scandal. It did not survive Margaret Thatcher. Her government's deregulation of key trading practices in London's markets in the so-called 'Big Bang' of October 1986 was one of the centrepieces of her economic programme. The intention was to unleash competitive appetites through liberalisation. Unusually, the reforms had their desired effect. The Big Bang decisively changed the City's fortunes, securing its position as the leading financial centre in Europe and establishing it alongside New York and Tokyo as one of the three global financial capitals. The Big Bang also secured London's comparative advantage over rival European financial markets, such as Frankfurt and Paris, that were less nimble in deregulating trading practices. The strategy was central to Thatcher's economic revolution, which sought to rebalance Britain's economy by abandoning its inefficient manufacturing industry to the competitive mercies of world markets and cultivating a dynamic financial services sector. The Thatcherite vision of Britain's future was of an economy led by and structured around the demands of global financial capital. Developing the City's comparative advantage was all important to this vision.

The City's comparative advantage over its rivals depended on many factors, but a crucial element was the regulatory regime. Regulation is important in all economic activity, but it is uniquely important in financial markets because the two components of economic activity in this sector – the provision of commercial services, such as legal and insurance services, and the trading of financial instruments – are both uniquely sensitive to regulation.

The Big Bang did away with the City's traditional system of financial self-regulation and led to a new regulatory structure built around the Securities and Investments Board (SIB). As set out in the Financial Services Act 1986, the reconstructed regulatory structure was designed simultaneously to provide a more robust system of controls while protecting the autonomy of markets from the 'usual suspects' that threatened to curtail competition, especially lawyers and politicians. The SIB was a complex half-public, half-private body, which presided over a convoluted system of 'self regulatory organizations' (SROs) and was supposed to supervise separate markets. Meanwhile, the Bank of England continued to control banking supervision.[5] However, the arrangements were discredited by successive regulatory failures and above all by the Barings fiasco of 1995, when one of the City's oldest names collapsed as a result of the 'rogue trader' Nick Leeson.[6] It was these arrangements, and the increasingly City-dominated economy, that an incoming Labour government would have to grapple with.

## Revising Labour's traditional economic programme

The second fateful change that occurred between 1979 and 1997 was in Labour's economic programme, which was adapted partly to reassure the City and partly to reassure the electorate. Labour's 'traditional' identity was founded on what one commentator termed the 'collectivist trinity' of public ownership, trade-union power and social welfare.[7] Clause IV of Labour's constitution committed it to the nationalisation of major industries and utilities or 'the common ownership of the means of production, distribution and exchange', a goal firmly associated with Marxist conceptions of socialism but which had increasingly embarrassed the party's leadership. Labour was not simply committed to the trade unions; it was, in many ways, the political expression of the union movement. This association too had caused embarrassment, especially after James Callaghan's government was brought down by the 1978–79 'Winter of Discontent'. Finally, Labour was formally committed to tax-and-spend welfare in its pursuit of social democracy or what Tony Crosland, following John Rawls, termed 'democratic equality'.[8] The party was certainly committed to some kind of progressive redistribution and used both taxation and expenditure to achieve it. This goal did not prevent some Labour supporters criticising welfare benefits or grumbling about taxes, but the party remained committed to the welfare state.

Throughout much of the post-war period, Labour's economic policies were partly framed by this trinity. Successive Labour governments were prepared to nationalise, they recognised the interests of organised labour, and they accepted high tax rates (especially income tax) to pay for the welfare state. Yet, as helpful as this trinity is for understanding post-war Labour programmes, it omits the party's view of the markets and financial regulation. Successive Labour governments, before and after 1945, had accepted the basic framework of a mixed economy despite the commitment to public ownership in Clause IV. In practice, Labour governments in the 1940s and the 1960s depended on the performance of private firms whose output and exports sustained jobs, fed economic growth and increased taxable income. Unfortunately, one of the enduring problems for Labour (and Conservative) governments in the 1960s and 1970s was that the British private sector was underperforming. In the 1960s a modernising Labour government tackled this underperformance by planning and intervening in the economy: a Department of Economic Affairs was established under George Brown and published a 'National Plan' in 1965. But the party as a whole did not develop a systematic approach to intervention and regulation.

There was one other important feature of Labour's traditional economic programme. It was widely associated with major economic crises, industrial unrest and forced devaluations of the currency. Ramsay MacDonald's minority government was unable to contend with the Great Depression and disintegrated in 1931. Clement Attlee's 1945 government presided over post-war fuel shortages, and its chancellor of the exchequer, Sir Stafford Cripps, was forced to devalue the pound in 1949. In 1967, another Labour chancellor, James Callaghan, devalued the pound during Harold Wilson's first administration. And the 1974–79 Labour governments of Wilson and Callaghan presided over high inflation, low growth and almost unending industrial strife, culminating in the 'Winter of Discontent'. At one point, in 1976, such was the state of the British economy that the then chancellor Denis Healey was forced to turn to the International Monetary Fund (IMF) for financial support. Voters, like industrialists and financiers, credited Labour's economic policies with a tendency to fail. One commentator observed that Labour had achieved 'an unenviable reputation for economic and industrial mismanagement'.[9] The party's reputation (for economic mismanagement) was a major factor – possibly the major factor – in explaining why Labour lost four consecutive elections to the Conservatives in 1979, 1983, 1987 and 1992.

Labour politicians were fully aware that they had to address their party's reputation for incompetence. Even before it lost to the Conservatives in 1992, Labour had sought to woo the City, which was prospering as an offshore financial centre after Conservative deregulation in the late 1980s (at a time when giant British manufacturing companies like GEC or ICI had apparently lost their way). The 'prawn cocktail offensive', as the wooing was known, began as a series of lunches in the early 1990s that brought together John Smith, Labour's then shadow chancellor, Gordon Brown, then shadow trade and industry secretary, and key figures from the City. The offensive continued when Brown succeeded Smith as shadow chancellor in 1992. The purpose of the lunches and meetings was to provide reassurance that Labour was generally committed to fostering the private sector and specifically in favour of the permissive regulatory regime that the City preferred. Michael Heseltine, the Conservative environment secretary, suggested the crustaceans were dying 'in vain'. They were not. Gradually, those in the City came to feel reassured: not only was a Labour victory no longer seen as a threat; it came to be seen by many in the City as an opportunity.

But the 'prawn cocktail offensive' was not just a short-term political tactic to make Labour appear more business friendly; it also signalled that some elements within the party were now actually buying into the Thatcherite vision of an economy built around financial services. The conversion was gradual. The most important policy changes were actually made under the leadership of Neil Kinnock, Labour's leader between 1983 and 1992.[10] But neither Kinnock nor his short-lived successor John

Smith questioned traditional symbolic attachments of the kind represented by Clause IV. Smith's sudden death in 1994 propelled Tony Blair to the leadership with Brown as economic overlord. This change allowed the two men, in alliance with the party's spin doctor supreme Peter Mandelson, to tell a story that, repeated endlessly over the years, was central to the New Labour narrative. This narrative accepted the diagnosis of the 1992 election that Labour's support had been damaged by Conservative warnings of a 'tax bombshell' if the party won. It accepted the diagnosis of inaccurate opinion polls in 1992 that had shown Labour winning. As one commentator put it, 'ours is a nation of liars. People lied about their intentions up to the moment of voting … People may say they would prefer better public services, but in the end they will vote for tax cuts.'[11] In short, Messrs Blair, Brown and Mandelson fashioned a narrative which concluded that aspirational middle-England voters would never support a party committed to redistribution through high levels of direct taxation and expenditure. This new story pictured the Labour past, especially the past of the 1970s, in terms of a kind of Neanderthal collectivism. The party now had to embrace openly the market and work with the forces of international financial capital to deliver social democracy.

The symbolic centre of the narrative was the new Clause IV, which Blair persuaded Labour to adopt almost immediately on his succession to the leadership. 'The Labour Party is a democratic socialist party', it now read:

> It believes that by the strength of our common endeavour we
> achieve more than we achieve alone, so as to create for each
> of us the means to realise our true potential and for all of us
> a community in which power, wealth and opportunity are in
> the hands of the many, not the few, where the rights we enjoy
> reflect the duties we owe, and where we live together, freely,
> in a spirit of solidarity, tolerance and respect.

In addition to the Clause IV rewrite, New Labour also promised to give the trade unions 'fairness, not favours', and it abandoned many of its tax-and-spend policies. Brown stunned commentators when he pledged not to raise the top rate of income tax ahead of the 1997 election – a pledge the party would repeat in 2001 and 2005 – and there would be welfare reform, with recipients being promised 'a hand up not a handout'. Above all, New Labour embraced the market. Fatalistic views about the inevitability of globalisation fostered highfalutin talk of a 'third way', in which governments could only respond to social, economic and technological changes by investing in education, infrastructure and other supply-side measures to enable society to compete in the global economy.[12] In fact, New Labour's whole economic programme would depend on flourishing markets making the most of their comparative advantage. It is now time to look at that programme of economic management in greater deal.

# New Labour's programme of economic management

One of the striking features of the bubble that preceded the 2007–08 financial crisis was that it was widely celebrated as heralding a new era of sustained growth and stability. Gordon Brown as chancellor was a prime beneficiary of this era of great complacency. Until virtually the end of his chancellorship he was widely viewed as outstanding. After his first four years in the Treasury, one acute observer of British politics described him as a 'genius', who had apparently presided over steady economic growth, low interest rates, low inflation and low unemployment.[13] In Labour circles, his economic management was credited with contributing to the party's post-1997 electoral dominance. It was only after he became prime minister that an increasingly accepted revisionist account cast him as an incompetent who bailed out of the Treasury just as the boom turned to bust.

The revisionist account needs to be viewed with care, however. As with most major policy legacies, the value of Brown's economic programme is contestable. Some achievements were undoubtedly positive, others questionably so. Six key and interrelated features of Brown's programme stand out. Some were his own invention, but collectively they demonstrated just how far New Labour's economic programme had embraced the Thatcherite economic programme of prosperity through enterprise.

## Light-touch financial regulation

One key feature of Brown's economic programme was the regulatory regime for banking and finance, which New Labour inherited from the Conservatives and then refined. Chancellor Brown moved to reshape the governing arrangements for City markets almost immediately after taking office in May 1997. Just four days after he entered the Treasury, he announced that the Bank of England's Monetary Policy Committee would henceforth be responsible for setting interest rates instead of the Treasury. The surprise announcement was a demonstration of the markets' centrality in the government's programme. It was also a calculated signal to the markets that interest-rate policy would no longer be subject to political influence. Policy would instead be decided by technocrats sensitive to the markets' needs. The business world was generally delighted by the move. Brown had asserted his authority and established his credentials as a chancellor to be reckoned with.

Less than a fortnight after this coup, Brown announced the creation of a new regime of financial supervision to replace the system of control administered by the Bank of England, a system that had been widely discredited by the collapse of Barings in 1995. The regime comprised a new Financial Services Authority (FSA), which acquired most of the Bank of England's supervisory authority over the banking system and additional authority over most other financial institutions, and a new Standing Committee, which was to coordinate the workings of the FSA, the Bank and the Treasury in matters relating to financial regulation. For the first time, the whole regime was embodied in a comprehensive piece of legislation, the Financial Services and Markets Act 2000.

With hindsight, these reforms are striking for the gap between their formal appearance and the reality of regulation. Formally, the Act endowed the British economy with a uniquely authoritative financial regulator: the FSA by itself exercised powers that in the United States were exercised by a number of Federal, and many state-level, supervisory agencies. In reality, as shown from post-mortems on the banking crisis, the strong central authority was accompanied by a self-consciously light-touch regulatory regime that was designed to be as accommodating as possible to City practices.[14] Labour swallowed the City's arguments that it needed light regulation to secure comparative advantage over other, more closely regulated, financial centres. The strength of the historically entrenched regulatory ideology, and the strength of various interests in the markets, ensured that the new FSA absorbed that ideology; its history until 2007 was a history of practising market-friendly, light-touch regulation in the belief that this promoted innovation and guaranteed London's superiority in the global financial market place. Unfortunately, light-touch regulation did little to discourage 'excessive risk-taking in the financial system' and was widely thought to have been an important contributor to the banking crash of 2007–08.[15]

In a revealing television interview broadcast three weeks before the 2010 election, Gordon Brown conceded that one of his biggest mistakes in office had been the weakness of post-1997 banking regulation: 'In the 1990s, the banks, they all came to us and said, "Look, we don't want to be regulated, we want to be free of regulation." ... And all the complaints I was getting from people was, "Look you're regulating them too much." The truth is that globally and nationally we should have been regulating them more.'[16]

## The growth of Treasury control

A second key feature of Brown's economic programme was very much his own personal legacy: a stronger Treasury that exercised increased control over domestic policy. Brown's uniquely long tenure as chancellor was tied to the unstable and fractious bargain that bound him and Tony Blair together at the top of the Labour party and subsequently the government. Part of that bargain gave Brown more authority than any chancellor in living memory to intervene across the range of domestic policy.[17] He reinforced his position by using public-spending control mechanisms to intervene in the details of domestic policy delivery. Before the 1997 election, Brown pledged to adhere strictly to the outgoing Conservative government's spending plans. In so doing, he wanted to reassure voters that this Labour government would not tax and spend like previous Labour governments. The assurance was consistent with the narrative that pictured 'Old' Labour as damaging and profligate; it happened to neglect the inconvenient fact that even Margaret Thatcher, under pressure of recession, had been herself a considerable taxer and spender. When the self-imposed restraints on public-sector expansion were removed in the 2000 comprehensive spending review, increases in resources were tied to public-service agreements that were designed to cen-tralise Treasury control over other government departments. As a result, the Treasury became a much more formidable domestic policy actor after 1997. It also left the Treasury in a much more central position than hith-erto in the management of economic crises. For instance, in the secondary banking crisis of the 1970s, the last great domestic *systemic* banking crisis, the Treasury was a marginal participant.[18] In the great systemic crisis of 2007–08, the Treasury would be the dominant domestic actor.

## The inexorable advance of the regulatory state

A third key feature of Brown's economic programme was his consolidation of the 'regulatory state'. Thatcher's revolution was not just economic; it had involved a fundamental reshaping of the historic relations between the central state and civil society and a shift from a culture of voluntarism and autonomy to one of target-led compulsion and central direction.[19] The auton-omy of key institutions in the public sector, including local government and the National Health Service, was drastically curtailed in a new regime of budgetary controls, targets and performance indicators. Education, which had been the preserve of more or less independent professional elites, was likewise subjected to the scrutinising, controlling gaze of a central state. Many of those who wanted and voted for a New Labour government in 1997, especially those working in the public sector, did so in the hope that the Thatcherite revolutionary storm would abate. They were disappointed. The regulatory state became even more deeply embedded under Brown's stewardship of the economy. The Treasury used its ascendancy over other departments to drive ever more in the direction of audit, performance indi-cators and target setting. Hospitals, schools, universities, prisons and a host of other organisation were all subject to far more regulatory controls in 2010 than in 1997.

## Consolidating managerial power

A fourth feature of Brown's economic programme also served to consolidate another of the post-1979 Conservative government's legacies: the empowerment of managers and owners in industry. The key Conservative reforms to the industrial-relations laws that dated from the 1980s remained fundamentally unaltered. The revolution in privatisation and of outsourcing the public sector was consolidated, and in some instances extended. Union membership, especially in the private sector, withered on the vine. One 2004 workplace survey showed that two-thirds of workplaces had no unions at all.[20] By 2010 the Thatcher revolution in respect of employer power in the private sector had been so successfully consolidated that Britain had perhaps the most flexible labour market in Western Europe. Managers had a freedom to hire, fire and redeploy workers that many managers in Europe envied.

## Creating a new plutocracy

A fifth feature of Brown's programme – and the feature that sat most uneasily with Labour's traditional economic programme – was the fostering of a new plutocracy. Labour inherited a Thatcherite taxation system that vastly increased the rewards enjoyed by the very top executives in the largest corporations and the most successful operators in the City. There was no attempt to disassemble that system. Under Brown, the gap that opened up between the corporate elite and the rest of the employed population was, by the standards of the post-war years, huge.[21] In respect of the very poorest 10 per cent, some of Brown's social policies, notably the introduction of tax credits and the funding of targeted pre-school programmes like Sure Start, did moderate the gap between the very poorest and the rest. But there is no argument that under Brown, both as chancellor and later as prime minister, the rise of the corporate plutocracy, especially the City-based plutocracy, continued apace.[22]

New Labour and Brown seemed to share a strong affinity for the City. They relaxed taxes on capital gains, maintained a Thatcherite limit on top-rate income tax (around 40 pence in the pound) and kept financial regulation light. They also championed shareholders' rights, which effectively meant championing the freedom of City fund managers. A brief flirtation with thinking of enterprises as involving a wide range of 'stakeholders', encompassing owners, employees, managers and customers, soon gave way to the full-throated reassertion of the doctrine of shareholder value. New Labour signed up to the view that it was the fundamental aim of management to extract the maximum return for just one group of stakeholders, those with legally enforceable property rights, and especially those with equity. As Peter Mandelon told an audience of American executives in 1998: 'We are intensely relaxed about people getting filthy rich'.[23] (To be fair, Mandelson immediately added: 'as long as they pay their taxes'.)

New Labour's support for the shareholder-value doctrine was crucial. The doctrine tended to foster a convergence of interests between top managers and holders of equity, because the most lucrative rewards secured by managers were bonuses in the form of share entitlements. It tended to tie corporate managers more closely to the judgements of equity markets since the critical index of success was share price. In the City, the doctrine created a whole class of traders in corporate property rights and advisers in mergers and acquisitions, who became fabulously rich 'working for themselves'.[24] Since an obvious way to maximise shareholder value was to sell up to the highest bidder, the doctrine of shareholder value also helped encourage a mergers-and-acquisitions boom. The enormous fees charged by traders and advisers fuelled the profits of investment bankers.

The activities of this new plutocracy had important structural consequences for the wider economy, which became 'one of permanent restructuring and churning of ownership … over the period from 1980 to 2003, for every pound spent on productive assets, FTSE firms collectively spent nearly 80 pence on buying other firms.'[25] Labour's acquiescence in the doctrine of shareholder value was just as important in facilitating the churning of ownership as it was in facilitating the emergence of the new plutocracy. The breakup of ICI in 1993 and the sale of Cadbury to Kraft in 2010 bookended a period of capitulation to shareholder value.

## Renewing public-sector employment and infrastructure

New Labour's friendliness with the City was not all about building a new plutocracy, however. There was a rationale for the party's relaxation about people getting 'filthy rich'. New Labour became convinced that a prospering City would stimulate economic growth and tax revenues, which in turn could fund investment in the public sector. Labour could thus pursue its social programmes without scaring aspirational voters fearful of high taxes. (The evidential basis of this bit of the New Labour narrative is examined below.)

The sixth feature of Brown's economic programme, then, was far from Thatcherite. It was about renewing public-sector employment and infrastructure. By the mid 1990s Labour was predominantly a party of the public sector, especially of the public sector in areas like local government, education and health. Many Labour voters worked in the public sector, as did a large part of its activist base. Moreover, the party's major institutional funders were trade unions whose strength increasingly lay in the public sector. As chancellor, Brown undoubtedly delivered to his party's public-sector supporters. The achievements are impressive: over ten years, real spending on health nearly doubled; that on education rose by over £25 billion in real terms.[26]

An obvious consequence of Labour's investment was that the size of the state grew. At first, as Figure 4.1 shows, government expenditure as a

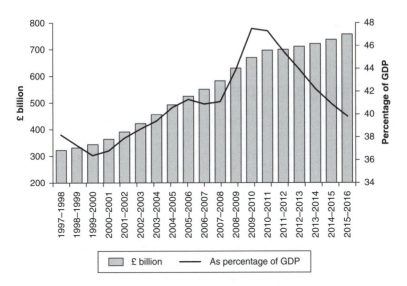

FIGURE 4.1    *Government expenditure, 1997–2016*

*Source*: HM Treasury, *Public Finances Databank*, Tables B1 and B2, available from http://www.hm-treasury.gov.uk/psf_statistics.htm. Last accessed 21 July 2010.

*Note*: Expenditure refers to total managed expenditure. Forecast figures from 2010–2011 to 2015–2016 are from the June 2010 budget.

percentage of gross domestic product (GDP) dipped, as Brown stuck to his Conservative predecessor's spending commitments. But from a low point in 1999–2000, when expenditure accounted for just 36.3 per cent, it rose year on year, so that by 2009–10, government expenditure accounted for some 47.7 per cent of GDP.

Brown's enlargement of the public sector amounts to an economic legacy, which, in its way, is as difficult to reverse as were the Thatcher economic reforms. For a start, there has been an irreversible physical transformation across whole parts of the public sector, and not even the most pessimistic observer expects any future government actually to demolish the schools, hospitals and laboratories built in these years. Furthermore, if Brown's strengthening of Treasury control has made the task of imposing public-spending cuts in the future easier, the expansion of a heavily unionised public-sector workforce has made it more difficult. And that difficulty is only compounded by recent changes within the trade-union movement. The creation of UNITE in 2007 as the country's largest union and the consolidation of UNISON (created in 1993) into a public-sector giant with 1.3 million members mark the most important institutional developments within organised labour since the creation of the Transport and General Workers' Union in the aftermath of the First World War. The trade-union movement is now configured around two giants with the will and capacity to defend the interests created by the Brown expansion.

## The thirty-year experiment: the evidence

New Labour's economic programme was not purely Thatcherite, but it did accept many Thatcherite solutions to some of the deep-rooted problems associated with Britain's economy. The end of the first long boom in the 1970s saw the ascendancy of a particular diagnosis of these problems: a weak and constrained private sector was being 'crowded out' by an over-large public sector; over-regulated labour markets inhibited managerial initiative; and trade unions with legal immunities obstructed innovation and challenged state authority. The Thatcherite prescription was a new economic order to liberate the private sector. Labour was initially opposed but in the 1990s came to accept the diagnosis and the medicine. In particular, Labour came to accept that market autonomy should be protected and that the state should intervene only minimally in the regulation of markets. It also came to accept that fostering the City's position as a global market place, and fostering the health of the financial-services industry, would compensate for the decline of Britain's manufacturing base. Deregulated labour markets and an unconstrained private sector were thought to be the key to wider economic regeneration. After 1979 Britain thus embarked on a thirty-year experiment to halt decline by constraining union power in the private sector, enhancing managerial authority in flexible labour markets, and creating a tax and corporate-reward system to match. The economic programme that collapsed during Gordon Brown's premiership was, in many ways, the end of this experiment.

There has been very little empirical analysis of how the private sector responded to Thatcher's new framework. The diagnosis established a presumption that the medicine should work. Quite fortuitously, North Sea oil came on stream as the Conservatives came to power in 1979, thus preventing any balance of payments crisis, the old index of economic failure. And the categories of official employment statistics obscured the record of private-sector job creation, the new index of success. Privatisation and outsourcing were a kind of bookkeeping adjustment, which, by effectively reclassifying public workers, steadily inflated measured private-sector employment. On our calculations, some 750,000 workers were transferred into the private sector in this way. This number accounts for some 71 per cent of the apparent overall increase in private-sector employment from 1979 to 1997.[27]

Closer examination of employment trends between these years reveals an economy with continuing problems about private-sector job creation.

TABLE 4.1    *Manufacturing, finance and state employees and total jobs, 1971–2008*

| | | No. | | | |
|---|---|---|---|---|---|
| | | Manufacturing (GB) | Finance (GB) | State employment (UK) | Total workforce jobs (UK) |
| Pre-Thatcher governments | 1971 | 7,886,059 | 620,324 | | |
| | 1978 | 7,123,476 | 730,294 | 5,598,000 | 26,861,000 |
| | Change | −762,583 | 109,970 | | |
| Pre-Thatcher government to immediate post-'Big Bang' | 1978 | 7,123,476 | 730,294 | 5,598,000 | 26,861,000 |
| | 1987 | 5,107,180 | 939,824 | 6,248,000 | 27,052,000 |
| | Change | −2,016,296 | 209,530 | 650,000 | 191,000 |
| Post-'Big Bang' to New Labour government | 1987 | 5,107,180 | 939,824 | 6,248,000 | 27,052,000 |
| | 1997 | 4,059,561 | 978,415 | 6,676,000 | 28,697,000 |
| | Change | −1,047,619 | 38,591 | 428,000 | 1,645,000 |
| New Labour | 1997 | 4,059,561 | 978,415 | 6,676,000 | 28,697,000 |
| | 2008 | 2,709,080 | 1,062,977 | 8,009,000 | 31,661,000 |
| | Change | −1,350,481 | 84,562 | 1,333,000 | 2,964,000 |

*Source:* Nomis, Office for National Statistics.

*Note:* Breaks in series end 1981, 1991 and 1997 related to changes in SIC classifications. The employment data for manufacturing and finance relate only to employees and excludes Northern Ireland. 1978 is used as the full year prior to the Conservatives winning the general election on 4 May 1979. 'Big Bang' reforms were enacted on 26 October 1986. New Labour won the general election on 2 May 1997. Total jobs and state employment relates to the United Kingdom, and the latter is the summation of jobs in public administration, education and health.

Manufacturing employment fell from 7 million in 1979 towards 4 million by the mid 1990s. The 1979–82 recession permanently destroyed 20 per cent of manufacturing employment. The Conservatives abandoned British manufacturing to global competition while welcoming inward investment by the Japanese, a development that brought few compensating jobs. They gambled on the service sector's capacity to create jobs and especially on the expansion of financial services after City deregulation in the Big Bang of 1986. As Table 4.1 shows, employment in financial services did indeed increase from a very small base of around 650,000 in the mid 1970s, but this increase was all over by the time the effects of deregulation kicked in at the end of the 1980s. In terms of job creation, the most substantial and durable achievement of the Conservative years was a one-million-plus rise in state employment sustained by Thatcher's pragmatic acceptance of public expenditure regardless of her rhetoric about rolling back the frontiers of the state.

All this set the scene for New Labour after 1997. It inherited Britain's palsied manufacturing sector, a policy bias towards finance and a heavy reliance on the state to fill in for a private sector that appeared incapable of creating jobs. Economic outcomes were again obscured by the categories of official statistics, which identified state employees as those working for public agencies. But official statistics failed to register how privatisation and outsourcing had expanded 'para-state employment', private-sector jobs that were dependent on government funding, such as those relating to nursery education and care for the elderly. State influence on job creation is best measured by adding together the number of state employees working in the public sector and the number of para-state employees working in the private sector. Calculations done by the Centre for Research on Socio-Cultural Change (CRESC) at the University of Manchester suggest that the para state employed 1.7 million in 2007, or roughly one-third again of the 5.7 million employed directly by the state.[28]

There were many who believed that the new 'knowledge economy' and 'creative industries' would provide fresh sources of employment. As Tony Blair put it in March 2000, the 'knowledge economy is our best route for success and prosperity'.[29] The holders of such views were living on a 'fantasy island', in Dan Atkinson and Larry Elliott's vivid coinage.[30] With low-wage imports from China and elsewhere rising, the number employed in British manufacturing continued to decline under New Labour, from 4 million in 1997 to 2.7 million in 2008. Nor was it the case that a burgeoning financial-services sector created new jobs. In the fifteen years after 1992, finance increased its share of output to 9.1 per cent and its share of profits to 12.8 per cent.[31] Over the same period, the numbers employed in the sector stayed flat and by 2008 accounted for less than 4 per cent of the total British workforce. Job creation in finance was limited because relatively few employees were needed in wholesale finance – the world of investment banks and trade in high-value financial instruments – and there was constant pressure to reduce staff numbers in retail finance – high-street banks – where large numbers were employed. The large increase in (non-financial) service-sector private employment actually includes many para-state jobs. State plus para-state employment increased by nearly 1.3 million between 1998 and 2007. This rise accounts for no less than 57 per cent of the total increase in the number of jobs in the period.

By 2007, therefore, the state and para-state sectors together employed 7.5 million, or 28 per cent of the employee workforce. This was never a deliberate economic strategy but an unintended effect of New Labour's spending on health and education. Initially after coming to office in 1997, Gordon Brown was 'prudence' personified and stuck to Conservative expenditure limits. In 2000, he tore up those limits. Real public expenditure increased sharply, as a glance back to Figure 4.1 shows. The public-sector deficit pushed towards 3 per cent, which was the formal limit under fiscal rules imposed on Britain by membership of the European Union. Any further expansion in state and para-state employment was plainly unsustainable even before the 2007–08 financial crash. Yet, no one in the government seemed willing to ask: what would come next?

Uncompetitive manufacturing had made the British economy one of the weakest of the big capitalist economies at the end of the first long boom in the 1970s. As a global economic downturn loomed in 2007, triggered by problems originating in the American banking system, confidence in Thatcher's revolution and Brown's economic stewardship licensed claims that the British economy was especially well prepared to weather the storm. But in a ghostly return to the 1970s, Britain's over-exposure to property and financial markets ensured that it was among the first major economies to enter into recession and among the last to emerge. The global recession thus challenged the narrative of national economic transformation that had been shared by almost the whole political class and the metropolitan elites.

Looking back, there seem to have been three main sources of delusion that prevented politicians from coming to terms with the full magnitude of the economic problems facing Britain.

## The over-estimation of the financial sector's economic contribution

From the early 1990s the City had sought to justify light-touch regulation and tax concessions by listing the many socio-economic benefits of finance. It did so by adding up the totals of jobs created, taxes paid and its contributions to the balance of payments. After the financial crisis, two quasi-official reports produced by the City – the Wigley and Bischoff reports – updated this narrative about finance as the goose that laid the golden egg.[32] The narrative was then re-used as a framing device in the Labour government's own 2009 White Paper on financial reform, a striking demonstration of how reform is often inhibited by policy makers' acceptance of the industry narrative.[33] Many of the claims were accepted by the political classes even though their empirical support was flimsy.

The most persistent of the City's claims was that tax revenues from finance were a key source of funding for New Labour's social programmes. But as a pro-cyclical sector built on tax avoidance, finance actually delivered remarkably little revenue in the boom years of the early 2000s. Table 4.2 below shows that, over the 5 years from 2002 to 2007, tax receipts from finance totalled £153 billion and averaged just 6.7 per cent of government receipts. In the same period, manufacturing employed many more workers, who all paid taxes under strict pay-as-you-earn (PAYE) rules, so that this sector delivered twice as much tax revenue. Moreover, as a report produced by Manchester University's CRESC demonstrated, the tax revenues of the pre-2007 boom were more than offset by the subsequent costs of bailing

TABLE 4.2  *Analysis of taxes paid by the finance and manufacturing sectors,*
*2002–2007*

| | Total taxes paid by employers and employees | | Employers share of sector's taxes | | Sector's taxes as a share of government receipts | |
|---|---|---|---|---|---|---|
| | Finance £million | Manufacturing £million | Finance % | Manufacturing % | Finance % | Manufacturing % |
| 2002–03 | 25,333 | 63,167 | 48.8 | 32.7 | 6.4 | 16 |
| 2003–04 | 25,184 | 62,273 | 50 | 32.8 | 6 | 14.7 |
| 2004–05 | 29,661 | 62,516 | 49.4 | 33.4 | 6.6 | 13.8 |
| 2005–06 | 34,366 | 62,993 | 52.4 | 33.8 | 7.1 | 12.9 |
| 2006–07 | 38,488 | 63,503 | 51.9 | 34.5 | 7.4 | 12.2 |
| Total (for 5 years) | 153,033 | 314,451 | 50.7 | 33.5 | 6.7 | 13.8 |

*Sources*: Nomis, Her Majesty's Revenue & Customs, Office for National Statistics and
PricewaterhouseCoopers.

*Note*: Employer taxes summate corporate tax plus employer's national insurance. Employee
tax summates income tax and national insurance.

out the banks after the 2007–08 crash.[34] The IMF has calculated the 'direct
up front financing' cost of bailouts to British taxpayers as £289 billion and
noted that the total cost including contingent liabilities could be as high as
£1,183 billion.[35]

## The over-reliance on public-sector employment

Under Gordon Brown's chancellorship, as under his Conservative predecessors', long-standing problems about regional imbalance between the
South East of England and the rest of Britain worsened. However, New
Labour's increased expenditure on health and education operated as a kind
of undisclosed regional policy. State and para-state employment expanded
right across the country but was particularly critical where private-sector
job creation was weak or failing. Table 4.3 shows that, in London and the South,
state and para-state jobs accounted for no more than between 38 and 44 per cent
of employment growth between 1998 and 2007. In the Midlands, the North,
Wales and Scotland, state and para-state jobs accounted for between 55
and 73 per cent of employment growth over the same period, with most
of the rest induced by public-expenditure multiplier effects. Increasing
state and para-state employment was crucially important in former industrial areas like the West Midlands and the North East, where manufacturing
was not replaced by any other autonomous private-sector activity. In the
North East, for instance, state and para-state employment accounted for
79 per cent of the total increase in jobs between 1998 and 2007. In the West

TABLE 4.3   *Change in employment by major region and source of change by major sector, 1998–2007*

| | Total change | | Sectoral contribution to change | |
|---|---|---|---|---|
| | **Privte sector** | **State and para-state sector** | **Private sector** | **State and para-state sector** |
| | **No.** | **No.** | **%** | **%** |
| London | 194,470 | 120,160 | 61.8 | 38.2 |
| Midlands | 114,771 | 304,047 | 27.4 | 72.6 |
| North | 186,212 | 337,793 | 35.5 | 64.5 |
| South | 332,101 | 260,317 | 56.1 | 43.9 |
| Wales | 66,606 | 81,935 | 44.8 | 55.2 |
| Scotland | 77,480 | 168,275 | 31.5 | 68.5 |
| Total | 971,641 | 1,272,526 | 43.3 | 56.7 |

*Source:* Annual Business Inquiry, Office for National Statistics.
*Note:* Data relate to employees and excludes Northern Ireland.

Midlands, where private-sector employment actually fell during the period, it accounted for 153 per cent of the net increase in employment.

The increased expenditures on health and education were equally important in meeting a new requirement for gendered employment. The Labour government's rhetoric about increasing women's participation in the labour market, combined with household calculations about the benefits of having two wage earners, worked to push the female participation rate to 70 per cent. State and para-state jobs were crucial because nearly 70 per cent of them were filled by women, and half of those jobs were part time. Thus, right across Britain under New Labour, the state worked to put a second, usually female, wage earner into the average household. Between 1998 and 2007, the state and para-state sectors accounted for 904,000 new female jobs, or 81 per cent of the total increase in female employment. Labour now had every incentive to postpone public-expenditure cuts – as it proposed doing ahead of the 2010 election – since postponement would avert the threat to all those voting households that now contained at least one state-funded job.

## The over-reliance on asset prices and imports of cheap goods and labour

A key source of economic 'feelgood' under New Labour was increasing property prices and the borrowing it underpinned. Asset-price inflation was sustained by a banking system that lent for speculation, not material investment. In 2007, at the end of the speculative bubble, lending on residential and commercial property assets, together with lending to other financial institutions trading in coupons derived from these assets, accounted for three-quarters of all British bank lending. This arrangement was wholly unstable but it kept large numbers of people optimistic about their financial prospects so long as households could fund consumption through equity withdrawal, that is, by borrowing money against the value of their house. During Brown's decade as chancellor, the real value of equity withdrawals was larger than the real increase in GDP, a pattern that had also occurred during the Thatcher years. The important difference was that the Thatcher boom had ended in a housing bust as real prices fell by 30 per cent, but the Brown boom did not. Labour avoided a housing bust thanks to massive cuts in interest rates. House prices stagnated but then started to rise again. By the spring of 2010, they were rising at an annualised rate of 10 per cent.

If rising house prices helped to sustain the nation's economic optimism after 1997, so too did a serendipitous conjuncture of low inflation in labour and product markets. The result was a steady increase in real incomes for those in work, especially those working in the expanding public sector. The government's good luck had little to do with the chancellor's policies, however. It rested largely on an overvalued currency, mass inward migration, which kept downward pressure on labour costs in the private sector, and the flood of cheap manufactured imports, especially from China.

Perhaps more importantly, the wider optimism was also at odds with the fundamental unsustainability of the British economy, especially those regional economies that relied so much on public-sector infrastructure investment, state and para-state employment expansion and the speculative property boom. Once the bubble burst, former industrial cities like Liverpool or Stoke might just as well have been Reykjavik or Dublin.

## The crisis and the fallout

The pin that pricked the bubble was, of course, the 2007–08 financial crisis, and especially the critical weekend of 10–13 October 2008, when the banking system came close to total collapse. As Nicholas Allen recounts in Chapter 1, Brown's government responded with various domestic and international initiatives as the crisis unfolded.[36] But beyond the crisis lies something of greater importance: what the unfolding events did to the politics of economic management in Britain. Four important consequences stand out, each of which was a repudiation of the thirty-year experiment begun by the Conservatives and continued by New Labour.

### The terms of the regulatory debate changed

One obvious consequence of the banking crisis was a change in the political discourse surrounding financial regulation. The regulatory regime created by New Labour after 1997 belonged primarily to the domain of low politics, of technical operations and bureaucratic manoeuvring between the responsible agencies. Its status was exemplified by the workings of the Standing Committee that coordinated the work of the FSA, the Bank of England and the Treasury. Nominally bringing together principals from these organisations – the chancellor of the exchequer, the governor of the Bank and the chairman of the FSA – in practice its meetings were attended and chaired by lower-ranking officials and the technicians of regulation. This practice was in tune with the whole regulatory philosophy, which marginalised political influences in the regulatory system. The run on Northern Rock in September 2007 transformed the terms of debate and the arenas where it took place. The issue of financial regulation was suddenly top priority for the prime minister and chancellor. The Standing Committee's role changed and from the Northern Rock crisis onwards drew the principals into attendance.[37] The systemic crisis of October 2008 deepened the transformation: it widened the range of regulatory issues now commanding elected politicians' attention beyond narrow questions about the stability of particular institutions, and the arrangements for depositor protection, to the stability of the whole banking system. The unfolding events also pulled in a wide range of other democratic actors. Of these, perhaps the most significant, because it succeeded in generating wide publicity about its activities, was the House of Commons Treasury select committee, which from 2008 published a series of reports on the crisis.[38]

Moreover, the international character of the crisis transformed financial regulation into the highest politics of international financial diplomacy, as senior politicians and their agents wrestled with the threat of global financial meltdown. G7 finance ministers, including Alistair Darling, met over the momentous weekend of 10–13 October 2008 in Washington, DC, where they helped to avert the possible collapse of the whole international banking system.[39] The acclaimed economist Paul Krugman heaped praise on the 'leadership' displayed by Darling and Brown.[40] G20 heads of government would later meet in November 2008, April 2009 and September 2009 to discuss the financial markets and the plight of the world economy. Gordon Brown's hosting of the April 2009 summit in London, where world leaders agreed to inject $1.1 trillion (£681 billion) into the global economy, was an all-too-rare personal triumph for the prime minister.

## State ownership in the economy

A second consequence of the financial crisis was the unexpected taking of several banks into public ownership. The privatisation movement was a key part of the thirty-year experiment described above. The scale of privatisation in Britain was greater than in any comparable economy.[41] But the crisis dramatically reversed this great legacy of the preceding three decades. With a number of British banks struggling amidst the credit squeeze, the initial response of policy makers was to resist public ownership. In the months immediately after the collapse of Northern Rock, the government spent millions of pounds on consultants in a failed attempt to offload the stricken bank and avoid its effective nationalisation. But in November 2008, the government was obliged to establish United Kingdom Financial Investments (UKFI) as a vehicle for managing public ownership of a huge tranche of the banking system. By July 2009 UKFI owned 70 per cent of the voting share capital of Royal Bank of Scotland (RBS), and 43 per cent of the Lloyds Banking Group. As John Kingman, UKFI chief executive at the time, put it in more homely terms: 'Every UK household will have more than £3,000 invested in shares in RBS and Lloyds.'[42] It was easy to enjoy the irony that all this had occurred under a Labour government that had renounced the party's old Clause IV.

## The fusing of the political and financial elite

A third consequence of the crisis was a rejection of one of the key principles of post-1979 market regulation: that there should be a clear separation between the roles of democratically elected politicians and financial regulators. The financial crisis broke this system, and reordered the relations between the political elite in the core executive and the financial elite. A coming together of the two groups began with the needs of crisis management, for it involved often difficult face-to-face negotiations between the ministerial figures – notably the chancellor and the prime minister – and leading bankers. The disastrous takeover of HBOS by Lloyds happened in part because of an informal deal struck on a social occasion between Brown and the Lloyds chairman that guaranteed Lloyds exemption from competition regulation.[43] In the depths of the crisis in 2008, the banking industry had to turn to the state for the resources and authority to prevent systemic collapse; but the complexities of crisis management also drove the state into close cooperation with the financial elite. Apart from instances like the Lloyds-HBOS deal, the most public sign of the fusing of politics and finance was the hurried recruitment of City grandees into the government via the House of Lords. Paul Myners, who had spent most of his professional career in the City, was appointed financial services secretary or 'City minister' in October 2008; and Mervyn Davies, a former chairman of Standard Chartered, was appointed as trade minister in January 2009.

## Creating narratives of incompetence and illegitimate reward

A fourth consequence of the financial crisis was the scapegoating of bankers and the development of new narratives about corporate greed and incompetence. In the decades before 2007, protecting financial markets from democratic control depended heavily on naturalising their functions: that is, on depicting the markets as responding to quasi-scientific laws of supply and demand. The doctrine of shareholder value and the exorbitant rewards claimed by the financial elite were justified on the basis that markets responded to impersonal economic forces, and that fund managers and wholesale bankers performed crucial functions such as allocating capital and packaging risk. Apart from the usual suspects on the radical left, only a few maverick journalists and politicians – the most notable of whom was Vince Cable, the Liberal Democrat Treasury spokesman – dissented from this orthodoxy.[44]

During the financial crisis, and in the parliamentary post-mortems, a new narrative developed that traced the crash to pathological features of the banking industry: it was a system that produced 'excessive' rewards, and stimulated excessive risk taking by a banking elite driven by the search for huge bonuses. The crisis was thus a result of institutional defects in markets and cultures of human greed. Opinion polls suggested that voters shared these perceptions. In October 2009, a YouGov poll found that 82 per cent of respondents thought it was a bad idea that banks were paying out bonuses because 'bankers are more interested in enriching themselves than benefiting the wider community'.[45] Two especially symbolic moments captured the public hostility. The first was the arraignment of several former heads of the stricken banks before the House of Commons Treasury select committee, which was widely reported on television news, and which led to critical newspaper headlines such as *The Sun*'s 'Scumbag millionaires'. The second was the extended and venomous campaign against Sir Fred Goodwin, also known as 'Fred the Shred', a former chief executive of the Royal Bank of Scotland, which focused on the huge pension that he had negotiated as the price of his departure.

Not surprisingly, given its importance, the crisis turned the regulation of markets into the stuff of adversarial party competition. For the Conservatives it created problems as they tried to create a new narrative to accommodate malign and rapidly changing economic circumstances. For Labour, and especially for Brown, it involved creating a new narrative that turned him from the wizard of economic growth to the rock of stability in the international economic storm. And for the Liberal Democrats, it simply propelled Vince Cable to media stardom.

But pitching the complex issues of financial regulation into the adversarial party arena also raised questions about the capacity of political debate to cope with issues of this complexity. Democratic pressures can unintentionally pull in more than one direction. On the one hand, for example, the crisis produced a reform moment, one when the style of market regulation built up over the preceding decades was subjected to potentially seismic forces. Amidst a wave of popular hostility to bankers, all the leading groups involved – politicians, regulators and even bankers – briefly disavowed the light-touch regulation that had characterised the City for so long.[46] Moreover, the enforced extension of public ownership made it impossible to avoid new questions about the banking industry, such as how far it should be treated as a closely regulated, part publicly-owned utility, rather than an instrument of global competition. The markets seemed to be opening up to the influence of democratic actors.

On the other hand, what had seemed like a democratic assault also turned out to provide a strong defence against radical reform. The ferocious criticism and scapegoating of Goodwin and others facilitated the development of a narrative separating 'bad' and 'good' bankers, thus pinning blame on individuals rather than institutions or systemic practices. Moreover, if the crisis led to democratic politicians getting more involved in questions of regulation, it also opened up politicians to members of the financial elite, in the form both of ministerial appointments and in the shaping of public institutions like UKFI in the image of the City elite.[47] Above all, however, serial bank failure and mass unemployment had only been avoided by huge outlay from the public purse. All three major parties were now committed to deep cuts in public spending and increases in taxation to fill the hole in the public finances that had been caused in part by the crash. The political elite had bailed out the financial elite, and yet, while the losses of the banking system had been socialised, the profits continued to be private. There were unanswered – and often unasked – questions about the disastrous effects of past banking practices on the public finances, what might be done to prevent similar crises occurring in future, and who should bear the burden of repairing the damage. These questions might have been expected to dominate the 2010 general election.

## The crisis and the 2010 election campaign

The 2010 election campaign was the most remarkable since at least 1945. So too was its outcome. Its main features are, of course, examined in other chapters in this volume. But three features of the campaign merit attention for what they reveal about the parties' response to the financial crisis. These features were 'negative', in that they were largely absent. They were dogs that seldom barked, if at all.

One notable feature of the election concerned the single most important outcome of the crash: the fiscal crisis confronting the British state. Everyone knew that an incoming government would impose draconian cuts on public spending, whatever political hue it happened to be. The Conservatives promised immediate cuts, Labour and the Liberal Democrats promised a temporary stay of execution so as to avoid a double-dip recession. Yet, nobody wanted to spell out in detail the scale of those cuts. The authoritative and independent think tank, the Institute for Fiscal Studies, analysed the three parties' spending plans and was damning in its judgement:

> ... the three main parties all accept that a significant fiscal tightening will be necessary over the coming Parliament, and perhaps beyond. Given that this is likely to be the defining task of the next administration, it is striking how reticent all three parties have been in explaining exactly how they would go about it. The Conservative and Liberal Democrat manifestos do not even state clearly how big a fiscal tightening they would seek to achieve, and by when, assuming that the public finances evolve as the Treasury currently expects. And all three parties are particularly vague about the cuts in public spending that they all think should deliver the majority of the fiscal tightening.[48]

Perhaps not surprisingly, none of the main parties in a close-fought election wanted to scare voters with details of the spending cuts and possible tax rises that they would impose if elected.

If this first absent feature of the campaign reflected the problems the parties had in managing voter expectations, the second reflected a fundamental problem of democratic politics, at least in the frenzy of an election campaign: the banking crisis was the root cause of the economic malaise, yet the reform of banking received very little attention. At the height of the banking crisis it was easy for politicians to scapegoat identifiable 'villains', apparently greedy bankers like Goodwin of RBS. Likewise it was easy for the Liberal Democrat leader Nick Clegg to score points in the first and third televised prime ministerial debates by referring to 'greedy' and 'irresponsible' bankers, or for the Conservative leader David Cameron to single out Goodwin for opprobrium in the third debate. But the technicalities of banking reform proved more difficult to package and were largely glossed over. The details were complex and ill suited to the cut and thrust of public debate.

During the campaign the parties occupied rather odd positions, at least relative to their historical alignments. Labour, the traditional party of the working man, was now the defender of the *status quo*: it had enacted a Banking Act just before the election that entailed only marginal changes in the institutional structure of banking regulation. The Conservatives, in contrast, promised to abolish the FSA and transfer most of its regulatory powers to the Bank of England. This was a surprising solution to the crisis of light-touch regulation since the Bank had lost its original supervisory role in 1997 because its own light-touch approach had led to the collapse of Barings in 1995. The Liberal Democrats, influenced by their Treasury spokesman, Vince Cable, offered the most radical policies, including breaking up the big banks to separate their high-street retail operations from their trading and investment arms in the financial markets. But all this detail was buried in the election manifestoes, and figured little in the campaign itself.

The third notable feature of the campaign concerned the apportionment of blame for the crisis. Labour was the author of the regulatory system that failed in 2007–08 and might have been expected to carry the can. In a sense it did, in that the party lost the election. But voters did not seem to pin as much blame on the government for this specific event as they might have done. In October 2008, the pollsters ICM asked the public to what extent they blamed different groups for 'the present financial crisis'. Nearly three-quarters of respondents, 74 per cent, placed 'a lot' of blame on 'poor decisions by banks and other financial companies', 69 per cent similarly blamed 'poor or weak supervision by the authorities of banks and financial companies', and 54 per cent blamed 'Consumers for borrowing too much money'. Only 45 per cent placed a lot of blame on 'the government here in the UK'.[49]

Moreover, while Labour lost the election, neither the run on Northern Rock nor the events of October 2008 seemed to inflict the kind of long-term damage on the party that 'Black Wednesday' – the day in September 1992 when Britain was forced to withdraw from the European Exchange Rate Mechanism – inflicted on the Conservatives. That event fatally damaged the Conservatives' reputation for economic competence for nearly two decades.[50] Not so the financial crisis and Labour's reputation. Indeed, in an ironic twist, Gordon Brown, the author of the failed regulatory system, actually had a 'good crisis', as did his chancellor, Alistair Darling. Brown garnered praise for his perceived role in helping to lead the international response at the height of the global banking crisis in October 2008, and he also garnered some public approval. The same ICM poll just referred to found that 61 per cent of respondents agreed that Brown had been handling the current financial crisis 'well' compared to 33 per cent who said 'badly'. Labour strategists were aware of this irony, and Brown made much of his role in responding to the crisis during the campaign, even if it was ultimately in vain.

## Conclusion

The 2010 election resulted in the first coalition government in London since 1945. The new government had to grapple immediately with two great issues created by the financial crisis: the future of taxation and public spending; and the future of the banking system. On the first, the Conservative and Liberal Democrat's coalition agreement produced some clarity on the fate of some of their campaign pledges: the Conservatives put proposals to raise the threshold for inheritance tax on the back burner; and the Liberal Democrat's secured a commitment to raise tax thresholds at the bottom so as to lift more low earners out of the tax net. Further details emerged in the government's emergency budget in June 2010, when the new chancellor George Osborne announced, amongst other measures, a 2.5 point increase in the rate of VAT from 17.5 to 20 per cent and a £1,000 increase in the personal income-tax allowance. The budget also made clear that the main burden of resolving the deficit would fall on spending cuts rather than tax increases: 77 per cent of the total consolidation would be achieved through slashing expenditure. There would be cuts in welfare spending, and real-term spending across all government departments would be cut by a quarter over four years, as shown in Figure 4.1 which shows the forecast decline in public expenditure as a percentage of GDP. The government claimed it was a 'progressive' budget, although analysis by the Institute for Fiscal Studies suggested that the overall package would hit the poor harder than the rich.[51] Needless to say, the real pain, unpopularity and potential difficulties for the coalition will come in 2011 and later.

There were also moves on the issue of banking reform. With Osborne heading up the Treasury, Vince Cable became the new business secretary. It soon became clear, however, that Gordon Brown's legacy of a dominant Treasury would endure. The cabinet committee concerned with banking would be chaired by Osborne, not the more radically inclined Cable. Moreover, the question of separating retail and investment banking – a key Liberal Democrat manifesto proposal – was farmed out to an independent commission. In short, structural reform of the banking system was kicked into the long grass. But changes were announced to the system of financial regulation. A week before the emergency budget, in the chancellor's traditional Mansion House speech to the City, Osborne announced 'a new system of regulation that learns the lessons of the greatest banking crisis in our lifetime.' In place of the existing tri-partite regulatory system based on the FSA, the Bank of England and the Treasury, the Bank would be given responsibility for both 'macroprudential' and 'microprudential' regulation. The FSA would be broken up and its successor would operate as a subsidiary of the Bank. There would also be a new independent Financial Policy Committee at the Bank, complementing Brown's Monetary Policy Committee, which would be responsible for considering and responding to any issues that might threaten economic and financial stability. The new system will be in place by 2012. It remains to be seen whether it succeeds where previous regimes failed.

Finally, the coalition will have to contend, at some point, with an even bigger economic issue. The financial crisis marked the end of a thirty-year experiment in freeing the private sector so as to maximise its ability to create jobs. The evidence presented in this chapter suggests that that experiment failed over large parts of Britain. There was some dim recognition of the long-term difficulties before the election. In March 2010, even before the election was called, Labour's business secretary Peter Mandelson observed to the annual conference of the Federation of

Small Businesses that 'Britain needs to build a new growth model for the future .... . The recovery can only be driven by private enterprise and investment.'[52] On the other side of the political divide, David Cameron acknowledged during the campaign that large parts of the economy, especially those outside the South East, had become hugely dependent on public-sector investment and jobs.[53] But both men's observations imply a faith in the private sector's capacity to create jobs that is unsupported by the evidence. Cameron's view reflects a diagnosis that goes back to the 1970s, that public-sector activity is crowding out the private sector, and that the solution is to shrink the public sector. Mandelson's diagnosis was accompanied by a characteristically neat phrase: 'more real engineering, less financial engineering.' But precisely how 'private enterprise and investment' can create employment when it has failed to do so over the last thirty years was not explained.

The mystery deepened after the emergency budget, which, on the Treasury's own figures, would cause more than 1 million job losses. Yet, forecasts by the Office for Budget Responsibility (OBR), a newly created body to provide independent assessments of the public finances and the economy, showed economy-wide employment increasing by 1 million to 30 million by 2014–15, which implied that the private sector could create 2 million new private-sector jobs within 5 years.[54] Thus, the whole of the coalition government's economic policy was staked on the assumption that the private sector could and would perform over the 5 years from 2010, as it had never done in the thirty years after 1979. The pursuit of fiscal prudence through deficit reduction was, therefore, combined with wishful thinking about the private sector's capacity to create the replacement jobs necessary for economic success. Events will test this assumption about job creation. Failure could well signal the end of the coalition and add yet another twist in the continuing story of the British political classes and their collective post-1979 delusions about what the private sector can do.

# Endnotes

1  Order of authorship does not indicate weight of contribution; in what follows, we are all equally guilty.

2  Brown's actual words in his budget statement of 21 March 2007 were: 'We will never return to the old boom and bust'.

3  P.J. Cain and A.G. Hopkins, *British Imperialism: Innovation and Expansion, 1688–1914* (London: Pearson Longman, 1993); Michael Moran, 'The company of strangers: defending the power of business in Britain, 1975–2005', *New Political Economy*, 11 (2006): 173–89.

4  For supporting detail, see Michael Moran, *The Politics of Banking: The Strange Case of Competition and Credit Control,* 2nd edn (London: Macmillan, 1986), pp. 9–28.

5  See Michael Moran, *The Politics of the Financial Services Revolution: The USA, UK and Japan* (London: Macmillan, 1991).

6  On the collapse of Barings, see Michael Moran, 'Not steering but drowning: policy catastrophes and the regulatory state', *The Political Quarterly*, 72 (2001): 414–27.

7  Ivor Crewe, 'The Labour Party and the electorate', in Dennis Kavanagh, ed., *The Politics of the Labour Party* (London: Allen and Unwin, 1982), pp. 9–49, at p. 37.

8  See Anthony Crosland, *Socialism Now and Other Essays*, edited by Dick Leonard (London: Cape, 1974).

9  Kenneth Newton, 'Caring and competence: the long, long campaign', in Anthony King, ed., *Britain at the Polls 1992* (Chatham, NJ: Chatham House, 1993), pp. 129–79, at p. 131

10 See Michael Moran and Elizabeth Alexander, 'The economic policy of New Labour', in David Coates and Peter Lawler, eds, *New Labour in Power* (Manchester: Manchester University Press 2000), pp. 108–21.

11 Robert Harris, 'We are a nation of liars', *Sunday Times,* April 12, 1992, quoted in Ivor Crewe, 'A Nation of Liars? Opinion Polls and the 1992 Election', *Parliamentary Affairs*, 45 (1992): 475–495, p. 489.

12 Anthony Giddens, *The Third Way: The Renewal of Social Democracy* (Cambridge: Polity Press, 1998).

13 Anthony King, 'Tony Blair's first term', in Anthony King, ed., *Britain at the Polls 2001* (Chatham, NJ: Chatham House, 2002), pp.1–44, at p. 2.

14 See, for example: Treasury Committee, *The Run on the Rock, Fifth Report of Session 2007–08,* Volume 1, HC 56–I (London: TSO, 2008); and Financial Services Authority, *The Supervision of Northern Rock: A Lessons Learned Review* (London: FSA Internal Audit Division, 2008).

15 Dominique Strauss-Kahn, 'A systemic crisis demands systemic solutions', *The Financial Times*, 25 September 2008.

16  Hélène Mulholland and Patrick Wintour, 'Gordon Brown admits banks needed more regulation', *Guardian*, 14 April 2010.

17 Colin Thain, 'Treasury rules OK? The further evolution of a British institution', *The British Journal of Politics and International Relations,* 6 (2004): 123–30.

18 Michael Moran, *The Politics of Banking*, pp. 97–112.

19 Andrew Gamble, *The Free Economy and the Strong State*, 2nd edn (Basingstoke, Hants: Macmillan, 1994); Michael Moran, *The British Regulatory State: High Modernism and Hyper-Innovation* (Oxford: Oxford University Press, 2003).

20 Barbara Kersley, Carmen Alpin, John Forth, Alex Bryson, Helen Bewley, Gill Dix and Sarah Oxenbridge, *Inside the Workplace: First Findings from the 2004 Workplace Employment Relations Survey* (London: Department of Trade and Industry, 2005), Table 4.

21 For measures and explanations encompassing the Anglo-American world, see Ismail Erturk, Julie Froud, Sukhdev Johal and Karel Williams, 'Pay for corporate performance or pay as social division? Rethinking the problem of top management pay in giant corporations', *Competition and Change*, 9 (2005): 49–74.

22 The complexities of measuring changes in inequality are authoritatively described in National Equality Panel, *An Anatomy of Economic Inequality in the UK: Report of the National Equality Panel* (London: Government Inequalities Office, 2010).

23  John Rentoul, 'Labour is unelectable again', *Independent*, 13 December 2009.

24  On the new working rich in the City, see Peter Folkman, Julie Froud, Sukhdev Johal and Karel Williams, 'Working for themselves?' Capital market intermediaries and present day capitalism', *Business History*, 49 (2007): 552–72.

25  Julie Froud, Adam Leaver, George Tampubolon and Karel Williams, 'Everything for sale: how non-executive directors make a difference', in Mike Savage and Karel Williams, eds, *Remembering Elites* (Oxford: Blackwell, 2008), pp. 162–86, at p.176.

26  HM Treasury, *Public Expenditure Statistical Analyses 2009* (London: HM Treasury June 2009), Table 4.2.

27  Our calculations of numbers transferred are based on numbers employed by privatized firms in the year of privatization as disclosed in reports and accounts.

28  John Buchanan, Julie Froud, Sukhdev Johal, Adam Leaver, and Karel Williams, 'Undisclosed and Unsustainable: problems of the UK national business model', CRESC Working Paper 75 (Manchester, University of Manchester, 2009), pp. 18–19, available at: www.cresc.ac.uk/publications/documents/wp75.pdf (last accessed 21 July 2010).

29  Tony Blair, 'Speech at the Knowledge 2000 Conference', 7 March 2000.

30  Dan Atkinson and Larry Elliott, *Fantasy Island: Waking up to the Incredible Economic, Political and Social Illusions of the Blair Legacy* (London: Constable 2007).

31  Buchanan et al., 'Undisclosed and Unsustainable', pp. 13–14.

32  These reports were: Win Bischoff and Alistair Darling, *UK International Financial Services – The Future: A Report from UK Based Financial Services Leaders to the Government* (London: HM Treasury, 2009); and Bob Wigley, *London: Winning in a Changing World* (London: Merrill Lynch Europe, 2008).

33  HM Treasury, *Reforming Financial Markets*, Cm 7667 (London: TSO, 2009).

34  CRESC, *An Alternative Report on UK Banking Reform: A Public Interest Report from CRESC* (Manchester: University of Manchester Centre for Research on Socio Cultural Change, 2009).

35  Mark Horton, Manmohan Kumar and Paolo Mauro, *The State of Public Finances: A Cross-Country Fiscal Monitor*, IMF Staff Position Note SPN/09/21 (Washington, DC: International Monetary Fund, 2009), p. 28, note 12.

36  The two authoritative primary accounts are: Treasury Committee, *The Run on the Rock*; and Treasury Committee, *Banking Crisis: Dealing with the Failure of UK Banks, Seventh Report of Session 2008–09,* HC 416 (London: TSO, 2009). The best reporting on the crisis was by the BBC's Robert Peston, whose reporting can be traced on his blog, available at: www.bbc.co.uk/blogs/thereporters/robertpeston/ (last accessed 21 July 2010).

37  Treasury Committee, *Banking Reform*, Seventeenth Report of Session 2007–08, HC1008 (London: TSO, 2008), para. 266.

38  Notably *Run on the Rock* and *Banking Reform*.

39  For insider accounts of these meetings, see Hank Paulson, *On the Brink: Inside the Race to Stop the Collapse of the Global Financial System* (New York: Business Plus, 2010); and Philip Swagel, *The Financial Crisis: An Inside View* (Washington, DC: Brookings Papers on Economic Activity, 2009).

40  Paul Krugman, 'Gordon does good', *New York Times*, 12 October 2008.

41  Harvey Feigenbaum, Jeffrey Henig and Chris Hamnett, *Shrinking the State: The Political Underpinnings of Privatization* (Cambridge: Cambridge University Press, 1999).

42  Jill Treanor, 'Recouping £70bn pumped into busted banks will need patience, says UKFI', *Guardian*, 13 July 2009.

43  Treasury Committee, *Banking Crisis,* paras 124–5.

44  Atkinson and Elliott, *Fantasy Island*; Vince Cable, *The Storm: The World Economic Crisis and What it Means* (London: Atlantic Books, 2009).

45  YouGov survey for the *Daily Telegraph*, October 2009, available at: www.yougov.co.uk/extranets/ygarchives/content/pdf/DT-toplines_29-OCT09.pdf (last accessed 21 July 2010).

46  For what became the new orthodoxy, see the review of the crisis produced by Lord Turner, the new chair of the Financial Services Authority: Adair Turner, *The Turner Review: A Regulatory Response to the Global Banking Crisis* (London: Financial Services Authority, 2009).

47  The evidence detailing this is in Julie Froud, Adriana Nilsson, Michael Moran and Karel Williams, 'Wasting a crisis? Democracy and markets in Britain after 2007', *The Political Quarterly,* 81 (2010): 25–38.

48  Robert Chote, Rowena Crawford, Carl Emmerson and Gemma Tetlow, *Filling the Hole: How do the Three Main UK Parties Plan to Repair the Public Finances?* (London: Institute for Fiscal Studies, 2010), p. 3.

49  ICM poll for the *Guardian*, October 2008, available at: www.icmresearch.co.uk/pdfs/2008_oct_guardian_poll2.pdf (last accessed 21 July 2010).

50  See Harold Clarke, David Sanders, Marianne Stewart and Paul Whiteley, *Political Choice in Britain* (Oxford: Oxford University Press, 2004), p. 60.

51  Larry Elliott and Patrick Wintour, 'Budget will hit poor harder than rich, according to IFS', *Guardian*, 23 June 2010.

52  Lord Mandelson, 'Speech to FSB Annual Conference', 19 March 2010.

53  Cameron made the acknowledgement in a television interview with Jeremy Paxman on 23 April 2010. See 'Cameron call on NI public sector', *BBC News* website, 25 April 2010, available at: news.bbc.co.uk/1/hi/uk_politics/election_2010/northern_ireland/8641358.stm (last accessed 21 July 2010).

54  For one commentator's incredulous response, see Phillip Inman, 'George Osborne needs 2m private jobs rise to balance public sector losses', *Guardian*, 30 June 2010. The OBR's full employment forecasts are available at: budgetresponsibility.independent.gov.uk/d/employment_forecast_300610.pdf (last accessed 21 July 2010).

# 5  THE GREAT DIVIDE: VOTERS, PARTIES, MPS AND EXPENSES

Oliver Heath

The 2010 general election took place against a backdrop of widespread dissatisfaction with politics and the political system. Voters were dissatisfied with Gordon Brown and Labour, as voters often are with long-serving governments; but they were also dissatisfied with Britain's politicians, political institutions and established political practices. In this respect, the public's mood was similar to what it had been in 2005, when the electorate exhibited signs of 'restlessness' and a sense of detachment from the main political parties.[1] Official turnout in 2005 rose from its historic low in 2001 but was still a mere 61.5 per cent, the second lowest in post-war history, and between them, Labour and the Conservatives, the two major parties in a supposedly two-party system, attracted the support of just 67.5 per cent of those who bothered to vote, a then post-war record low. Five years later, little seemed to have changed. The social and psychological bonds between voters and parties were just as weak, perhaps weaker, and politicians found it just as hard to mobilise and win over voters who were more conditional in their support for any of the parties. Turnout in 2010, at 65.1 per cent, was still historically low, while the two main parties' combined share of the vote, also 65.1 per cent, was a new record.

The public's mood in 2010 was also similar to what it had been in 2005 in another respect. It was laced with anger. In 2005, a number of people had been angry at Britain's involvement in the Iraq war and especially at the way that Tony Blair had used dubious evidence about weapons of mass destruction to justify the invasion. There had also been anger, especially among students, at the introduction of university top-up fees despite previous assurances that this would not be done. Five years later, people had something new to be angry about: the parliamentary expenses scandal of May 2009 and allegations that many MPs were misusing or abusing their official allowances. Following an explosion of outrage, almost every MP became an object of vilification, and the media soon characterised the men and woman who sat at Westminster as 'the rotten parliament'. The scandal reinforced the impression that politicians as a class were increasingly divorced from those they represented, if not completely divorced from reality. It also reignited long-running concerns about voters being disengaged from mainstream politics, and it forced politicians to work even harder to persuade a sceptical and hostile electorate that they were not all crooks.

The expenses scandal meant that 'trust in politics' would be a major issue during the 2010 election campaign, although it was unclear how much the scandal would affect the result since all parties were implicated. From a longer-term perspective, it was also unclear how much the scandal would change how members of the public felt towards politics and politicians. It certainly did nothing to lessen voters' general dissatisfaction, but nor did it greatly increase that dissatisfaction either; the public's anger merely reflected and reinforced the prevailing mood. What is clear, however, is that the scandal confirmed the existence of a vast gulf between voters, on the one hand, and politicians and their small coterie of advisers, helpers and followers, on the other. For some commentators, this gulf had already supplanted the traditional two-party contest between the Labour and Conservative parties as the pre-eminent divide in British politics.[2] Months before the scandal broke, one professor wrote: 'On the far side of a chasm stand politicians of all parties and their hangers-on. On the near side is almost everyone else.'[3] Months after the scandal, it was difficult to deny the existence of such a chasm or, as one newspaper commentator wrote, 'the huge gulf of distrust, disbelief and lack of interest that now separates the political class from everyone else.'[4]

This chapter explores the nature of this divide between voters and politicians, its relationship to the expenses scandal and its significance in 2010. It highlights how politicians – both as individuals and as members of political parties – increasingly lack connections with those 'ordinary people' who do not make their living off politics. It also highlights how voters have become steadily more conditional in their support for parties. The first section sets out some of the long-term indicators of the divide, while the second examines the public response to the expenses scandal. The third section assesses the impact of the anti-politics mood at the 2010 election, focusing on the parties' different strategies for responding to the scandal, on turnout and on the performance of minor parties operating outside the mainstream. The final part then looks at some of the long-term factors that may explain the estrangement between Britain's voters and its politicians.

## Moving apart: signs of the divide

The contemporary divide between voters and party politicians has multiple indicators. The most commonly discussed is the long-term decline in turnout

TABLE 5.1    *Turnout and the Labour-Conservative share of the vote in general elections, 1945–2010*

| General election | Turnout | Lab-Con % share of vote |
|---|---|---|
| 1945 | 72.8 | 88.1 |
| 1950 | 83.9 | 89.6 |
| 1951 | 82.6 | 96.8 |
| 1955 | 76.8 | 96.1 |
| 1959 | 78.7 | 93.2 |
| 1964 | 77.1 | 87.5 |
| 1966 | 75.8 | 89.8 |
| 1970 | 72.0 | 89.4 |
| 1974 Feb | 78.8 | 74.9 |
| 1974 Oct | 72.8 | 75.0 |
| 1979 | 76.0 | 80.9 |
| 1983 | 72.7 | 70.0 |
| 1987 | 75.3 | 73.1 |
| 1992 | 77.7 | 76.3 |
| 1997 | 71.4 | 74.0 |
| 2001 | 59.4 | 72.4 |
| 2005 | 61.5 | 67.5 |
| 2010 | 65.1 | 65.1 |

*Sources:* House of Commons Research Papers 08/12, *Election Statistics: UK 1918–2007*, and 10/36, *General Election 2010*. Available from http://www.parliament.uk/business/publications/research/research-papers. Last accessed 26 August 2010.

at general elections (see Table 5.1). Put simply, fewer people today seem to think it worthwhile taking part in the activity of choosing a government. Official turnout averaged over 80 per cent in the 1950s and as recently as 1992 was as high as 77.7 per cent. Then, in 2001, it plummeted to 59.4 per cent, and has since risen only slightly. If anything, official figures underestimate the decline in the proportion of potential voters who bother to cast a ballot. There is clear evidence of a gradual long-term decline in the number of citizens who actually register to vote.[5]

There is, moreover, a growing tendency for voters to cast votes for non-mainstream parties when do they bother to vote. Immediately after 1945, elections were dominated by two mass parties, the centre-left Labour party and the centre-right Conservatives. Until the early 1970s, these two parties consistently attracted about 90 per cent of the vote in general elections. But the proposition that Britain has a two-party system akin to that in the US looks increasingly threadbare. Not only does the third party, the Liberal Democrats, regularly attract the support of about 20 per cent of voters, but recent years have seen growing levels of support for single-issue and other fringe parties, notably the United Kingdom Independence Party (UKIP) and the British National Party (BNP) on the right, and the Greens on the left. The Scottish and Welsh nationalist parties (the Scottish National Party and

Plaid Cymru) have also consistently attracted large numbers of votes in the respective nations since the 1970s. The 2009 European parliamentary elections were a striking illustration of these developments. The Conservatives came top but with a mere 27.7 per cent of the vote, Labour came third with 15.7 per cent, and the Liberal Democrats came fourth with 13.7 per cent. The second-placed party was the supposed 'minor' party UKIP, which polled 16.5 per cent of the vote, while the Greens got 8.6 per cent and the BNP 6.2 per cent. Between them, the three major parties attracted the support of only 57.1 per cent of the vote on a turnout of just 34.5 per cent.

Another commonly identified indicator of the divide between voters and politicians is the declining number of party members. Many fewer citizens today pay membership fees and get involved than those of two generations ago.[6] To be sure, the parties' own membership records are notoriously unreliable – they often reported inflated figures in the past – but the basic downward trend cannot be doubted. During the heyday of mass parties in the 1950s, the Conservatives claimed close to 3 million members and Labour claimed close to 1 million (leaving aside, for a moment, the millions of trade union members who were affiliated by paying the 'political levy' that invariably wound up in Labour coffers). As the decades passed, however, both parties found it more and more difficult to attract members. So did the Liberal Democrats. As recently as 2008, the Conservatives claimed 250,000 members, Labour 166,000 and the Liberal Democrats a mere 60,000. In marked contrast, the National Trust, an organisation which aims to conserve the environmental heritage of England, Wales and Northern Ireland, had well over 3 million members.

There are also clear long-term signs of voters becoming psychologically disconnected from politicians. The notion of party identification, commonly

TABLE 5.2   *Approximate individual party memberships, 1951–2008*

|      | Conservatives | Labour | Liberal Democrats |
| --- | --- | --- | --- |
| 1951 | 2,900,000 | 876,000 | |
| 1965 | 2,250,000 | 817,000 | |
| 1975 | 1,120,000 | 675,000 | |
| 1983 | 1,200,000 | 274,000 | 145,000 |
| 1987 | 1,000,000 | 289,000 | 138,000 |
| 1992 | 500,000 | 280,000 | 101,000 |
| 1997 | 400,000 | 405,000 | 87,000 |
| 2001 | 311,000 | 272,000 | 73,000 |
| 2005 | 300,000 | 198,000 | 73,000 |
| 2008 | 250,000 | 166,000 | 60,000 |

*Source*: House of Commons Standard Note SN/SG/5125, *Membership of UK political parties*, available at http://www.parliament.uk/documents/commons/lib/research/briefings/snsg-05125.pdf. Last accessed 26 August 2010.

understood as an enduring commitment or attachment to a particular political party, has long been one of the most important – if contested – concepts in research on electoral behaviour. Party identification is thought to serve a number of functions that help to integrate citizens with political processes. It serves as a 'perceptual screen' that helps voters to organise their political evaluations and judgements.[7] That is, once voters acquire a partisan identity, they tend to view politics from a more partisan perspective, using parties as the key reference points. A sense of party identification also performs a mobilising function. It creates and reinforces a sense of loyalty towards a political party and encourages individuals to vote for it. According to some, it may even reinforce support for the system of party democracy.

Successive British Election Studies (BES) have measured levels of party identification by asking voters whether they usually think of themselves as being Conservative, Labour, Liberal or what, and how strongly they think of themselves in that way. The data show clearly that the strength of these attachments has declined considerably over the last four decades. As Figure 5.1 shows, the percentage of the electorate who identified 'very strongly' with a political party has fallen from 45 per cent in 1964 to 11 per cent in 2010. At the same time, the proportion of non-identifiers has increased from 5 to 19 per cent during the same period, while those who still express some form of identification have weaker (not very strong) attachments. This process of 'dealignment' may have important implications for

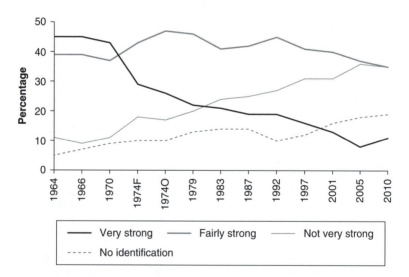

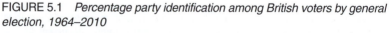

FIGURE 5.1   *Percentage party identification among British voters by general election, 1964–2010*

Source: British Election Study.

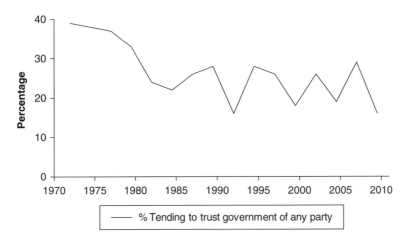

FIGURE 5.2   *Political trust, 1974–2009*

*Sources*: 1974, Political Action Study; 1986-2009 British Social Attitudes.

*Note*: Figure shows combined responses – 'just about always' and 'most of the time' – to the following question: 'How much do you trust a British government of any party to place the needs of this country above the interests of their own political party?'

the functioning of democratic politics. Parties are less important reference points and less important sources of political information. Voters' attachments to parties now probably serve as weaker perceptual screens, and voters are more likely to absorb information that undermines party loyalty. Voters are, accordingly, likely to be more easily swayed by cues from other sources, such as the media. Perhaps more importantly, voters are less tribal. Party loyalty has gradually given way to more conditional forms of support, based on government performance and, in particular, management of the economy.[8]

There are also unmistakable signs of a growing attitudinal divide between voters and parties. Among the few survey questions that have been asked more or less consistently over several decades is one that asks respondents how much they trust governments of any party to place the country's needs above the interests of their own political party. The question was first asked in 1974 and the British Social Attitudes survey has been collecting responses to this question since 1986. The evidence is displayed in Figure 5.2. Although the trend is uneven, the general direction is clear: there has been a marked decline in the proportion of voters who say they trust governments to put the interest of the nation above the party's, either 'just about always' or 'most of the time'. In 1974, 39 per cent responded this way. In 2009, just 16 per cent did so.

A more recent indication of voters' attitudes towards parties and politicians is suggested in the responses to a series of questions asked by the BES in

March 2009.[9] Taken together, these suggest that the public has a grudging acceptance of representative democracy but little liking for how parties and politicians operate in practice. Nearly two-thirds of respondents, 65 per cent, 'strongly agreed' or 'tended to agree' with the statement that 'we need people who are able to consider and debate the many and complex issues that face us', and three-quarters agreed that they could usually find a political party to vote for that reflected at least some of their views. But there was only minority agreement with the views that 'politicians discuss the issues that are most important to Britain' (48 per cent), that parties 'bring together different types of people to achieve common goals' (42 per cent) and that 'parties try to represent their supporters, not just those who fund them' (32 per cent). The most obvious point to emerge was that members of the public seem to feel they have little in common with politicians or others party members. Just 18 per cent agreed that 'people involved in political parties are people just like me', and only 17 per cent agreed with the statement that 'politicians share the same goals and values as me'. Perhaps most damning of all was the widespread belief that parties and politicians simply could not be trusted to do what they said they would. Just 16 per cent agreed with the statements that parties in power 'do what they say they would', and only 12 per cent that 'politicians deliver on their promises'.

Other surveys confirm citizens' disregard for their politicians. In the Hansard Society's 2007 'Audit of Political Engagement', for instance, 36 per cent of respondents with dissatisfied with how MPs in general were doing their job compared to the 31 per cent who were satisfied.[10] At the same time, and in common with similar surveys, respondents tended to hold their own MP in higher regard than MPs in general, and they also seemed to be more satisfied than not with the work their own MP does. Some 41 per cent claimed to be satisfied with their own MP compared to 12 per cent who were dissatisfied. MPs in general, however, are viewed as prioritising their own careers or being craven to their party machine. For example, a survey fielded by the polling firm Ipsos MORI in May 2009 found that 62 per cent of respondents said MPs generally put their own interests first, with exactly a quarter putting their party's interests firsts.[11] Tiny minorities seemed to think that MPs put the national interest (7 per cent) or their own constituency's interest first (5 per cent). All of this stands in marked contrast to what the public claim to prefer. In the same survey, 52 per cent said they thought MPs should generally put the country's interests first, and 43 per cent said their constituents'.

## The expenses scandal and the public backlash

It was against this general backdrop that the 2009 MPs expenses scandal occurred. In the context, it was not surprising that the allegations of impropriety struck such a chord with the public, who were already suspicious of politicians' personal motives. In many respects, the public had reason to be suspicious. Allegations of misconduct are frequent in British politics, and there was no shortage of scandals after 2005. Party funding was a particularly big concern, with all three major parties caught up in varying degrees of impropriety. Labour was implicated in the 'loans for peerages' controversy and allegations that it had awarded peerages to wealthy benefactors, and it also suffered from allegations that a wealthy businessman, David Abrahams, had made donations to the party in other people's names. The Tories were implicated in their relationship with Lord Ashcroft, a billionaire who donated enormous sums of money but who also used his residency in Belize to avoid paying taxes in Britain. And the Liberal Democrats were stung by their association with Michael Brown, a convicted fraudster who donated £2.4 million of other people's money to the party. Yet no scandal in recent history had quite the impact of the expenses controversy. No event came to symbolise more just how great the gulf between people and politics had become.

## The scandal

Previous years had seen a number of apparently isolated incidents of MPs misusing their official allowances. Then in May 2009, the *Daily Telegraph* began exposing how many MPs from all parties had been making dubious claims for official allowances and expenses. Now there was evidence of systemic impropriety centring in particular on the Additional Cost Allowance (a scheme intended to help MPs who represent constituencies far from London maintain a second home in the capital). The steady publication of details over many days kept the story running and meant it dominated newspapers, television news, online blogs and radio phone-in shows for weeks. Some of the claims – for things like bath plugs, biscuits and lavatory-seat repairs – seemed extraordinarily petty. Others – for things like ducks houses, chandeliers, moat-cleaning services and repairs to helipads – seemed wildly extravagant. Yet other claims – for already paid-off mortgages, for example – implicated a handful of MPs in accusations of fraud and tax evasion. At any rate, it was extremely dubious that many of the items being claimed for were needed to help MPs perform their parliamentary duties, the central premise underpinning all allowances and expenses.

Before the *Telegraph's* exposé, the House of Commons authorities had spent months trying to avoid publishing details of MPs' expense and allowance claims under new freedom of information laws. From a cynic's point of view, it was easy to see why. Once the claims were out in the open, MPs were unsure how to react. Some sought to surf the tide of public anger and called for root-and-branch reforms to what was clearly a bad system. Others, seeking to defend their own conduct, claimed they had done nothing wrong because they had acted within the rules. Many privately, and a handful publicly, blamed the media frenzy and hinted that the public's outcry was an unreasonable over-reaction. Anthony Steen, a Conservative MP who claimed tens of thousands of pounds to maintain his large country home, insisted: 'I've done nothing criminal, that's the most awful thing, and do you know what it's about? Jealousy … I've got a very, very large house. Some people say it looks like Balmoral [the Queen's Scottish residence]. It's a merchant's house of the 19th century. It's not particularly attractive, it just does me nicely.'[12]

A few MPs even blamed the whole affair on successive governments' reluctance to increase MPs' salaries, which was currently about £65,000. It was suggested that ministers, mindful of the likely hostile reaction to any pay rise, had colluded with MPs to increase their effective salary by increasing their opportunities to claim allowances and expenses. Parliament was now reaping the whirlwind of this systemic dishonesty. The solution was to pay MPs properly and further to ensure that the parliamentary wage attracted top talent. Douglas Hogg, a former Tory cabinet minister who infamously claimed for his moat to be cleaned, suggested to an official inquiry that: 'A parliamentary salary does not support the lifestyle to which most professional and business classes aspire'. He suggested that MPs should be paid around £100,000 per annum together with appropriate expenses.[13] Such suggestions were largely at odds with public opinion and fed suspicions that many MPs saw holding office as less of a public service and more of a career choice, and one to be financially exploited at that.

Whatever the vices and virtues of individual MPs, the nature of the media coverage tended to lump all of them together. While a few MPs were praised as 'saints' for not claiming the second-home allowance, all were still implicated to some extent if only by association. Most MPs, however, were not as rotten as the frenzied media coverage at times implied.[14] A hastily organized audit headed by Sir Thomas Legg investigated the past claims of 752 incumbent and former MPs made between April 2004 and March 2009.[15] Mindful of the public mood, Legg followed a very strict interpretation of the rules and recommended that 392 individuals repay varying sums of money. Most sums were comparatively small as a proportion of the total claims involved: 182 sitting and former MPs were asked to repay between £5,000 and £1,000 and a further 149 less than £1,000. Following appeals, a total of 372 individuals (less than half) were finally asked to repay some money, including all three main party leaders.[16] Amongst all those directly implicated in the scandal, a few had broken the law – four were later charged by police – and some were disciplined by the House of Commons for breaching its code of conduct.[17] Others had certainly milked the system for as much as the rules allowed. Yet others had simply gone along with the rules without questioning or understanding them.

## The immediate response

A sense of the public's immediate anger at the *Telegraph's* allegations is suggested by BES polling data from June 2009, just after the expenses scandal first erupted. An overwhelming majority of respondents, 91 per cent, tended to agree that the way some MPs had claimed expenses made them very angry, and a large majority, 65 per cent, rejected the line of defence put forward by some MPs that they had done nothing wrong and were just claiming expenses that the rules allowed. Most members of the public had little doubt as to what should happen. Some 82 per cent agreed that MPs who had abused their expense claims should be required to resign immediately. The allegations also confirmed a large number of citizens' jaded views about the honesty and probity of their representatives. Over half, 56 per cent, agreed that the reports on MPs' expense claims proved that most MPs are corrupt.

The expenses scandal cut across party lines and affected members from all three main political parties, but it was the Labour government that seemed to suffer most since the scandal occurred on its watch and it had most MPs. Since April 2004 – before the previous general election – the BES had asked members of the public each month whether they thought that the government had, on balance, been honest and trustworthy, or not. The responses, shown in Figure 5.3, show considerable variation since Labour's win in

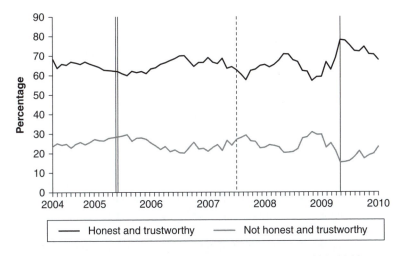

FIGURE 5.3   *Government honesty and trustworthiness, 2004–2010*

*Source*: BES Continuous Monitoring Survey, available from http://www.bes2009–10. org. Last accessed 26 August 2010.

*Note*: Respondents asked: 'Do you think that the Government has, on balance, been honest and trustworthy, or not'? The three vertical lines represent, chronologically, the 2005 general election, Gordon Brown's accession to the prime ministership and the height of the expenses scandal in May 2009.

2005 (the vertical double line) and either side of Gordon Brown's accession (the vertical dotted line) with a dramatic increase in the proportion answering that the government had not been honest and trustworthy in the first half of 2009. These months saw allegations that several Labour members of the House of Lords had been willing to amend legislation in return for cash as well as allegations that two Labour ministers, home secretary Jacqui Smith and employment minister Tony McNulty, had abused their parliamentary allowances over claims made for their second homes. (Smith had also mistakenly claimed for a pornographic film apparently ordered by her husband from a cable television channel.) The public's apparent belief in their government's dishonesty and untrustworthiness peaked just after the *Daily Telegraph* broke its story. In January 2009, just under 30 per cent had said the government was honest and trustworthy and just under 60 per cent said it was not. In May 2009 (the vertical single line), these views were now shared by 15 per cent and 78 per cent respectively, a gap of 63 points. As the scandal began slowly to subside, the gap began to narrow.

## The response in context

It was clear to all that the public was angry with individual MPs, the government and politicians more widely. Given the media attention lavished on MPs' expenses, this was not surprising. What was less clear was the nature of the scandal's wider impact.

All systems of government require the support of those they govern if they are to remain legitimate. According to a standard way of thinking about such things, it is possible to distinguish between diffuse support – that is, an individual's approval for something in principle – and specific support – an individual's approval for something in practice.[18] It is further helpful to distinguish between support for different levels of political object, ranging from specific holders of political office, such as individual MPs or ministers, through the institutions and offices of government, such as parliament, to the wider political community and system. To retain legitimacy, political systems need reserves of diffuse support to tide them over during periods when governments and other actors lose specific support through unpopular policies and errors. But it is also thought that when actors lose specific support for long periods of time, dissatisfaction can infect attitudes towards the political system.

In the context of an existing gulf between voters and their representatives, a number of commentators feared that the expenses scandal might undermine confidence in established political institutions and democracy itself. One commentator suggested that the crisis had caused 'a collapse in public trust in politicians so comprehensive that the entire basis of parliamentary democracy might well be in jeopardy.'[19] Another, focusing on the immediate response, suggested that 'the MP expenses scandal has significantly

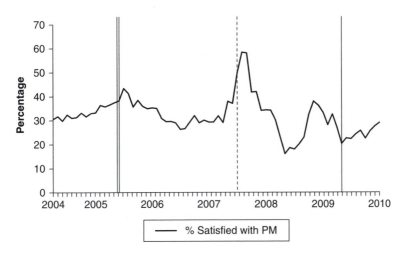

FIGURE 5.4    *Satisfaction with the prime minister, 2004–2010*

*Source*: BES Continuous Monitoring Survey, available from http://www.bes2009-10. org. Last accessed 26 August 2010.

*Note*: Respondents asked: 'Are you satisfied or dissatisfied with Mr Blair/Mr Brown as Prime Minister?' The three vertical lines represent, chronologically, the 2005 general election, Gordon Brown's accession to the prime ministership and the height of the expenses scandal in May 2009.

reduced public confidence, faith and trust in politics.'[20] With hindsight, such warnings seem greatly exaggerated.

To demonstrate this point, it is necessary to examine support for various aspects of the political system before and after the scandal. A glance back to Figure 5.3 shows clearly how the expenses scandal immediately undermined specific support for the government's reputation for honesty and trustworthiness, but that its reputation gradually began to recover. Likewise, Figure 5.4, which tracks satisfaction with the prime minister of the day, provides another indicator of a sudden fall in specific support, this time for Gordon Brown and how well he was doing his job. As suggested by the data, the expenses scandal (again indicated by the vertical single line) seemed to dent his already weak satisfaction ratings. Yet afterwards, these ratings began to return slowly to pre-scandal levels.

A remarkably similar pattern – a sharp drop in support followed by a gradual return to normality – applies to the public's satisfaction with the way parliament works and with democracy more widely. Table 5.3 reports responses to questions asked intermittently by Ipsos MORI. It suggests that, before May 2009, the proportion of people dissatisfied with the way parliament works was relatively stable at around 30 per cent. In the wake of the expenses scandal, the number of respondents dissatisfied with parliament

TABLE 5.3   *Satisfaction with parliament*

|              | May 1995 | Aug 2000 | May 2001 | Dec 2003 | Nov 2006 | May 2009 | Nov 2009 |
|--------------|----------|----------|----------|----------|----------|----------|----------|
| Satisfied    | 34       | 43       | 45       | 36       | 35       | 20       | 33       |
| Dissatisfied | 31       | 29       | 30       | 32       | 33       | 63       | 38       |

*Source:* Ipsos MORI, 'Satisfaction with the way Parliament works 1995–2009, available at http://www.ipsos-mori.com/researchpublications/researcharchive/poll.aspx?oItemId=2453&view=wide. Last accessed 26 August 2010.

*Note:* In 1995 and 2000, the question asked was: 'To what extent are you satisfied or dissatisfied with the way each is doing its job these days? The way Parliament works'. In 2001, the question was: 'To what extent are you satisfied or dissatisfied with the way each is doing its job these days? The way the Westminster Parliament works'. In May 2009, the question was: 'To what extent are you satisfied or dissatisfied with the way each is doing its job these days? The Westminster Parliament'.

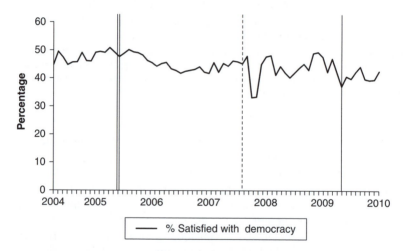

FIGURE 5.5   *Satisfaction with democracy, 2004–2010*

*Source*: BES Continuous Monitoring Survey, available from http://www.bes2009–10.org. Last accessed 26 August 2010.

*Note*: Respondents asked: 'Thinking about how well democracy works in this country, on the whole, are you very satisfied, fairly satisfied, a little dissatisfied, or very dissatisfied with the way that democracy works in this country?' The figure combines those who replied 'very satisfied' and 'fairly satisfied'. The three vertical lines represent, chronologically, the 2005 general election, Gordon Brown's accession to the prime ministership and the height of the expenses scandal in May 2009.

leapt to 63 per cent, yet by November 2009, public opinion seemed to be heading back towards its pre-scandal levels. Meanwhile, Figure 5.5 displays responses to a question asked each month by the BES about voters' satisfaction with the way democracy works. It combines the responses of those who said 'very satisfied' and 'fairly satisfied'. The graph makes clear that reported satisfaction varies greatly over time and is sensitive to specific events. The sudden dip in satisfaction in October and November 2007 – greater than the post-expenses dip – coincided with the government's loss of important data disks and the controversy surrounding David Abrahams' party donations. When viewed in this context, the smaller drop in satisfaction in May 2009 seems less dramatic.

Taken together, it seems that that the expenses scandal may not have affected the public's underlying attitudes towards politicians, political institutions and democracy that greatly. Whatever backlash there was, it did not appear to last long. It might have helped that all three party leaders queued up to apologise, with Gordon Brown, David Cameron and Nick Clegg all competing with each other to demonstrate the most anger on the public's behalf and to be the most responsive to demands for reform. It might also have helped that there were a few sacrificial lambs, in the shape of Speaker Michael Martin, who ultimately lost his job, and other MPs who were promptly prevented from running for parliament again by their local parties or national organisation. It almost certainly helped that the media gradually grew tired of the subject. At any rate, within a few months, public trust and confidence in politicians, democracy and even parliament, whose standing seemed to suffer the most damage, were slowly returning to their pre-scandal levels.

## Anti-politics at the 2010 election

The expenses scandal and the divide between voters and politicians that it came to symbolise inevitably cast a shadow over the 2010 election. There was no getting away from the anti-politics mood, either in terms of what politicians talked about or in terms of expectations about the public's behaviour.

The politicians, for their part, tried to address the public's disaffection head-on, notably in the three televised prime ministerial debates (see Chapter 7). There were apologies, such as David Cameron's in the first debate: 'The expenses saga brought great shame on parliament. I'm extremely sorry for everything that happened'. There were attempts to show empathy with the public's anger, as Gordon Brown tried to do in the second debate: 'I was ashamed by the behaviour of some of the MPs in the House of Commons. What they did was completely unacceptable. And no punishment is too great for them'. There were attempts to blame the other parties, with Nick Clegg proving particularly effective at attacking the 'old parties' for their failings and their links to wealthy donors. And reforms were proposed that would restore the public's trust in politicians. Brown promised recall elections for MPs found guilty of misconduct, parliamentary debates on public petitions and an elected House of Lords. Clegg suggested that a new voting system would stop people feeling that they were being ignored by politicians. Cameron even used the public's disaffection with politics as a reason to reduce the size of government: 'politicians in this country have been treating the people as mugs for far too long. They've been sort of saying, we can do everything, vote for us and we'll solve all your problems.'

The public's response was unpredictable. Large numbers watched the debates, but voters were also typically distrustful of the parties' promises. When asked in April whether they thought the parties were being honest with voters about a number of issues, large majorities of the public said that the parties were 'only partly honest' or 'not honest at all' about 'their tax plans', 'their commitment to cleaning up politics' and various other policies.[21] But two broader questions would only be answered when the votes were in: would turnout be greatly affected, and would the election witness a dramatic increase in support for anti-establishment parties? In both regards, there was surprisingly little change on the results in 2005.

Turnout did rise a little, from 61.5 per cent to 65.1 per cent, yet it remained far below the levels that once characterised British elections (see Table 5.1). In six constituencies, turnout was below 50 per cent, with Manchester Central taking the wooden spoon with 44.3 per cent.[22] The Scottish seat of Renfrewshire East, where 77.3 per cent of eligible voters went to the polls, had the highest turnout, yet this was still below the national average as recently as 1992. After the 2001 election, when national turnout slumped to a post-war low of 59.4 per cent amidst a contest that everyone expected Labour to win, one commentator wrote: 'Just provide the voters with a closely fought election at which a great deal is at stake and, make no mistake, they will again turn out in their droves.'[23] In 2010, voters were provided with a closely fought election – there was enormous uncertainty surrounding the outcome – and most commentators thought there was a great deal at stake. The new government would be responsible for shepherding the country's fragile economic recovery, it would have an opportunity to enact wholesale political reform, and its decisions about tackling the national deficit would affect nothing less than the future size and scope of the British state. Yet large numbers of voters still did not turn out to vote. They looked at the parties and saw few differences between the policies on offer. In the past the choice presented to voters was between more or less spending and taxes. In 2010 the choice concerned the timing, scale and focus of the cuts to be pursued.

In addition to the small rise in turnout, there was an even smaller rise in the proportion of votes cast for non-mainstream parties. The combined Labour–Conservative–Liberal Democrat share of the vote in 2010 was 88.1 per cent, only slightly down on the 89.6 per cent the three parties secured in 2005. Across the country, UKIP increased their share of the vote to

3.1 per cent and the BNP to 1.9 per cent (making them the fourth and fifth most popular parties respectively), yet only the Greens (who remained stuck on 1 per cent) made inroads where it mattered: in the House of Commons. When the party's leader Caroline Lucas won in Brighton Pavilion, she became the first ever Green MP at Westminster. Otherwise, the minor parties were disappointed. The Greens came a lowly fourth in their other key target seat, Norwich South, while neither UKIP nor the BNP came close to winning in any constituency. UKIP's flamboyant former leader, Nigel Farage, challenged the Speaker of the House of Commons John Bercow in Buckingham but could only manage third place and 17.4 per cent of the vote. In no other seat did the party get more than 10 per cent. As for the BNP, its leader Nick Griffin fared poorly in the east London seat of Barking, where he had hoped to win, and came third, and in only two other seats, in nearby Dagenham and Rainham and in Rotherham in Yorkshire, did the party's candidates obtain more than a tenth of the vote.

Interestingly, none of the myriad of independent – and usually anti-establishment – candidates achieved much success in 2010. The three sitting independent MPs who sought re-election – Dai Davies in Blaenau Gwent, Richard Taylor in Wyre Forrest and George Galloway in Bethnal Green and Bow – were all defeated (Galloway was actually defeated in Poplar and Limehouse, which he had decided to contest), and there were no new independents to take their place. The most prominent of the independent anti-sleaze candidates was the former television presenter Esther Rantzen, who sought to emulate the journalist Martin Bell's success in Tatton in 1997, when he defeated the unsavoury former Conservative minister Neil Hamilton. Despite investing considerable time and energy in the Luton South constituency, Rantzen fared poorly and managed to win only 4.4 per cent of the vote. If the casting of protest votes provides any indication on the subject, the backlash against the expenses scandal had fizzled out by the time of the election.

## Coming to terms with the divide

The expenses scandal may have had a limited impact on the election, but the wider divide between voters and politicians that the scandal highlighted is likely to be more enduring. The causes of that divide – as suggested by indicators such as declining turnout, shrinking party memberships and weakening levels of party identification – are long term, inter-connected and complex. A chapter of this length cannot possibly provide a full explanation, so it will confine itself to discussing three distinct sets of explanations, each of which sheds some light on the public's disengagement with politics.

## The media

One view advanced by commentators is that the media and their coverage of politics are to blame for voters' detachment from politics. Typifying this argument, a professor of mass communications suggests that 'the increasingly hostile tenor of political journalism in the twenty-first century may be helping to undermine faith in the democratic system itself'.[24] If journalists were once deferential to politicians, they are now contemptuous, and their confrontational and derisive coverage has contributed to a 'process which is degrading democracy's institutions and undermining political representatives'. Not surprisingly, such arguments appeal to many politicians. In a speech on the media and public life, outgoing prime minister Tony Blair voiced similar concerns about the ways in which journalists go about their business. 'Fear of missing out means today's media, more than ever before, hunts in a pack. In these modes it is like a feral beast, just tearing people and reputations to bits.'[25]

Some of the more interesting attacks on media coverage come from within the media ranks. Alastair Campbell, a former journalist who became Blair's director of communications, has blamed the media for encouraging cynicism by obsessing about process and personalities rather than covering substance.[26] The journalist John Lloyd has suggested that contemporary media coverage in Britain is framed by a 'master story' that portrays politics as 'a degraded profession' and criticizes a tendency to cherry-pick and present individual facts within this context.[27] Meanwhile, the journalist Peter Oborne has criticised many of his colleagues not for their hostility but for their complicity with politicians. Since 1997 there has been an era of 'client journalism', in which journalists have been more worried about maintaining good relations with the government in order to maintain a steady supply of good news.[28] As a result, journalists have come to see the world through the eyes of politicians and become obsessed about their intrigues and interests, not the concerns of ordinary people.

It is very difficult to demonstrate that such developments have contributed to the divide between voters and parties. Media effects are notoriously difficult to establish, while some of the developments are relatively recent and occurred after links between the voters and political parties had already begun to weaken. But it is likely that media coverage has exacerbated these trends. At any rate, a tendency to focus on scandal and controversy (as was evident during the expenses scandal) and to sensationalise coverage almost certainly primes voters to share the sentiments sometimes attributed to a former editor of the *Sunday Times*: 'Always ask yourself, when interviewing a politician, why is that bastard lying to me?'

## Voters

Another set of explanations of voters' detachment from politics focuses not on the media but on the voters themselves. As seen, they have become less likely to join parties, less likely to identify themselves strongly as being the supporters of a party and less tribal in their politics. In short, voters seem to have become more politically individualistic, and the received wisdom is that this reflects wider social changes.

The crucial social changes need only be listed briefly. First, since 1945, there has been a rapid increase in access to education, especially higher education, and there are now more graduates in Britain than ever before. This rapid increase in educational standards, it is argued, has led to an electorate that is more sophisticated, more demanding and critical of government activity, less deferential, and more likely to challenge authority than in the past.[29]

Second, there has been an increase in geographic and social mobility, which has undermined in particular the strong working-class communities that traditionally formed the bedrock of Labour support and further undermined the salience of traditional group-based identities. At the same time, key civic institutions, notably the Church of England and trade unions, have witnessed declining memberships, all the more significant since Church membership, informally, and union membership, often formally, were associated with support for the Conservatives and Labour respectively. If these institutions once promoted crucial individual-group linkages that sustained support for the two major parties, they now do so to a lesser extent, if at all. Such developments in tandem with wider changes in the class structure of society have led to an erosion of class-based politics and the weakening of partisan attachments. Voters in turn have become more individualistic. Their voting behaviour is less heavily influenced by group ties and values and more influenced by questions of governmental performance and management. Put another way, politics for most voters is now more about the politics of delivery, or what political scientists call 'valence politics', rather than the politics of fixed ideological preferences.[30]

Third, British society, like many other advanced western societies, seems to have experienced a shift in its values. A growing proportion of voters have acquired a 'post-materialist' outlook, that is, a preoccupation with 'quality of life' issues like the environment, world peace and democracy.[31] As a result, voters are more ideologically diverse and their preferences are now much more loosely organised, and it has become correspondingly harder for political parties to aggregate and accommodate citizens' preferences. For their part, voters, who seem more inclined to focus on narrow issues rather than the broad policy bundles offered by the mainstream parties, prefer to participate in unconventional and less institutionalised forms of political action, such as taking part in protests and demonstrations, signing petitions and boycotting goods or services, which allow them to prioritise their specific causes.

The received wisdom – that social change has led to an individualisation of politics – provides a compelling narrative, at least on the surface, of why voters have become detached from political parties and more critical of their political representatives. But like many received wisdoms the reality is somewhat different. One obvious problem with placing too much emphasis on the significance of social change is that the process has been gradual, and if political engagement was merely a consequence of social transformation, then there should be a gradual long-term decline in all the indicators of political engagement. Yet some changes have been abrupt, most obviously the slump in turnout in 2001, and some changes, such as changing levels of political trust and satisfaction with democracy, show considerable volatility.

Another problem is that there are actually good reasons to be sceptical about the scale of social change and whether society really has become all that individualistic. According to available survey data, social identities, based on individuals' attachments to their class, religion and nationality, are as strongly held as ever, and there is little evidence of any decline in levels of inter-personal trust or institutional trust in non-political bodies such as the police.[32] In addition, other forms of social behaviour, such as volunteering and associational membership, continue to flourish.[33] Thus, while there appears to have been a dramatic weakening of the link between social and collective identities and mainstream party politics, there is little evidence that citizens have become more individualistic in all areas of life. Voters have changed, but the crucial point is that these changes are confined largely to the political realm, specifically the formal confines and practices of representative democracy. If the links between voters and parties have weakened, this detachment is perhaps more likely to reflect changes that have taken place at the elite level rather than at the societal level.

## Politicians and parties

The third general set of explanations focuses on changes amongst politicians and parties. One line of argument is that politicians themselves have changed in their orientation towards politics. In a 2008 speech to the Hansard Society, Hazel Blears, Labour's secretary of state for communities, warned of 'a trend towards politics being seen as a career move rather than a call to public service.' Instead of attracting people with varied backgrounds and a wide experience of life, the typical political career now followed a '"transmission belt" from university activist, MPs' researcher, think-tank staffer, Special Adviser, to Member of Parliament, and ultimately to the front bench.'[34] Others have made this point before. Writing almost thirty years ago, Anthony King commented upon the rise of 'the career politician' in Britain, that is, of the men and women in parliament being increasingly dominated by those who are committed to politics, who seek fulfilment in politics, who see their future in politics and who would like

TABLE 5.4   *Selected occupations of MPs (% Labour, Conservative and Liberal Democrat MPs), 1979–2005*

|  | 1979 | 1983 | 1987 | 1992 | 1997 | 2001 | 2005 |
|---|---|---|---|---|---|---|---|
| Professions | 44.9 | 44.2 | 41.7 | 41.1 | 43.2 | 42.9 | 39.3 |
| Business | 22.3 | 25.8 | 25.6 | 24.2 | 18.0 | 17.0 | 19.2 |
| Publisher/journalist | 7.4 | 7.2 | 6.7 | 7.0 | 7.5 | 7.9 | 7.0 |
| Farmer | 3.7 | 3.3 | 3.0 | 1.9 | 1.1 | 1.0 | 1.3 |
| Politician/political organiser | 3.4 | 3.2 | 5.4 | 7.3 | 9.5 | 10.5 | 14.1 |
| Manual workers | 15.8 | 11.8 | 11.6 | 10.0 | 8.9 | 8.4 | 6.2 |

*Source*: House of Commons Research Paper 10/33, *Members 1979–2010*, available at http://www.parliament.uk/documents/commons/lib/research/rp2010/RP10-033.pdf. Last accessed 26 August 2010.

*Note*: Columns do not total 100 per cent since a number of miscellaneous occupational backgrounds have been excluded.

to spend most of their adult life working in politics.[35] The potential advantages of this development, he suggested, were that MPs were likely to be more politically experienced and hard working. The potential disadvantages were that MPs could end up being more partisan, would have less experience of the world outside politics and would probably be 'less in touch with the mass electorate'.[36]

Table 5.4 provides an indication of the growing number of MPs who were formerly politicians or political organisers before entering the Commons. In the 1979 parliament, the body of MPs that King was writing about, only 3.4 per cent of Members had such a background. By 2005, the 'rotten parliament' at the heart of the expenses scandal comprised 14.1 per cent of MPs with such a background. Needless to say, such MPs were most unlikely to have spent time in factories, in firms, in call centres or in most of the other places where the vast majority of the British population spend their time working. Meanwhile, there has been a marked decline in the proportion of working-class MPs. Although never high, the number of MPs with a background in manual work has fallen still further, from 15.8 per cent in 1979 to just 6.2 per cent in 2005. Much of this decline has occurred among Labour MPs, those who were traditionally expected to represent working-class people. The result has been a parliament with many fewer voices able to speak from blue-collar experience. There has also been a gradual decline in the proportion of MPs with backgrounds in business and in the professions – medicine, the law, teaching and the civil service – though these declines have been less pronounced.

Such changes in MPs' occupational background and the 'transmission belt' career path many now follow are almost certainly weakening the links between voters and politicians. In the words of one commentator, most politicians' outlook is increasingly 'metropolitan and London-based. They perceive life through the eyes of an affluent member of London's middle and upper-middle class. This converts them into a separate, privileged elite, isolated from the aspirations and the problems of provincial, rural and suburban Britain.'[37] This separation and isolation compounds the huge (if narrowing) gulf between what voters look like and what their representatives look like. Fewer than 20 per cent of MPs in the 2005 parliament were women (up from 3 per cent in 1979), and only 2.3 per cent of the MPs were from a non-white background (there were none in 1979). In contrast, more than half the population were women and about 8 per cent were from a non-white background according to the 2001 Census.

There is also still a gulf between voters and politicians in terms of educational background. According to the Sutton Trust, an organisation that promotes social mobility through education, the number of privately-educated MPs has been gradually declining since 1951, but MPs are still unduly likely to have attended fee-paying independent schools: in 2005, just under one-third of all MPs had been educated in this way compared to 7 per cent of the population.[38] Moreover, those MPs who had been privately educated were more likely to find themselves on the front bench than their state-educated counterparts. Whereas 29 per cent of backbenchers had been to a private school, 42 per cent of those holding ministerial office in the Labour government or shadow posts in the Conservative or Liberal Democrat opposition teams had done so.

Since the 1950s, the proportion of MPs with a university education has been gradually increasing – which is also true of voters – so that by 2005, 72 per cent of MPs from the three main parties had been to university. But among the adult population, only about one in five have been to university, and MPs remain disproportionately likely to have attended Oxford or Cambridge (27 per cent in 2005). At a time when there is concern about the representation of women and ethnic minorities in parliament, it is worth remembering that education does more than anything else to shape the life chances and experiences of people living in Britain. In this respect the *un*representativeness of MPs is all too often overlooked.

In one respect, however, the links between MPs and those they represent have been strengthening in recent years. MPs today are more active than ever, at least in the sense of acting for or on behalf of individual constituents. MPs generally place far more emphasis on being 'good constituency Members' than they did sixty years ago.[39] They tend to spend far more time in the constituency, far more time communicating with constituents and far more time seeking redress for constituents' grievances. In the mid 1980s, it was estimated that as many as 6 million letters were sent to Members each year, half of them coming from constituents, which represented a ten-fold increase since the 1950s.[40] The total number of communications from constituents – whether by email or post – has greatly increased in the intervening years. Between 2009 and 2010 it was estimated that the House of Commons received some 2 million letters and the Commons and Lords combined received nearly 38 million emails.[41] However, the zeal with which many MPs throw themselves into micro-managing their constituency casework seems to have done little to improve their overall standing. It is unclear why this is so, but it might have something to do with the highly individualised and localised style of representation that constituency case-work fosters. If more MPs are spending less time acting for groups and wider interests, activities that perform a broader integrative function, it may become harder for voters to see their MPs representing their constituents either individually or as a whole.

If the divide between voters and politicians is partly a consequence of changes in the typical political career structure, it may also be a consequence of changes in the nature of party competition. One idea commonly put forward concerns the perceived ideological convergence in the party system. As suggested by their election manifestos (see Figure 6.1), recent years have witnessed a general narrowing of the policy differences between the two main parties, with the Conservatives gradually moving to the centre and Labour, especially under Tony Blair and Gordon Brown after 1994, abandoning its old left-wing policies and becoming an essentially centrist or just-to-the-left-of-centre party.[42] A similar convergence in the 1950s and early 1960s – in the era of the so-called 'post-war consensus' – coincided with high-levels of turnout and party membership, yet the convergence since the mid 1990s seems to have fostered a mindset that there is now very little policy difference between the parties and that there is accordingly less at stake during elections. This mindset not only weakens the incentive to vote, but it also weakens voters' attachments to parties and erodes the social base of party support still further.[43]

The ideological convergence of recent years has probably had this effect at least in part because it has coincided with voters having increasingly diverse and diffuse policy preferences. It is always difficult for parties to fashion programmes that attract broad support in pluralistic societies. It is more difficult for them to do so at a time when the logic of party competition and the demands of vote maximisation oblige politicians to move to the centre ground. Because Labour and the Conservatives have followed that logic in recent elections, the policy choices on offer to voters appear even more constrained than they otherwise would. The upshot has been a double disconnect. Not only are parties now less integrated with society at large, because of weakening attachments among voters and potential activists, but the policies they focus on are less likely to reflect the diversity of views within the electorate. Although the 2010 election campaign was notable for addressing issues such as climate change, immigration and an aging population, it was a seemingly rare foray into these policy areas by the main political parties. Voters can be forgiven for thinking that there is often little critical debate on a number of issues that interest them.

A further feature of the convergence of recent years is that it is part cause, part consequence of a tendency for politicians to focus on issues of management and performance, or 'valence politics'. In essence, party strategists have almost entirely accepted the dictum that 'it's the economy stupid'. As the independent Power inquiry into the health of British democracy noted in 2006, '*managarialism* [sic] *has replaced vision ...* the main political parties are no longer distinct enough and no longer base their policies on core principles'.[44] The focus on valence politics may well reflect the increasingly professional view of politics engendered by politicians' career paths. It may also be a rational response to voters' preferences for a booming economy and high-quality public services. But the absence of exciting and inspirational ideas has arguably impoverished public debate.

The emphasis on 'the economy stupid' may also have had the effect of making parties and politicians seem much more concerned with the interests of big business than with the concerns of ordinary people. In a bid to maintain the confidence of the City, politicians often court the very wealthy but such associations can be risky. The 'Yachtgate' affair of 2008, when Labour's business secretary Lord Mandelson, the then shadow chancellor George Osborne, their mutual friend the multimillionaire financier Nat Rothschild and the Russian Oligarch Oleg Deripaska dined together on a £60 million yacht off Corfu, is a case in point. Osborne was alleged to have solicited party donations, but more damage was probably done by the impression of senior politicians mixing in a world entirely detached from wider society.

The sense that politicians are primarily concerned with the interests of big business was also given credence by the massive bailouts for the banks in the wake of the 'credit crunch'. An October 2008 survey of voters in Labour-held constituencies found that 49 per cent agreed that 'The Government had to spend what it did to bail out the banks, in order to keep them going and keep people's savings safe' but 33 per cent agreed that 'The Government has been too generous towards the banks'. In the same survey, a majority of respondents, 53 per cent, also agreed that the Tories were only 'pretending' to be tough on bankers to win votes.[45] Later, there was real anger when, having been bailed out by the taxpayers, the banks announced their intention to pay big bonuses to their staff. When YouGov asked members of the public in January 2010 how this made them feel, 37 per cent replied 'quite angry' and a further 52 per cent said 'livid'.[46] For most voters, financial elites were in cahoots with most politicians on the other side of the divide.

## Conclusions

The 2009 expenses scandal pulled into sharp focus a growing rupture in British politics between politicians and voters. Politicians, aware of their low standing, have been seeking to engage with citizens and restore citizens' trust in a number of ways for a number of years. Widespread concerns about MPs' financial impropriety in the 1990s triggered a wave of ethics reforms throughout public life. Parliament has done much in recent years to 'modernise' its procedures and 'engage the public with its work and activities'.[47] Labour in the early 2000s sought to reduce the cost of participation by making it easier for voters to cast postal ballots. Political parties have sought to find new ways of involving members in policy-making processes, even as parties have become more centralised. And a number of local councils have used referendums to settle policy questions, most frequently to determine whether or not they would institute directly-elected mayors.[48]

The rhetoric in the wake of the expenses scandal suggested a renewed commitment by politicians to re-engage. The new Conservative–Liberal Democrat government's coalition agreement contained no fewer than 27 specific pledges to mend the 'broken' political system, including: electoral reform; the introduction of recall elections for when MPs have engaged in serious wrongdoing; the introduction of a wholly or mainly elected upper chamber in place of the largely appointed House of Lords; funds for 200 all-postal primary elections; and several further measures to open up parliament to the public.[49] It remains to be seen whether such changes will reconnect politicians and the public or not. Current levels of political disengagement have much to do with the composition and behaviour of elites: politicians have become more socially isolated, and contemporary political debate fails to represent the pluralism within the electorate. It is not impossible but it would be ironic if a government led by David Cameron, an old Etonian, and packed full of Etonians and Oxbridge graduates were able to close the gap.

## Endnotes

1  Nicholas Allen, 'A restless electorate: stirrings in the political system', in John Bartle and Anthony King, eds, *Britain at the Polls 2005* (Washington, DC: CQ Press, 2006), pp. 54–77.

2  See, for example, Peter Oborne, *The Triumph of the Political Class* (London: Simon & Schuster, 2007). In line with this general sentiment, Oborne (pp. xvi–xvii) suggests that 'The real divide in British public life is no longer between the main political parties, but between the Political Class and the rest.'

3  Anthony King, 'As the Queen opens Parliament, the chasm between politics and people widens', *Daily Telegraph*, 3 December 2008.

4   Daniel Finkelstein, 'Westminster chatter won't change the result', *The Times*, 3 March 2010. Philip Gould, the Labour party's polling guru, even suggested that there was now nothing less than a divide 'between politics and anti-politics.' Quoted in Peter Riddell, Tom Baldwin and Roland Watson, 'Politicians fear angry electorate will lead to hung parliament', *The Times*, 14 April 2010.

5   Electoral Commission, *The Completeness and Accuracy of Electoral Registers in Great Britain* (London: The Electoral Commission, 2010), p. 3.

6   Paul Whiteley, 'Where have all the members gone? The dynamics of party membership in Britain', *Parliamentary Affairs*, 62 (2009), 242–57.

7   See Russell J. Dalton, 'Decline of party identifications', in Russell J. Dalton and Martin P. Wattenberg, eds, *Parties without Partisans: Political Change in Advanced Industrial Democracies* (Oxford: Oxford University Press, 2000), pp. 19–36, at p. 21.

8   See Harold D. Clarke, David Sanders, Marianne C. Stewart and Paul Whiteley, *Performance Politics and the British Voter* (Cambridge: Cambridge University Press, 2009).

9   British Election Study Continuous Monitoring Survey data, available at: www.bes2009-10.org (last accessed 26 August 2010).

10  Electoral Commission and the Hansard Society, *An Audit of Political Engagement 4* (London: Electoral Commission and the Hansard Society, 2007), p. 40.

11  Ipsos MORI, 'MPs' Motives 1994–2009', available at: www.ipsos-mori.com/research-publications/researcharchive/poll.aspx?oItemId=2443&view=wide (last accessed 26 August 2010).

12  Quoted in Sam Coates and Philip Webster, 'MPs quit – and blame the voters', *The Times*, 22 May 2009.

13  Philip Webster, 'Grandees who demand double pay don't speak for the party, says leader', *The Times*, 20 August 2009.

14  Matthew Flinders, 'Everyone should sing out in praise of politics', *Yorkshire Post*, 4 May 2010.

15  For details of Legg's audit, see Members Estimate Committee, *Review of past ACA payments, First Report of Session 2009–10*, HC348 (London: TSO, 2010).

16  Gordon Brown repaid £13,723.04, David Cameron £965.45 and Nick Clegg £989.50. See Polly Curtis and Hélène Mulholland, 'MPs' expenses: system "deeply flawed", says Sir Thomas Legg', *Guardian*, 4 February 2010.

17  The police later charged the Labour MPs Elliot Morley, David Chaytor, Jim Devine and Eric Illsley with offences involving false accounting.

18  David Easton, *A Framework for Political Analysis* (Englewood Cliffs, NJ: Prentice-Hall, 1965).

19  See Alexandra Kelso, 'Parliament on its knees: MPs expenses and the crisis of transparency at Westminster', *The Political Quarterly*, 80 (2009): 329–38: p.330.

20  Matthew Flinders, 'Bagehot smiling: Gordon Brown's "New Constitution" and the revolution that did not happen', *The Political Quarterly*, 81 (2000): 57–73: p. 59.

21  Populus survey for *The Times*, April 2010, available at: populuslimited.com/uploads/download_pdf-120410-The-Times-The-Times-Poll---April-2010.pdf (last accessed 26 August 2010).

22  May 6th 2010 British General Election Constituency Results Release 5.0, available at: www.hks.harvard.edu/fs/pnorris/Data/Data.htm (last accessed 26 August 2010).

23  Anthony King, 'Why a poor turnout points to a democracy in good health', *Daily Telegraph*, 17 May 2001.

24  Steven Barnett, 'Will a crisis in journalism provoke a crisis in democracy?', *The Political Quarterly*, 73 (2002): 400–8, p. 400.

25  Tony Blair, 'Tony Blair's "Media" speech: the prime minister's Reuters speech on public life', *The Political Quarterly*, 78 (2007): 476–87.

26  Alastair Campbell, 'It's time to bury spin', *British Journalism Review*, 13 (2002): 15–23.

27  John Lloyd, *What the Media are Doing to Our Politics* (London: Constable and Robinson, 2004), p. 8

28  Oborne, *The Triumph of the Political Class*, pp.233–70.

29  See Pippa Norris, ed., *Critical Citizens: Global Support for Democratic Government* (Oxford: Oxford University Press, 1999); and Russell J. Dalton, *Citizen Politics: Public Opinion and Political Parties in Advanced Industrial Democracies*, 4th edn (Washington, DC: CQ Press, 2006).

30  For the classic introduction to valence politics, see Donald E. Stokes, 'Spatial models of party competition', *American Political Science Review*, 57 (1963): 368–77.

31  Ronald Inglehart, *The Silent Revolution: Changing Values and Political Styles among Western Publics* (Princeton, NJ: Princeton University Press, 1977).

32  Anthony Heath, Jean Martin and Gabriella Elgenius, 'Who do we think we are? The decline of traditional social identities', in Alison Park, John Curtice, Katarina Thomson, Miranda Phillips and Mark Johnson, eds, *British Social Attitudes: The 23rd Report – Perspectives on a Changing Society* (London: Sage, 2007), pp.1–34.

33  Peter A. Hall, 'Social Capital in Britain', *British Journal of Political Science*, 29 (1999): 417–61.

34  Hazel Blears, 'Tackling political disengagement: speech to the Hansard Society', 5 November 2008.

35  Anthony King. 'The rise of the career politician in Britain – and its consequences', *British Journal of Political Science*, 11 (1981): 249–85; p. 250.

36  King, 'The Rise of the Career Politician in Britain', p. 285.

37  Oborne, *The Triumph of the Political Class*, p. 9.

38  The Sutton Trust, *The Educational Backgrounds of Members of the House of Commons and House of Lords* (London: Sutton Trust, 2005), pp. 8–11, available at: www.suttontrust. com/reports/politiciansbackgrounds_09-dec-05.pdf (last accessed 26 August 2010).

39  Donald D. Searing, 'The role of the good constituency member and the practice of representation in Great Britain', *The Journal of Politics*, 47 (1985): 347–81.

40  Philip Norton and David M. Wood, *Back from Westminster: British Members of Parliament and their Constituents* (Lexington: University Press of Kentucky, 1993), p. 43.

41  According to data supplied by the House of Commons Information Office.

42  Judith Bara, 'The 2005 manifestos: a sense of déjà vu?', *Journal of Elections, Public Opinion, and Parties*, 16 (2006): 265–81, p. 270.

43  Oliver Heath, 'Explaining turnout decline in Britain, 1964–2005: party identification and the political context', *Political Behavior*, 29 (2007): 493–516.

44  Power Commission, *Power to the People: The Report of Power – An Independent Inquiry into Britain's Democracy* (London: The POWER Inquiry, 2006), p. 100.

45  YouGov survey for Channel 4 News, October 2008, available at: www.yougov.co.uk/extranets/ygarchives/content/pdf/C4%20results%2008%2010%2022%20topline.pdf (last accessed 26 August 2010).

46  YouGov survey for the *Sunday Times*, January 2010, available at: www.yougov.co.uk/extranets/ygarchives/content/pdf/ST-toplines_Jan10.pdf (last accessed 26 August 2010).

47  Alexandra Kelso, 'Parliament and Political Disengagement: Neither Waving nor Drowning', *The Political Quarterly*, 78 (2007): 364–73, p. 364.

48  For a brief overview of the various democratic initiatives introduced in recent years, see Anthony King, *The British Constitution* (Oxford: Oxford University Press, 2007), pp. 249–96.

49  HM Government, *The Coalition: our programme for government* (London: Cabinet Office, 2010), pp. 26–8.

# 6 THE POLICY MOOD AND THE MOVING CENTRE

John Bartle, Sebastian Dellepiane Avellaneda and
James A. Stimson

## A matter of perspective

As the preceding chapters have demonstrated, the 2010 general election
was one of the most eventful and dramatic in British electoral history.[1]
The Labour party's share of the vote declined by some 6.4 points and the
Conservative party's share increased by 3.8 points. The resulting 5.1 point
swing from Labour to the Conservatives was the second largest since 1945.
Britain's 'first-past-the-post' electoral system translated this adjustment of
electoral support into a dramatic transformation of the electoral map, with
large parts of the country turning from Labour red to Conservative blue,
though Labour was still able to deny the Tories an overall majority. The
Conservatives made a net gain of some ninety-five seats, while Labour
made a net loss of ninety. And for all the excitement ignited by the first
leadership debate and a few campaign polls that put them in first place,
the Liberal Democrats gained just 0.9 points compared with 2005 and
made a net loss of six seats (see Table 8.1). To state the obvious, therefore, the outcome of the 2010 general election was largely due to a decline
in the Labour vote and also, but secondarily, to a smaller increase in the
Conservative vote share.

It is only natural that election analysts should seek to explain change.
The challenge, however, is to select an appropriate perspective and reference point from which change is measured. The most obvious approach,
simply because it is the most immediate, is to focus on the formal campaign
and assess the performance of the party leaders and the impact of unpredictable events. In 2010, all three party leaders were leading their party in
a general election for the very first time, and the leadership factor might
have been expected to have an unusually significant impact (though, to be
sure, Gordon Brown had been a major figure for a long time and public
perceptions of him were largely formed). In the campaign there were two
events that could have affected people's perceptions of the leaders. The first

was the first leadership debate when Nick Clegg's performance temporarily succeeded in styling the Liberal Democrats as the party of 'real change' and seized the imagination of the media and parts of the public alike. The second was 'Bigotgate', when Gordon Brown was caught on tape calling Gillian Duffy, a lifelong Labour voter, a 'bigoted woman' merely for raising the issue of immigration during his visit to Rochdale in Lancashire. Yet for all the media attention that was devoted to these two events, it is difficult to see that they had a significant impact. To be sure, the Labour party lost a little support during the campaign. The Tories, however, ended up pretty much where they began (see Figure 7.1). The immediate effect of the first leadership debate was a sharp rise in Liberal Democrat support that saw them leapfrog into second or even sometimes first place. Yet Liberal Democrat support usually rises by 3 to 4 points from the start of the campaign to the final vote and that is broadly what happened in 2010; they started off at 19–20 points in the poll of polls at the start of the campaign and ended up with 23.6 per cent of the vote. 'Bigotgate' blew up in the final week of the campaign and, for all the media coverage it produced, had no measurable effect: it merely served to remind people that the British media could act like a 'pack of shrieking gibbons'.[2]

Yet it would be a mistake to view the election campaign as simply focussed on who said what and when. Other aspects of the 2010 campaign, such as the row about Labour's plans to increase national insurance, touched on more enduring issues such as the effect of the tax system on personal incentives, as well as distributional issues about who should ultimately pay the bill for bailing out the banks. Several questions in the leadership debates focussed on the issue of welfare dependency and why the system did not support those 'who have worked and contributed towards the country's economy'.[3] The Conservative campaign alleged that the state was inefficient. In the first debate, for example, David Cameron argued 'There is a lot of waste, and it needs to be cut', in the second he proclaimed 'I want less waste, less bureaucracy', and in the third 'What we're saying is, save government waste to put money back in people's pockets'.[4] These were all old, familiar arguments but in 2010 they resonated with public in a way that they had not done in the three previous elections. 'Bigotgate', moreover, highlighted the issue of immigration; it did not create it. Disagreements about how to deal with the burgeoning government deficit touched on that most enduring of issues: the limits of state activity. The 2010 campaign was about much more than personalities and events. It was about politics too. At its heart many of the political issues in 2010 were the same as those that had featured in most other post-war elections.

If the first approach to explaining change focuses on campaign events, the second approach shifts the focus back still further to consider what changed between two adjacent elections. In 2010 several obvious developments influenced the outcome: David Cameron's attempts to modernise the

Conservative party; the resignation of Tony Blair and his replacement by his long-serving chancellor and rival, Gordon Brown; the ballooning budget deficit; Charles Kennedy's resignation as Liberal Democrat leader and the eventual emergence of Nick Clegg; the 'bottled' election that never was in the autumn of 2007; the impact of the MPs expenses scandal; and, above all, the financial crisis that altered all the parties' strategic calculations.

An examination of these events and developments is clearly important to understanding the outcome. But yet again some of these developments have deep roots. The Conservative party's problems did not start in 2005. They pre-dated Michael Howard's, Iain Duncan Smith's, William Hague's and even John Major's leaderships. The deficit had its origins in Labour's enduring commitment to equality and the public services, the long-term weaknesses of the British economy, as well as the decision – taken by Gordon Brown and Tony Blair in early 1997 – not to raise the basic or top rates of income tax, a decision that was itself a response to Labour's defeat in 1992. As Philip Gould noted of Labour's electoral strategy in 1997:

> Tax was central to our strategy of reassurance. If the election campaign had one crucial battle, one defining fight, it was over tax. We lost the 1992 election and won the 1997 one in large part because of tax. Tony Blair and Gordon Brown both believed the shadow Budget in 1992 had been a mistake: it revealed our hand and raised taxes for middle-income earners . . . Blair and Brown had a gut feeling that hard-working families paid enough tax; why should they pay any more?[5]

While the campaign and inter-election perspectives provide clues about the outcome of the election, they miss important parts of the story. A third perspective views the 2010 election as merely the latest round in the competitive struggle for the vote.[6] To be sure, such a perspective cannot provide everything that one needs to know about the 2010 election; the first two perspectives add necessary detail to the story. Yet, unless one consciously adopts a long-term perspective, it is all too easy to overlook those factors that influence behaviour in the long haul – in particular those predictable, cumulative and powerful movements of opinion – and instead focus on the unpredictable impact of recent events.

Studies in the US, Britain and elsewhere have shown that public opinion across a whole series of issues can be usefully summarised by the concept of the 'policy mood'. This refers to the electorate's preferences for more or less government activity and can be thought of as an indicator of the 'political centre'.[7] To foreshadow the rest of this chapter the evidence laid out below suggests that the policy mood moved rightwards, away from 'bigger' government and towards 'smaller' government between 1997 and 2010, contrary to the policies of Labour. This movement in the political centre had been underway ever since Labour came to power in 1997. Tellingly, moreover, the reverse occurred under the Conservative government between 1979 and 1997, which favoured smaller government; the electorate steadily moved to the left and demanded more government throughout this period.

This 'thermostatic effect' – the tendency of public opinion to move in the opposite direction to government policy first identified by Chris Wlezien – seems to be a regular and predictable feature of the British political system.[8] It explains why Labour lost support in 2010 and why the Conservatives gained it (though, to be sure, additional evidence is required to explain why the Tories did not 'seal the deal' and win a majority). It may also offer some clues as to why the 'Brown bounce' in the summer of 2007 proved to be so limited and why Labour's campaign arguments about the need for government activity apparently had less effect in 2010 than in previous elections. It may even help explain why the political momentum appears to have favoured a Conservative–Liberal Democrat coalition and why the new government felt able to announce plans to cut the size of government. Movements in the mood and the political centre do not simply account for electoral change; they point the way to the future too.

## Long-term perspectives on electoral change

A long-term perspective goes beyond the proximate causes of electoral outcomes. It identifies the influence of remote causes that have indirect effects via other factors that in turn influence the vote. The difficulty with such a perspective, however, is that there is no obvious starting point. Explaining electoral outcomes is rather like peeling an onion: each and every explanation itself demands explanation. In the technical language of causal modelling, there are few genuinely exogenous variables that are not caused by something else. All explanations are endogenous – that is, caused by something else – at least to a degree.

The starting point for the analysis laid out in this chapter is determined in part by normative considerations and in part by empirical considerations. It is normative because voters' preferences (or opinions) are supposed to be *the* driving force in democratic politics.[9] It is empirical because it is only with the introduction of nationally representative surveys that there is any independent evidence about opinions. The masses of data gathered by polling organisations means that it is possible to trace the dynamics of preferences from 1950 right through to 2010, to assess their relation to election outcomes and to explain why they changed. Before this can be done, however, preferences across a large number of distinct issues need to be expressed in terms of a standard unit. Just such a *numeraire*, however, is provided by the political system: the left-right dimension.

# The political system: government, voters and parties

There are three basic actors in British democracy: governments, voters and parties (setting aside the hugely complicating fact of the media.)[10] These three actors make up a system because they interact with each other over long periods of time. In order to understand the consequences of these inter-actions it is useful to consider what government does and the motivations of voters and parties.

## What does government do?

Government, of course, does many things. In the context of democratic elections and party competition, however, it has two particularly important functions: it *taxes* and *spends*. Governments identify social, economic and political problems and then develop programmes and mobilise resources using tax-levying powers to fund them. Correction, governments do *three* things: they tax, they spend and they *borrow*. This qualification is particu-larly necessary in 2010 when the deficit, then estimated to be somewhere in the region of £175 billion, loomed over the entire election. The issue of the deficit is set aside here because, at least from one point of view, bor-rowing represents either a deferred tax rise or a spending cut. And even if this view is not accepted, ignoring borrowing simplifies analysis and cuts out inessential detail.[11]

The importance of the public services provided by the government is a fact that is all too easily ignored. In 2009, the state spent some £671 billion in total, including £189 billion on welfare benefits, £119 billion on the National Health Service (NHS), £88 billion on education, £38 billion on defence and £35 billion on law and order. These vast sums provide some indication of the size of the state but do not fully convey the extent to which most Britons are dependent on it for some of the things they most value. This dependence is particularly striking in the case of healthcare. The British Social Attitudes (BSA) survey suggests that only around one in five Britons were covered by any form of private health insurance between 2005 and 2009.[12] Even this lucky few, moreover, rely on the NHS for the majority of their care – espe-cially day-to-day consultations with general practitioners and accident and emergency services. Similarly, most British children attend state schools or state subsidised nurseries. And when the same children go on to university their places are heavily subsidised again.

The role of the state goes far wider than health and education. Some six million people claim welfare benefits of one kind or another (income sup-port, employment support and so on).[13] Many elderly people rely on the state for their pensions, for subsidies to meet fuel costs, for meals on wheels and for winter fuel allowances. Those who live in urban Britain are heavily dependent on publicly subsidised transport to get them to and from work. And, as a result of all this activity, many people rely on the state for their jobs. By the fourth quarter of 2009 the public sector employed six million people or about 20 per cent of the labour force. Under Labour, public spending as a proportion of GDP initially fell from 38 per cent in 1997 to 36.3 per cent in 1999 because Gordon Brown chose to stick to Conservative spending plans. It subsequently increased to 41 per cent in 2007 as a result of increases in the NHS, education and welfare (see Figure 4.1). In addition to all the usual running costs of a modern welfare state, the government also engages in discretionary expenditure, such as the bail out of the banks in 2008–09 that cost some £289 billion.[14] This had a dramatic impact on the nation's finances. Total managed expenditure rose to 44 per cent of GDP in 2008–09 and to 48 per cent by 2010–11.

The other side of the equation is taxation. In 2009–10 the British state raised £496 billion in revenue, including £141 billion from income tax, £98 billion from national insurance, £64 billion from VAT, £35 billion from corporation tax and £44 billion from duties on tobacco, alcohol and other goods.[15] From 1997 Labour introduced a range of taxes, labelled 'stealth taxes' by their opponents. Revenue did not rise as a proportion of GDP, however. In 1997 it represented 37.5 per cent of GDP but fell to 36.6 per cent by 2009, producing the deficit.[16] Yet, according to the Institute for Fiscal Studies, the authoritative independent research organisation, the average UK family paid £970 more tax per year in 2010, than in 1997. This would have increased to £1,420 per family under the plans announced by Alistair Darling in Labour's spring 2010 budget.[17] Not surprisingly, many voters took the view that taxes were likely to rise, whoever won the election.

The centralised nature of British government is another fact that is all too easily ignored in commentary about elections and party competition. Both the levying of taxation and the provision of public services are subject to an unusual degree of central influence compared with federal systems such as the US. Indeed, only 5 per cent of all tax revenue is raised locally in Britain.[18] There is political resistance, moreover, to any attempt to devolve responsibility from Westminster. Britons expect a degree of uniformity in the provision of services. Accusations about 'postcode lotteries', where services are available in one part of the country and not the other, are generally thought to be politically damaging. Most issues relating to public services are, therefore, matters for central government, and it is implicated in most controversies about expenditure.

## What do voters want?

Individual voters know little about the detail of politics and do not have coherent preferences.[19] Nevertheless, it seems obvious that they want two things from government: higher spending and lower taxes. Or, in the words of Polly Toynbee, they want Scandinavian levels of welfare with US levels of taxation. [20] This proposition about voter motivation tends to scandalise those with a keen awareness of budget constraints. It is not possible, they argue, to have both higher spending and lower taxes unless there is higher borrowing. They might add further that it is not possible to borrow indefinitely. It is, however, perfectly possible to *prefer* these things, and the empirical evidence provides ample support for the proposition that people are ambivalent about tax and spending: many people *do* prefer higher spending and lower taxes.[21] Individuals do not always have coherent positions and often fail to recognise the (implicit) trade-offs between things they prefer, the need to balance the books and the implications of their choices. Most have a mixture of – often conflicting – 'considerations' (reasons for deciding one way or another) so that the opinion they express depends in part on those considerations that have been highlighted in the question they have been asked.[22] Those who enquire what individual voters (singular) want quickly discover some very confusing results. Indeed, such findings have led some to speculate that voters respond to questions about preferences at random.[23] It seems that they do not really have opinions at all and their opinions do not respond to changes in information.

Preferences relating to tax and spending are enormously important but other preferences matter too. These are also characterised by a degree of ambivalence.[24] Voters want a welfare system that acts as safety net but does not erode individual responsibility or remove incentives. They generally want an immigration system that welcomes those with skills and a genuine fear of persecution but not economic migrants. They also generally want trade unions that are strong enough to protect their members but not so strong as to challenge the authority of governments. Even attitudes on issues like abortion are characterised by a degree of ambivalence. Some individuals with generally anti-abortion views are prepared to accept the need for abortion in certain extreme circumstances, while even those who believe in a woman's right to choose are prepared to accept the need for limits on that right.

In their details, individual preferences can appear bewildering and unpredictable. Unlike politicians, ordinary citizens are not called on to elaborate and defend their opinions. They get by with opinions of varying degrees of consistency, and changes in individual preferences may reflect random variation rather than real changes. Democracy does not, however, depend on everyone having fully-worked-out opinions: it depends on the aggregation of preferences across individuals. Moreover, the major political parties conveniently structure issues in terms of 'left' and 'right'. This enables a summation of preferences across issues to estimate the political centre: the preference (or position) of the average voter. Once this double summation (across individuals and issues) has taken place public opinion appears to respond to political and economic developments in reasonable ways. In short, the electorate is a lot smarter than the average individual in it.[25]

Voters want other things that do not require them to work out their 'positions'. Some things are universally desired and the only issue is which party is best able to deliver these things.[26] Classic examples of a so-called 'valence issue' are honesty in government, corruption-free government and crime. Few, if any, voters would actually choose more dishonesty, more corruption and more crime. The question is which candidate or party is 'better' or 'worse' at achieving what virtually everyone wants.

While the distinction between position and valence issues is useful, the boundary can easily blur. On the one hand, most choices can be framed as valence judgements. For instance, if one takes the view that no one values taxation in itself and that everyone would like to spend more on things such as education and the relief of poverty, then both tax and an awful lot of spending can be seen as 'valenced'.[27] On the other hand, most valence issues mask trade-offs between universally desired things. Economic growth, another classic valence issue, usually entails a trade-off between low inflation and full employment. Such trade-offs often result from a scarcity of resources and compel decision makers to reveal their preferences. Political parties, for example, must prioritise their values and goals if they are to produce coherent bundles of policies: they present voters with choices between programmes that can be located on a left–right scale. And while voters' evaluations of government performance matter, voters cannot evaluate something before they know what is of value, which is obviously a matter of preference. In practice, therefore, individual vote choices – and election outcomes – are influenced by both position and valence judgements.

## What do parties want?

Political parties want to win elections. But parties have ideological or programmatic goals too. People join parties because they share certain basic views about the way the world is, the way the world should be and how to get from the one to the other.[28] They may also join a party to express their disagreement with another party or out of some combination of agreement and disagreement. In any event political parties are based on preferences, disagreements and conflicts. And the sorts of things that parties have disagreed about have not fundamentally altered since the formation of socialist, or, perhaps more accurately, social democratic parties, in the late nineteenth century.[29] These left-wing parties advocated more state activity to improve the lives of ordinary people and to achieve greater political, social and economic equality. This basic program proved to be so popular (because it appealed directly to voters' self-interest) that all other parties had to take positions on this one 'super issue'. To this day, left-wing parties such as Labour continue to advocate more government activity while right-wing parties such as the Conservatives tend to advocate less state activity and greater individual responsibility. The Liberal Democrats on the other hand have tended to take a position somewhere between these two parties, depending on the precise circumstances.

This extent of disagreement between the parties can be easily demonstrated by examining the content of party programmes or manifestos. The Comparative Manifestos Project (CMP) has coded every party programme from 1945 right through to 2010 (see Figure 6.1). Their evidence shows that Labour has always been to the left of the Conservatives, while the Liberal Democrats have generally been somewhere in between (but not always equidistant from) the major parties. To be sure, the differences between the parties have varied over time. The major parties converged on the left in the 1950s but moved apart in the early 1970s and again in 1983, a development that probably led to the growth in support for the Liberal Democrats (or rather their predecessors, the Liberal Party and then the SDP-Liberal Alliance).[30] The parties converged again in the late 1990s largely as a result of New Labour's move to the right. Critically, however, British elections have always posed the question of more or less, where both the 'more' and the 'less' refer to government activity. In 2010 the differences between the two major parties were broadly similar to those in the 1950s, 1960s and the previous three elections. According to the CMP estimates the Liberal Democrats were located at almost exactly the same position as Labour in

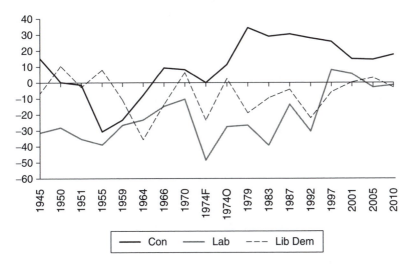

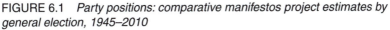

FIGURE 6.1   *Party positions: comparative manifestos project estimates by general election, 1945–2010*

*Source*: Comparative manifestos project data, kindly provided by Judith Bara, Queen Mary, University of London.

2001, 2005 and 2010, a finding that provides some foundation to the commonly held pre-election assumption that these two parties were natural coalition partners.

Not all issues naturally relate directly and logically to the scope of government activity.[31] New issues, such as nuclear power, the environment and Europe, arise that do not obviously relate to the issue of government activity. Yet as new issues arise the existing parties take positions on them and these issues acquire an association with left or right. Opposition to nuclear weapons could, for example, be a right-wing opinion and be made to go together with opposition to state activity. Similarly environmentalism might be associated with a preference for small government. However, simple observation shows that opposition to nuclear weapons and environmentalism have become associated with left-wing positions. This makes it possible to summarise the position of the parties and the electorate by simply aggregating across diverse issues.

## Government activity, taxes and spending: the 2010 general election

The scope of government activity (or tax and spending) has often been the defining issue in British general elections, leading one commentator to suggest that, in Britain at least, 'it's the economy *and public services* stupid'.[32] In 1987 the Labour campaign quickly ran into trouble because of its ill-thought out income tax proposals. In 1992 Conservative allegations that a Labour government would produce a 'double whammy' of tax rises and inflation were central to the Tory campaign.[33] In 1997 Blair and Brown felt that Labour had to promise not to make any changes in the basic and top rates of income tax for an entire parliament in order to win the election. By 2001 and 2005 the debate was framed in somewhat different terms but remained basically the same. Labour alleged that the Conservatives could only reduce taxes by cutting spending on key services, and this allegation was thought to have damaged the Tories' prospects. This was reflected in the determined efforts of the Tory leader and his shadow chancellor not to promise up-front tax cuts and to reassure voters that the public services were safe in their hands (see Chapter 2).

In 2010 there were clear differences, particularly relating to the deficit:

- How quickly should the deficit be reduced? Labour promised to halve the deficit over a full parliament. The Conservatives promised to reduce the 'bulk' of the deficit in the same period. The Liberal Democrats promised to identify and cut £15 billion of lower priority spending and to protect frontline services, cutting the structural deficit at least as quickly as Labour.

- Should the burden of adjustment fall primarily on public expenditure or taxation? All the parties supported a combination of spending cuts and tax rises. According to the Institute for Fiscal Studies, however, Labour plans implied spending cuts to tax rises in the ratio of 2:1, while the Liberal Democrats plans implied a ratio of 2.5:1 and the Conservatives a ratio of 4:1.[34]
- Which spending budgets had to be cut? Labour promised to protect frontline services in the NHS, education and the police, while the Conservatives promised to protect spending in the NHS and international development. The Liberal Democrats suggested that there would be no 'no go' areas.
- Which taxes would rise? Labour advocated an across the board 1 pence rise in the rate of national insurance and an increase in the top rate of tax to 50 pence in the pound for those earning £150,000 or more. The Conservatives rejected the rise in national insurance (which they labelled a 'tax on jobs') and promised to abolish inheritance tax on estates above £1 million. The Liberal Democrats regretted the national insurance rise but accepted it in the circumstances. They argued that no one earning under £10,000 should pay income tax and pledged to introduce a special tax on homes worth more than £2 million.

Given the size of the deficit in 2010 it was not possible for Labour to characterise the choice as one between 'Labour investment and Tory cuts'. All the parties accepted the need to cut the deficit by some combination of spending cuts and tax rises. Nevertheless, there were still very significant differences between the parties. Government would have been significantly larger under Labour than the Conservatives. The choice was not as stark in the past but it was still a choice. The Labour manifesto was entitled *A Future Fair for All* and promised to help people through the recession. The Conservative manifesto on the other hand was entitled *Invitation to Join the Government of Britain* and advocated a 'big society', which provided an interesting spin on their commitment to smaller government. The Liberal Democrats portrayed themselves as the party that would be honest about the tough decisions that would have to be made on the deficit.

The clash of preferences was not just clear from the parties approaches to the deficit or the content of their manifestos. It was also obvious in the leadership debates for anyone who looked for it. Gordon Brown continually stressed the need for government to support people in hard times and warned that removing this would risk generating a double-dip recession. David Cameron warned that more government was not the answer to Britain's problems. In the second debate he argued for greater individual responsibility:

> [T]he politicians in this country have been treating the people as mugs for far too long. They've been sort of saying, we can do everything, vote for us and we'll solve all your problems. Let us pass a few more laws, spend a bit more money, pass more regulation and all the trouble will be fixed. It is not really true, it is a big lie. The truth is, if you really want to change things, if you want safer streets, if you want better schools, yes, the Government's got its role, but we've all got our responsibilities, too.

Most media attention focussed on the leaders' performance in the debates. Yet, as this snippet demonstrates, the debates contained more than their fair share of political conflict too. While some of the media of political debate – the blogs, the stream of Twitter comment and the leaders' debates – were new, they contained much that was familiar. And although the parties competed on valence issues – such as honesty about the deficit – they also offered different choices.

## The political centre and the thermostatic effect

Political ideology and preferences matter to political parties and voters alike. People join parties because they agree with a party's basic goals and policy prescriptions but they also want to win elections and so have to moderate their appeals. Voters want higher spending and lower taxes, so their willingness to tolerate both poor services and higher taxes has limits. These motivations can interact to produce a thermostatic effect.

The interaction goes something like this. A right-wing Conservative government tends to reduce spending and taxes. This results in increasing concern about the public services and leads the electorate to want more spending. Voters now indicate a willingness to tolerate higher taxes and become more sympathetic to welfare recipients. A purely office-seeking party might moderate its policies in response to this movement. The government, however, follows its ideological impulses and continues reducing spending so the leftwards movement continues. Eventually there reaches a point where voters switch to Labour. Public opinion acts like a thermostat, judging policy too cold and signalling a preference for a warmer temperature. The same pattern then operates in reverse. Labour governments increase spending and taxes. Over time, voters become increasingly concerned about waste, inefficiency and the effect of welfare on personal responsibility. Policy is too hot and preferences move rightwards. The movement of opinion across issues is slow but its cumulative effect can be dramatic.

The obvious question here is why a governing party would continue to move policy in a right or left direction if it is likely to result in defeat. Part of the reason is that no one can ever be sure when the government has gone too far.[35] If the opposition is not credible – as Labour was in 1983–92 and the Conservatives in 1997–2005 – what constitutes too far might, moreover, vary over time. The other part of the story, however, is the powerful motivating force of ideology. Without this impulse politicians could sense the mood of the electorate and alter their policies accordingly. But ideology – perhaps together with policy stickiness – makes it difficult for even the most ambitious office-seeking politician to respond. Tony Blair and Gordon Brown, the authors of New Labour, denied that theirs was a tax-and-spend party but – as the record shows – New Labour in office certainly spent and it did increase some taxes (though not enough to keep the deficit down). David Cameron and George Osborne sought to reassure voters that the public services would be safe in their hands but immediately announced massive cuts in public expenditure on a larger scale than those imposed by the Thatcher governments. Whether it is a result of ignorance or ideology, government is unlikely to be able to achieve a Goldilocks solution, one that is neither too hot nor too cold. The political centre is, accordingly, likely to be moving for long periods of time.

# Estimating the policy mood and the political centre

There are good reasons to think that voters and parties' motivations tend to interact and produce an observed thermostatic effect. To establish whether this is the case what is needed is evidence and some way of measuring preferences over time. Such technology has long been available but the data has hitherto been scattered in many different sources: dusty archives, the reports of market research organisations and various electronic data archives. This data has now been pulled together in the policy-mood database held at the University of Essex and University of North Carolina, Chapel Hill, in the United States. The resulting dataset constitutes one of the largest and richest sources of evidence about the shifting preferences of an electorate anywhere in the world. The evidence stretches from 1938 to 2010. There is little data in the period between 1938 and 1950 but from the 1950s onwards there is enough data to infer the broad preferences of British voters.[36] Before the estimates are laid out it is useful to have a brief technical account of where they come from. Those who are more interested in the destination rather than the journey can skip the following two sections and rejoin the chapter at the section headed 'The moving centre, 1950–2010'.

## The policy-mood database

The policy-mood database contains responses to questions asked in the seventy-two years between 1938 and 2010. The original questions all refer to controversial issues, where two otherwise reasonable people might have difference preferences or take different positions.[37] None of the questions make any reference to specific political actors because such partisan cues make it extremely difficult to separate preferences from voters' evaluations of these actors.

All the relevant questions are asked in at least two different years because the method of estimating the policy mood uses evidence about changes in responses to draw inferences. One long-running question on trade unions was asked in forty separate years, while many others were asked on just two or three years. Unfortunately, it is only recently that analysts have begun to ask the same questions year after year. Further back there is little consistency. In some cases questions are asked twice in the same year and then never again and thus reveal nothing about annual changes. Even so the database contains 703 separate questions that were asked a total of 4,236 times.

The marginal distributions (the proportion supporting a statement, or selecting a particular position) are entered in the database and then expressed as an index of preferences representing the proportion of left responses among those respondents who provide a substantive response (i.e. left/ left + right). The generality of the left–right framework is illustrated by the fact there are very few responses that cannot be coded as left or right. Even if the wrong coding decision is made – and a 'right' response coded 'left' or vice-versa – the computer program will use the available information to produce the right answer. All that is required is consistency.

## Some simple intuitions

The key to inferring the political centre lies in the fact that every survey question that seeks to measure public opinion contains its own biases. Even minor variations in the wording of questions or the response categories offered to respondents can produce disconcertingly large variations in the distribution of responses.[38] Responses to a range of questions about the budget deficit in 2010, for example, were difficult to reconcile with each other: the electorate gave different responses on the timing of cuts, whether the burden should fall on spending or tax rises and much else besides, depending on the precise wording of the question. This fact, of course, allows politicians to make selective use of evidence to suit their purposes and means that it is difficult to compare responses to different questions.

These biases are, however, constant over time. Comparison of responses to the *identical* question asked at different times can, therefore, provide information about changes in preferences. If preferences on one question related to tax become more left-wing, this fact represents a suggestion that the electorate have shifted leftwards. If this is repeated across other questions tapping attitudes to taxation then this provides clear evidence of such a shift. And if preferences become more left-wing across a whole series of issues

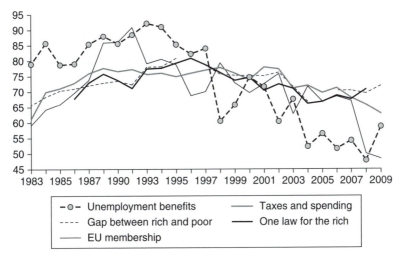

FIGURE 6.2   *Intuitions about the policy mood*

*Sources*: British Social Attitudes and Eurobarometer.

*Note*: For information about what the questions in the chart refer to, see text.

from taxes to welfare, to trade unions, public ownership, abortion and environmental issues, this provides compelling evidence of a general left-wards movement in preferences that cannot be easily dismissed as mere sampling error or idiosyncratic variation: something altogether more fundamental is happening. Aggregation across both individuals and issues, therefore, provides compelling evidence of changes in underlying preferences.

Changes in recorded preferences provide the key to measuring the policy mood. This is something that policy makers have long understood.[39] And if policy makers can detect variations in mood then some traces ought also to be found in responses to survey questions. Such longitudinal variation can be used to infer how public opinion is shifting over time. This intuition is illustrated in Figure 6.2, which displays responses to a fairly diverse set of questions between 1983 and 2010 that ask whether:

- Taxes and spending should be increased or reduced
- Unemployment benefits are too low or too high
- The gap between rich and poor is too high
- There is one law for the rich and one for the poor
- Membership of the EU is good or bad for Britain.

Despite the differences in wording, response category and issue, it is clear that there is some common variation over time: the series move together.[40] The existence of such parallelism makes it plausible to suggest that each of these series is – to varying degrees – picking up something deeper and more fundamental. This something is the policy mood. Its content is, for the moment, left open. Intuition, theory and evidence from similar studies elsewhere all suggest that this something is likely to be 'attitudes towards government activity' or what are generally called left-right positions.

The usual way of inferring unobserved variables from observations is a technique called principal component analysis. This technique will not work in this case because some questions are asked infrequently and there is a lot of missing data for each year. Instead, a different form of estimation is required that makes full use of all the information about preferences. The algorithm that is used to infer the policy mood has been widely used in a range of studies.[41] The estimation details need not be laid out here. Suffice it to say that it simply finds a common metric that makes responses to diverse questions comparable and then averages them.[42]

## The moving centre, 1950–2010

The policy mood represents the best estimate of the political centre that can be inferred with all the available evidence. Like all inferences it is subject to a degree of uncertainty. Yet while the precise details are uncertain the broad details are not. As Figure 6.3 shows the series starts off high and to the left in 1950 and then drifts downwards to the right for around the next thirty-three years.[43] It reaches its trough, or most right-wing position, around 1979–80, just after Margaret Thatcher's first election victory. Thereafter,

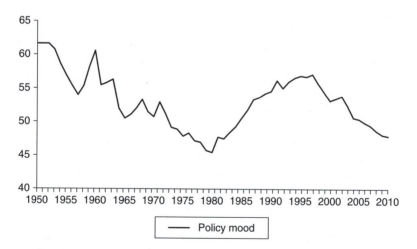

FIGURE 6.3   *The moving centre, 1950–2010*
*Source*: See text.

the series starts increasing (moving leftwards) until 1997, when it peaks and reaches its most left-wing point since the 1950s. It subsequently falls rapidly (moves rightwards) until it reaches its nadir in 2010.

Although these three broad movements are important, it must be noted that the movements of the political centre take place within a relatively narrow range. Mood can range from 0 (where all responses are right-wing) to 100 (where all responses are left-wing). The average score is 53; suggesting that the electorate has tended to be slightly left of the 'neutral' point of 50.[44] Changes in the mood are quite small. Indeed, the average annual change, ignoring the signs, is just 1.1 unit. The proposition that the electorate moved to the right between 1950 and 1979 should not, therefore, be read as implying that it became Thatcherite and fully converted to a low-tax and deregulated economy. It simply means that, across a wide range of issues (including tax and spending, welfare, Europe and immigration), a very large number of people moved, sometimes slightly, sometimes drastically, to the right.[45] Similarly, the drift to the left over the subsequent eighteen years should not be taken to imply that the electorate had become socialist. In both these phases the electorate collectively remained ambivalent, conflicted and usually moderate.

A sceptic might reasonably ask how they could be sure that the data are picking up the left-right movement of the electorate. The short answer is that one can never be sure. The series does, however, have a degree of face validity; it conforms to some standard accounts of post-war opinion. The leftward mood inferred for the early 1950s, for example, accords with the conventional history, typified by Andrew Marr's contention that in this period, 'the mood was for big government, digging deep into people's lives to improve them'.[46] And that weathervane of opinion in the 1950s, the pre-Thatcherite Conservative party, appears to have agreed: it shifted significantly to the left in the 1950 and 1951 general elections by accepting the vast majority of the post-war Labour government's reforms (see Figure 6.1).

According to the estimates displayed in Figure 6.3 the drift to the right unfolded over the next thirty years. This confirms the findings of Ivor Crewe and Anthony Heath, who both documented a drift to the right in the years between 1964 and 1979. The evidence outlined here adds to this interpretation by suggesting that the drift may have started a little earlier than this.[47] Crewe and his colleagues in particular identified a decline in support for what they labelled the 'collectivist trinity' of public ownership, trade unions and the welfare state.[48] Crewe and Heath also identified a shift to the left under the Thatcher and Major Conservative governments.[49] Concern about the state of the key public services was one of the factors underlying the Conservatives' spectacular defeat in 1997.[50]

The shift to the right that has taken place more recently has received relatively little attention from commentators. One exception is John Curtice, who has drawn attention to the increasing reluctance of respondents to support further tax rises to increase spending on the public services.[51] Another exception is Anthony King, who, in May 2008, just *before* the financial crisis, wrote in his regular *Daily Telegraph* column:

> Without naming David Cameron, YouGov went [on to ask] respondents whether they agreed or disagreed with the claim of 'a leading politician' that 'we have reached the limits of acceptable taxation and borrowing. With the rising cost of living taxpayers can't take any more'.
>
> No fewer than 85 per cent of YouGov's respondents echo Mr Cameron's sentiments.[52]

The policy mood displayed in Figure 6.3 supports this conclusion. Intriguingly, it also suggests that the financial crisis did not lead to a reversal in the rightward movement, even though increases in unemployment tend to shift preferences left. Overall, however, there was no increased demand for government activity in 2009 or 2010. It seems entirely plausible to suggest that many people had indeed come to the conclusion that taxes and public spending were high enough.

## The relationship between preferences and election outcomes

Figure 6.3 suggests that there is a subtle relationship between the policy mood and electoral outcomes. The outcome of the three recent elections that resulted in a change of government are, however, fully anticipated by prior movements in the policy-mood series. The Conservative party's victory in 1979 followed a long period of rightward movement. Similarly, New Labour's triumph in 1997 followed eighteen years of generally leftward movement (the electorate only appeared to drift right in three of those eighteen years and these changes are so small that they are probably due to sampling error). Finally, the electoral swing back to the Conservative party in 2010 came as little surprise given the rightward shift in the mood between 1997 and 2010. It is likely that prior shifts in mood may also account for some of the 3.5 point swing from Labour to the Tories in 2005 (though the swing was almost entirely the result of a sharp reduction in the Labour vote share). Quite clearly, there were other factors that limited the Conservative recovery in 2005 and meant that they failed to win an outright majority in 2010. Yet, equally clearly, the changing electoral fortunes of the parties are related to a prior shift in public opinion.

It is clear that changes in the policy mood do not have a law-like relationship with vote share. In the 1960s and in 1974, for example, Labour was capable of winning elections, despite a prior general rightward drift of opinion. More generally, the picture is complicated by the fact that preferences shift long before this is revealed in vote shares. The mood in 1979 – the year of Margaret Thatcher's first election victory – were no more right-wing than it had been five years earlier in October 1974 when Labour, under Harold Wilson, won a narrow majority. This finding challenges some understandings of the period, such as the much-quoted explanation of the Conservatives victory in 1979 offered by James Callaghan, the Labour prime minister:

> You know there are times, perhaps once every thirty years, when there is a sea-change in politics. It then does not matter what you say or what you do. I suspect there is now such a sea change – and it is for Mrs Thatcher.[53]

Callaghan was correct that there was a sea change but this pre-dated Thatcher's election as Tory leader and the so-called 'Winter of Discontent' (the series of strikes that had so disrupted life in the winter of the 1978–79 and that became forever associated with Labour's defeat). The 1979 general election merely made what was latent observable. Similarly, the policy mood was only slightly more to the left in 1997 than in 1992 but that second election produced a Labour lead of 13 points compared with a Tory lead of 7 points five years earlier. The prior shift in the policy mood clearly created the conditions for Labour's subsequent revival but it was not sufficient by itself.

According to most accounts it was after 'Black Wednesday', when Britain was forced to leave the European exchange rate mechanism (ERM) and the Conservative party's reputation for economic competence was destroyed, that Labour finally made the breakthrough.[54] The less than law-like relationship between policy mood and vote share, however, may also stem from the failure to consider the parties' positions and assessments of party competence. Spatial models of electoral competition, such as those associated with Anthony Downs, suggest that the party located nearest to the political centre will be greatly advantaged in the competitive struggle for the vote. Figure 6.1 provides the CMPs estimates of the parties' overall left-right positions while Figure 6.3 provides estimates of the voters' positions. In principle these two separate bits of evidence could be brought together to estimate how far each party was from the average voter at each election and to see if the party closest to the political centre was advantaged, as spatial theories suggest. Unfortunately, it is difficult to map parties and voters onto the same metric without imposing strong and untestable assumptions.[55]

Nevertheless, the CMP evidence about party movements and spatial theory make a valuable contribution to the long-term explanation of election outcomes. Labour's leftward lurch in 1974, for example, must have harmed the party's fortunes because the electorate had already moved rightwards. In contrast, Labour's damaging leftward move in 1983 would probably have done more damage had the electorate not shifted to the left over the same period. Since the policy mood was moving left between 1987 and 1992, one can similarly conclude that Labour's sharp move to the left, coupled with the Conservatives' own leftwards move in 1992, probably contributed to Labour's fourth consecutive defeat. The same evidence suggests that Labour's move to the centre (or right) between 1992 and 1997 must go some way to explaining New Labour's triumph at the polls. Commenting on that election, David Sanders was clearly correct to argue that: 'In true Downsian fashion, Labour moved towards [the voters]. In equally Downsian fashion, they responded.'[56] In 2010 the finding that the policy mood moved rightwards, while Labour moved ever so slightly to the right and the Conservatives nudged rightwards, provides a plausible account of why the Tories ultimately failed to win the election. It does not seem fanciful to suggest that the Conservatives may have won the election had they continued to move to the centre or had Labour moved left. Conservative warnings about the need for an 'age of austerity' and cuts in public spending in the autumn of 2009, and their demand to make an immediate start on cutting the deficit, may have won marks for honesty but – with the benefit of hindsight – may not have been entirely wise.

It must be noted that the changes in party position between 2005 and 2010 were very small. This suggests that the main cause of any spatial contribution to the swing resulted from the shift in the policy mood. To be sure, shifting evaluations of party competence must also have contributed to these changes. Most commentators rightly attributed part of the decline in Labour's share of the vote to memories of the Iraq war, a growing reputation for dishonesty and declining evaluations of Tony Blair and Gordon Brown. Yet underpinning all this was a largely unnoticed shift in the mood that may also account for the declining evaluations of the two leaders.[57]

The long-term movements in mood may well explain more about the 2010 election than the actual outcome. Blair's resignation and replacement by his then successful chancellor of the exchequer in 2007 created the 'Brown bounce' that fuelled speculation about a snap election. In the event this bounce proved short-lived and was followed by plummeting levels of support. At the time many commentators attributed this reversal of fortunes to a series of events such as the loss of personal data by the government and allegations relating to the funding of the Labour party. It seems entirely plausible, however, to suggest that both the relatively limited bounce and its short duration may have reflected the continued rightward shift of the mood. This is not the only consequence. The policy mood may also influence which political arguments are accepted and which are rejected.[58] In the 2010 election Labour argued that government support was needed to bring the country through the recession but the policy mood was already moving away from more government. Gordon Brown's basic political pitch was, accordingly, about as attractive to the electorate as it had been in the early 1980s (see Figure 6.3). The generally negative reactions to Brown in the leadership debates probably reflected this fundamental political fact as much – if not more than – any personal failings.

These movements in the policy mood may finally provide part of the explanation as to why the Liberal Democrats formed a coalition with the Conservatives. One senior Liberal Democrat at the time expressed reservations about the party tying itself to the 'rotting corpse' of Labour.[59] At the time this comment seemed to refer to the idea of associating the party with an unpopular prime minister and government but it may also have referred to Labour's basic policy programme and its commitment to 'big government' or statist solutions. Yet again, something more fundamental than personality was at stake.

## What shifts the policy mood?

The implication of Figure 6.3 is that the policy mood shifts gradually and in the long haul. This fact alone suggests that it is subject to systemic influences such as that suggested by the thermostatic model. If the party in government is a proxy for policy, the policy mood should shift left under Conservative governments and right under Labour governments. Figure 6.4 breaks down changes in the policy mood for each government since 1951. It shows that such naïve expectations are wrong in the earlier period. Setting aside the Labour government from 1950 to 1951, the policy mood moves to the right under the Conservatives (1951–64), to the left under Labour

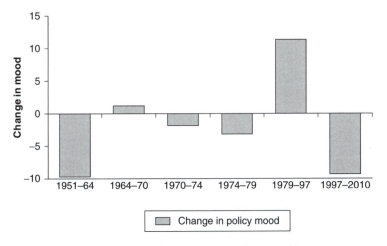

FIGURE 6.4   *Percentage changes in the policy mood by government, 1951–2010*

*Source*: See text.

(1964–70) and right again under the Conservatives (1970–74). It is only under more recent Labour (1974–79), Conservative (1979–97) and Labour governments (1997–2010) that the thermostatic model appears to operate. This, however, may be because party control is a poor proxy for policy. The Conservative government from 1951–64 oversaw a steady expansion of the welfare state, compromised with organised labour and broadly accepted Keynesian demand management techniques. The Wilson Labour government of 1964–70 presided over rises in unemployment, abandoned national planning and tried to control the trade unions. The Heath Conservative government of 1970–74 was muddled, beginning with a Thatcherite commitment to roll back the state, then executing an embarrassing policy U-turn and ending up by massively expanding the power of government. Yet when parties are true to their ideological roots (right-wing parties contract the state, left-wing parties expand it), the thermostatic effect appears to operate.

More detailed statistical analyses suggests that the policy mood shifts left when unemployment increases (presumably because voters want the government to act to reduce it) and to the right when government spending as a proportion of GDP and income tax as a proportion of average income rises.[60] The detailed statistical analysis is not reported here but the broad argument is illustrated by Figure 6.5, which displays the policy mood and total managed expenditure as a proportion of GDP between 1965

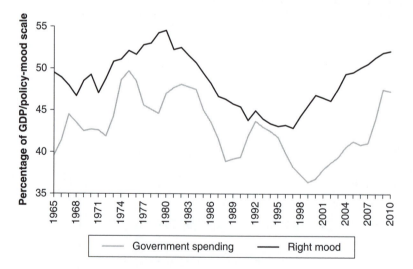

FIGURE 6.5  *Relationship between the size of government and right mood, 1965–2010*

Source: HM Treasury, available from http://www.hm-treasury.gov.uk/psf_statistics. htm. Last accessed 4 May 2010.

Note: 'Right mood' is 100 – policy mood (see text for details). Government spending refers to total managed expenditure as a proportion of GDP.

and 2010.[61] In this case the policy mood is inverted so that higher scores represent right-wing positions. There is a pretty clear relationship between the two: as spending increases the electorate move right; and as it falls the electorate move left.

Statistical models and diagrams might not persuade everyone that the thermostatic effect is real. Sceptics might find this account of why Labour lost so many elections, provided by a young Labour politician writing in 1992, to be a little more persuasive:

> When the majority were have-nots, and the vested interests that held them back were those of wealth and capital, the idea of people acting together, through the state, to reform social conditions and redistribute power became a strong political force ..... But, the state as it grew, itself became a potential vested interest with tremendous power over people's lives... the majority of people, as they prospered, earned more and began to pay the tax to fund the state, became more sceptical of its benefits.[62]

The young Labour politician was none other than Tony Blair. His exposition of the thermostatic model is incomplete because it does not consider what happens when a government tries to shrink the state – as the Conservative governments did between 1979 and 1997. Yet it also neatly points to a paradox: a government that successfully pursues ideological goals is likely to sew the seeds of its own destruction as the electorate – individually ignorant, collectively rational and generally moderate – move in the opposite direction.

## Conclusions

The outcome of the 2010 general election turned on a 5 point swing from Labour to the Conservatives. The account provided here suggests that this swing was in part a consequence of a long-term rightward movement in the policy mood that was a predictable consequence of the growth in the size of government. This in turn had its origins in both Labour's enduring commitment to the public services and prior public concerns about the plight of those services, which made the electorate more receptive to Labour's programme. In short, a significant part of the decline in Labour's vote was long-term and systemic.

There are – to be sure – alternative accounts of the election and the long-term decline. It has, for example, been suggested that support for all governments falls as a result of the 'costs of ruling'.[63] According to some estimates parties in government lose on average around 3 points in vote share per election, almost irrespective of how well they perform in office.[64] This might be simply because governments are blamed when things go wrong and receive little credit when things go right. Labour's decline, however, was far steeper than this: it lost 2 points between 1997 and 2001, 7 points between 2001 and 2005 and 6 points before 2005 and 2010; on average 5 points per election (see Appendix). Labour's decline goes well beyond the 'cost of ruling'. The thermostatic explanation outlined above also has the merit of treating aggregate behaviour as a reasonable collective response to political developments. Indeed, it generally confirms Daniel Finkelstein's prediction made in March 2010 that:

> We will have two separate elections this year, held at the same time but in different worlds. One will feature the traditional knockabout, complete with press conferences, posters and battle buses. The other will screen out the political noise, ignore the political claims, only skim the coverage and feature instead the issues and experiences that voters encounter in their daily life. The result of this second election will be the decisive one.[65]

Some accounts of the 2010 general election inevitably focus on Gordon Brown's unpopularity and specific events, such as the various party funding scandals, that damaged Labour. For some people at least, political history really is just one thing after another. Those who seek a more general account, however, may prefer the systemic explanation offered above, not least because it produces predictions about the future.

Since it is difficult to map party positions and the electorate on the same scale, it is not possible to determine categorically whether the positions of the new coalition partners were closer to the political centre than Labour's and whether they have a mandate to cut government spending along the lines they propose. What *is* clear in the late summer of 2010 is that the coalition has either interpreted the outcome as an instruction to make deep cuts in spending or, like governments before it, plans to pursue its ideological goals irrespective of opinion. The willingness of the Liberal Democrats to contemplate joining a coalition with the Conservatives that cuts back the state took some people by surprise. It should not have done: the centre party was willing to expand state activity in 1997 when public expenditure constituted 37 per cent of GDP, but as this increased to 48 per cent, the party, like all liberal parties, became increasingly concerned about the effect of the growth of the state on personal freedom. The coalition agreement explicitly states that the two parties believe that 'the days of big government are over'.[66] The proposed cuts in spending and reductions in income tax are both likely to produce a predictable thermostatic effect and shift the mood leftwards. As previous experience shows, this may not prevent the coalition partners – either standing together in a pre-election pact or as two separate parties – from winning elections, particularly if their policies produce growth, low inflation and falling unemployment, and if the Labour party moves left. It does suggest, however, that a moderate Labour party will in future be able to launch a campaign without the considerable handicap of a continued rightward shift in the public mood. Indeed, if the past is any guide to the future, the mood should drift slowly back to the left. This will certainly not guarantee a Labour victory but it will help.[67]

# Endnotes

1   This research was supported by the Economic and Social Research Council under award number: 000-22-2053.
2   Armando Iannucci, 'The Duffy affair turned the media into a pack of shrieking gibbons', *Independent*, 4 May 2010.
3   This particular question was asked in the first debate, the transcript of which is available at: news.bbc.co.uk/1/shared/bsp/hi/pdfs/16_04_10_firstdebate.pdf (last accessed on 26 August 2010).
4   The BBC transcripts for the second and third debates are available at: news.bbc.co.uk/1/shared/bsp/hi/pdfs/23_04_10_seconddebate.pdf, and news.bbc.co.uk/1/shared/bsp/hi/pdfs/30_04_10_finaldebate.pdf (last accessed on 26 August 2010).
5   Philip Gould, *The Unfinished Revolution: How Modernisers saved the Labour Party* (London: Little Brown, 1998), pp. 283–4.
6   Joseph Schumpeter, *Capitalism, Socialism and Democracy* (London: Allen and Unwin, 1987).
7   James A. Stimson, *Public Opinion in America: Moods, Cycles and Swings* (Boulder, CO: Westview Press, 1991).
8   Christopher Wlezien, 'The public as thermostat: dynamics of preferences for spending', *American Journal of Political Science*, 39 (1995): 981–1000.
9   John. D. May, 'Defining democracy: a bid for coherence and consensus', *Political Studies*, 26 (1978): 1–14.
10   It is necessary to distinguish between parties and government because the party in government has particular powers not available to others.
11   To be sure, economic growth can also erode deficits as tax revenues rise. A reliance on this fact was attributed to Gordon Brown by some of his friends and critics.
12   See British Social Attitudes Information System, available at: www.britsocat.com (last accessed on 20 April 2010).
13   Tom Peck, 'Six million Britons to claim benefits', *Independent*, 6 August 2009.
14   CRESC, *An Alternative Report on UK Banking Reform: A Public Interest Report from CRESC* (Manchester: University of Manchester Centre for Research on Socio Cultural Change, 2009), p. 6.
15   See 'Overview', in HM Treasury, *Budget 2009: Building Britain's future*, HC 407 (London: TSO, 2009).
16   The term 'structural deficit' refers to that portion of the deficit that is not due to the economic cycle.

17  Robert Chote, *The Tax Burden under Labour* (London: Institute of Fiscal Studies, 2010).

18  Stuart Adam, James Browne and Christopher Heady, *Taxation in the UK* (London: Institute for Fiscal Studies, 2010), p. 3.

19  David Butler and Donald Stokes, *Political Change in Britain: The Evolution of Electoral Preference* (London: Macmillan, 1974).

20  Polly Toynbee, 'After the lie of the free lunch comes a real political choice', *Guardian*, 24 April 2009.

21  Peter Taylor-Gooby, *Public Opinion, Ideology and State Welfare* (London: Routledge, 1985).

22  John R. Zaller, *The Nature and Origins of Mass Opinion* (Cambridge: Cambridge University Press, 1992).

23  Evan Davis, *Public Spending* (London: Penguin, 1998), chap. 4.

24  See Ipsos MORI, 'Economist poll – do voters know what they want?', 23 April 2010, available at: http://www.ipsos-mori.com/researchpublications/researcharchive/poll.aspx?oItem Id=2598 (last accessed 7 September 2010).

25  Robert S. Erikson, Michael D. MacKuen and James A. Stimson, *The Macro Polity* (Cambridge: Cambridge University Press, 2002).

26  Donald Stokes, 'Spatial models of party competition', *American Political Science Review*, 57 (1963): 368–77.

27  Stokes, 'Spatial models of party competition', p. 373.

28  Anthony Downs, *An Economic Theory of Democracy* (New York: Harper and Row, 1957).

29  Judith Bara and Albert Weale, eds, *Democratic Politics and Party Competition* (London: Routledge, 2006).

30  Jack H. Nagel and Christopher Wlezien, 'Centre-party strength and major party divergence in Britain, 1945–2005', *British Journal of Political Science*, 40 (2010), 279–304.

31  Philip E. Converse, 'The nature of belief systems in mass publics', in David Apter, ed., *Ideology and Discontent* (New York: Free Press), pp. 209–61.

32  Ivor Crewe, 'Now relax, it's a dead cert', *New Statesman*, 12 February 2001.

33  See David Butler and Dennis Kavanagh, *The British General Election of 1992* (Basingstoke, Hants: Macmillan, 1992).

34  Carl Emmerson, *Filling the Hole: How do the Three Main UK Parties Plan to Repair the Public Finances?* (London: Institute of Fiscal Studies, 2010).

35  Ian Budge, 'A New Spatial Theory of Party Competition: Uncertainty, Ideology and Policy Equilibria Viewed Comparatively and Temporally', *British Journal of Political Science*, 24 (1994): 443–67.

36  George H. Gallup, *The Gallup International Public Opinion Polls, Great Britain, 1937– 1975* (London: Random House, 1976), 2 volumes; Anthony King, ed., *British Political Opinion 1937–2000: The Gallup Polls* (London: Politicos, 2001).

37  Stokes, 'Spatial Models of Party Competition'.

38  Howard Schumann and Stanley Presser, *Questions and Answers in Attitude Surveys: Experiments on Question Form, Wording and Context* (Thousand Oaks, CA: Sage, 1996).

39  John W. Kingdon, *Agendas, Alternatives and Public Policy* (Boston: Little Brown, 1984), p. 153.

40  The means in Figure 6.2 have been standardised to improve the visual presentation.

41  Stimson, *Public Opinion in America*; Jeffrey E. Cohen, 'The polls: public favourabil-
    ity toward the First Lady', *Presidential Studies Quarterly*, 30 (2000): 575–85; Virginia A.
    Chanley, Thomas J. Rudolph and Wendy M. Rahn, 'The origins and consequences of pub-
    lic trust in government: a time series analysis', *Public Opinion Quarterly*, 64 (2000): 239–
    56; Paul M. Kellstedt, *The Mass Media and the Dynamics of American Racial Attitudes*
    (Cambridge: Cambridge University Press, 2003); Erik Voeten and Paul R. Brewer, 'Public
    Opinion, the War in Iraq, and Presidential Accountability', *Journal of Conflict Resolution*,
    50 (2006): 809–30; Frank R. Baumgartner, Suzanna L. De Boef and Amber E. Boydstun,
    *The Decline of the Death Penalty and the Discovery of Innocence* (Cambridge: Cambridge
    University Press, 2008)

42  Stimson, *Public Opinion in America,* Appendix 1.

43  The reason for the sharp peak in the late 1950s is unclear. We interpret it as a consequence
    of the little data available but it may have a more substantive cause.

44  The neutral point is not the same as the centre.

45  'Most' issues does not mean 'all'. As John Curtice points out, public attitudes towards
    homosexuality have become progressively more liberal. See John Curtice, 'Britain in 2010:
    more tolerant, more Conservative, but less likely to vote', *Independent*, 26 January 2010.

46  Andrew Marr, *A History of Modern Britain* (Basingstoke, Hants: Macmillan, 2007), pp. xi,
    28 and 70.

47  Ivor Crewe, Bo Sarlvik, B. and James Alt, 'Partisan dealignment in Britain 1964–1974',
    *British Journal of Political Science*, 7 (1977): 129–90; Anthony Heath, Roger Jowell
    and John Curtice, *How Britain Votes* (Oxford: Pergammon Press, 1985); Anthony Heath,
    John Curtice, Roger Jowell, Geoffrey Evans, Julia Field and Sharon Witherspoon,
    *Understanding Political Change: The British Voter, 1964–1987* (Oxford: Pergammon
    Press, 1991).

48  Crewe et al., 'Partisan dealignment in Britain 1964–1974'.

49  Ivor Crewe and Donald D. Searing, 'Ideological change in the British Conservative Party',
    *American Political Science Review*, 82 (1988): 361–84; Anthony Heath, Roger Jowell and
    John Curtice, *The Rise of New Labour: Party Policies and Voter Choices* (Oxford: Oxford
    University Press, 1997).

50  Anthony King, 'Why Labour won – at last', in Anthony King, ed., *New Labour Triumphs:
    Britain at the Polls* (New York: Chatham House, 1998), pp. 177–208.

51  Curtice, 'Thermostats or weathervane?'

52  Anthony King, 'Labour crisis: no way back for Gordon Brown', *Daily Telegraph*,
    29 May 2008.

53  Bernard Donoghue, *Prime Minister: The Conduct of Policy under Wilson and Callaghan*
    (London: Jonathan Cape, 1987), p. 191.

54  King, 'Why Labour won – at last'.

55  See Erikson et al., *The Macro Polity*, chap. 7.

56  David Sanders, 'The new electoral battleground', in King, ed., *New Labour Triumphs*,
    pp. 207–48, p. 217.

57  cf. John Bartle, *New British Politics: Election Update* (London: Pearson, 2005).

58  James A. Stimson, *Tides of Consent: How Public Opinion Shapes American Politics*
    (Cambridge: Cambridge University Press, 2002).

59  Patrick Wintour and Nicholas Watt, 'Lib Dems rule out coalition government', *Guardian*, 14 February 2010.

60  John Bartle, Sebastian Dellepiane Avellaneda and James A. Stimson, 'The moving centre: preferences for government activity in Britain, 1950–2005', *British Journal of Political Science* (forthcoming). See also Stuart N. Soroka and Christopher Wlezien, *Degrees of Democracy: Politics, Public Opinion and Policy* (Cambridge: Cambridge University Press, 2010).

61  Total managed expenditure data is only available from 1965.

62  Andy McSmith, *John Smith: A life, 1938–1994* (London: Mandarin, 1994), p. 300.

63  Peter Naanstead and Martin Paldam, 'The Costs of Ruling', in Han Dorussen and Michael Taylor, eds, *Economic Voting* (London: Routledge, 2002), pp. 17–44.

64  Michael D. McDonald and Ian Budge, *Elections, Parties, Democracy: Conferring the Median Mandate* (Oxford: Oxford University Press, 2005).

65  Daniel Finkelstein, 'Westminster chatter wont change the result', *The Times*, 3 March 2010.

66  HM Government, *The Coalition: our programme for government* (London: Cabinet Office, 2010), p. 7.

67  Martin Kettle, 'The coalition honeymoon is over but the marriage has plenty left', *Guardian*, 24 June 2010.

# 7 A MUCH DEBATED CAMPAIGN

Nicholas Allen, Judith Bara and John Bartle

When prime minister Gordon Brown confirmed Thursday 6 May as the date of the 2010 general election, he triggered one of the most anticipated campaigns in modern times. For the first time since 1992, there was genuine uncertainty about the eventual outcome. In particular, there was doubt over whether David Cameron and the modernised Conservative party could translate their slender opinion-poll lead into a majority in the House of Commons. For the first time since 1979, moreover, the three main parties entered the campaign led by someone who had not led them in the previous election and who had no experience of fronting a general election campaign. And, for the first time ever, there would be televised debates between the leaders of the three main UK parties. These debates would have made the 2010 election interesting in any circumstances. They were a democratic innovation and suggested to some a further step towards the 'presidentialisation' of British politics.[1] In the context of a close fight, the debates not only fuelled the uncertainty but contributed to the most topsy-turvy contest in recent political history.

In many respects, the 2010 campaign was entirely conventional. Between 6 April, when Brown called the election, and polling day, voters – especially those undecided voters in marginal constituencies – were subject to the political parties' usual frenetic attentions. Activists put up posters, pounded the streets, distributed leaflets and knocked on doors. Senior politicians attended public meetings, rallied the party faithful and took to the airwaves. Parties launched their manifestos, produced their election broadcasts and organised their morning press conferences. And journalists documented the campaign's many twists and turns. In other respects, however, the campaign was entirely unconventional. Bloggers posted their comments on the unfolding campaign in greater numbers than ever before. Social networking sites such as Facebook provided new forums for politicians and voters to communicate with and among each other. Twitter, an even newer technology, enabled users to exchange instant comments. Many commentators looked across the Atlantic to Barack Obama's victory in the 2008 US presidential election and mused on the implications of Britain's first 'new media' election.[2]

New media technologies certainly played a prominent part in 2010, and the broadcasters and newspapers made much of them. But it was the old media, and especially television, that dominated to a truly remarkable extent; the new merely complemented.[3] This chapter analyses the televised debates and the national campaign that evolved around them. As polling day loomed, the parties' proximity in the opinion polls, coupled with the prevailing anti-politics mood among voters, made for an unusually volatile mix. Some commentators still predicted a smooth Conservative procession to victory. Others claimed to notice an improvement in Labour's standings and wondered whether Brown might engineer a remarkable recovery and become Britain's own 'comeback kid'. Virtually no one paid much attention to Nick Clegg, the Liberal Democrat leader. In the event, most commentators' expectations were confounded. From the first debate onwards, the buzz was about 'Cleggmania', multi-party politics and hung parliaments. It was all very un-British, just like the final outcome.

## No debates please, we're British[4]

Many countries hold televised election debates between leaders of major parties, or, more accurately, between prospective heads of government. The most famous and commented on are those held in the United States.[5] In September 1960, Richard M. Nixon and John F. Kennedy broke new ground by taking part in four presidential debates. The first of these, held in Chicago, generated a mythology all of its own. It has ever since been remembered for the fact that television viewers thought the handsome, relaxed and confident Kennedy won against a tense, sweaty and shifty Nixon, while radio listeners thought an inexperienced and shallow senator from Massachusetts lost to the vastly experienced vice president from California. This case has constantly been used to demonstrate the importance of television imagery, not to mention the potential influence of debates on electoral outcomes.

Americans had to wait another sixteen years before the next debates were held, between President Gerald Ford and Governor Jimmy Carter. Since then, at least two debates involving presidential candidates have been held before every election. All have been extensively and intensively covered by the media.

Televised debates are logical extensions to presidential campaigns in an era of mass communication. Voters are expected to choose directly between two or more candidates for high office, and televised debates provide an opportunity for millions of voters actually to see the candidates engage with each other, discuss substantive issues and try to persuade voters of their abilities. From the broadcasters' point of view, debates can also make good television. But debates are an unpredictable forum. They do not always fulfil their dramatic or educative potential. Some debates are fascinating, others spectacularly dull. Some candidates shine, others find their campaigns knocked off course because of inadvertent slips in front of the cameras. Gerald Ford's infamous statement that: 'there is no Soviet domination of Eastern Europe and there never will be under a Ford administration' was endlessly looped during the 1976 campaign, much to the president's chagrin. More generally, presidential debates have acquired some of the worst trappings of television talent shows. The campaign teams plan and rehearse their candidates' performances, the media focus on style over substance and wait to pounce on any gaffe, and the teams spin their candidate's performance even before the cameras stop recording. To be sure, debates have provided a fair amount of bread; but they retain their circus elements.[6]

Debates are also now a staple feature of elections in many other countries. France has hosted televised debates between presidential candidates intermittently since 1974. In 2007, some 20 million viewers watched the debate between the neo-Gaullist Nicolas Sarkozy and the Socialist Ségolène Royal. Germany, a parliamentary system, has had televised debates between the chancellor candidates since 1972, most recently in September 2009 when Angela Merkel of the Christian Democrats took on the Social Democrats' Frank-Walter Steinmeier.[7] Other parliamentary systems have held election debates since the late 1960s, but Britain entered the twenty-first century without having held a televised leaders' debate.

## Previous attempts to produce a debate

None of this is to say that British party leaders have evaded scrutiny at the hands of broadcasters during election campaigns. In 1964, the BBC (Britain's public service broadcaster) developed *Election Forum*, a programme screened before the start of the campaign in which the three main party leaders appeared on separate shows and answered questions submitted by the public. A more enduring fixture has been the in-depth interview with individual party leaders. The BBC's current affairs programme *Panorama* has a long tradition of interviewing the leaders during the campaign, a tradition which it maintained in 2010. In 2005, the three main party leaders even appeared separately on the same edition of the BBC's *Question Time*, when Liberal Democrat leader Charles Kennedy, Conservative leader Michael Howard and Labour prime minister Tony Blair each endured thirty minutes of questioning by the audience. They did not, however, debate head to head.

British television executives have long wanted to host such a debate. Before the 1964 election, an unofficial committee comprising the then two terrestrial broadcasters, the BBC and ITA (Britain's main commercial terrestrial broadcaster, later ITV), and representatives of the main parties discussed proposals from the BBC for a televised 'confrontation' between the party leaders.[8] On that occasion, and others, the parties welcomed the proposals in principle but found reasons to reject them in practice. One objection was that Britain was a parliamentary system and any debate between leaders would run against the grain of collective government. British prime ministers, it was argued, were merely first among equals. It would be misleading to focus on individuals. Another objection, at least for Labour and the Conservatives, was the involvement of the third party in British politics, the Liberals. Once a major party of government in the early twentieth century, they were marginalised by the early 1960s. However, they were still a national party that could – in theory – supply a prime minister. The problem of how to involve the Liberals without detracting from the main event of a Labour–Conservative debate vexed television producers. It also provided the two major parties with an excuse not to participate.

From 1978, opponents of televised debates could draw on yet another objection. The radio broadcasting of parliament meant that the public could listen to the party leaders jousting with one another in prime minister's questions (PMQs). And from 1988 they could watch the leaders in action when parliament was televised. This ritual required prime ministers to answer questions from party leaders and other MPs on almost any issue. Who needed televised election debates when the public could watch the leaders clash each week?

In truth, the principal reason why there were no election debates before 2010 was because it had never been in the mutual interest of the two main parties. For the party ahead in the polls, it would create unnecessary risks. Any slips by its leader could be picked up by millions of viewers and pored over by thousands of journalists. For the party in government, it also risked throwing away some of the advantages of incumbency since other party leaders would get equal exposure. As prime minister, the leader of the governing party has a unique profile and authority. All things being equal, it is unlikely to be to a prime minister's advantage to share a stage – and some of that authority – with others.

Ever since 1964, the stars were rarely aligned so as to favour a debate. In that year, Labour's 'modernising' leader Harold Wilson challenged the Conservative prime minister Sir Alec Douglas Home to a debate, safe in the knowledge that negotiations had already broken down and that Home would say no. In 1966, the incumbent Wilson had no reason to debate with the new Conservative leader Edward Heath and rejected the latter's challenge. In 1979, the Labour prime minister Jim Callaghan became the first incumbent prime minister to propose such a debate, but Margaret Thatcher, whose Conservative party was ahead in the polls, declined citing the standard collective-government objection.[9] There was similarly no reason for the now incumbent Thatcher to risk her lead in 1987 when the new Labour leader Neil Kinnock challenged her. John Major, her successor, likewise rejected Kinnock's challenge in 1992. As Major put it: 'Every party politician that expects to lose tries that trick of debates and every politician who expects to win says no.'[10] Major expected to win. He said 'no'.

Major again followed his dictum in 1997, this time when he did not expect to win, and challenged Tony Blair, the new Labour leader. In this year, Britain came closer to having a televised debate than ever before. Major and Blair both signalled their willingness to debate many months before polling day, and discussions between the broadcasters and parties ensued. However, the talks were unable to overcome a number of sticking points.[11] The two parties disagreed over the length and number of debates and whether to allow audience participation. The Conservatives were especially reluctant to involve the Liberal Democrat leader Paddy Ashdown. The talks finally collapsed amidst mutual blame and recriminations. Commenting afterwards, the BBC's chief negotiators suggested that, while the negotiations had been hindered by insufficient time and too little co-operation between broadcasters, the crucial factor had been the parties' lack of enthusiasm.[12] In particular, Labour, with its huge lead, had nothing to gain from the debates proceeding.[13]

Curiously enough, political parties and broadcasters have been able to agree terms for televised election debates that did not involve the national party leaders. In 1992, the BBC organised a three-way debate between the Conservative chancellor of the exchequer, Norman Lamont, and his Labour and Liberal Democrat counterparts. A similar debate took place in 1997, and that year also saw a televised debate between the leaders of the four main parties in Scotland (the Conservatives, Labour, the Liberal Democrats and the Scottish National Party).[14] Televised leaders' debates have also taken place before the 1999, 2003 and 2007 Scottish parliamentary elections, while the candidates for the London mayoral election debated in 2008. The parties have even organised televised debates for their own leadership elections: Labour did so in 1994, the Conservatives did so in both 2001 and 2005. But national televised leaders' debates remained elusive.

## The campaign for debates in 2010

As seen, it had become something of a ritual in recent years for at least one of the party leaders to challenge their rivals to debate with them.[15] There were few raised eyebrows, then, when David Cameron initiated the ritual in May 2007 and challenged the then soon-to-be prime minister Gordon Brown. Someone in the Labour camp ritually dismissed the challenge as 'a silly stunt'.[16] There was more grandstanding during Brown's brief honeymoon period in September 2007, when Cameron called on Brown to take part in a televised debate and even offered to 'pay for the taxi to take him to the studio'.[17] Cameron repeated his challenge again in February 2008, this time claiming that televised debates could capture 'people's imagination' and 'restore some invigoration in our politics'.[18]

Cameron's repeated challenges were driven by political calculations. He was reckoned to be a better television performer than Brown, and it was thought that debates would play to his strengths. But basing his challenge on the need to capture 'people's imagination' gave his challenge added force, especially in the wake of the 2009 MPs expenses scandal. In July 2009, the business secretary Peter Mandelson, always personally in favour of debates, hinted that Brown might accept Cameron's challenge.[19] By now, the Conservatives were well ahead in the polls, and such was Labour's standing that Brown had little to lose – and potentially much to gain – by taking part. The prime minister was allegedly planning to make an announcement himself in his forthcoming annual conference speech and was furious at Mandelson's indiscretion.[20] Both Cameron and Clegg responded enthusiastically.

At around this time, the terrestrial broadcasters, the BBC and ITV, made contact with the main parties in case Brown called an autumn election. They were conscious that previous attempts to arrange debates had failed, partly because of insufficient cooperation between the broadcasters, and partly because there had been insufficient time to complete negotiations. Whether or not the broadcasters' behind-the-scenes approach would have delivered agreement in 2010 is unclear. The parties professed willingness to debate, but they had professed willingness in the past. What is clear, however, is that the prospect of success was given a significant boost at the beginning of September by John Ryley, the Head of Sky News (one of Rupert Murdoch's 24-hour news stations). Riley wrote publicly to each of the three party leaders inviting them to 'reinvigorate our democratic process' by taking part in the 'UK's first televised Leaders' Debate'.[21] He simultaneously launched an online petition. To crank up the pressure still further, Sky News promised to offer the debate 'live and unedited' to any of its competitors and further threatened to have an empty chair in the place of any leader who declined to participate. Cameron and Clegg immediately said 'yes'. Brown's response was hesitant but suggested a willingness to discuss further.

Sky's unilateral initiative did not go down well at the BBC and ITV, who preferred to proceed by consensus. It was felt that the initiative jeopardised the discussions that had already taken place; in any event, it was unlikely that the leaders would agree to appear on a Murdoch-owned station and not the terrestrial channels. Yet, Sky News' initiative was undoubtedly a shot in the arm to the process, as it was intended to be, and made success more likely. Discussions now started, involving the broadcasters and the parties. Following separate meetings with each of the parties, a panel comprising representatives of the BBC, ITV and Sky News and senior Labour, Conservative and Liberal Democratic figures was duly convened. Its members met on an ongoing basis throughout the autumn and winter. Although there were inevitable disagreements, including over the roles of the moderator and audience, there was a shared commitment to make the debates happen. Gradually, the broadcasters' and the parties' positions on various issues moved closer together. By December, the panel had agreed on seventeen key principles to guide the debates. There would be three ninety-minute live debates, one in each full week of the election campaign, and each of the broadcasters would be responsible for producing one programme subject to a set of common rules. On 1 March 2010, all those involved finally signed up to a detailed document of seventy-six rules that would govern the broadcasts.[22]

Through lengthy negotiations, the broadcasters and parties thus achieved what had eluded their predecessors in previous elections. With the important exception of Sky New's initiative, the debates had been delivered by the broadcasters working together and by the consensual discussions between all the interested parties. Negotiations had almost certainly been helped by all the parties' collective sense that they had to engage with voters. But most importantly, the stars had aligned: all the parties finally believed that it was in their interests to take part. Labour hoped the debates would enable Brown to project his gravitas and command of detail. The Conservatives expected Cameron to shine in front of the cameras. The Liberal Democrats knew that simply by being on stage, Clegg would have an unprecedented platform to communicate with voters.

The agreement to hold prime ministerial debates unleashed a cascade of debates between other party spokespersons (see Table 7.1). A week before the start of the formal campaign, Channel 4, another terrestrial broadcaster,

TABLE 7.1   *Other televised debates during the 2010 election campaign*

| Broadcaster | Show | Date |
| --- | --- | --- |
| Channel 4 | Ask the Chancellors | 29 March 2010 |
| Sky News | Sky News Wales Debate | 18 April 2010 |
| BBC | Daily Politics, 'Foreign Affairs Debate' | 19 April 2010 |
| BBC | Daily Politics, 'The Crime Debate' | 20 April 2010 |
| ITV | Scotland Debates | 20 April 2010 |
| ITV | Welsh Leaders' Debate | 20 April 2010 |
| BBC | Daily Politics, 'The Chancellors Debate' | 21 April 2010 |
| UTV | The UTV Leaders' Debate (Northern Ireland) | 22 April 2010 |
| Sky News | Sky News Scotland Debate | 25 April 2010 |
| BBC | Daily Politics, 'The Environment Debate' | 26 April 2010 |
| BBC | Daily Politics, 'The Business Debate' | 27 April 2010 |
| BBC | Daily Politics, 'The Health Debate' | 28 April 2010 |
| BBC | The Scottish Leaders' Debate | 2 May 2010 |
| BBC | Welsh Leaders' Debate | 2 May 2010 |
| BBC | Northern Ireland Leaders' Debates | 2 May 2010 |
| BBC | Daily Politics, 'The Education Debate' | 3 May 2010 |
| BBC | Daily Politics, 'The Immigration Debate' | 4 May 2010 |
| BBC | Daily Politics, 'The Trust in Politics Debate' | 5 May 2010 |

*Note:* Channel 4's 'Ask the Chancellors' was broadcast before the start of the formal campaign.

organised *Ask the Chancellors*, a debate among the three parties' finance spokespersons, chancellor of the exchequer Alistair Darling, the Conservative shadow chancellor George Osborne and the Liberal Democrats' Vince Cable. During the campaign, the BBC's *Daily Politics* programme organised nine debates bringing together the main parties' spokespersons – and on occasion some of the smaller parties' principal spokespersons – on foreign affairs, crime, the economy (a second chancellors' debate), the environment, business, health, education, immigration and British democracy.

## Format of the leaders' debates

From the very beginning, and throughout the negotiations, the broadcasters had assumed that the debates would involve just the leaders of the three major national parties. There remained, however, the potentially thorny problem of the Scottish and Welsh nationalists. The Scottish National Party and Wales' Plaid Cymru criticised their exclusion from the debates on the grounds that both were in power in their respective devolved institutions. To fulfil their legal obligations, the broadcasters gave these parties an early opportunity to reply to the national leaders' debates. The broadcasters also held additional national debates in Scotland and Wales, as well as in Northern Ireland. Such concessions did not stop the SNP protesting to the BBC Trust and subsequently mounting an unsuccessful high-court challenge to be included in the final debate.[23]

Unlike in some US presidential election years, when up to three different debate formats have been tried, the 2010 British leaders' debates would all follow the same basic format, which was set out in the seventy-six rules. There would be a live audience, selected by the pollsters ICM to be broadly representative of the voting public, and each debate would have a different moderator, who would be responsible for keeping the leaders to agreed time limits and for ensuring a free-flowing debate. The three leaders would stand behind lecterns and would debate only with each other. Some members of the audience would be allowed to ask pre-screened questions; otherwise they were to sit and be quiet, only applauding all the leaders at the programme's end. To avoid viewers' judgements being biased by the reactions of the live audience, there were strict rules governing cutaways to the audience when leaders were speaking.

Each debate would comprise two halves, one with questions relating to pre-arranged themes, the other with questions on potentially any issue. The first debate, to be produced by ITV, would have as its theme 'domestic affairs' (see Table 7.2). The second debate, to be produced by Sky News, would have as its theme 'international affairs'. The third debate, the BBC's, would centre on 'economic affairs'. It was up to each broadcaster to compile a list of both themed and unthemed questions. To that end, each established their own selection panel to choose from among the many

TABLE 7.2    *The prime ministerial debates*

| Broadcaster | Date | Moderator | Location | Theme and topics[1] | Audience |
|---|---|---|---|---|---|
| ITV1 | 15 April 2010 | Alastair Stewart | Manchester | Domestic affairs including: NHS, education, immigration, law and order, family, constitution, trust in politics, political reform. | 9.7m |
| Sky News[2] | 22 April 2010 | Adam Boulton | Bristol | International affairs including: international relations, Afghanistan, Iraq, Iran, Middle East, UK defence, international terrorism, Europe, climate change, China, international development. | 4.2m |
| BBC1[3] | 29 April 2010 | David Dimbleby | Birmingham | Economic affairs including: financing of public services, taxation, debt, deficit, public finances, recession, recovery, banking and finance, business, pensions, jobs. | 8.6m |

*Note:* [1]Permissable topics according to clause 65, 'Programme format agreed by all parties 1st March 2010'. [2]Simultaneously broadcast on BBC News and later broadcast by BBC2 on the same night. [3]Also shown on BBC News BBC HD and Sky News. Audience figures cover all broadcasts and are those provided by the Broadcasters' Audience Research Board (BARB).

questions submitted by both the audience and the wider public. Their choices had to meet the broadcasters' legal obligations to provide fair and impartial coverage – no question could focus on the policies of just one party, for example – and the panels also had to select topical questions that would make for lively television. All three panels met in private, and their final decisions were made just ahead of the broadcasts.[24]

The agreed rules also contained strict time limits on the leaders' contributions. At the beginning of each programme, the three leaders – who would draw lots beforehand to determine the order – would take it in turns to make a one-minute opening statement. The leaders would also have an opportunity to make a one-and-a-half minute closing statement at the end of each pro-gramme. They would also be strictly limited in how long they could talk in response to individual questions. Each leader would have one minute to reply to each question and would then be given an additional minute to respond to the others' answers. A four-minute free debate would then ensue. To make sure that no leader hogged the stage, the broadcasters would bring in an inde-pendent time keeper to help the moderator ensure balance. In case any party felt their leader was being treated unfairly, they would be able to contact the broadcasters on specially installed hotlines during the programme.

## The debates

As the broadcasters prepared for the debates, so too did the parties. Even before the rules were finally agreed, Labour and the Conservatives had sought advice from those in the US with relevant experience of planning for and performing in front of the cameras. Joel Benenson, who had helped to prepare Barack Obama for the 2008 presidential debates, advised Gordon Brown's team. Two other former advisers to Obama, Anita Dunn and Bill Knapp, advised David Cameron.[25] With a month to go, the three leaders began their rehearsals. Alastair Campbell, Tony Blair's former director of communications, played Cameron in Brown's rehearsals, while Theo Bertram, a special adviser, played Clegg. For the Conservatives, Michael Gove, the party's education spokesperson, played Brown, while Jeremy Hunt, the culture spokesperson, played Clegg. For the Liberal Democrats Chris Huhne played Brown, while David Laws played Cameron.[26]

### Expectations

In February, an Ipsos MORI poll found that 60 per cent of respondents agreed that the performance of the leaders in the debates would be very important or fairly important in helping them to decide who to vote for.[27] The belief that an unusually large number of voters had yet to make up their minds ahead of the election, coupled with the novelty of the medium, raised the stakes on the eve of the first debate. It was widely supposed that if any of the leaders performed better or worse than expected, it could be a 'game changer' that would alter the course of the campaign and possibly the outcome of the election.

The burden of expectation fell heaviest on the shoulders of David Cameron. The Tory leader was an accomplished and stylish television per-former. In 2005, he had surprisingly defeated David Davis, the then front-runner in the Conservative leadership contest, partly as a result of assured performances in front of the cameras. His party hoped that Cameron would be able to frame the election as a referendum on Labour's performance and position the Conservatives as the agent of 'change'. Some wondered, however, whether Labour's gibes about Cameron's lack of substance were true and whether Brown – who Tony Blair once described as Labour's 'clunking fist' – would knock him out.

Brown's goal was to frame the election as a choice between the major parties rather than as a referendum on his government. He already had some limited experience of television debates having participated in the chancellors' debate in 1997. But his brief on that occasion was narrower and the event lower profile. In 2010, some of his more optimistic supporters thought that Brown's mastery of policy detail would expose Cameron's inexperience. Yet even Brown's closest friends realised that it was precisely his command of detail – and, in particular, his tendency to recite statistics – that could make him appear unsympathetic. The prime minister's demeanour and odd facial expressions, especially his infamous rictus smile, were also thought to count against him. He had a 'radio face', as Neil Kinnock, the former Labour leader, noted. To alter such perceptions Brown appeared on a television chat show just before the election campaign. He captured headlines, some favourable, some cynical, by shedding a tear as he recounted the death of his baby daughter (just as Cameron had done when discussing the death of his son). Nevertheless, Brown was clearly ill at ease with the style-conscious politics of the sort that people associated with debate performances.

Nick Clegg was simply delighted to share a platform and equal billing with one prime minister and one potential prime minister. 'We want Nick just to be Nick' said one member of the Liberal Democrat campaign team. Otherwise, Clegg was encumbered with few expectations. Such was the advantage of being the largely unknown third man, or 'invisible Nick' as some of his colleagues had labelled him.

Voters' expectations ahead of the debates reflected their perceptions of the three leaders' qualities and assumptions about what influenced their fellow voters. They also inevitably reflected partisan loyalties. The prevailing political mood was decidedly unsympathetic to Labour, as Chapter 6 describes in detail, and the party entered the campaign behind the Conservatives. Moreover, voters had already had the opportunity to observe Brown versus Cameron in PMQs for three years. Even the most loyal Labourite had to concede that the Conservative leader was capable of delivering a devastating sound bite. Not surprisingly, an ICM poll fielded at the beginning of the campaign found that Cameron was expected to perform best in the debates by 44 per cent of the voting public, Brown by 20 per cent.[28] Fully 80 per cent of Conservative voters expected their man to win. Among Labour supporters 51 per cent expected Brown to triumph, and, tellingly, 32 per cent of them expected Cameron to win. Clegg, who had risen without trace before becoming Liberal Democrat leader in December 2007, hardly registered in the public consciousness. A mere 13 per cent of respondents in the same survey expected him to perform best.

## The first debate: 'I agree with Nick'

The first live election debate took place on the second Thursday of the campaign on 15 April in Manchester in the North West of England. ITV, the host broadcaster, was understandably anxious for their programme to be a success. Not surprisingly, the debate received extensive (and possibly excessive) attention in the media. For that reason, and because first impressions matter, it merits special attention.

As with the two subsequent encounters, this first debate conveyed information about both the parties' policies and their leaders' personal qualities. It is difficult to disentangle the influence of one from the other, but it is important to try to do so. The substance of the debates merits more detailed analysis than can be provided here, but the leaders' opening statements provide a good indication of their general pitches.

Clegg spoke first. He combined populism with a promise of change:

> You're going to be told tonight by these two [Brown and Cameron] that the only choice you can make is between two old parties who've been running things for years. I'm here to persuade you that there is an alternative. I think we have a fantastic opportunity to do things differently for once. If we do things differently, we can create the fair society, the fair country we all want: a fair tax system, better schools, an economy no longer held hostage by greedy bankers, decent, open politics.[29]

Brown's opening statement predictably emphasised what he thought was his strongest card: his experience and ability to steer the economy through the current crisis:

> Now, every promise you hear from each of us this evening depends on one thing: a strong economy. And this is the defining year. Get the decisions right now, and we can have secure jobs, we can have standards of living rising, and we can have everybody better off. Get the decisions wrong now, and we could have a double-dip recession.

Cameron spoke third. He tried to reassure voters that he was not a risk to public services and promised change.

> Now, there is a big choice at this election: we can go on as we are, or we can say no, Britain can do much better; we can deal with our debts, we can get our economy growing and avoid this jobs tax [a rise in national insurance], and we can build a bigger society. But we can only do this if we recognise we

need [to] join together, we need to come together, we need to recognise we're all in this together. Now, not everything Labour has done in the last 13 years has been wrong – they've done some good things and I would keep those, but we need change, and it's that change I want to help to lead.

After the opening statements the programme moved on to the four themed questions, which covered immigration, crime, MPs' credibility and testing in schools. These were then followed by four general questions relating to the budget deficit, the equipping of the armed forces, healthcare and long-term care of the elderly.

Although the questions structured the debate, it was the leaders' responses that mattered most. By utilising specialist computer software, it was possible to undertake a fuller content analysis of how much was said by whom about what.[30] Table 7.3 shows a breakdown of the first debate – and the second and third debates – in terms of the proportion of sentences that reflect more or less the three designated themes – 'domestic affairs', 'international affairs' and 'economic affairs' – as well as two further issues of particular interest in this election, 'immigration' and 'political reform'. It reports the proportion of content for both the debate as a whole, which included

TABLE 7.3   *Content of prime ministerial debates by theme (%)*

|  | Total debate | Brown | Cameron | Clegg |
|---|---|---|---|---|
| *First debate* | | | | |
| Economy | 14.6 | 19.3 | 18.6 | 12.4 |
| Immigration | 4.6 | 5.4 | 4.0 | 5.7 |
| Political reform | 3.4 | 6.6 | 2.9 | 3.6 |
| Other domestic | 27.6 | 38.9 | 32.4 | 27.3 |
| Foreign & defence policy | 6.4 | 10.4 | 5.5 | 5.0 |
| *Second debate* | | | | |
| Economy | 15.4 | 28.2 | 14.3 | 12.5 |
| Immigration | 3.3 | 1.5 | 5.0 | 4.7 |
| Political reform | 3.2 | 3.4 | 3.9 | 3.2 |
| Other domestic | 13.3 | 17.6 | 17.1 | 11.9 |
| Foreign & defence policy | 12.4 | 17.2 | 13.9 | 11.8 |
| *Third debate* | | | | |
| Economy | 37.2 | 61.1 | 38.1 | 33.9 |
| Immigration | 3.5 | 3.6 | 2.9 | 5.1 |
| Political reform | 1.5 | 3.2 | 0.7 | 1.2 |
| Other domestic | 24.4 | 31.7 | 27.9 | 22.8 |
| Foreign & defence policy | 1.6 | 2.3 | 2.2 | 1.6 |

*Note:* Figures represent the percentage of sentences in the debate transcripts devoted to the respective themes. The analysis is carried out by means of a computer assisted computer package, HAMLET II, according to categories constructed by the authors. The columns do not total 100 since some sentences mention more than one issue. See text for further information.

audience and facilitator input, and also for the aggregated contributions by Brown, Cameron and Clegg. For methodological reasons, the domestic-theme percentages exclude references to immigration and political reform, even though the official 'domestic theme' specifically covered questions on these issues. Aggregating these three categories provides a loose approximation of the content that accorded with the official theme, but it is only a loose approximation. During the debates, for example, the issue of immigration was talked about in both a domestic- and foreign-policy context.

As might be expected, domestic policy dominated the leaders' contributions. Table 7.3 suggests that, according to the computerised content analysis, Brown focussed most on the designated theme of domestic policy in the first debate (50.9 per cent when the 'immigration', 'political reform' and 'other domestic' categories are aggregated), Cameron was somewhat less focussed on domestic policy (39.3 per cent) and Clegg least (36.6 per cent). Indeed, a large portion of Clegg's contributions did not fall into any of the five categories.

Throughout their responses, the leaders returned to their initial pitches again and again. Cameron criticised the planned rise in national insurance, which he labelled 'the jobs tax', and he stressed the need to make early progress on reducing the deficit. Fending off claims that his party's proposed immediate £6 billion spending cuts would curtail the economic recovery, he noted that that sum was just 'one out of every £100 the government spends'. Brown returned again and again to the short-term risks from cutting public spending and the threat of a double-dip recession. Clegg professed the need for honesty, especially when it came to handling the deficit: '[W]e all know we're going to have to make cuts. The question at this election is who is trying to be straight with you about the scale of those cuts.'

Brown's performance probably did little to alter the public's perceptions of his qualities. The prime minister did not look comfortable. He was the least likely of the leaders to look directly into the camera and the least likely to appear to speak to the audience beyond the studio. At times his intonation suggested that he was addressing a party rally or a rowdy House of Commons. Brown was also the gloomiest of the three leaders. His opening statement was portentous, his contributions were peppered with references to 'risk', 'fear' and 'concern', and he seemed unable to smile spontaneously or naturally. He was also the most likely to interrupt or to try to get the last word: 'This is not Question Time', he goaded Cameron, 'It's answer time, David'. Such an approach served to reinforce his reputation as a bully.

Cameron, like Brown, looked uneasy throughout the debate. Perhaps the weight of expectation was taking its toll. Like Brown, Cameron addressed the studio audience most of the time, though he looked directly in the lens during his opening and closing remarks. He also paid tribute to various groups – including people who worked in the NHS, teachers and soldiers – but his performance sounded somewhat scripted.

Clegg's performance was a considerable success. Unlike the other leaders, he usually talked directly to the camera. He appeared entirely at ease, engaging with the audience and interacting in a wholly natural and apparently unscripted manner. He made a point of returning to the question and singling out the questioner by name to establish a rapport. He moved his hands in order to emphasise points. Most importantly, he expressed anger at the inability of previous governments to reform the political system. Consciously or unconsciously he positioned himself as the spokesman for the angry voter.

During the broadcast, various polling organisations used 'people metering' methods to track responses to the debates. Participants were given a control and told to press one key when they liked what they heard and another when they did not. The rating or 'worm' could then be superimposed on television footage to provide evidence about the precise moment when responses changed.[31] Ipsos MORI, as well as others, found that little Brown said appeared to move the electorate.[32] Whenever he talked about the government's record his worm went down; otherwise, his worm remained stubbornly flat. It was as if people had already made up their minds about him. The other leaders were able to elicit more positive responses. Cameron's statement about the need to limit non-EU immigration, for example, was very well-received. Clegg also appeared to do well, especially in his criticisms of the other two parties: 'I'm not sure if you're like me, but the more they attack each other, the more they sound exactly the same'. Up jumped the worm.

One very striking feature of the first debate was the failure of the leaders to follow up on the campaign themes of their party manifestos. Brown rarely mentioned 'fairness', despite the fact that the Labour manifesto promised *Fairness for All*. Indeed, Clegg used the word more often than Brown. And although Cameron had launched his idea of the 'big society' in his manifesto, he mentioned it only in his opening and closing statements. The idea was otherwise lost both in responses to questions and in the ensuing debates.

The most striking feature of the debate, however, was the reluctance of the two major party leaders to criticise Clegg. Cameron did raise questions about Liberal Democrat attitudes towards those convicted of criminal offences but this was a mild exception. The easy ride may have reflected an assumption that Clegg was a sideshow to the confrontation between Brown and Cameron. Yet, it also undoubtedly reflected the polls, which indicated that a hung parliament was a likely outcome and that the Liberal Democrats might be pivotal. Brown in particular was keen to assert his – hitherto hidden – affinity with the Liberal Democrats. 'I agree with Nick', he declared on three occasions, and twice he claimed that 'Nick agrees with me.' Nick's reactions suggested otherwise.

The immediate polls largely confirmed the message of the people-metering exercises. Although the details varied from polling organisation to polling organisation, Clegg was generally judged the clear winner, Cameron was generally placed second and Brown was generally placed third. YouGov's findings, reported in Table 7.4, show that Clegg still trailed in third place as the best prime minister in people's minds, but his 26 per cent was undoubtedly a major improvement on the 12 per cent recorded in March. Nick Clegg had suddenly become *the* star of the campaign.

TABLE 7.4    *Public responses to the television debates (% agreeing with statement)*

(a)  'Leaving aside your own party preferences, who do you think performed best overall in tonight's debates?'

|  | 15 April | 22 April | 29 April |
|---|---|---|---|
| Gordon Brown | 19 | 29 | 25 |
| David Cameron | 29 | 36 | 41 |
| Nick Clegg | 51 | 32 | 32 |
| Don't know | 2 | 3 | 2 |

(b)  'Which of them was most evasive, and least willing to give straight answers to straight questions?'

|  | 15 April | 22 April | 29 April |
|---|---|---|---|
| Gordon Brown | 48 | 30 | 29 |
| David Cameron | 44 | 45 | 49 |
| Nick Clegg | 4 | 21 | 19 |
| Don't know | 4 | 4 | 3 |

(c)  'Who would make the best prime minister?'

|  | 15 April | 22 April | 29 April |
|---|---|---|---|
| Gordon Brown | 29 | 31 | 28 |
| David Cameron | 39 | 40 | 41 |
| Nick Clegg | 26 | 25 | 25 |
| Don't know | 6 | 6 | 5 |

*Source:* YouGov survey for *The Sun*, available at http://today.yougov.co.uk/sites/today.yougov.co.uk/files/YG-Archives-Pol-SunDebate3-100429.pdf. Last accessed on 26 August 2010.

The apparent effect on the opinion polls was dramatic. Figure 7.1 displays average vote intentions as recorded in various polls for each day of the campaign. Such daily polling enables precise identification of turning points and assessments of specific campaign events such as the debates, which are represented by vertical lines. The results show that Liberal Democrat support leapt by around 8 points in the two or three days after the first debate. In most polls, Clegg's party pushed Labour into third place, and in a small number of others it actually came out on top. Nothing had been seen like this since the heady days of the early 1980s when the SDP–Liberal Alliance had taken advantage of the Thatcher government's unpopularity and Labour's unelectability to rise like a shooting star, only to crash back to

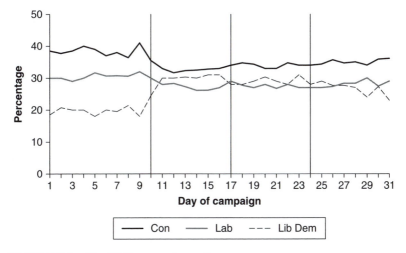

FIGURE 7.1   *The 2010 campaign polls*

*Source*: UK Polling Report, 'Voting intention', available at http://ukpollingreport.co.uk/blog/voting-intention.

*Note*: Average findings of all polls (by survey end date) published by Angus Reid, BPIX, Communicate, ComRes, Harris, ICM, Ipsos MORI, Marketing Sciences, Opinium, Populus, TNS BMRB and YouGov between 6 April 2010 and 5 May 2010. The final voting intentions on day 31 of the campaign are the actual results. The vertical dotted lines represent the three debates.

earth later. But Clegg's success was just three weeks away from polling day. In late April 2010, Britain appeared to be within days of a genuine three-party system in which the Liberal Democrats might hold up to 100 seats and act as the 'kingmaker' in the new parliament, choosing between supporting the Conservatives or Labour.

## The second debate: turning fire on Nick

Voters had the opportunity to learn much about the leaders' abilities and qualities during the first debate. There was probably little more that they could learn from the second and third debates. But these later debates did allow the public to learn gradually more about the parties' policies and strategies, and what they liked and disliked about them.

The two largest parties certainly learnt from the first debate. Previously, they had paid little attention to the Liberal Democrats. The size of the Clegg boost forced them to respond. The Conservatives in particular became aware that the rise in the Liberal Democrat vote might deny them an outright victory, and they promised to subject Clegg's policies, especially on immigration and defence, to greater scrutiny. Labour's response to Clegg's success was ostensibly more positive. With his party struggling to maintain second place in the polls, Brown called for Labour and Liberal Democrat voters to combine to form a 'progressive alliance' that could keep the Conservatives from winning.[33] He hoped to attract voters inspired by Clegg's earlier rhetoric of political reform and prepare the ground for a possible coalition.

The second debate, hosted by Sky News, was a glitzy affair that took place in Bristol in the South West of England on 22 April, the third Thursday of the campaign. Before the debate the *Daily Telegraph*, a Conservative-leaning newspaper, had tried to prick the Cleggmania bubble by running a story alleging that Clegg had received payments from party donors directly into his private bank account.[34] As potential scandals go, it was pretty meagre stuff, and it only briefly interrupted the parties' preparations.

In this debate it was Brown's turn to deliver the first opening statement. His remarks contained an admission that he lacked some of the gloss of his opponents but he sought to turn this to his advantage:

> This may have the feel of a TV popularity contest, but in truth, this is an election about Britain's future, a fight for your future, and for your jobs. If it's all about style and PR, count me out. If it's about the big decisions, if it's about judgment, it's delivering a better future for this country, I'm your man.[35]

The admission did not have the effect intended. The evidence from Ipsos MORI's worm indicates that Brown's approval actually fell as he tried to sell himself.

Cameron's opening statement was generally a refined version of what he had delivered a week before. He again warned of the 'jobs tax', he again pledged to build a 'big and strong society', and he again promised 'real change'. Clegg's opening statement also echoed his own from the previous week. He again contrasted the Liberal Democrats with the other two 'old parties' and emphasised his party's commitment to nuclear disarmament and tackling climate change.

The second debate's theme was international affairs. The themed questions covered Britain's relations with the European Union, future British participation in anti-terrorist operations, the leaders' use of sustainable forms of transport and the Pope's impending visit to Britain.[36] The four general questions addressed the parliamentary expenses scandal (again), the adequacy of state pensions, political cooperation in the event of a hung parliament and immigration (again). Despite the supposed focus on global issues, the leaders seemed to prefer talking about domestic politics and the economy. Table 7.3 suggests that as little as 12 per cent of the programme content focussed on international affairs. Brown spoke most about this theme but even he focussed more on economic and domestic issues.

In marked contrast to the first debate, both Brown and Cameron turned their fire onto the Liberal Democrats. Brown criticised Clegg's attitudes towards the US and the British nuclear deterrent, whereas Cameron attacked Clegg's policies on Europe and immigration. But once again the two leaders failed to develop their campaign themes or provide a compelling narrative. Cameron mentioned his 'big society' in the opening and closing remarks but did little to incorporate the phrase in his other answers. Later polls suggested few knew much about this idea.[37] Brown did little to expand on his campaign theme of fairness and only addressed the issue indirectly when criticising Conservative plans to abolish inheritance tax on estates below £1 million.

Clegg's major achievement in this debate may have been to reassure voters about what might happen in the event of a hung parliament. He declared: 'I do think there is potential for politicians to work with each other. Don't believe all these ludicrous scare stories about markets and political Armageddon'. For those looking for clues as to what might happen in the event of a hung parliament, Clegg added:

> [I]f politicians are going to talk to each other, then I think what we need to do is be upfront about what our priorities are. We need to be upfront about what we would seek in any discussion with other parties. I've been very upfront, dealing obviously with the fiscal deficit, we've been much more open about how we would do that than the other two parties. But also tax reform, educational reform, political reform.

As the prospect of a coalition government increased, so the issue of financial stability and dealing with the deficit appeared to have become more of a priority for the Liberal Democrats. In the circumstances this was hardly surprising, but few commentators seemed to notice it at the time.

The Ipsos MORI people-metering exercise indicated that Cameron again scored well on immigration in the second debate. However, his suggestion that the Conservatives were best placed to offer change did not go down well among panel members. The exercise also indicated that people generally responded negatively to Brown's attacks on Cameron and particularly Clegg. One of Brown's jibes provided the Liberal Democrat leader with his own *Love Actually* moment. Responding to Brown's criticism of his supposed anti-Americanism, Clegg said: 'I have a simple attitude towards our relationship with America. It is an immensely important, special relationship, but it shouldn't be a one-way street. We shouldn't always automatically do what our American friends tell us to do.' Clegg's ratings jumped.

YouGov polling figures reported in Table 7.4 suggest that Cameron emerged the narrow winner after this debate, though he was – by some margin – also adjudged the least likely to give straight answers. Other polls suggested that Clegg had won again, but less emphatically than before. All the polls agreed that Brown had done better than in the first debate but was still trailing behind Cameron and Clegg. The polls also suggested that this debate had no dramatic impact on the parties' overall appeals. As Figure 7.1 shows, there was no bounce for any of the contenders as there had been for Clegg after the first debate. With the parties still neck and neck, the anticipation ahead of the last debate was now all the greater.

## The third debate: Gordon's last chance

The third and final debate was hosted by the BBC and took place in Birmingham in the Midlands on 29 April, the fourth Thursday of the campaign. Its theme was the central issue of the election, as well as Gordon Brown's specialist subject: the economy.

Brown's hopes of using this debate as a springboard were shattered by a bizarre event the day before. On a trip to Rochdale in northern England, Brown was overheard referring to a woman he had just spoken to, Gillian Duffy, a pensioner and Labour voter, as 'bigoted' after she had made a number of remarks about immigrants. The prime minister's words were picked up as he drove away by a Sky microphone that he had forgotten to remove. Unfortunately for him, the Sky feed was being used as a pool for all the broadcasters, who immediately relayed Brown's words to the nation and to Mrs Duffy. The words were also replayed to a visibly mortified Brown during a live radio interview. He later issued a series of abject and very public apologies. In retrospect, Brown's gaffe is most noteworthy for the coverage it generated rather than its impact on the election. 'Bigotgate', as the incident was called, fired journalists' imagination far more than it did the voters'. One writer likened the media's response to a 'pack of shrieking gibbons'.[38]

The furore discomfited the prime minister, but he dealt with it calmly in his opening remarks in Birmingham: 'There's a lot to this job, and as you saw yesterday, I don't get all of it right'.[39] With that admission out of the way, he went on to make clear his well-worn pitch to the country: 'but I do know how to run the economy in good times and in bad.'

As with the second debate, this final encounter again allowed the public to learn a little more about the parties' policies. The themed questions selected by the BBC addressed the need for honesty about government spending cuts, taxes for those on average earnings, bankers' bonuses and the decline in manufacturing. The unthemed questions covered immigration (yet again), housing, the abuse of state benefits and education opportunities for children in deprived areas. The designated theme, in this case the economy, featured to far a greater extent than it had in either of the two previous debates (see Table 7.3). Over a third of this debate was on this theme, and all contributors spoke at length about it. Brown's comfort in talking about the economy was especially evident: according to the content analysis of the transcript, nearly two-thirds of his contributions related to economic matters, far in excess of either Cameron's or Clegg's contributions.

On this occasion Cameron did refer to his 'big society' in response to a question, but he did not introduce it in his opening remarks and failed to follow it up in his closing remarks. He also repeated his argument that his planned £6 billion spending cuts merely meant 'saving one out of every £100 that the government spends'. Brown again largely failed to follow up on the Labour manifesto's emphasis on fairness. And he again repeatedly emphasised that the Tories' planned cuts could trigger a 'double dip recession'. He was also more likely to quote precise economic figures, which made him look either knowledgeable or boring depending on one's predispositions. Labour strategists must have despaired.

Clegg played his usual hand, attacking the political system. 'Can I try to move beyond the political point-scoring?', he asked. But by now this sort of trick appeared tired. Clegg also took the opportunity to address the financial deficit and raised the spectre of cuts and tax rises. He promised not to fool the audience 'into thinking that just efficiency savings are enough. You can't fill the black hole by just a few savings on pot plants and paper clips in Whitehall.'

Brown's performance was better in this debate, but it was on his specialist subject and still fell short of expectations. The general verdict of the polls was that Cameron had won, despite the finding that he was again – by some margin – seen as the most evasive of the leaders (see Table 7.4). This verdict raises questions about what the instant polls were actually measuring. They probably reflected the public mood of the time rather than objective judgements about the leaders' performances: fewer people seemed receptive to Labour's message that national insurance rises were the best and the fairest way to deal with the deficit. Brown and Labour were swimming against the tide.

## The impact of the debates

And so the debates were over. The election was still a week away but the campaign now lost much of its sense of purpose. The media gave the appearance of suffering from collective withdrawal symptoms. So too did the parties. When the last debate was over, one commentator asked, half tongue-in-cheek: 'What are we going to do for the rest of the election campaign? What are they going to do, the leaders, the strategists and the entourages?'[40] The debates had structured the campaign; indeed, in some respects, they had been the campaign. Now all that was left was to take stock.

## Impact on the media's campaign coverage

There was a self-fulfilling collective expectation that the debates would dominate the media's campaign coverage. On the one hand, the debates had enormous novelty value. On the other hand, they created an obvious weekly news cycle with one debate taking place in each of the first, second and third full weeks of the campaign. Incidents like 'Bigotgate' offered distractions, but the debates provided the central campaign story. News coverage before the debates always looked forward towards them; news coverage afterwards always looked back. Many journalists and commentators were genuinely excited by the debates and wanted to write about them. It also helped that the broadcasters wished to capitalise on the time and energy they had invested in securing them. ITV, Sky News and the BBC all wanted to make the most of their historic achievement.

The saturation coverage of the debates was at times otherworldly. Journalists gave the impression of behaving as if the debates were all that mattered to the public. Before and after each programme, there were extended discussions in print, online and over the airwaves about who would win or lose, or who had won and lost, and what it all meant. Commentators were quick to pass judgement, and their instant verdicts affected the subsequent mood of the campaign. Some actively sought to influence the mood by passing partisan and sometime bizarre judgements to the effect that their favoured man had won convincingly. Given the lack of knock-out blows, it was hard to square such judgements with reality. Huge importance was attached to instant polls, and to what individuals using Twitter and Facebook were saying, even if most social-media users only ever talked to likeminded social-media users.[41] Back in 1992, before the advent of instant online-polling technology, one commentator had said of debates: 'the public won't make up their minds until pundits and commentators decide who won the debate. Then the public will decide.'[42] Not now, it seemed. Pundits and commentators were making up their minds after the public had decided.

## Impact on the parties

If journalists decided in advance that the debates would dominate the campaign, so too did the party strategists. At the local level, campaigning went on much as usual. At the national level, energies were focused on preparing for the debates and campaigning around them. Visits, speeches, interviews and policy launches were all carefully choreographed to fit with the debate timetable. The parties also took pains to ensure their people were on hand in 'spin alley' to provide an instant and highly favourable analysis immediately after the event. The post-debate spin was usually in full swing before the programmes had ended. The instant polls sometimes made this task harder, especially for Labour spin doctors who had to contest the evidence that Clegg and Cameron were ahead of Brown.

As the campaign unfolded, the political parties showed some willingness to learn from each debate. By the end of the third debate, all the leaders, including Brown, appeared much more comfortable with the format and better able to use it to make their case. The parties' strategies were also flexible. After the first debate, Labour and the Conservatives turned their fire on the Liberal Democrats and started to treat them not only as a serious competitor but also as a potential partner in the event of a hung parliament. Clegg's success provided further motivation for Liberal Democrat activists as they revised their expectations. It may also have caused the Conservatives to shift their focus away from Conservative–Liberal Democrat marginals, which would now be harder to win, to Conservative–Labour contests. Indeed, Clegg's first-debate upset led many Conservatives to question Cameron's judgement in agreeing to debate in the first place. He had been ahead in the polls, and some senior colleagues were reported as saying that it was Clegg's performance that cost the party an outright majority.[43]

## Impact on the public

The debates undoubtedly attracted a great deal of attention from the watching public. Despite concerns that the rules would stifle debate and produce dull television, many voters tuned in to watch the leaders interact with each other. The audiences varied between 9.7 million for the first, 4.2 million for the second (not broadcast live on terrestrial free-to-air television) and 8.6 million for the third, far larger than the audiences who tune in to watch PMQs. Furthermore, many of those who did not watch the debates would have seen or heard clips on the various news reports on television and radio, or read about the debates in the newspapers or on the internet.

The debates stimulated interest in politics and, if some are to be believed, may even have saved the election from the clutches of the prevailing anti-politics mood. Survey data from Ipsos MORI show a remarkable jump in the proportion of voters who reported being interested in election news during the campaign. A week after polling day in 2010, 41 per cent said they had been very interested in such news, compared with 19 per cent in 2001, 12 per cent in 1997 and 13 per cent in 1992.[44] Some of that interest was almost certainly a consequence of the debates. Nick Clegg's performances in particular aroused enthusiasm, especially amongst younger voters, and he was warmly greeted by crowds and audiences wherever he spoke.[45] However, given the explosion of television channels, there were clear limits on the ability of the debates to draw in new voters. In 2010, those who wanted to opt out of all election coverage could still exercise this choice by watching satellite channels that contained little or no real coverage of the election. And at the end of the day, turnout in 2010 increased only slightly from 61.5 per cent in 2005 to 65.1 per cent in what was a close election, when turnout would have been expected to increase anyway.

The debates themselves probably had a small effect on voters' choices. Most individuals were likely to have made their mind up before watching them, though according to Ipsos MORI, a larger proportion of voters in 2010, 43 per cent, claimed to have decided which party to vote for during the campaign than the 34 per cent in 2005.[46] For interested viewers, the debates contained a great deal of information about the issues at stake and – despite Brown's comments – did not focus excessively on style. But the leaders were not always clear with their central messages, sometimes because their messages were not always clear. Few people knew much about David Cameron's 'big society' before the first debate, for example. Few people knew much about it after the third. Likewise, few voters probably understood Brown's warnings about why the Conservatives' proposed spending cuts might trigger a double-dip recession or how Clegg proposed to fill the 'black hole' of Britain's structural deficit.

Most importantly, of course, there were no knock-out blows. A glance back to Figure 7.1 suggests that, after all the ups and downs, the Tories and Labour ended up on 6 May not far from where they had started on 6 April. The rise in support for the Liberal Democrats after the first debate cannot be doubted but its significance can. It may well have been an artefact of media-priming effects and the tendency for people to say they would vote for the party whose leader they had been told had won the debate. At any rate, the last three election campaigns – in 1997, 2001 and 2005 – all witnessed increases in support of around 3 to 4 points for the Liberal Democrats, and this is exactly what happened in 2010. According to this rule of thumb the debates may not have had a significant effect, separate from general campaign exposure, on the party's share of the vote. The campaign would obviously have unfolded very differently without the debates but there is little evidence to support the contention that the Conservatives failed to secure an outright majority because of Clegg's performance in the first debate. It is perhaps worth noting that at the March 2010 Political Studies Association conference in Edinburgh, two directors of the authoritative British Election Study gave different presentations based on very different models, both forecasting a hung parliament.[47] Their long-term predictions made ahead of the campaign were entirely correct.

## Conclusion: debates and British elections

Although the debates defined the 2010 campaign, and although Nick Clegg's exposure in them probably prepared the ground in the public's mind for his party entering into coalition with David Cameron's Conservatives, their impact on the actual election outcome was probably marginal. Their long-term impact, however, is likely to be significant. Televised prime ministerial debates are here to stay. Party leaders will find it impossible not to take part in future debates, and parties and the media will plan campaigns and campaign coverage respectively around them.

That is not to say the debate format in 2010 is here to stay. The parties and broadcasters may well choose to relax some of the rules to allow greater audience participation and more free-flowing debate. Moreover, thought will need to be give to the involvement of other parties – notably the Greens whose leader Caroline Lucas became their first MP in 2010 – which will almost certainly fight harder to be involved in any future debates. Having seen how Clegg's exposure boosted the Liberal Democrats after the first debate, they may want similar treatment. Thought will also need to be given to how any future debates accommodate coalition partners. If the current Conservative–Liberal Democrat coalition holds until the next election, and especially if both parties hope for it to continue afterwards, it may be awkward for Cameron and Clegg to debate with each other in front of the cameras.

Finally, and perhaps most importantly, politicians and party strategists now believe that debates have the potential to change the game, and this belief will alter their behaviour.[48] A good performance can boost a leader's authority, while a poor performance can greatly undermine it. At any rate, party leaders will probably train even more thoroughly for future debates. And parties may well select future leaders on the basis of how well they are expected to perform in this particular arena. Alistair Darling might have made a good prime minister in the Clement Attlee mould, but it was Ed Miliband, a more confident television performer, who became the new Labour leader in September 2010. If British democracy continues to follow the American lead in this respect, the quality of politics and government could become poorer. Engaging voters requires a touch of the circus. It would be unfortunate, however, if voters were simultaneously to be deprived of bread.

## Endnotes

1   See, for example, Daniel Finkelstein, 'A presidential leader in No 10? Bring him on', *The Times*, 10 February 2010. The evidence on the 'presidentialisation' of British politics is mixed. While election campaigns have become increasingly focused on the leader, the nature of Britain's parliamentary system makes talk of a British presidency misleading. See Richard Heffernan and Paul Webb, 'The British Prime Minister: much more than "first among equals"', in Thomas Poguntke and Paul Webb, eds, *The Presidentialization of Politics: A Comparative Study of Modern Democracies* (Oxford: Oxford University Press, 2005), pp. 26–63.

2   Toby Helm, 'Parties race to harness new media as poll battle begins', *Observer*, 3 January 2010.

3  Andy Williamson, '2010: the internet election that wasn't', *Political Insight*, 1 (2010): 58–60.

4  A similar phrase provided the title of a short comment on the 2005 election campaign. See Philip Davies 'no election debates please, we're British', *Contemporary Review*, 286 (2005): 257–62.

5  For an excellent overview of American debates, see Alan Schroeder, *Presidential Debates: Fifty Years of High-Risk TV*, 2nd edn (New York: Colombia University Press, 2008).

6  It was the Roman poet Juvenal who coined the phrase 'bread and circuses', or *panem et circenses*, in his *Satires*. Juvenal was suggesting that his fellow Romans had given up their political responsibilities and become concerned only with cheap food and frivolous entertainment.

7  Andrew Rawnsley, 'Will TV debates change face of election?', *Observer*, 4 October 2009. See also House of Commons Standard Note SN/PC/05241, *Televising Leaders or Prime Ministerial Debates*, available at: www.parliament.uk/documents/commons/lib/research/briefings/snpc-05241.pdf (last accessed on 26 August 2010).

8  Martin Harrison, 'Television and Radio', in D.E. Butler and Anthony King, *The British General Election of 1964* (London: Macmillan, 1965), pp. 156–84, at pp. 157–8.

9  Michael Cockerell, 'Why 2010 will see the first TV leaders election debate', *BBC News* website, 10 April 2010, available at: news.bbc.co.uk/1/hi/uk_politics/election_2010/8612153.stm (last accessed on 26 August 2010).

10  Quoted in Cockerell, 'Why 2010 will see the first TV leaders election debate'.

11  Richard Tait, 'The debate that never happened: television and the party leaders', in Ivor Crewe, Brian Gosschalk and John Bartle, eds, *Political Communications: Why Labour Won the General Election of 1997* (London: Frank Cass, 1998), pp. 205–16.

12  Tony Hall and Anne Sloman, 'The televised debate that never was', *Independent*, 2 July 1997.

13  It was later suggested by a party insider, Lance Price, that the party 'didn't really want this debate to take place.' Quoted in Cockerell, 'Why 2010 will see the first TV leaders election debate'.

14  Stephen Coleman, *Televised Leaders' Debates Revisited* (London: Hansard Society, 2001).

15  This section draws on interviews with representatives of ITV, the BBC and Sky News and contemporary newspaper reports. A particularly useful post-election overview is provided in Anne McElvoy, 'The box that changed Britain', *Sunday Times Magazine*, 13 June 2010.

16  'Call for Brown to face TV debate', *BBC News* website, 19 May 2007, available at: news.bbc.co.uk/1/hi/uk_politics/6671931.stm (last accessed on 26 August 2010).

17  George Pascoe-Watson, 'I'll give EU vote', *The Sun*, 6 September 2007.

18  *House of Commons Debates*, Vol. 472, Part 55, 27 February 2008, column 1084.

19  Anne McElvoy, 'Brown "ready for live TV debate with Cameron"', *Evening Standard*, 29 July 2009.

20  Andrew Porter, 'Gordon Brown's anger at Lord Mandelson over TV debate plan', *Daily Telegraph*, 1 August 2009.

21  A copy of Riley's letter to Gordon Brown can be found on the Sky News website at: blogs.news.sky.com/editorsblog/Post:69139385-4abb-4ba3-936d-6aaadfcef4fd (last accessed on 26 August 2010).

22  ITV, Sky, and BBC, 'Programme Format Agreed By All Parties 1st March 2010', available at: www.itv.com/utils/cached/common/ProgrammeFormat2.pdf (last accessed on 26 August 2010).

23  Severin Carrell, 'SNP continues action against BBC despite court verdict', *Guardian*, 28 April 2010.

24  The process resulted in a list of questions. The final selection would be made during the programme and would be sensitive to how the debate unfolded.

25  See Philip Webster and Francis Elliott, 'Brown calls in Obama team for help with television debate', *The Times*, 8 February 2010; Roland Watson, 'Cameron hires Obama advisers to prepare for TV election debates', *The Times*, 26 February 2010.

26  Philip Webster, 'Alastair Campbell plays David Cameron as Brown rehearses for TV debates', *The Times*, 15 March 2010.

27  Ipsos MORI, 'February 2010 Political Monitor', available at: www.ipsos-mori.com/researchpublications/researcharchive/poll.aspx?oItemId=2553&view=wide (last accessed on 26 August 2010).

28  ICM poll for the *Sunday Telegraph*, April 2010, available at: www.icmresearch.co.uk/pdfs/2010_apr_ST_campaign_poll1.pdf (last accessed on 26 August 2010).

29  This quotation, like all others from the first debate, is taken from the BBC transcript, available at: news.bbc.co.uk/1/shared/bsp/hi/pdfs/16_04_10_firstdebate.pdf (last accessed on 26 August 2010).

30  The programme utilised for this was Hamlet II. See Alan Brier and Bruno Hopp, *HAMLET II, Software for Computer-assisted Text Analysis* (Southampton/Cologne: 1998–2010), available at: apb.newmdsx.com/hamlet2.html. The texts analysed were the transcripts made available by the BBC.

31  'Election 2010: How PM debate audience "worm" works', *BBC News* website, 22 April 2010, available at: news.bbc.co.uk/1/hi/uk_politics/election_2010/8636745.stm (last accessed on 26 August 2010).

32  Ipsos MORI, 'The Leaders' debates: Immediate public reaction – Clegg wins the first round', available at: www.ipsos-mori.com/Assets/Docs/News/ipsos-mori-public-reaction-to-leaders-debate.pdf (last accessed on 26 August 2010).

33  Andrew Grice, 'Brown trains his sights on a "new politics" – with the help of the Lib Dems', *Independent*, 21 April 2010.

34  Robert Winnett and Jon Swaine, 'Nick Clegg, the Lib Dem donors and payments into his private account', *Daily Telegraph*, 22 April 2010.

35  This quotation, like all others from the first debate, is taken from the BBC transcript, available at: news.bbc.co.uk/1/shared/bsp/hi/pdfs/23_04_10_seconddebate.pdf (last accessed on 26 August 2010).

36  The question about the Pope's visit had originally been selected as a general question. However, the leaders' discussions had already ranged over areas covered by the other 'themed questions' on Sky's list, so this question was chosen to avoid repetition.

37  'Reading the runes', *The Economist*, 27 May 2010.

38  Armando Iannucci, 'The Duffy affair turned the media into a pack of shrieking gibbons', *Independent*, 4 May 2010.

39  This quotation, like all others from the first debate, is taken from the BBC transcript, available at: news.bbc.co.uk/1/shared/bsp/hi/pdfs/30_04_10_finaldebate.pdf (last accessed on 26 August 2010).

40  Steve Richards, 'What have these showdowns taught us?', *Independent*, 1 May 2010.

41  Charles Arthur, 'We need your Twote', *Guardian*, 3 May 2010.

42  Ivor Crewe quoted in Joe Joseph, 'Presidential-style TV debate threatens hype and novelty, but little light', *The Times*, 14 March 1992.

43  Andrew Rawnsley, 'After all the drama, their poll ratings hardly shifted', *Observer*, 9 May 2010.

44  Unfortunately, the question was not asked in 2005. See Ipsos MORI, 'Interest in Election News 1992 – 2010', available at: www.ipsos-mori.com/researchpublications/researcharchive/poll.aspx?oItemId=2426&view=wide (last accessed on 26 August 2010).

45  Peter Riddell, 'Clegg effect could mobilise the young and boost turnout', *The Times*, 21 April 2010.

46  See Ipsos MORI, 'When did you decide how to vote?', available at: www.ipsos-mori.com/researchpublications/researcharchive/poll.aspx?oItemId=2410&view=wide (last accessed on 26 August 2010).

47  Harold Clarke and Paul Whiteley, the two directors, were speaking in a round-table discussion on: 'The UK General Election 2010: Prospects, Challenges and Implications'.

48  Anne McElvoy, 'The box that changed Britain'.

# 8 THE LOCAL CAMPAIGNS AND THE OUTCOME

Ron Johnston and Charles Pattie

Labour dominated British politics throughout the late 1990s and 2000s. As chronicled in earlier books in this series, a combination of strong economic growth and a Conservative opposition in disarray kept Labour in office from 1997 on. Even in 2005, when the government had to defend its unpopular decision to go to war in Iraq, the party was able to win re-election with apparently little difficulty (though with a substantially reduced share of the vote). Thereafter, however, Labour's remarkable run of electoral luck began to run out. The leadership of Tony Blair, the party's most successful ever election winner, was fatally weakened by his association with the Iraq adventure and, his popularity waning rapidly, he was forced to stand aside in 2007 to make way for his chancellor of the exchequer, Gordon Brown, who had long coveted the post of prime minister.

After a brief honeymoon with the public, however, Brown's premiership ran into increasing difficulties and both he and his party lost substantial support. A number of factors contributed to Labour's mounting woes. First, following their 2005 defeat, the Conservatives elected a new leader, David Cameron, who began to make the Conservatives look like a credible party of government for the first time since the early 1990s.[1] In the autumn of 2007, Cameron's success forced Brown to abandon clumsily-trailed plans to hold an early election to cash in on his honeymoon. As a result, Brown began to be thought of as a ditherer, unravelling his previously unassailable reputation for competence and decisiveness that he had gained while chancellor. For the Labour government worse was soon to follow when the long economic boom which had marked Labour's time in office (and Brown claimed as evidence of his successful economic stewardship) came to an abrupt end in late 2007 with the onset of the credit crunch, an international banking crisis and then a deep recession. The economy, previously Labour's trump card, was in serious trouble and remained so right up to the 2010 election. Labour's poll ratings, predictably, slumped, while the Conservatives' rose. As if this was not enough, Brown's leadership of Labour became a source of internal party discontent and rumours abounded of possible challenges from other leading figures in the party. And, to add insult to injury, in May 2009 the *Daily Telegraph* broke a major news story regarding MPs' expenses: the resulting scandal dominated the press for many weeks, placing extra pressure on the prime minister.

An increasingly beleaguered and unpopular prime minister; a lost reputation for economic competence; and a mounting scandal over political sleaze. In the 1990s, a combination of these factors had been enough to bring down a Conservative government that had ruled for eighteen years, ousted by one of the largest landslide defeats in modern British political history. Their reappearance on the political stage in the run-up to the 2010 election should, one would have thought, have presaged a similar fate for Labour, and a comfortable win for its Conservative rivals. But, in the event, 2010 was not quite 1997 in reverse. Labour lost, but did not see its parliamentary representation decimated to the same extent as had the Conservatives thirteen years before. The Conservatives, meanwhile, emerged as the largest party but failed to gain an overall majority: only by forming a coalition with the Liberal Democrats was David Cameron able to enter Number 10 Downing Street. How could an opposition facing such an open goal fail to score? To understand why, we need to consider two things: the electoral system and local campaigning.

The result of the 2010 general election was thus both decisive and inconclusive. It was decisive in that, as Table 8.1 shows, the incumbent governing party, Labour, experienced a substantial decline in both its share of the votes and its number of seats in the House of Commons; the electorate clearly no longer wished it to remain in office. It was inconclusive because its main opponent, the Conservatives, failed to increase their vote share to the same extent and fell considerably short of the 326 seats needed for an overall majority. The eventual outcome was a coalition between the Conservatives and the Liberal Democrats, the most likely one on the numbers although for a few days Gordon Brown hoped that a multi-party coalition involving Labour, the Liberal Democrats and some at least of the 'others' would be feasible.[2] In the end, the political arithmetic and the realpolitik ended his hopes.

TABLE 8.1    *The result of the 2010 general election in Great Britain (excluding the Speaker)*

|  | Conservative | Labour | Liberal Democrat | Other | Total |
|---|---|---|---|---|---|
| Vote share (%) | 36.9 | 29.7 | 23.6 | 9.9 | 100 |
| Vote share change | +3.7 | −6.4 | +0.9 | +1.9 | |
| Seats won | 305 | 258 | 57 | 11 | 631 |
| Change in seats won | +95 | −90 | −5 | −1 | |

*Source*: House of Commons Research Paper 10/36, *General Election 2010*, p. 11. Available at http://www.parliament.uk/documents/commons/lib/research/rp2010/RP10-036.pdf. Last accessed 26 August 2010.

Labour's defeat was widely expected by the time the country went to the polls on 6 May 2010. After their landslide victories of 1997 and 2001 it had been re-elected in 2005, with a much reduced majority, largely because the electorate was unconvinced that the Conservatives offered a satisfactory alternative. Indeed, from 2002 on more people were dissatisfied with the Labour government's performance than were satisfied as the data in Figure 8.1 show very clearly. There were brief periods when the party's popularity recovered somewhat, notably when Brown replaced Blair in 2007 and, even more briefly, when he was responding to the global financial crisis in early 2009, but the omens for Labour were always bad. For them, the 2010 general election result reflected that situation. But the main opposition party was not able to benefit from this sufficiently to form a government with its own majority; the Conservatives increased their share of the votes by 3.7 points while Labour's fell by 6.4 points, which was insufficient to produce a Conservative majority (Table 8.1). This chapter explores why, focussing not on the characteristics of those who voted for the different parties but rather on the geography of the election, on where the Conservatives gained and failed to gain seats from their opponents.

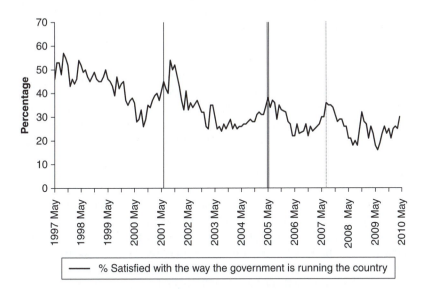

FIGURE 8.1    *Satisfaction with the Labour government, 1997–2010*

*Source*: Ipsos MORI, 'Political Monitor: Satisfaction Ratings 1997-Present', available at http://www.ipsos-mori.com/researchpublications/researcharchive/poll. aspx?oItemID=88&view=wide. Last accessed 26 August 2010.

*Note*: Ipsos MORI's question asks: 'Are you satisfied or dissatisfied with the way the Government is running the country?' The three vertical lines represent, in order, the 2001 general election, the 2005 general election and Gordon Brown's accession to the premiership.

Political parties run two inter-dependent sets of campaigns at UK general elections. Their national campaigns focus on their policies and – especially in 2010 given the importance of the televised debates – their leaders, to sustain support among those inclined to vote for them and to win over others who might have been thinking of voting for an opponent or abstaining. These campaigns are almost entirely addressed either to the country at large – as with policies on defence and security, for example – or to identified key groups, such as families. There is little geography to such appeals.

The local campaigns are conducted separately in each of the 650 constituencies. By the 1970s some commentators considered them of minor importance, having very little impact on the outcome.[3] But it was always the case that the more intensively candidates campaigned in their constituencies the better their performance there.[4] Such activity included not only campaign meetings, walkabouts, poster displays and leafleting but also careful canvassing, creating databases of likely supporters, encouraging them to vote and contacting them on polling day to ensure that they did.

From the 1990s on, the central party organisations increasingly realised there were substantial potential returns from more intensive, professionally-organised and -run local campaigns, involving their candidates and local party members, especially in those constituencies where the election could be won or lost – the marginals. The social and economic geography of Great Britain means that a large number of constituencies are 'natural' territory for one of the main political parties only. They are likely to win there by large majorities, and not much effort is needed to mobilise enough of their supporters to vote and ensure the anticipated victory – appreciating that other parties know they are very unlikely to win there and would not invest much effort to win a little extra support where those votes would not in any case count. Much of the country comprises seats that are 'safe' for the incumbents and 'hopeless' for their opponents. General elections are won and lost in the marginal constituencies, increasingly the focus of campaigning attention.[5]

Each major party's strategy now combines a national campaign with a centrally-directed, partly locally-delivered, geographically-focused set of local campaigns.[6] The latter often start long before the date of the expected general election, with parties ensuring visibility for their candidates through events and various publications (newsletters, leaflets, videos, email and text messages, etc.) and conducting polls and other surveys to identify their potential supporters and their local concerns. Other activities are organised and run centrally, such as the use of call centres to contact voters in the targeted constituencies to determine whether they were likely to support the party, producing a database that could then be used by the local organisation.

The nature of those local campaigns has changed very considerably recently, in particular through lengthening the time period in which the parties actively seek local support. The Liberal Democrats have long deployed local activists in key constituencies on relatively inexpensive tasks designed to sustain and grow their support base – in some cases operating in effect a continuous campaign, perhaps peaking at the time of local, European Parliament and, in Northern Ireland, Scotland, and Wales, national devolved-assembly elections.[7] Other parties – especially the Conservatives – now follow their lead. The campaigning climaxes in the few weeks immediately before the election, when it is constrained by legal limits on the amount that can be spent promoting a candidate's cause – although expenditure on such items as leaflets and posters can be boosted by 'cost-free' activities provided by supporters' time.[8] Numerous studies have shown that however campaigning activity is measured, the more intensively that candidates campaign the better their performance. This is especially true of challengers.[9]

A third campaign period has been recently introduced: if a parliament is going full term, the parties know when this is; if not, they – and the media – are often able to predict the date of an election very successfully. The parties increase the intensity of their campaigns during the final months before the contest. During 2007 and 2008 inter-party negotiations regarding party funding considered whether there should be a cap on local spending throughout the inter-election period, but no agreement was reached.[10] The Labour Party was concerned over the large sums donated to Conservative constituency parties by Lord Ashcroft and others prior to the 2005 general election, which had a clear impact on the party's fortunes in a number of seats.[11] As a by-product of the failure to reach agreement, section 21 of the Political Parties and Elections Act 2009 limits spending between the end of the fifty-fifth month after a parliament first sat and the date at which the candidate is formally adopted for the election after the parliament's dissolution; the amount that could be spent during the period January–April 2010 under these regulations was about £30,000 in an average constituency.[12]

There are now thus three campaign periods for constituency electioneering:

1    the long campaign, in which there are no limits on candidate expenditure;
2    the proximate campaign, covering the last months of a parliament (five if it runs for its full term, and one less for each month short of that); and
3    the climax campaign, covering the period after parliament is dissolved, for which the spending limits per candidate average some £12,000.

At the time of writing, comprehensive data are only available on the first of these three, thus the analyses reported below focus on the foundations laid by the parties during the long campaign.

## Preparing for 2001

After new constituencies were designated in 2007 for England, Wales and Northern Ireland (Scotland's were introduced before the 2005 election) the parties identified their key marginal seats and began to formulate campaign plans for them. That identification was necessarily based on estimates ('notional vote shares') of the pattern of voting commissioned by the main broadcast media using well-established methods.[13]

The pattern of marginality for each of the three parties that contested all British seats in 2010 (save that being defended by the Speaker) is shown in Table 8.2. The margins represent the percentage point differences between the party's notional share of the vote (real vote in Scotland) in 2005 and that of the winning party. Negative values are seats it was estimated that the party did not hold going in to the election, positive values refer to the seats that they were defending. Thus the Conservatives were defending 160 seats with margins of 10 points or more over their nearest challenger, where they might reasonably assume that victory was secure and there was no need for a great deal of local effort to turn out their supporters. On the other hand, the upper section of the 'Conservative' column shows relatively few constituencies held by the other parties that needed only a small swing to return

TABLE 8.2   *Marginal constituencies prior to the 2010 general election by marginality and by party (Great Britain only)*

| Margin (%) | Conservative | Labour | Liberal Democrat |
|---|---|---|---|
| Negative | | | |
| −20< | 225 | 173 | 458 |
| −15: −20 | 52 | 45 | 54 |
| −10: −15 | 49 | 19 | 27 |
| −5: −10 | 50 | 14 | 15 |
| −4: −5 | 7 | 5 | 5 |
| −3: −4 | 12 | 3 | 1 |
| −2: −3 | 10 | 6 | 2 |
| −1: −2 | 6 | 9 | 3 |
| 0: −1 | 10 | 8 | 5 |
| Positive | | | |
| 0: 1 | 9 | 9 | 4 |
| 1: 2 | 9 | 9 | 4 |
| 2: 3 | 5 | 9 | 3 |
| 3: 4 | 3 | 11 | 1 |
| 4: 5 | 9 | 5 | 2 |
| 5: 10 | 9 | 45 | 14 |
| 10: 15 | 26 | 42 | 12 |
| 15: 20 | 50 | 49 | 12 |
| 20< | 84 | 172 | 10 |

*Note:* Negative values are for the constituencies that the party lost in 2005; positive values are for those the party won.

a Tory MP in 2010: the Conservatives trailed the winning candidate by less than 2 points in just sixteen seats, and in a further twenty-two where it was 2–4 points behind. A large number of seats were less vulnerable to a pro-Conservative shift in support, requiring a substantial shift in voter preferences if the constituency was to be won.

The Liberal Democrats faced a more difficult situation; only sixteen seats could be won by overturning a deficit of less than 5 points, and the party was defending fourteen held by the same slender margin. Finally, Labour was not expecting to gain seats save in a small number of very marginal seats held by the other two parties. It held forty-three marginal seats vulnerable to a loss of 5 points or less – although if it lost all of them it would still be the largest of the three parties in the House of Commons, with 308 seats, only eighteen short of an overall majority.

The Conservatives thus faced a very difficult challenge in 2010. To form a government required winning a considerable number of constituencies where they had a substantial margin to make up. To become the largest party involved overturning deficits of more than 5 points in some fifty seats. For an outright majority, they additionally needed to win at least half of the seats where they trailed by between 10 and 15 points.

Labour's strategy was clearly defensive. For most of the previous two years opinion polls indicated that although the Conservatives led in terms of popular support they were unlikely to win more than a small majority of seats. If Labour could retain control of many of its marginal seats, therefore, it could probably deny the Conservatives a parliamentary majority and be able either to form a minority government or join a sustainable coalition with the Liberal Democrats.

Their focus of campaigning has recently been a difficult issue for the Liberal Democrats. Their heartlands were in a few rural areas where non-conformist religion provided the basis for opposition to Conservative landowners – in the South West of England (especially Cornwall) and parts of central Wales and non-urban Scotland (see Chapter 3). From the 1970s on they used successes at local government elections as the foundations for parliamentary advances in areas with strong non-conformist, liberal traditions – parts of the Lancashire and Yorkshire textile areas, for example – and in some relatively affluent suburban areas, such as South West London. Elsewhere, by-election successes formed isolated pockets of support sustained over several elections (the Isle of Ely was won in 1973 and held at the next four general elections; Bermondsey and Old Southwark was won in 1983 and held since). But in much of the country their support was low, and their chances of winning seats remote. Table 8.2 shows the Liberal Democrats trailing by more than 15 points in over 500 constituencies before the 2010 contest and behind by less than 5 points in only sixteen. By focusing their limited resources at recent elections on increasing their tally of MPs and largely ignoring a large number of constituencies where they had only a weak local presence, they increased their parliamentary contingent but made further gains of seats difficult without a major swing of support towards them. Meanwhile, more than a fifth of the seats they already held were vulnerable to relatively small shifts in support to the other parties, many of them to the Conservatives.

This last point highlights a feature of the recent geography of British politics. If two parties predominate they are the main contestants in almost all constituencies, with others occupying distant third and lower places; in the 1950s and 1960s Labour and Conservative candidates took the first two places in over 90 per cent of seats. That is no longer the case. The Liberal Democrat surge from the 1970s to the 1990s was almost entirely focused on Conservative-held seats, where Labour support declined substantially: the Liberal Democrats replaced it as the Conservatives' main opponents there. From 1997 on, however, Liberal Democrats began to challenge Labour in many of its heartlands – cities like Liverpool, Newcastle upon Tyne and Sheffield, where the party was increasingly successful in local-government elections. This advance accelerated somewhat in 2005, the Liberal Democrats winning many votes in urban areas through opposition to the Iraq invasion and increases in university tuition fees. They became Labour's main competitor there, with the Conservatives languishing in third place in many constituencies.

Britain is now split into three main areas according to the nature of the local electoral competition, therefore. Prior to the 2010 election, approximately half of all constituencies had Conservatives and Labour as the two major contestants; in one-fifth Conservatives and the Liberal Democrats provided the main contenders; and in a further fifth Labour and the Liberal Democrats were the front runners.[14] Relatively few constituencies were genuine three-way marginals (let alone four-way in Scotland and Wales): only six had the third-placed party less than 10 points behind the winner in 2005 (the third-placed Conservatives won two of them, Camborne and Redruth and Watford, in 2010). The three main parties are thus each facing two different opponents in different places, which imposes considerable campaigning difficulties, exacerbated in some places where the two parties opposing each other at the general election are working together in local government where no party has overall control. Marginal constituencies can be found in all three types of battleground.

## A brief interlude

Prior to the general election being called on 6 April 2010, the marginal seats were widely accepted as the arena where the contest would be won and lost – with most commentators emphasising the difficulty of the

Conservatives' task. The situation changed after the first televised party leaders' debate on 15 April. The Liberal Democrat leader Nick Clegg was widely perceived to have 'won' that debate, and this was accompanied by a substantial surge in his party's support in opinion polls (see Figure 7.1). The Conservative lead was substantially reduced, and many polls placed Labour third. However, calculations suggested these poll positions might not be reflected in the translation of votes into seats. Labour in third place at a little under 30 per cent could still be the largest parliamentary party, and the Liberal Democrat surge into second place might still see it come a poor third in the allocation of seats.

For a time, polls suggested that the Conservative vote share might not be substantially larger than in 2005 (33.2 per cent in Great Britain; all of the data analysed here exclude Northern Ireland). This would not guarantee victory if any increase was relatively uniform across the country. The distribution of any additional votes became increasingly crucial; they had to be focused on the marginal seats. But Labour's lower share of vote intentions (from 36.2 per cent in 2005 to perhaps 27–28 per cent) put a larger number of its seats at risk. This implied that if the Conservatives had the available resources they could direct their campaign toward seats that might otherwise have been considered unwinnable – which they did, for example, in Morley and Outwood where Ed Balls (a key Brown aide and likely candidate to replace him as leader) was defending a 'notional' majority of some 21 points. Unseating such a prominent figure would be the Conservatives' equivalent of Labour's Stephen Twigg defeating Michael Portillo in 1997.[15] However, the Liberal Democrats appeared to be picking up many alienated Labour supporters, which made winning Labour's marginally-held seats more difficult for the Conservatives. This problem was exacerbated when two cabinet ministers called for Labour–Liberal Democrat tactical voting in the last week of the campaign. The Labour-supporting *Daily Mirror* and Liberal Democrat-supporting *Guardian* newspapers, moreover, helpfully listed those constituencies where Labour supporters should vote Liberal Democrat to deny a Conservative victory and those where Liberal Democrats should switch their vote to Labour. Whether or not those campaigns were successful, there was nevertheless considerable evidence of patterns consistent with tactical voting, involving perhaps 15 per cent of the electorate. British Election Survey data, for example, indicate that of those who recalled having voted Labour in 2005, 58 per cent did so again in 2010. That figure was 63 and 65 per cent in the seats Labour was contesting with Conservative and Liberal Democrat candidates respectively, but only 39 per cent where it came third or lower in 2005 and the Conservatives and Liberal Democrats were the main contestants (35 per cent of former Labour voters switching to the Liberal Democrats in 2010, compared to 17 and 19 per cent in the other two seat types).

The first leaders' debate appeared to change the situation to one with three more-or-less equal parties rather than, as at recent elections, two main parties and a third which was not a threat in most of the constituencies (a two-and-a-half party system). The result in many constituencies appeared to be less predictable, depending on which party the Liberal Democrats were drawing most of their expanded support from.

The Liberal Democrat surge was short-lived, however, and not sustained by the subsequent leaders' debates. The party was caught in a campaigning pincer between the other two: Labour argued that 'a vote for the Liberal Democrats was a vote for Cameron', and the Conservatives 'vote Clegg, get Brown'. The Liberal Democrat estimated vote share declined somewhat as election day approached. But much of that shift came very late in the campaign and was only fully picked up by the election-day exit poll which showed that the national swing to the Conservatives was insufficient to generate a parliamentary majority and accurately predicted a reduction in the number of Liberal Democrat MPs.

## Translating votes into seats

Why might a victory by 6–7 points over their nearest rival not guarantee a Conservative majority? The Conservatives were only 3 points behind Labour in 2005, suggesting that their 2010 goal to replace Labour with a majority of seats was readily achievable, given their substantial opinion poll leads since 2008. But such was the disproportionality and bias in the 2005 result that the Conservatives needed to gain at least 116 marginal constituencies to guarantee a majority of just one, and the gap between the Conservative and the incumbent party's share in that one-hundred-and-sixteenth seat was 12 points.

Labour won 36.2 per cent of British votes in 2005 to the Conservatives' 33.2 per cent, and 55.4 per cent of House of Commons seats to the Conservatives 33.4 per cent. A uniform swing from Labour to the Conservatives of just over 1.5 points should therefore give the latter party victory in the battle for a plurality of public support – with 34.8 per cent of the votes to its opponent's 34.6 per cent. But such a lead would not deliver a Conservative victory in the seat allocation: Labour would still have a small majority. Furthermore, a reversal of the vote totals (Conservatives 36.2 per cent and Labour 33.2 per cent) would also not produce a Conservative majority. Labour won 55.4 per cent of the seats with 36.2 per cent of the votes, but the Conservatives would have obtained only 42.9 per cent.

This marked difference in the translation of votes into seats reflects the operation of the electoral system which has recently been very biased towards Labour. If Labour and the Conservatives had each obtained 34.7 per cent of the votes in 2005 then, assuming that the number of votes for all of the other parties and the number of abstentions in each constituency remained the same and that there was a uniform redistribution of votes from Labour to the Conservatives across all constituencies, Labour would have obtained 111 more seats than the Conservatives.[16] In the new constituencies introduced in 2007, it would still have won ninety-five more with those equal vote shares.[17]

In 2005, therefore, Labour got a much better return in the translation of votes into seats than the Conservatives: it won a seat for every 26,921 votes whereas for the Conservatives the ratio was one seat for every 44,517 votes. (For the Liberal Democrats it was even worse, at 96,485 votes per seat.) This unequal treatment of the two largest parties can be evaluated using a bias decomposition method, which indicates how many of the 111 seats in that differential – the total bias – result from a number of interacting mechanisms.

- *Differences in constituency electorates.* Assuming that there are no abstentions in a constituency, then 50 per cent +1 of the votes guarantee victory there; 35,001 are needed for victory in a constituency with 70,000 electors, but only 30,001 in one with only 60,000 electors. If one party is more popular in constituencies with smaller electorates it will gain more seats for a given number of votes than one whose main electoral strength is in the larger constituencies.
- *Differences in turnout rates.* If we relax the assumption regarding turnout, the larger the number of abstentions the fewer votes needed for victory, as with electorate size. A party that is strong in the constituencies with low turnouts will therefore gain more seats for a given number of votes than one whose main electoral strength is in those with higher turnouts.
- *Differences in the performance of other parties.* If all voters in a constituency turn out but 10 per cent of them vote for a party other than the largest two, then again fewer votes are needed for one of the larger two to win the seat. A strong party in constituencies with substantial 'other party' support will gain more seats for a given number of votes than one whose main electoral strength is where 'other parties' are relatively weak. If one of the other parties wins a seat, however, this will impact on which of the two largest might otherwise have done so.
- *Differences in the efficiency of a party's vote distribution.* Constituencies vary in their support for the main parties: in general, the Conservatives perform better in middle-class and rural areas, and Labour in working-class urban areas. If each is equally successful in its 'heartlands' there should be no bias. But if one tends to win by much larger majorities than the other, it will have many more votes that are 'surplus to

requirements'; in a constituency with 70,000 electors and all voting for one of two parties, victory with 55 per cent of the votes means that 3,500 are surplus (i.e. more than enough to guarantee victory), whereas in one won with 65 per of the votes the surplus is 10,500. The smaller the surplus – plus the fewer wasted votes a party gets in constituencies where it loses, because they win it no representation – the greater the party's vote efficiency.

Table 8.3 gives the size of these various bias components at the 2005 general election; a positive figure indicates a bias favouring the Labour party and a negative one a pro-Conservative bias. The bias component for constituency size (i.e. variations in electorates) is divided into two subcomponents. The first is for differences between countries. The House of Commons (Redistribution of Seats) Act 1944 guaranteed thirty-five seats for Wales and seventy for Scotland; subsequent boundary redistributions increased these to forty and seventy-two respectively by 1997. Those countries were over-represented, with average electorates of some 55,000 relative to England's 69,000. The number of Scottish MPs was reduced to fifty-nine after the creation of its parliament, and in 2005 Scottish constituencies were closer to the English average (65,287 and 70,202 respectively). There was no similar reduction of Welsh MPs following the creation of the National Assembly, however; the average constituency there had 55,762 voters in 2005. Labour is by far the stronger of the two largest UK parties in those two countries, which delivered a small bias of six seats in 2005. Labour also tends to win the smaller constituencies more generally which produced it a further bias of twenty seats.

TABLE 8.3   *Biased results at the 2005 and 2010 British general elections*

| Bias component | 2005 | 2005E | 2010 |
| --- | --- | --- | --- |
| Size | | | |
|   Between country | 6 | 6 | 9 |
|   Within country | 20 | 6 | 9 |
| Abstentions | 38 | 38 | 31 |
| Third party | | | |
|   Votes | −17 | −16 | −17 |
|   Victories | 26 | 24 | 21 |
| Vote efficiency | 35 | 34 | 0 |
| TOTAL | 111 | 95 | 54 |

*Source*: Colin Rallings, Ron Johnston and Michael Thrasher, 'Changing the boundaries but keeping the disproportionality: the electoral impact of the fifth periodical reviews by the Boundary Commissions for England and Wales', *The Political Quarterly*, 79 (2008): 80–90, p. 86.

*Note*: 2005 – 2005 general election, actual result; 2005E – 2005 general election if it had been fought in the 2010 constituencies; 2010 – 2010 general election, actual result.

Although Labour benefited substantially from being stronger in the smaller constituencies, both abstentions and the efficiency component provided even greater pro-Labour bias, worth thirty-eight and thirty-five seats (out of the total of 111) respectively. Labour was much more likely than the Conservatives to win the constituencies with low turnout, and its support was much more efficiently distributed (fewer surplus and wasted votes) than its main opponent's.

Only one component favoured the Conservatives in 2005, the distribution of votes for other parties. These – especially the Liberal Democrats – tend to win more votes in seats where the Conservatives are strong than where Labour is. As a consequence, many of those seats need slightly fewer votes for one of the largest two parties to gain victory, commonly the Conservatives. However, if a party other than Labour and the Conservatives wins the seat, that is to the Conservatives' disadvantage and Labour's benefit. When the two are combined, however, the extent of the bias is small, favouring Labour in 2005 by some nine seats.

The new constituency boundaries introduced in England and Wales after the 2005 election had little impact on the bias, recomputed as if that election had been fought in the new constituencies (Table 8.3, central column). The main goal of a Boundary Commission redistribution is to reduce variation in electorate sizes, so not surprisingly that component declines although still giving Labour a slight advantage.[18] But the other components are largely unaffected and had virtually no impact on the scale of the Conservatives' task in winning a majority in the 2010 election.

Countering many of these bias components was not straightforward for the Conservatives. Labour's advantage from the geography of abstentions could be reduced, if not eliminated, by encouraging greater turnout. But if more people voted in the seats with high abstention levels, it is very likely that many of them would support Labour rather than the Conservatives. This would reduce the size of that bias component but be unlikely to deliver more seats to the Conservatives – who would have to expend resources promoting turnout in seats they are unlikely to win rather than focusing on those they need to win!

## The long campaign

Efficiency bias was the only component of bias that the Conservatives could influence in the short term. A uniform swing of 6.9 points between the two largest parties was needed for the Conservatives to gain a majority in the House of Commons in 2010. Few parties have ever achieved such a swing. Even if it had been achieved, the Conservatives would have only a tiny majority; a much larger swing was needed for a working majority. Such calculations assumed that there was no change in the level and geography of support for the other parties, particularly the Liberal Democrats. Switches between them and the two largest parties could considerably influence the outcome of any swing from Labour to the Conservatives.

The Conservatives did not need such a large uniform swing across the country in order to gain a majority, however; they needed it in a minority of seats only. In most constituencies the Tories would still either win or lose, whatever the swing. Where they still won, their surplus votes would increase; where they still lost, their wasted votes tally would grow – and their vote inefficiency increase. What they needed was more votes in the marginal seats where the larger the swing the greater the possibility of victory.

Of course, the Conservatives wanted to win more votes everywhere, to boost their overall standing and legitimacy. But with limited resources, there was little reason to expend effort (including money) where the likelihood of either winning or losing the seat was slight. If they could gain more votes in their safe and hopeless seats without much local effort – through the impact of the national campaign – that would be good. But resources needed to be focused in three areas: in the seats that the Conservatives held by only small majorities, that they wanted to make safer; to a lesser extent, on the seats held by other parties where, even if they could not win them in 2010, the Conservatives could build a strong foundation for victory at the next election; but, especially, on the seats held by other parties by small margins over the Conservatives which were needed for an overall victory.

The Conservatives could not entirely ignore those seats held by relatively small majorities even with an overall swing towards them, being threatened there not only by possible Labour–Liberal Democrat tactical voting but also by competition from some smaller parties. Of particular concern was the United Kingdom Independence Party (UKIP), which contested 547 of the constituencies with its main policy platform of withdrawal from the European Union. It offered not to stand in constituencies where the Conservative candidate was a clear Eurosceptic, and did not contest some seats held by Conservative leaders (such as William Hague and George Osborne). As with other smaller parties, it got little national coverage, so much depended on its local campaigns.[19] It won substantial support at the 2009 European Parliament elections, coming second to the Conservatives with 16.5 per cent of the votes. Although it was not expected to perform anything like as well in a general election it was a clear potential threat to the Conservatives in some seats – both those they held by relatively small margins and those they hoped to win. In the event, UKIP obtained only 3.2 per cent of the votes nationally. Nevertheless, there were twenty-one constituencies in which the Conservatives came second by a margin less than the UKIP vote total there. Without UKIP's presence in key seats a Conservative-majority government may have been elected.

Against this, there was less of a threat to Labour from smaller parties, although the British National Party's (BNP) anti-immigration and anti-EU campaign was focused on disaffected working-class Labour supporters: it targeted fifteen constituencies, thirteen Labour-held and two Liberal Democrat-held. The Greens' threat was focused on three constituencies – especially Brighton Pavilion, won by its leader Caroline Lucas with 31.3 per cent of the vote compared to 21.9 per cent in 2005. The contests with the left-leaning nationalist parties were uncertain: many of the issues central to the 2010 election campaign had been devolved to the Scottish Parliament and the National Assembly of Wales – but both Plaid Cymru and the Scottish National Party campaigned for increased representation at Westminster so as to put a strong case for public services in their countries not to be cut, perhaps as parts of a deal that might be brokered should there be a hung parliament. Labour had slightly better prospects in Scotland than Wales, however, because it was in opposition to the SNP administration but in coalition with Plaid Cymru. (Labour's share of the vote increased between 2005 and 2010 in Scotland – from 38.9 to 42.3 per cent – but fell in Wales – from 42.7 to 36.7 per cent.)

Marginal constituencies – those that it was defending as well as those held by either Labour or the Liberal Democrats – were thus at the core of the Conservatives' local campaigning strategy once the new constituencies were formally adopted by parliament in 2007. The strategy was led by the party's vice-chairman, Lord Ashcroft. He had realised the importance of marginal seats during the 2005 campaign and donated money to local parties he considered had viable plans to defeat a Labour incumbent – a largely successful strategy in the small number of seats where he and a few others made large donations to the local party organisation.[20] For the 2010 election, this strategy was substantially enhanced and operated through Conservative Central Office, to which Ashcroft and his wife made large donations of both cash and cash-in-kind. Ashcroft directed a dedicated marginal constituencies section which had three main tasks:

1  identifying possible Conservative voters in target seats (through polling, much of it by telephone) and sending them materials promoting the party's cause and its candidates – many of whom were standing for the first time and needed to increase their visibility with the local electorate;[21]

2  providing cash grants to local parties with viable business plans showing that they could organise campaigning activities there to promote the party's candidate; and

3  redirecting resources towards key constituencies, including during the final campaigning weeks.

The party also encouraged candidates who had fought and lost a constituency in 2005 to contest it again, arguing that their visibility and local activity during the intervening five years would be an advantage in the 2010 campaign.

Of the constituencies where Conservatives came second in 2005, thirty-one fielded the same candidate in 2010, twenty-seven in Labour-held seats. Many were contesting marginal seats with incumbent Labour and Liberal Democrat MPs. And the local parties raised moneys – through fund-raising events as well as individual and corporate donations – to support the campaign.

It is not currently possible to identify and analyse all of the elements of this strategy, because some of the needed data are not yet available – such as candidate spending during the proximate and climax campaigns. Under the Political Parties, Elections and Referendums Act 2000, all local accounting units associated with a registered political party (most of them individual parliamentary constituencies) must return annual audited accounts to the Electoral Commission if either their income or their expenditure exceeds £25,000 during the year in question. Local party accounts indicating grants received from Central Office in 2007 and 2008 have been published by the Electoral Commission, as have data on donations to local parties over the period from 2007 to the end of the first quarter of 2010. In addition, all donations to those accounting units of £1,000, or of smaller amounts from the same donor that sum to £1,000 in any quarter, must also be reported to the Commission. All of these data are available on the Commission's website and are analysed here, along with comparable data for the Labour and Liberal Democrat parties.[22] The amount of money spent campaigning is, of course, only a surrogate for its intensity; as Justin Fisher has argued, how money is spent can be as important as how much, which reflects the tactical nous and local knowledge of the candidates and, especially, their agents.[23] But the materials used in much of the campaigning have to be bought, and knowing how much was spent on them – and on associated activities such as voter surveys and polls – is a very valuable indicator of the amount of activity in a constituency.

One aspect of the contest difficult to factor in to these analyses is the impact of the MP expenses scandal. Many of those whose behaviour was the focus of much of the obloquy did not stand (or were not allowed to stand) for re-election and it is difficult to evaluate whether their successor candidates – some of them in considerably changed seats – suffered from their predecessors' behaviour. Some MPs who were publicly criticised did stand, but it is not straightforward to identify them from available data because what some were criticised for – such as 'flipping' first and second homes for tax purposes – was outside the scope of the independent inquiry.[24] As it happened, commentators found no general evidence suggesting that candidates implicated in the scandal suffered at the polls in 2010.

In this preliminary analysis of the impact of local campaigns, therefore, we focus mainly on the long campaign. This was when the Conservatives laid the foundations of their marginal-seats strategy, beginning to mobilise the electorate in the constituencies they had to win if they were to form the next government. Our analyses explore the impact of this foundation-laying and the extent to which their opponents responded, along with some material on the penultimate campaign, as revealed by donations to local political parties during the first quarter of 2010.

## The long campaigning pattern in the constituencies

However strong the central direction and provision of resources, intensive local campaigns need active local parties as their foundations. Table 8.4 examines two features of those local Conservative parties that returned their annual accounts to the Electoral Commission: their membership – an indicator of the size of the voluntary labour force that can be mobilised during campaigns; and their declared income in 2008 – an indicator of the local party's financial health and the resources available for campaigning. It also reports the number and value of donations received by each local party between January 2007 and December 2009.[25]

Not all constituency parties provided membership data. Those that did included a majority of the seats won by the Conservatives in 2005 (180 of the 211 constituencies). Where Labour came second then, in general the larger the victory, the larger the local Conservative party (611 members on average in seats that the Conservatives won by more than 20 points, but 426 where they won by less than 5 points); local parties were larger where the Conservatives got more votes. Parties in seats being contested with the Liberal Democrats, on the other hand, were substantially larger (averaging 750 members) than in the seats where Labour came second in 2005 (527 members). The same was true in the seats that the Conservatives lost in 2005: where the Liberal Democrats won, the local Conservative party had more members on average (480) than was the case where Labour was the victor (290). Prior to the 2010 election, therefore, the Conservatives were better placed, in terms of potential local activists, where they were challenging a Liberal Democrat rather than a Labour incumbency.

Most parties where the Conservatives won in 2005 reported a 2008 income of £25,000 or more – as did almost all of those where the Liberal Democrats provided the winner. Only a minority of local Conservative parties with a Labour victor had a sufficient income to make a return, however, most of them where Labour's majority was less than 10 points. (Of the 143 constituencies where Labour led the Conservatives by 10 points or more, only thirty-nine had an income of £25,000 or more in 2008.) Again, the clear impression is that local Conservative parties were better placed to counter the Liberal Democrats than they were Labour, especially in the more marginal seats: the mean 2008 constituency party income where the Conservatives were beaten by less than 10 points in 2005 was over £92,000 where the Liberal Democrats won but only £28,000 where Labour was victorious. However, Liberal Democrat parties appeared

TABLE 8.4   *Conservative constituency party memberships, incomes and donations*

| Margin (%) | NC | CM | MM | CI | IM (£) | CD | DM | DVM (£) |
|---|---|---|---|---|---|---|---|---|
| *Conservative-Labour contests* | | | | | | | | |
| Conservative won 2005 | | | | | | | | |
| 20< | 49 | 39 | 611 | 42 | 57,628 | 30 | 6.1 | 19,600 |
| 15: 20 | 33 | 26 | 483 | 28 | 23,276 | 17 | 3.6 | 11,673 |
| 10: 15 | 14 | 10 | 540 | 12 | 46,586 | 7 | 6.3 | 18,461 |
| 5: 10 | 7 | 6 | 514 | 7 | 25,150 | 5 | 5.0 | 20,383 |
| 0: 5 | 27 | 21 | 426 | 23 | 34,941 | 21 | 5.0 | 23,136 |
| Labour won 2005 | | | | | | | | |
| 0: 5 | 32 | 20 | 447 | 26 | 34,534 | 26 | 8.8 | 32,568 |
| 5: 10 | 40 | 19 | 256 | 26 | 21,503 | 32 | 7.3 | 29,123 |
| 10: 15 | 34 | 10 | 292 | 15 | 15,216 | 24 | 4.5 | 15,845 |
| 15: 20 | 35 | 12 | 211 | 12 | 11,805 | 16 | 3.8 | 15,796 |
| 20< | 74 | 12 | 158 | 12 | 12,549 | 13 | 2.4 | 13,874 |
| *Conservative-Liberal Democrat contests* | | | | | | | | |
| Conservative won 2005 | | | | | | | | |
| 20< | 35 | 33 | 734 | 35 | 95,516 | 23 | 6.5 | 21,985 |
| 15: 20 | 17 | 18 | 745 | 16 | 84,937 | 10 | 3.8 | 9,424 |
| 10: 15 | 12 | 11 | 728 | 11 | 68,717 | 7 | 4.1 | 11,552 |
| 5: 10 | 9 | 9 | 856 | 9 | 78,509 | 7 | 4.0 | 17,001 |
| 0: 5 | 8 | 7 | 834 | 8 | 97,725 | 7 | 7.3 | 34,089 |
| Liberal Democrat won 2005 | | | | | | | | |
| 0: 5 | 10 | 10 | 518 | 10 | 58,313 | 9 | 5.5 | 18,488 |
| 5: 10 | 8 | 8 | 415 | 8 | 135,924 | 5 | 4.6 | 27,942 |
| 10: 15 | 11 | 10 | 490 | 11 | 47,476 | 9 | 6.4 | 14,940 |
| 15: 20 | 10 | 7 | 566 | 8 | 65,847 | 5 | 4.2 | 13,028 |
| 20< | 6 | 6 | 412 | 6 | 40,948 | 5 | 4.2 | 11,160 |

*Note*: NC – number of constituencies; CM – constituencies for which membership data available, 2008; MM – mean number of members per constituency, 2008; CI – constituencies for which income data available, 2008; IM – mean constituency income, 2008; CD – constituencies that received recorded donations, 2007–09; DM – mean number of recorded donations per constituency, 2007–09; DVM – mean value of recorded donations, 2007–09.

generally better placed to respond to Conservative local campaigns than their Labour counterparts.

The last three columns in Table 8.4 look at the number of separate recordable donations received during 2007–09. Constituency parties in the more marginal seats that the Conservatives lost in 2005 were more likely to have received such donations (twenty-six of the thirty-two most marginal Labour-held constituencies, for example, and nine of the ten Liberal Democrat-held). The average total value of the donations received was also generally higher in the more marginal constituencies, again suggesting that

TABLE 8.5   *Conservative constituency parties in receipt of target seat grants, 2007 and 2008*

| Margin (%) | NC | CT07 | TM07 (£) | CT08 | TM08 (£) |
|---|---|---|---|---|---|
| *Conservative-Labour contests* | | | | | |
| Conservative won 2005 | | | | | |
| 20< | 49 | 0 | | 0 | |
| 15: 20 | 33 | 0 | | 1 | 16,068 |
| 10: 15 | 14 | 0 | | 1 | 3,658 |
| 5: 10 | 7 | 1 | 652 | 2 | 2,393 |
| 0: 5 | 27 | 7 | 8,354 | 5 | 5,959 |
| Labour won 2005 | | | | | |
| 0: 5 | 32 | 12 | 14,811 | 18 | 6,388 |
| 5: 10 | 40 | 11 | 11,185 | 14 | 5,862 |
| 10: 15 | 34 | 5 | 3,589 | 7 | 4,841 |
| 15: 20 | 35 | 4 | 4,048 | 4 | 4,571 |
| 20< | 74 | 1 | 8,237 | 3 | 4,628 |
| *Conservative-Liberal Democrat contests* | | | | | |
| Conservative won 2005 | | | | | |
| 20< | 35 | 0 | | 0 | |
| 15: 20 | 17 | 2 | 7,035 | 0 | |
| 10: 15 | 12 | 1 | 8,201 | 1 | 5,990 |
| 5: 10 | 9 | 1 | 5,184 | 1 | 5,184 |
| 0: 5 | 8 | 3 | 25,784 | 3 | 13,996 |
| Liberal Democrat won 2005 | | | | | |
| 0: 5 | 10 | 7 | 15,864 | 7 | 11,366 |
| 5: 10 | 8 | 3 | 9,648 | 3 | 16,331 |
| 10: 15 | 11 | 3 | 3,356 | 5 | 8,442 |
| 15: 20 | 10 | 1 | 3,223 | 1 | 12,240 |
| 20< | 6 | 0 | | 1 | 1,500 |

*Note:* NC – number of constituencies; CT07 – number of constituencies receiving a target seat grant, 2007; TM07 – mean value of target grants, 2007; CT08 – number of constituencies receiving a target seat grant, 2008; TM08 – mean value of target grants, 2008.

the local parties where the contest was most likely to be intense were better prepared financially to fight it.

Some of the income reported in Table 8.4 comprised grants from Conservative Central Office as part of its 'target seats' campaign (the so-called 'Ashcroft money' although the full cost of the campaign was more than he donated to the party).[26] Table 8.5 summarises those grants for the calendar years 2007 and 2008. In both years, and in the contests with both of the other parties, there was a clear concentration on the more marginal seats. A few seats won by the Conservatives with majorities of less than 5 points received grants but most went to local parties where the Conservative lost in 2005 – mainly where the margin of defeat was less than 10 points. On average, local parties in the more marginal constituencies received larger grants.[27] A substantial number of local parties received no grant, however, even those where Labour's margin of victory was 5 points or less (twenty of the thirty-two in 2007, for example, and fourteen in 2008), indicating that in the long campaign many local parties did not convince the Central Office team that they offered a good potential return on money intended to sustain their campaigning efforts – in some cases because national and other polls suggested either that the Conservative candidate was going to win there or that they had no chance of success, so that further investment was unnecessary. (These assessments were re-evaluated every six months.) The absence of a grant does not, however, mean that the Conservatives' target seats unit was not actively campaigning everywhere, only that it was not funding campaign activities by the local parties.[28]

Turning to the other two parties, only forty-six Labour accounting units made a return in 2008 (out of a possible total of 632).[29] The comparable figures for the other parties were 325 for the Conservatives and ninety-eight for the Liberal Democrats. The vast majority of Labour's local parties had turnovers below £25,000, suggesting poor financial health, and most of those that did make a return had an income was little more than the minimum requirement.[30] Most of the local parties in constituencies that Labour won in 2005 received a considerable number of donations over the years 2007–09 inclusive, but the average sum received by such a party was less than half that donated to a comparable Conservative party. Local parties in safe Labour seats were as likely to attract donations as those in the marginals, however, undoubtedly reflecting the long-established links between trade unions and the party organisations in Labour's heartlands.

Most of the local parties in the sixty-two constituencies won by the Liberal Democrats in 2005 made a financial return in 2008; their average turnover was relatively large (some £40,000). Most of the parties in Liberal Democrat-held seats also attracted substantial numbers of donations in 2007–09, raising on average £20–40,000 over the period. Relatively few local parties where the party lost in 2005 had a turnover of £25,000 or more, however, and although more attracted donations the sums raised were not large.

The Labour party did not operate any target seat grant programme that appeared in the local party accounts during 2007–08. The Liberal Democrats operated two, one for local-government campaign development and the other for the general election: they have been combined here as success in each has impacts on the other. Table 8.6 shows that approximately the same number of grants was made in each year, mainly to parties in marginal constituencies – both those held by the Liberal Democrats after 2005 and those where it came a fairly close second. The grants were on average small, save for a few larger ones in some constituencies where the party had little apparent chance of success at the 2010 general election but appeared to be building a local presence.[31]

These data, except those for donations, indicate the situation more than a year before the 2010 election. They suggest that, at that stage at least, local

TABLE 8.6    *Liberal Democrat constituency parties in receipt of target seat grants, 2007 and 2008*

| Margin (%) | NC | CT07 | TN07 (£) | CT08 | TM08 (£) |
|---|---|---|---|---|---|
| Liberal Democrat won 2005 | | | | | |
| 20< | 10 | 1 | 650 | 1 | 9,061 |
| 15: 20 | 12 | 1 | 5,491 | 1 | 3,638 |
| 10: 15 | 12 | 3 | 6,577 | 4 | 6,123 |
| 5: 10 | 14 | 2 | 5,242 | 2 | 7,022 |
| 0: 5 | 14 | 8 | 9,148 | 8 | 9,894 |
| Liberal Democrat lost 2005 | | | | | |
| 0: 5 | 81 | 9 | 9,309 | 9 | 8,613 |
| 5: 10 | 61 | 10 | 6,888 | 12 | 6,467 |
| 10: 15 | 70 | 3 | 8,540 | 3 | 9,299 |
| 15: 20 | 100 | 5 | 21,344 | 4 | 36,402 |
| 20< | 258 | 7 | 12,030 | 8 | 8,396 |

*Note:* NC – number of constituencies; CT07 – number of constituencies receiving a target seat grant, 2007; TM07 – mean value of target grants, 2007; CT08 – number of constituencies receiving a target seat grant, 2008; TM08 – mean value of target grants, 2008.

Conservative parties were better placed to mount strong campaigns (with more members and more money) in those marginal constituencies held by Liberal Democrats than in those held by Labour, and that this greater preparedness was to some extent matched by the target seat grants received from Central Office. Labour seemed ill-prepared to counter those campaigns, however, with very few apparently active local parties in the seats the Conservatives were targeting. In contrast the Liberal Democrats had not only active local parties in most of the seats they were defending but also in a considerable number of those that they had lost by small margins in 2005.

## The long campaign and the result

Two arguments have been developed here with regard to the long campaign preceding the 2010 general election in Great Britain. First, unless either the Conservatives or the Liberal Democrats expected a major swing towards them and away from, especially, Labour, they needed to have a well-focused marginal-seats campaign integrated with their national strategy, because of the inherent biases against them in the electoral system. The Liberal Democrats have traditionally fought such focused local campaigns and the Conservatives began to do so centrally after the 2005 election. These tactics were modified as the campaign progressed and involved substantial expenditure on voter surveys and contacts – as a number of affected Labour MPs noted. This suggests a first argument that within the context of the overall change in each party's fortunes in the national vote tally compared to the 2005 election result, the greatest changes in vote shares should have been in the marginal constituencies.

Secondly, each of the parties varied in the intensity of its preparations for the 2010 election across the marginal constituencies. Even the Conservatives, who invested more than the Liberal Democrats in their target seat campaigns, did not put the same amount of resource into each constituency. Local Labour parties seemed ill-prepared to counter these tactics, with most of them apparently relatively moribund and raising little money with which to contest their challengers' onslaughts.[32] From this it follows that across the marginal constituencies, variations in the intensity of the local campaigns will have been reflected in variations in the electoral outcome – the more intense the campaign, the greater the electoral return.

## The pattern of change overall

The first argument suggests that there would be substantial variations in each party's change in vote share between 2005 and 2010 if the marginal-seat strategies had succeeded. Extra votes won elsewhere (in each party's safe and hopeless seats) would boost its overall standing but not necessarily increase its parliamentary representation.

Overall, the Conservative share of the votes cast across the 630 contested British constituencies increased by an average of 3.8 points, though the associated standard deviation of 3.4 indicates very substantial variation around that mean value (Table 8.7).[33] Its increase was substantially larger in the most marginal seats – 6.8 points in those that it won by a majority of less than 1 point in 2005 and 4.5 points where it lost by less than a single point – although large standard deviations again indicate substantial variation around the average. Given the importance of winning seats where it lost by between 5 and 15 points in 2005 if it were to achieve a majority, however, the higher averages of 6.8 and 4.5 point increases there suggest that the target seat strategy had an important impact.

Labour's share of the vote fell by an average of 6.4 points across all constituencies, but by much more in those that it lost in 2005 than those where it won. It necessarily fought a defensive strategy, and was relatively successful, especially in those constituencies which it held by a margin of less than 2 points. The very large standard deviations (6.0 and 6.8 respectively, against means of 5.4 and 3.8) indicate considerable variation around the mean gains, however. But although it was somewhat better able to sustain its vote share in some of those constituencies, as later tables show this was insufficient to prevent a Conservative victory there and it lost them all.

The Liberal Democrats were even more successful in a similar strategy; their average vote share increased by just under 1 point overall,

TABLE 8.7   *The mean change in a party's percentage share of the votes cast in a constituency between 2005 and 2010 (standard deviations in brackets)*

| Margin (%) | Conservative | | Labour | | Liberal Democrat | |
|---|---|---|---|---|---|---|
| *Constituencies lost in 2005* | | | | | | |
| −20< | 3.5 | (3.4) | −6.3 | (3.5) | 1.2 | (4.0) |
| −15: −20 | 3.7 | (4.0) | −8.2 | (12.2) | 0.7 | (4.8) |
| −10: −15 | 4.8 | (3.6) | −9.6 | (4.7) | 0.9 | (6.2) |
| −5: −10 | 4.5 | (3.3) | −8.1 | (4.8) | −0.6 | (4.2) |
| −4: −5 | 3.0 | (2.9) | −11.2 | (4.0) | −3.9 | (4.8) |
| −3: −4 | 3.9 | (2.1) | −7.6 | (5.3) | −5.1 | – |
| −2: −3 | 3.6 | (2.1) | −10.2 | (4.9) | −0.9 | (2.9) |
| −1: −2 | 2.2 | (5.7) | −8.3 | (5.1) | −0.9 | (5.7) |
| 0: −1 | 4.5 | (2.9) | −10.6 | (5.6) | −1.3 | (4.0) |
| *Constituencies won in 2005* | | | | | | |
| 0: 1 | 6.8 | (3.0) | −5.4 | (6.0) | 5.4 | (8.1) |
| 1: 2 | 4.5 | (3.1) | −3.8 | (6.8) | 7.1 | (5.3) |
| 2: 3 | 3.1 | (2.6) | −6.7 | (3.6) | 4.9 | (6.2) |
| 3: 4 | 4.5 | (2.4) | −7.4 | (4.4) | 4.7 | – |
| 4: 5 | 5.6 | (3.4) | −6.1 | (3.8) | 7.0 | (5.2) |
| 5: 10 | 5.1 | (3.8) | −6.6 | (5.8) | 0.2 | (4.1) |
| 10: 15 | 4.4 | (2.6) | −5.6 | (5.6) | −2.1 | (5.6) |
| 15: 20 | 3.5 | (3.0) | −4.5 | (5.3) | −0.9 | (5.0) |
| 20< | 3.0 | (3.5) | −5.8 | (7.3) | −6.7 | (6.8) |
| ALL SEATS | 3.8 | (3.4) | −6.4 | (6.3) | 0.9 | (4.5) |

but by more than five times that in their marginally-held constituencies – although large standard deviations yet again indicate considerable variation; their defence was better in some than others. But the party's offensive against its opponents was not successful; on average its vote share fell in the marginal constituencies where it hoped to make gains, but with large standard deviations suggesting better fortune in some seats than others. (In the light of the excitement and boost to the party's poll rating after Nick Clegg's performance in the first televised debate, and the expectation that it created of a substantial increase in the number of Liberal Democrat MPs that then did not materialise, it should be remembered that many in the party had previously thought it would be very difficult to increase substantially on their tally of sixty-two MPs elected in 2005. Until that surge of interest in April 2010, the party was realistically preparing to concentrate on defending its 2005 gains – so that the lack of any substantial advance in the marginal seats it failed to win then is less surprising than might at first appear.)

Some of the variation in performance across constituencies could have been because the parties differed in the success of their strategies according to which of the others was their main opponent. Table 8.8 thus looks separately at the three main groups of constituencies identified in Table 8.2. In

TABLE 8.8   *The mean change in a party's percentage share of the votes cast in a constituency between 2005 and 2010 (standard deviations in brackets) in the three main contest types*

| | Mean | (SD) | Mean | (SD) |
|---|---|---|---|---|
| *Conservative-Labour contests* | | | | |
| **Change in** | **Conservative percentage** | | **Labour percentage** | |
| Labour won 2005 | | | | |
| −20< | 4.3 | (3.1) | −7.3 | (6.2) |
| −15: −20 | 4.8 | (3.6) | −5.6 | (4.9) |
| −10: −15 | 4.4 | (3.1) | −5.8 | (5.4) |
| −5: −10 | 4.9 | (2.7) | −7.4 | (5.1) |
| 0: −5 | 4.2 | (2.4) | −7.7 | (3.8) |
| Conservative won 2005 | | | | |
| 0: 5 | 5.2 | (2.8) | −10.2 | (4.7) |
| 5: 10 | 5.8 | (5.1) | −10.7 | (3.1) |
| 10: 15 | 3.7 | (2.4) | −11.0 | (3.1) |
| 15: 20 | 3.5 | (2.6) | −11.0 | (2.7) |
| 20< | 1.5 | (8.5) | −8.7 | (3.6) |
| *Conservative-Liberal Democrat contests* | | | | |
| **Change in** | **Conservative percentage** | | **Lib Dem percentage** | |
| Liberal Democrat won 2005 | | | | |
| −20< | 1.2 | (4.5) | −0.3 | (4.8) |
| −15: −20 | 5.3 | (4.2) | −1.8 | (5.7) |
| −10: −15 | 5.3 | (4.3) | −1.8 | (5.7) |
| −5: −10 | 3.7 | (4.6) | 1.6 | (3.5) |
| 0: −5 | 2.1 | (4.3) | 4.8 | (5.9) |
| Conservative won 2005 | | | | |
| 0: 5 | 5.2 | (4.4) | −1.8 | (5.4) |
| 5: 10 | 4.6 | (2.5) | 0.3 | (4.4) |
| 10: 15 | 5.3 | (2.7) | −1.7 | (6.6) |
| 15: 20 | 3.7 | (3.8) | 1.4 | (4.9) |
| 20< | 3.5 | (3.7) | 1.4 | (3.6) |
| *Labour-Liberal Democrat contests* | | | | |
| **Change in** | **Labour percentage** | | **Lib Dem percentage** | |
| Liberal Democrat won 2005 | | | | |
| −20< | 0.0 | (2.9) | −3.3 | (9.3) |
| −15: −20 | −3.9 | (2.1) | −4.0 | (6.7) |
| −10: −15 | −8.5 | − | −5.6 | − |
| −5: −10 | −4.8 | (5.1) | −1.5 | (−3.2) |
| 0: −5 | −6.8 | (5.6) | 7.3 | (4.4) |
| Labour won 2005 | | | | |
| 0: 5 | −0.7 | (4.7) | −2.6 | (3.1) |
| 5: 10 | 0.3 | (6.1) | −1.6 | (4.1) |
| 10: 15 | −6.0 | (5.8) | 2.3 | (6.3) |
| 15: 20 | −2.2 | (5.2) | 0.1 | (6.5) |
| 20< | −5.9 | (7.6) | 0.8 | (5.9) |

the Conservative-Labour contests (335 constituencies) Labour performed much less well in the Conservative-held seats than in those it was defending. Its vote share also declined more in the marginal constituencies than in its safer seats, although this difference is not replicated in the pattern of Conservative vote increase. In the constituencies where the Conservatives and the Liberal Democrats were the main contenders, the ability of the latter to defend their marginal seats is clear (their vote increased on average by 4.8 points in those won in 2005 by a margin of less than 5 points). In the constituencies where Labour and the Liberal Democrats were the main contenders, too, the Liberal Democrats performed very much better than the average in the seats with small margins that they were defending. In some constituencies the outcome was very much out of line with the general trend, however, reflecting either particular local circumstances or/and a very intensive campaign by one of the parties – as in Redcar, where Vera Baird, the incumbent Labour MP and solicitor general, had a 31-point lead over the Liberal Democrats in 2005 (over 12,000 votes), but lost by 5,214 votes in 2010.

The overall pattern suggested by Tables 8.7 and 8.8, therefore, is that the Conservative focus on the marginal constituencies was at least partly repelled, notably by the Liberal Democrats. But while the average performance was strong, did the considerable variation indicated by the standard deviations mean that the Conservatives failed to win many of their target seats? Table 8.9 addresses this question by looking at the pattern of Conservative gains, and draws a clear contrast between the two types of seat where it was the main challenger.

There were ninety-five constituencies in which the gap between the incumbent party and the Conservative challenger was 10 points or less. The Conservatives gained sixty-nine of them; twenty-six were held by the incumbent party, therefore, most of them constituencies where the gap was

TABLE 8.9   *Conservative seat gains in 2010 in all seats and in the two contest types involving the Conservatives*

| Margin (%) Conservative gain | All Seats | | Con-Lab | | Con-LibDem | |
|---|---|---|---|---|---|---|
| | Yes | No | Yes | No | Yes | No |
| 20< | 2 | 223 | 1 | 73 | 1 | 5 |
| 15: 20 | 6 | 46 | 5 | 30 | 1 | 9 |
| 10: 15 | 22 | 27 | 17 | 17 | 4 | 7 |
| 5: 10 | 34 | 16 | 32 | 8 | 2 | 6 |
| 4: 5 | 4 | 3 | 4 | 1 | 0 | 1 |
| 3: 4 | 10 | 2 | 9 | 0 | 0 | 1 |
| 2: 3 | 9 | 1 | 8 | 0 | 1 | 1 |
| 1: 2 | 3 | 3 | 3 | 0 | 0 | 3 |
| 0: 1 | 9 | 1 | 7 | 0 | 2 | 1 |

5–10 points. The overall increase in the Conservative share was just under 4 points, but seven seats where the gap was less than that did not change hands. Six were held by the Liberal Democrats and only one by Labour: the latter (Watford) does not appear in Table 8.9 because it was one of the small number of three-way marginals; the Conservatives came third there in 2005, 4 points behind the successful Labour candidate.

The Conservatives won all of the Labour-held seats with margins no greater than the overall increase in their share of the vote between the two elections, but were less able to achieve similar victories against incumbent Liberal Democrats. In order to become the largest party, let alone secure a parliamentary majority, the Conservatives needed to advance much further than the average in seats where they were 5–15 points behind – most of them Labour-held. Achieving those victories was the goal of the target seats strategy.

## The success of targeting?

Our second argument suggests that the more intensive their local campaign in the marginal constituencies the greater the probability that the Conservatives would achieve their overall goals. To establish whether this was the case, we focus on aspects of the pattern of seat gains in their separate contests with Labour and the Liberal Democrats.

Were incumbent Labour and Liberal Democrat candidates better able to withstand the Conservative attacks than new candidates? In Labour-held seats with margins of 4 points or more (the Conservatives having won all of those with smaller majorities), there is no difference (Table 8.10): Labour was as likely to retain the seat with a new candidate contesting it as with an incumbent MP. Against the Liberal Democrats, on the other hand, Conservatives were much more likely to defeat a new candidate than an incumbent. As to the Conservatives' own candidates there is little evidence that those standing again in seats they lost in 2005 had any greater success than new candidates.

Were the Conservatives more successful in those constituencies where their local party was in good health, as reflected in their financial condition; and were their opponents better able to resist the Conservative advances where their local parties were relatively well-off? In general, the Conservatives were more likely to gain a seat where they had a local party with an annual turnover of £25,000 or more and the margin of defeat in 2005 was between 4 and 15 points (thirty-five gains and only nine not gained) than where the local party was relatively weak (eighteen gains and sixteen not gained). The presence of a relatively healthy local Labour party did not appear to constrain the number of Conservative gains. In the constituencies contested by the Conservatives and Liberal Democrats there is

TABLE 8.10   *Conservative seat gains in 2010 according to whether the incumbent MP was contesting the seat, in the two contest types involving the Conservatives*

|  |  |  |  | Incumbent Standing | | | |
|  | All Constituencies | | | Yes | | No | |
| Margin (%) | N | G | NG | G | NG | G | NG |
|---|---|---|---|---|---|---|---|
| Labour won 2005 | | | | | | | |
| 20< | 74 | 1 | 73 | 0 | 50 | 1 | 23 |
| 15: 20 | 35 | 5 | 30 | 1 | 27 | 4 | 3 |
| 10: 15 | 34 | 17 | 17 | 10 | 10 | 7 | 7 |
| 5: 10 | 40 | 32 | 8 | 20 | 5 | 12 | 3 |
| 4: 5 | 5 | 1 | 4 | 2 | 1 | 2 | 0 |
| 3: 4 | 9 | 9 | 0 | 5 | 0 | 4 | 0 |
| 2: 3 | 8 | 8 | 0 | 4 | 0 | 4 | 0 |
| 1: 2 | 3 | 3 | 0 | 1 | 0 | 2 | 0 |
| 0: 1 | 7 | 7 | 0 | 4 | 0 | 3 | 0 |
| Liberal Democrat won 2005 | | | | | | | |
| 20< | 6 | 1 | 5 | 1 | 4 | 0 | 1 |
| 15: 20 | 10 | 1 | 9 | 1 | 8 | 0 | 1 |
| 10: 15 | 11 | 4 | 7 | 1 | 7 | 3 | 0 |
| 5: 10 | 8 | 2 | 6 | 1 | 6 | 1 | 0 |
| 4: 5 | 1 | 0 | 1 | 0 | 0 | 0 | 1 |
| 3: 4 | 1 | 0 | 1 | 0 | 1 | 0 | 0 |
| 2: 3 | 2 | 1 | 1 | 0 | 1 | 1 | 0 |
| 1: 2 | 3 | 0 | 3 | 0 | 3 | 0 | 0 |
| 0: 1 | 3 | 2 | 1 | 1 | 1 | 1 | 0 |

*Note:* N – number of constituencies; G – Conservative gain; NG – Conservative did not gain

little evidence that the more affluent local parties were better at winning or retaining seats.

Turning to income from donations to the local parties in 2007–09, for the Conservative–Labour contests Table 8.11 divides the local Conservative parties into those that received any donations and those that received none. In the key area – seats won by Labour with margins of 4–15 points in 2005 – the local parties that received donations were much more likely to experience a Conservative gain in 2010 than those that did not. The local Labour parties that received relatively substantial donations (more than £5,000 over the period) were not more likely to prevent gains than those that received less, however. Donations appear to have been unimportant as determinants of the outcome in the Conservative–Liberal Democrat contests. In 2010, as at previous elections, it seems that campaign spending by the opposition parties was more efficacious than that by the incumbent governing party.[34]

TABLE 8.11   *Conservative seat gains in 2010 according to whether the constituency party and its opponent received donations 2007–2008, in the two contest types involving the Conservatives*

| | Conservative Donations | | | | Opposition Donations | | | |
| | Yes | | No | | Yes | | No | |
| Margin (%) | G | NG | G | NG | G | NG | G | NG |
|---|---|---|---|---|---|---|---|---|
| Labour won 2005 | | | | | | | | |
| 20< | 0 | 13 | 1 | 60 | 0 | 29 | 1 | 44 |
| 15 : 20 | 4 | 12 | 1 | 19 | 1 | 15 | 4 | 15 |
| 10 : 15 | 16 | 8 | 1 | 9 | 8 | 8 | 9 | 9 |
| 5 : 10 | 25 | 7 | 7 | 1 | 18 | 5 | 3 | 16 |
| 4 : 5 | 4 | 1 | 2 | 0 | 1 | 1 | 0 | 3 |
| 3 : 4 | 7 | 0 | 1 | 0 | 6 | 0 | 0 | 3 |
| 2 : 3 | 7 | 0 | 1 | 0 | 3 | 0 | 0 | 5 |
| 1 : 2 | 2 | 0 | 1 | 0 | 3 | 0 | 0 | 0 |
| 0 : 1 | 5 | 0 | 2 | 0 | 6 | 0 | 0 | 1 |
| Liberal Democrat won 2005 | | | | | | | | |
| 20< | 1 | 4 | 0 | 1 | 0 | 2 | 1 | 3 |
| 15 : 20 | 1 | 4 | 0 | 5 | 0 | 5 | 1 | 4 |
| 10 : 15 | 4 | 5 | 2 | 0 | 3 | 4 | 1 | 3 |
| 5 : 10 | 1 | 4 | 2 | 1 | 2 | 3 | 0 | 3 |
| 4 : 5 | 0 | 1 | 0 | 0 | 0 | 0 | 0 | 1 |
| 3 : 4 | 0 | 0 | 0 | 1 | 0 | 1 | 0 | 0 |
| 2 : 3 | 1 | 1 | 0 | 0 | 1 | 1 | 0 | 0 |
| 1 : 2 | 0 | 3 | 0 | 0 | 0 | 3 | 0 | 0 |
| 0 : 1 | 2 | 1 | 0 | 0 | 2 | 1 | 0 | 0 |

*Notes:* G – Conservative gain; NG – Conservative did not gain. Conservative local parties are divided into those which received no donations and those which received one or more whereas the Labour and Liberal Democrat parties are divided into those receiving donations of less than £5,000 and those receiving £5,000 or more.

Table 8.12 looks at the outcome in constituencies that received target seat grants ('Ashcroft money') in 2007 and 2008. Again focusing on the key seats that the Conservatives lost to Labour by 4–15 points in 2005 (those won by less than 4 points were all Conservative gains in 2010; those won by more than 15 points were outside the range where gains were needed for an overall victory), eighteen constituencies received grants in 2007, and fifteen of them were Conservative gains in 2010. (A further sixty-three constituencies in that range did not receive a grant, however, and thirty-eight of them were nevertheless Conservative gains.) Twenty-two of the twenty-five constituency parties in receipt of grants in 2008 were the locations of Conservative gains in 2010, compared to thirty-one of the fifty-four that did not receive grants. Such money in those first two years of the campaign was not necessary to success, therefore, but it apparently helped. Similar

TABLE 8.12   *Conservative seat gains in 2010 according to whether their constituency party received a target grant in 2007 and 2008, in the two contest types involving the Conservatives*

| | Target Grant 2007 | | | | Target Grant 2008 | | | |
| | Yes | | No | | Yes | | No | |
| Margin (%) | G | NG | G | NG | G | NG | G | NG |
|---|---|---|---|---|---|---|---|---|
| **Labour won 2005** | | | | | | | | |
| 20< | 0 | 1 | 1 | 72 | 0 | 3 | 1 | 70 |
| 15 : 20 | 1 | 3 | 4 | 27 | 1 | 3 | 4 | 27 |
| 10 : 15 | 5 | 0 | 12 | 17 | 6 | 1 | 11 | 16 |
| 5 : 10 | 9 | 2 | 23 | 8 | 13 | 1 | 19 | 7 |
| 4 : 5 | 1 | 1 | 3 | 0 | 3 | 1 | 1 | 0 |
| 3 : 4 | 3 | 0 | 6 | 0 | 5 | 0 | 4 | 0 |
| 2 : 3 | 3 | 0 | 5 | 0 | 4 | 0 | 4 | 0 |
| 1 : 2 | 3 | 0 | 0 | 0 | 2 | 0 | 1 | 0 |
| 0 : 1 | 1 | 0 | 6 | 0 | 3 | 0 | 4 | 0 |
| **Liberal Democrat won 2005** | | | | | | | | |
| 20< | 0 | 0 | 1 | 5 | 0 | 1 | 1 | 4 |
| 15 : 20 | 1 | 0 | 0 | 9 | 1 | 0 | 0 | 9 |
| 10 : 15 | 1 | 2 | 3 | 5 | 2 | 2 | 2 | 4 |
| 5 : 10 | 1 | 2 | 1 | 4 | 1 | 2 | 1 | 4 |
| 4 : 5 | 0 | 1 | 0 | 0 | 0 | 1 | 0 | 0 |
| 3 : 4 | 0 | 1 | 0 | 0 | 0 | 1 | 0 | 0 |
| 2 : 3 | 1 | 1 | 0 | 0 | 0 | 1 | 1 | 0 |
| 1 : 2 | 0 | 1 | 0 | 2 | 0 | 2 | 0 | 1 |
| 0 : 1 | 1 | 1 | 1 | 0 | 1 | 1 | 1 | 0 |

*Notes:* G – Conservative gain; NG – Conservative did not gain.

grants to local parties contesting a Liberal Democrat-held seat were not as effective, however: only five of the fourteen receiving grants in 2007 won for the Conservatives in 2010, as did five of the sixteen in 2008.

## The proximate campaign

Data on spending by candidates after January 2010 are not yet available, and the only material available for exploring the extent and intensity of the proximate campaign are the data on recorded donations to local parties during the first quarter of 2010 (January–March). During that period, 202 different Conservative constituency parties received a total of 347 donations exceeding £500; the total sum received was £1,454,356, with an average donation of £4,191. Among local Labour parties, 249 received a total of 395 donations, but the average was much smaller than for the Conservatives, at £2,427; the total received was £958,804. Finally, 102 Liberal Democrat constituency parties received 135 donations averaging £3,480 and totalling £469,903.[35]

TABLE 8.13    *Donations to local parties during the first quarter of 2010*

| Margin (%) | Conservative | | | Labour | | | Liberal Democrat | | |
|---|---|---|---|---|---|---|---|---|---|
| | NC | CD | MD (£) | NC | CD | MD (£) | NC | CD | MD (£) |
| Constituencies lost in 2005 | | | | | | | | | |
| −20< | 225 | 27 | 5,778 | 173 | 4 | 4,757 | 458 | 30 | 2,521 |
| −15 : −20 | 52 | 17 | 6,711 | 45 | 6 | 2,925 | 54 | 10 | 3,093 |
| −10 : −15 | 49 | 24 | 6,075 | 19 | 3 | 5,500 | 27 | 12 | 3,791 |
| −5 : −10 | 50 | 26 | 7,560 | 14 | 6 | 4,721 | 15 | 3 | 5,333 |
| −4 : −5 | 7 | 6 | 9,381 | 5 | 3 | 5,489 | 5 | 3 | 4,923 |
| −3 : −4 | 12 | 6 | 11,460 | 3 | 3 | 1,513 | 1 | 0 | − |
| −2 : −3 | 10 | 7 | 7,857 | 6 | 2 | 5,225 | 2 | 1 | 3,900 |
| −1 : −2 | 6 | 2 | 8,750 | 9 | 4 | 3,996 | 3 | 3 | 6,481 |
| 0 : −1 | 10 | 5 | 9,551 | 8 | 4 | 1,287 | 5 | 3 | 1,750 |
| Constituencies won in 2005 | | | | | | | | | |
| 0 : 1 | 9 | 3 | 9,283 | 9 | 7 | 3,906 | 4 | 4 | 2,820 |
| 1 : 2 | 9 | 4 | 5,631 | 9 | 4 | 8,266 | 4 | 3 | 11,066 |
| 2 : 3 | 5 | 3 | 8,847 | 9 | 4 | 3,662 | 3 | 1 | 1,000 |
| 3 : 4 | 3 | 2 | 10,000 | 11 | 5 | 6,368 | 1 | 0 | − |
| 4 : 5 | 9 | 7 | 13,095 | 5 | 4 | 1,217 | 2 | 2 | 3,824 |
| 5 : 10 | 9 | 9 | 5,628 | 45 | 31 | 3,141 | 14 | 8 | 5,632 |
| 10 : 15 | 26 | 8 | 6,193 | 42 | 32 | 5,944 | 12 | 10 | 8,199 |
| 15 : 20 | 50 | 15 | 5,573 | 49 | 27 | 3,327 | 12 | 5 | 7,950 |
| 20< | 84 | 31 | 7,169 | 172 | 100 | 3,179 | 10 | 4 | 2,950 |

*Note:* NC – number of constituencies; CD – number of constituency parties receiving donations; MD – mean value of all donations by constituency party.

Where were these donations received? The greatest local benefit would be if they went to the local parties in the more marginal constituencies. But many donors are likely to give to their local party, which may not have a great need for their money, although local parties in marginal seats may seek donations more actively.[36] Table 8.13 shows the pattern of giving by party and marginality, indicating the number of local parties that received donations and the mean total sum received. Both Labour and, to a lesser extent, Liberal Democrat donors concentrated their largesse in the parties' safer seats. Conservative donors were somewhat less likely to give money to local parties in the safest seats. In addition, donations – averaging some £7,000 per party – were received in a majority of the marginal constituencies that the Conservatives had to win if they were to form the next government. In both types of contest where the Conservatives came second in 2005 there was a positive significant relationship between the total amount of money donated to the local Conservative party and the probability of it gaining the seat. There was, however, no significant negative relationship between that probability and the total sum received in donations by the defending party.

TABLE 8.14  *Modelling Conservative seat gains in Conservative-Labour and Conservative-Liberal Democrat contests*

|  | Coefficient | SE | Exponent |
|---|---|---|---|
| *Conservative-Labour contests* | | | |
| Constant | −0.884 | −0.309 | |
| Labour incumbent | −0.531 | −0.335 | 0.588 |
| Total target grant 2007–8 (£000) | **0.134** | **−0.031** | **1.143** |
| Conservative donations 2010 (£000) | **0.109** | **−0.036** | **1.115** |
| Labour donations 2010 (£000) | 0.029 | −0.036 | 1.03 |
| N = 215 | | | |
| Nagelkerke $R^2$ = 0.296 | | | |
| per cent correct classification = 74 | | | |
| *Conservative-Liberal Democrat contests* | | | |
| Constant | −0.074 | −0.963 | |
| Liberal Democrat incumbent | **−2.932** | **−1.021** | **0.053** |
| Total target grant 2007–8 (£000) | 0.001 | −0.037 | 1.001 |
| Conservative donations 2010 (£000) | **0.203** | **−0.113** | **1.224** |
| Libdem donations 2010 (£000) | 0.064 | −0.063 | 1.007 |
| N = 45 | | | |
| Nagelkerke $R^2$ = 0.440 | | | |
| per cent correct classification = 87 | | | |

*Note:* Significant relationships at the 0.10 level or better are shown in bold.

## Modelling seat gain

The preceding discussion has looked at various relationships between aspects of the constituency campaigns and the pattern of Conservative gains. A number of the variables considered may be related (financially healthy local parties attract more donations, for example), however, and to unravel the various impacts on Conservative gains we need to undertake statistical modelling. For this, we use binary logistic regression to identify which aspects of the local parties and their campaigns had the most significant and substantial impact on the outcome; knowledge of the technique is not necessary for an appreciation of the results and the interpretation here.

Two models – one each for the Conservative contests with Labour and the Liberal Democrats – are reported in Table 8.14.[37] For the 215 constituencies held by Labour, the model has only two significant variables, both relating to Conservative money. The larger the amount received in target grants by the local party in 2007–08, the greater the probability of a Conservative gain; the exponent of 1.143 shows that for every additional £1,000 received, that probability increased by some 14 per cent. Secondly, the larger the amount received in donations during the first quarter of 2010 the larger the probability of a Conservative gain; an increase of some 12 per cent for every £1,000 received. The amount received in donations by the local Labour party did not significantly counter that impact. The presence of a Labour incumbent MP defending the seat did, however, although the substantial coefficient was not statistically significant; the exponent indicates that the probability of a Conservative gain in a seat with a Labour incumbent was only 0.6 of that where a new candidate was defending the seat, but there was considerable variability around that general pattern.

A similar model for the forty-five Conservative-Liberal Democrat constituencies won by the latter party in 2005 also shows that Conservative money was linked to the outcome, though in this case only the amount received in donations during the proximate campaign; for every £1,000 received, the probability of a Conservative gain increased by some 22 points. The other significant relationship was with Liberal Democrat incumbency: compared to a seat with a new candidate, there was only a 5 per cent chance of a Conservative gain where there was a Liberal Democrat incumbent.

As the results came in to the television studios on the night of 6–7 May, commentators claimed to discern no pattern save one that incumbents seemed to be faring better in stemming the Conservative advance than were novice candidates. These analyses substantiate that interpretation; indeed, they show that it was a very strong relationship in those seats being defended by the Liberal Democrats. These regressions also show the importance of the intensity of the local campaigns, as indexed by the amount of money available. In the seats where the Conservatives were challenging Labour, the amount given to the local Conservative parties as target grants in 2007–08, laying the foundations during the long campaign, clearly had an important influence.[38] Where they were challenging the Liberal Democrats, the money made available by donors in the last months before the election was more important; variation across those seats suggests that the proximate and climax campaigns were very important there, but this can only be analysed when further data become available.

## Conclusions

The outcome of the 2010 election differed in two main ways from its 2005 predecessor. First, with an increase of just under 4 points in its overall share of the vote in Great Britain the Conservative party gained eighty-seven seats from Labour, and lost none to them. All twenty-seven of the seats where the gap between the two parties was less than 4 points changed hands. That was far from sufficient for the Conservatives to become the largest party in the House of Commons, however, let alone win a parliamentary majority. Another ninety seats were needed for that particular outcome. Of the constituencies held by Labour with a larger majority, the Conservatives gained fifty-three where the gap was between 4 and 15 points, but failed to gain a further twenty-six; only six of the 109 where Labour's majority was even larger changed hands. Where the margin that the Conservatives had to overturn was small, Labour was unable to stem the tide flowing from it and lost all of those seats, but where the margin was larger its defensive strategy was successful in enough constituencies to prevent a flood to the Conservatives.[39]

The second main feature was that there was no general pattern to the results where the Conservatives were contesting a Liberal Democrat-held constituency. Of the nine where the margin was below the 4 points average overall increase in Conservative vote share, the Liberal Democrats retained all but three, suggesting that the strength of the local parties there enabled them to mount intensive campaigns to sustain their incumbent MPs' hold on the seats. The regressions reported in Table 8.14 indicate that the important variable was whether an incumbent MP was defending the seat rather than the resources available to sustain that defence. Whereas the Conservatives defeated all of the Labour candidates in the most marginal seats, they were unable to achieve a similar result where they were contesting with the Liberal Democrats. But they won eight others that the Liberal Democrats held with larger margins, four of them being defended by incumbent MPs – while at the same time losing three seats to their opponents.[40]

The election outcome was very different in those two types of seat, therefore, which makes it difficult to draw any overall conclusion. In the third type of seat, where Labour and the Liberal Democrats occupied first and second places in 2005, only eight of the 125 changed hands: the Liberal Democrats won five from Labour; Labour won a single seat from the Liberal Democrats; and the Conservatives won one each from the other two, having occupied third place only in those seats in 2005. And in thirty-five seats where one of the nationalist parties came either first or second in 2005, only one changed hands – a Plaid Cymru gain from Labour.[41]

As outlined at the outset of this chapter, for the Conservatives to win an overall majority in the House of Commons they had to counter the efficiency component of bias that has favoured Labour at each of the last three general elections; the other two major contributors to that bias – constituency size and turnout variations – could not readily be countered within a vote-winning campaign. To attack the efficiency bias, the Conservatives launched a target seats strategy in 2007, based on the successful local campaigns coordinated and funded by Lord Ashcroft in 2005. For 2010 this combined activities funded from and undertaken within Conservative Central Office – masterminded by Lord Ashcroft – with grants to many constituency parties to enhance their local campaigns over the three years in the run-up to the 2010 election. We have been able to evaluate only the first two years of that activity (data for 2009 and 2010 not yet being available), and have suggested that the foundations laid by the campaigns then were substantially but not totally successful.

The greatest apparent success of the Conservatives' local campaigns came in the constituencies held by the Labour party. All of the seats held by Labour with majorities of less than 4 points over their main rival were lost, indicating that the general shift towards the Conservatives across the country held there. Beyond that level, the Conservatives were more likely to gain a seat from Labour the more money granted to the local parties to fund their campaigns; investing in the long-term search for extra votes paid off. Not all of the seats within the target range fell to the Conservatives, however; those being defended by Labour incumbent MPs were less likely to be won over. Donations given to the local Conservative parties in the months immediately prior to the election also helped to advance the party's cause. But there was clearly some resistance, of the type provided by the UNITE trade union. It spent over £2 million promoting Labour candidates, not by giving money to the local parties but by contacting its members in eighty-four key constituencies, where their number exceeded the margin being defended, and encouraging them to vote Labour. Of those eighty-four, the Conservatives won only fifty-six, with UNITE leaders claiming that their action prevented a Conservative overall victory. Money apparently mattered there, but it was money spent centrally rather than locally, and not by the party organisation itself.[42] Elsewhere, particular local factors were important, as in Birmingham, Edgbaston, where the popular Labour MP, Gisela Stuart, successfully defended a majority of only 4.1 points, winning by 3.1 points.

Whereas the target seats strategy worked to a considerable degree in the contests against Labour, the same cannot be said about those where the Conservatives were seeking to replace the Liberal Democrats. Some very marginal seats remained in Liberal Democrat hands, whereas others that were less marginal fell to the Conservatives. Overall the Liberal Democrats were much more likely to retain seats where they had an incumbent MP as a candidate than where a new candidate was fielded, and there was no evidence that the amount of money provided by Conservative Central Office to constituency parties was effective.[43] Again, however, extra money made available by donors to local Conservative parties in early 2010 apparently had an impact, allowing the campaigns to intensify.

Despite this failure to make advances in Liberal Democrat-held seats consistent with those held by Labour, the Conservatives' target seats strategy was, according to this preliminary evaluation, successful enough to remove the efficiency bias that favoured Labour in the elections up to and including 2005. Table 8.3 shows that the overall pro-Labour bias was almost halved to fifty-four, with the major change being the total elimination of the efficiency component. For the first time in five elections, the Conservatives were as successful as Labour as winning votes in the right places. But they were not as successful as Labour had been in the previous three elections (the pro-Labour efficiency bias in 1997, 2001 and 2005 was forty-eight, seventy-four and thirty-five seats respectively), nor as the Conservatives had been in the 1980s elections (there was a pro-Conservative efficiency bias of twenty-eight and thirty-four seats respectively in 1983 and 1987). The 2010 strategy was sufficient to eliminate Labour's advantage but no more.

The British electoral system remains biased against the Conservatives, therefore, largely because of the geography of turnout that favours Labour and, to a lesser extent, differentials in electorate size. The Conservatives have plans to attack the latter in the coalition government's proposal to have all constituencies across the United Kingdom having electorates within 5 points of the national average by the time of the next election, but the former bias cannot readily be tackled.[44] Their target seats strategy enabled them to eliminate the pro-Labour efficiency bias, but not to regain a similar advantage for themselves that existed in the 1980s. The reason for that failure, according to the current analyses, is because their strategy was not entirely successful in the seats they were contesting with Labour, and even less so in those held by the Liberal Democrats. Although data for the long-campaign period indicate that the Conservatives were better placed to contest marginal seats held by the Liberal Democrats than those held by Labour, they also show that their opponents were better able to respond to such targeting: this response was successful in a number of cases, especially those where incumbent Liberal Democrat MPs defended their seats. Only further analyses, when later data become available, can explore this partial failure in greater detail. The provisional conclusion is that the focused local long campaigns were more effective in some situations than others, and that incumbent MPs had an advantage over newly-selected candidates in defending marginal constituencies.

Overall, although Labour clearly lost, the Conservatives did not in consequence have a decisive victory – which was always a fairly remote possibility because of the pro-Labour bias. Their target seats campaign was designed to counter that bias, but it was only partly successful. In the contests with the Liberal Democrats, the outcome was stalemate: the Conservatives made few gains in the marginal seats they needed to win, but the Liberal Democrats in their turn failed to win any of their targets held by the Conservatives with small majorities. The Conservatives performed much better in their contests with Labour, winning all of the seats held by Labour by margins less than the Conservative overall vote gain. But the Conservatives failed to win enough of the Labour-held seats where the majorities were larger – and that variation in success can only be analysed in detail when we have data on the intensity of the proximate and climax campaigns. The long campaign laid down firm foundations for winning many seats, but there were still many voters in target constituencies waiting to be convinced.

# Endnotes

1  See Tim Bale, *The Conservative Party from Thatcher to Cameron* (Cambridge: Polity, 2010).

2  Brown's view immediately after the results were known was: 'But this is not the final word'. See Peter Mandelson, *The Third Man: Life at the Heart of New Labour* (London: HarperPress, 2010), p. 541.

3  This was the view expressed by David Butler and Dennis Kavanagh in *The British General Election of 1987* (London: Macmillan, 1988) and *The British General Election of 1992* (London: Macmillan, 1992). See also Dennis Kavanagh, *Constituency Electioneering in Britain* (London: Longman, 1970).

4  As indicated in *The Times* obituary for former MP Denzil Freeth: 'Denzil Freeth: former MP and junior minister', *The Times*, 12 May 2010. On long-term trends in campaign spending and its impact see Ron Johnston, *Money and Votes: Constituency Campaign Spending and Election Results* (London: Croom Helm, 1987).

5  Using spending as a surrogate index of the intensity of campaigns in the constituencies, there is plenty of evidence of rational behaviour by the parties – i.e. concentrating their effort in marginal constituencies – although in general the Conservatives have spent more in their 'safe seats' than have the other parties. See Johnston, *Money and Votes*; Charles Pattie and Ron Johnston, 'Local battles in a national landslide: constituency campaigning at the 2001 British general election', *Political Geography*, 22 (2003): 381–414.

6  See, for example, David Denver and Gordon Hands, 'Labour's targeted constituency campaigning: nationally directed or locally produced?', *Electoral Studies*, 23 (2004): 709–26; Justin Fisher and David Denver, 'From foot-slogging to call centres and direct mail: a framework for analysing the development of district-level campaigning', *European Journal of Political Research*, 47 (2008): 794–826, and 'Evaluating the electoral effects of traditional and modern modes of constituency campaigning in Britain, 1992–2005', *Parliamentary Affairs*, 62 (2009): 196–210.

7  David Cutts, 'Continuous campaigning and electoral outcomes: the Liberal Democrats in Bath', *Political Geography*, 25 (2006): 72–88; David Cutts, '"Where we work we win": a case study of local Liberal Democrat campaigning', *Journal of Elections, Public Opinion and Parties*, 16 (2006): 221–42; and David Cutts and Nick Shrayne, 'Did Liberal Democrat activism really matter? Liberal Democrat campaigning and the 2001 British general election', *The British Journal of Politics and International Relations*, 8 (2006): 427–44.

8  See Justin Fisher, 'Political finance and local party activity in Britain', paper given at the Political Studies Association Conference, Edinburgh, April 2010, and cited with the author's permission, in Keith Ewing, Joo Cheong Tham and Jacob Rowbotham, eds, *The Funding of Political Parties* (London: Routledge, 2011).

9  See Charles Pattie and Ron Johnston, 'Still talking, but is anyone listening?: The changing face of constituency campaigning in Britain, 1997–2005', *Party Politics*, 15 (2009): 411–34.

10 The reports produced by Sir Hayden Phillips on the funding of political parties are available from www.partyfundingreview.gov.uk/download.htm (last accessed 21 May 2010).

11   Ron Johnston and Charles Pattie, 'Funding local parties in England and Wales: donations and constituency campaigns', *The British Journal of Politics and International Relations*, 9 (2007): 365–95.

12   Ron Johnston and Charles Pattie, 'Local parties, local money and local campaigns: regulation issues', in Ewing et al., *The Funding of Political Parties*.

13   Colin Rallings and Michael Thrasher, *Media Guide to the New Parliamentary Constituencies* (Plymouth: Local Government Chronicle Elections Centre, 2007).

14   Ron Johnston and Charles Pattie, 'The British general election of 2010: a three-party contest or three two-party contests?', *The Geographical Journal*, 176 (2010).

15   There was a major redistribution of seats in that part of West Yorkshire and the new seat contained only one-third of Balls' former seat of Normanton. The intensity of the campaign there is illustrated by the three donations totalling £7,000 received by the Labour constituency party during January–March 2010 and the two totalling £13,212 received by the local Conservative party.

16   This is the basis of most evaluations of the bias, as in Ron Johnston, Charles Pattie, Daniel Dorling and David Rossiter, *From Votes to Seats: The Operation of the UK Electoral System Since 1945* (Manchester: Manchester University Press, 2001).

17   Colin Rallings, Ron Johnston and Michael Thrasher, 'Changing the boundaries but keeping the disproportionality: the electoral impact of the fifth periodical reviews by the Parliamentary Boundary Commissions for England and Wales', *The Political Quarterly*, 79 (2008): 80–90.

18   For a full discussion of the size issues see Galina Borisyuk, Ron Johnston, Colin Rallings and Michael Thrasher, 'Parliamentary constituency boundary reviews and electoral bias: how important are variations in constituency size?', *Parliamentary Affairs*, 63 (2010): 4–21.

19   Its former leader and highest profile candidate chose to stand against the Speaker, who – following tradition – was not challenged by the three main parties. He came third.

20   Johnston and Pattie, 'Funding local parties in England and Wales'. See Lord Ashcroft's books *Dirty Politics Dirty Times* and *Smell the Coffee*, available on his website at: www.lordashcroft.com/publications/index.html (last accessed 21 May 2010).

21   The Labour MP for the marginal constituency of Pendle claimed that substantial sums of money were being spent there by the Conservatives during the long campaign. See Brian Brady, 'Can Ashcroft put a spell on Pendle? Tories spend heavily in the Pennines', *Independent on Sunday*, 14 March 2010. On a comparable situation in Hove, see Toby Helm, Jamie Doward and Rajeev Syal, 'Lord Ashcroft goes from Tory saviour to election liability in marginal seats', *Observer*, 7 March 2010.

22   These data are available at: www.electoralcommission.org.uk/party-finance (last access 21 May 2010).

23   Fisher, 'Political finance and local party activity'. Some studies, however, have found close relationships between a range of indicators of campaign intensity – as in Charles Pattie, Paul Whiteley, Ron Johnston and Patrick Seyd, 'Measuring local campaign effects: Labour Party constituency campaigning at the 1987 General Election', *Political Studies*, 42 (1994): 469–79, and David Denver and Gordon Hands, *Modern Constituency Electioneering: Local Campaigning in the 1992 General Election* (London: Frank Cass, 1997).

24 Of those who did stand, Hazel Blears in Salford and Eccles experienced a drop in her share of the vote from 55 to 40 per cent. Sir Thomas Legg's findings are set out in an Appendix to Members Estimate Committee, *Review of past ACA payments, First Report of Session 2009–10*, HC348 (London: TSO, 2010).

25 Most of those accounting units are individual constituency parties, but in some places – Milton Keynes and Swindon, for example – there is a single unit covering two or more adjacent constituencies. In these cases the income and other data have been divided equally across the constituencies. In some cases the Ashcroft money was probably focused on one constituency more than another, but we made no attempt to suggest such differentials. Accounting units covering larger areas –such as regions of the UK – are excluded from these analyses.

26 These grants are separately identified in the party accounts, although in a few cases it was not clear whether a grant was 'Ashcroft money' from Central Office. The nature of such grants is rarely mentioned, let alone discussed, in the Annual Report appended to most of the Statements of Accounts, suggesting a party policy.

27 The small number of grants to parties in non-marginal constituencies reflects the combination of two or more constituencies in a single accounting unit, one of which may not be marginal.

28 Of the thirty-two constituencies won by Labour with a margin of less than 5 points over the Conservatives in 2005, six did not return their accounts in 2008 (i.e. had a turnover of less than £25,000) and four others reported incomes in excess of £100,000.

29 Of those forty-six, six were by accounting units covering two or more constituencies.

30 Averages below the £25,000 figure are because of the presence of several local parties that covered more than one constituency.

31 This was the case, for example, in Streatham where the Liberal Democrats were in second place but 17 points behind Labour according to the 2005 notional results; their candidate – an accountant in a city firm – is reputed to have spent some £250,000 campaigning there over the three years prior to the election, which Labour won by 7 points. See Nigel Morris, 'Lib Dem candidate accused of "buying seat"', *Independent*, 4 March 2010, and Mike Watts, 'Lib Dem candidate Chris Nicholson "attempting to buy a parliamentary seat" says Labour MP Keith Hill', *Streatham Guardian*, 11 March 2010.

32 In some constituencies, however, the local Labour party was able to mobilise substantial numbers of voluntary workers, as in the successful campaign to stem the growth of the BNP vote in Barking, where the party's leader came third with only 14.6 per cent, less than the 17 per cent obtained by the BNP's candidate in 2005. Labour performed better in London than in most of the rest of England in 2010, perhaps reflecting the strength of its campaigning organisation there; the Barking constituency party obtained donations of £22,372 in 2009 to sustain its campaign against the BNP.

33 We omit two constituencies: Buckingham was held by the incumbent Speaker and according to convention was not contested by candidates from the main political parties; the Thirsk and Malton contest was postponed because of the death of one of the candidates and was held three weeks later.

34 Pattie and Johnston, 'Still talking but who's listening?'

35  As with the earlier data, a few donations went to local accounting units covering two constituencies and these have been divided equally among the member units.

36  The main exceptions are the trade-union donors to local Labour parties, many of which have links to candidates in relatively safe seats.

37  We explored a range of other models to identify the most informative; no others found that further factors were significantly related to the pattern of Conservative seat gain.

38  It may not be a straightforward relationship between money and vote-winning. As the local parties were required to submit business plans in order to qualify for such grants, the Central Office unit identified those most likely to run successful campaigns. However, without the money from the grants, they may not have been able to run such an intensive campaign; the money probably mattered.

39  Anecdotal evidence suggests that Labour recognised that it was very likely to lose those seats held by small majorities and so concentrated its campaigning resources on the seats where the margin was larger and the possibility of a successful defence greater.

40  Again, some of these cases reflect particular local situations. In Oxford West and Abingdon, for example, Evan Harris was defending a majority of 16,602 but lost by 176 votes – in considerable part because of campaigns opposing his pro-abortion position and by an Animal Protection Party candidate.

41  Within England, the main regional pattern was that Labour's vote fell by much less (on average only 2.6 points compared to an overall average of 7.5) in London.

42  See Patrick Wintour and Nick Watt's blog, 'Unions claimed they stopped a Tory majority government', 21 May 2010, available on the *Guardian* website at www.guardian.co.uk/politics/wintour-and-watt/2010/may/21/general-election-2010-unite (last accessed 21 May 2010). The union claims to have sent out over 1.9 million letters from its headquarters plus 2.5 million e-mails, and to have made some 52,000 phone calls to members from its phone bank. However, of the constituencies held by Labour with margins of 5–10 points, the Conservatives gained nine of the sixteen where UNITE did not campaign and twenty-three of the twenty-nine where it did.

43  There were clear exceptions, notably in Montgomeryshire where the incumbent Liberal Democrat MP, Lembit Öpik, defeated a Conservative by some 23 points in 2005. A combination of Öpik's unpopularity locally and the popularity of the Conservative candidate who stood again (having lost his list seat in the Welsh Assembly in 2007) saw a Conservative victory by some 4 points.

44  See Ron Johnston, Iain McLean, Charles Pattie and David Rossiter, 'Can the Boundary Commissions help the Conservative Party? Constituency size and electoral bias in the United Kingdom', *The Political Quarterly*, 80 (2009): 479–94.

# 9  THE POLITICS OF COALITION

Philip Norton

Coalitions in British government – two or more parties combining to form the government of the day – have occasionally been anticipated, sometimes favoured by some political parties, but rarely come to fruition, and when they have it has not been as a consequence of the uncertain outcome of a general election. Coalition government in one form or another existed in the twentieth century for a period of twenty-one years, but for eighteen of those years the Conservatives could have governed on their own as a majority party. There were also in total twelve years of minority government, only four of those occurring in the period since 1931. The United Kingdom thus has limited experience of minority government at Westminster and no experience of successful post-election bargaining to create a minimal winning coalition (or indeed any coalition).[1] The only attempt at coalition building in recent history was in February 1974 when Edward Heath sought to bring the Liberal party into a minority coalition, but the attempt failed.[2] The only formal deal done between parties, falling well short of coalition, was a short-lived parliamentary pact between 1977 and 1978 involving the Labour government and the Liberals.[3] Otherwise, single-party dominance has been the norm. The political system has been geared to that political reality. Both the administration of government, and of parliament, proceeds essentially on the basis that a single party will be returned to office, usually with an absolute majority.

The outcome of the 2010 general election thus created a unique situation in British politics. It induced post-election, and part public, negotiations for the creation of a coalition and resulted in a situation in parliament that bore no resemblance to previous parliaments. For much of the two years prior to the election, the general assumption, as Tim Bale and Paul Webb note in Chapter 2, was that there would be a Conservative government and that it would be a majority government. There was therefore no sustained planning for a hung parliament, in which no party had an overall majority, and certainly no preparation based on learning from the experience of countries where coalition forming was well established. What happened in 2010 was largely a case of muddling through and much of what happened can be understood as much by comparison to practice elsewhere as to British history.

Harold Wilson's observation that a week can be a long time in politics was borne out in the days following Thursday 6 May 2010. David Cameron had largely succeeded in transforming the Conservatives from an unelectable into an electable party.[4] Most people had expected Labour to lose the general election, coming second to the Conservatives, but – as Ron Johnston and Charles Pattie show in Chapter 8 – it was less certain that the Conservatives would achieve an absolute majority. Though many commentators were inclined to discount the election-evening exit polls, which predicted a hung parliament, the polls proved remarkably accurate. As Friday 7 May dawned, Cameron knew he would not be called to Buckingham Palace that morning to form a majority administration. Indeed, he feared he would not be called at all. The situation was unprecedented. For all three party leaders, there was no win-win situation. Each faced difficult choices. This chapter identifies the dilemma confronting the party leaders and explains how it was resolved in terms of the available options, the inter-party negotiations and the key variables that determined the final outcome.

## The dilemma

Gordon Brown had led his party to defeat, though not on the scale which many in the party had feared. Labour had lost, coming second not only in seats but also (unlike the Conservatives in February 1974) in votes. The constitutional position was simple. Brown remained as prime minister and would stay so until he chose to resign or (following the older tradition) until the new parliament met and he was defeated in the House of Commons. The politics, however, were far from simple. Although Brown had lost, there was no outright winner with an uncontestable moral or constitutional right to succeed him. He could elect to go to the Palace immediately and advise the Queen to send for David Cameron. Alternatively, he could wait, following the precedent of Edward Heath in 1974, to see if he could come to some arrangement with Nick Clegg and the Liberal Democrats, even though the numbers would not be sufficient for an overall majority.

David Cameron now led the party with the largest number of seats in the House of Commons. However, he stood as the heir presumptive to the premiership rather than the heir apparent. He could make some sort of moral claim to the keys of 10 Downing Street but, since he lacked an absolute majority of his own, he had no way of enforcing the claim. He could only bide his time, or publicly call for Brown to resign, and/or plan an approach to the Liberal Democrats with a view to some agreement, possibly falling short of a coalition (much like the Lib–Lab Pact of 1977–78), to sustain a Conservative government in office.

Nick Clegg had achieved a personal success in the leaders' televised debates, but this had not translated into increasing the number of seats held by the Liberal Democrats (see Chapter 7). His party now held the balance of power in the House of Commons, but it was a party diminished in size. He was also constrained in having declared prior to the election that the party gaining 'the strongest mandate' in the election should have the first opportunity to form a government.[5] He was also known to have poor personal relations with Gordon Brown, but he led a party where the ideological difference between it and the Conservative party, though not as wide as before, was greater than between it and the Labour party.

The picture was complicated by Clegg's own position on the ideological spectrum, being one of the *Orange Book* Liberal Democrats (see Chapter 3) and thus not as adverse to the Conservatives as many in his party. He had worked with Conservative politicians before (notably Leon Brittan in the European Commission, who had tried to recruit him to the Conservative cause), and he took a notably different stance to his predecessors, Paddy Ashdown, Charles Kennedy and Sir Menzies Campbell, on relations with the two major parties.

In many respects, the dilemma facing the Liberal Democrats had been neatly encapsulated three years earlier by a one-time contender for the party leadership, Mark Oaten. In his work on coalitions, he recorded:

> Cameron's Conservatives have held out the olive branch to a number of Liberal MPs, most notably David Laws, one of the party's brightest MPs, who has admitted that he was asked to defect in 2005. Others, such as Jeremy Browne and, the biggest prize of all, Nick Clegg, must also be in their sights. These MPs and a cluster of others would have little difficulty working with Conservatives in a hung Parliament. They don't, however, represent a majority of the Parliamentary Party.[6]

For each party leader, there was no obvious solution. They proceeded on the basis of only two points of agreement. First, that the Queen must not be embarrassed by having to exercise any discretion. Instead, the matter had to be resolved by the party leaders (as in February 1974) and the result reported to the Palace. Second, the matter had to be resolved within a matter of days rather than weeks. The preparation for the Queen's Speech, the traditional unveiling of the government's legislative programme, normally takes two weeks, and even that means it is usually done in something of a rush after an election. Though the Queen's Speech had been put back by a week from when it would normally be held, there was still pressure to form a government as quickly as possible. The economic situation was one source of pressure. Cabinet secretary Sir Gus O'Donnell, Britain's most senior civil servant, was convinced that agreement had to be reached quickly in order to stabilise the financial markets and made this clear to the party leaders. A further source of pressure was the media coverage. Television companies created an encampment opposite the houses of parliament and provided virtually continuous coverage of the unfolding events. Some sections of the right-wing press made clear their preferences for an entirely new government, portraying the defeated Brown as the 'squatter' in Downing Street.[7]

The issue might conceivably have been resolved in a matter of hours rather than days had Gordon Brown decided to resign as prime minister once the results were known. He elected not to do so, stating that it was his duty to remain in office until it was clear as to who could command a majority in the House of Commons. A more political interpretation of his announcement was that he was keen to remain until it was clear that *he* could not form a new government. As one retiring Labour MP had previously noted in his diary: 'Letting go is not in Gordon's DNA.'[8]

## Resolving the dilemma

Once it was clear on 7 May, the day after polling day, that no party had gained an overall majority, there was bilateral contact between the parties. Gordon Brown emerged from Downing Street to announce that he would remain in office while the other parties negotiated and that he was prepared to provide the necessary civil service support for such negotiations to take place. He also made clear that he was available to talk to the Liberal Democrats should their negotiations with the Conservatives fail. The scene was thus set for a frantic and unprecedented round of private and public negotiations.

### The options

By convention, the return of a party with an overall majority of seats in the House of Commons results in the leader of that party being summoned to Buckingham Palace. Other options for government formation are effectively foreclosed. A hung parliament brings other options into play. The outcome of the 2010 election created a number of options, some viable, some not.

Three theoretically possible but politically non-viable options can be excluded from consideration. A *minority Labour government*, with no formal support from any other party, would have had no political credibility and was a non-starter. Although performing better than many expected, the Labour government had clearly 'lost' the election and would have been vulnerable to defeat as soon as it met the new parliament. The non-viability of this option was recognised by Gordon Brown who made no attempt to pursue it. A *grand coalition* (Conservative + Labour) of the sort occasionally employed in Germany, but never employed in the United Kingdom in conditions in which both principal parties remained united, was also not contemplated. Neither was a *super-, or surplus-, majority coalition* (Conservatives + Labour + others), which has been employed in Britain only in exceptional conditions of wartime (1940–45). Since a grand coalition was not politically feasible, a super-majority coalition was not an option either.

The viability of any option was greatly affected by the new configuration of party support in the House of Commons. The election results had handed the parties 'not just the first hung Parliament for thirty-six years, but the most complicated Commons arithmetic since the 1920s.'[9] The Liberal Democrats in alliance with the Conservatives (57 + 306) could deliver an overall majority in a 650-member House, but the Liberal Democrats in alliance with the Labour Party (57 + 258) could not. There were twenty-nine other MPs elected, though six of these were non-voting (five Sinn Fein MPs who would not take their seats and the Speaker, John Bercow). Of the twenty-three who were voting Members, only the eight members of the Democratic Unionist Party were likely to have much empathy with the Conservatives. The remaining parties were closer ideologically to Labour. However, complicating the picture were the other two key variables to be discussed below, politics and personality. In Scotland, for example, the principal political antagonists were the Scottish Nationalist Party (SNP) and Labour, and there was little personal empathy between prime minister Gordon Brown and Scottish first minister Alex Salmond.

Taking such factors into account, there were five viable options. A *Labour–Liberal Democrat pact,* that is, a minority Labour government with contingent support from the Liberal Democrats primarily on a 'confidence and supply' basis (backing it in confidence votes and on supply votes, such as the budget) – though it could extend to other votes – was technically possible, but potentially the most unstable of the five. The votes of the other party would not be sufficient to deliver a majority. If the Liberal Democrats supported Labour in a confidence vote this would mean that the Conservatives would need the support of some minor parties that were not their natural allies in order to bring the government down. Labour and the Liberal Democrats could muster 315 votes and the Conservatives with Democratic Unionist support could deliver 314. In practice, the Labour vote would go down by two, and the Conservative vote by one, once three non-voting deputy speakers were elected, so the numbers would be equal at 313 each. Given that the three Social Democratic and Labour Party (SDLP) MPs from Northern Ireland could be expected to support Labour, the government's total would be boosted to 316. With Green MP Caroline Lucas, independent MP Lady Sylvia Hermon and Alliance MP Naomi Long most likely to support Labour, that would raise it further to 319.[10] Only if the nine nationalist MPs (six SNP, three Plaid Cymru) voted against, as opposed to abstain, would the government lose in any vote in the Commons. Yet Labour MPs with long memories would find it difficult to forget that the nationalist parties had contributed to bringing down James Callaghan's government in a vote of confidence on 28 March 1979. For them, and others, there would always be the uncertainty deriving from the prospect of a repeat performance.

A *Labour–Liberal Democratic coalition* offered the prospect of a more formal and enduring alliance: the Liberal Democrats would be part of government, holding some ministerial posts, and deliver fifty-seven additional votes on a regular rather than a contingent basis. Though such a coalition would always face the possibility of losing divisions in the House, the experience of minority government from April 1976 to March 1979, and even the period of minority Labour government in the short parliament of 1974 (which effectively sat for only five months, from March to July), demonstrated that a government without an overall majority could achieve the passage of a considerable body of legislation.[11] For Gordon Brown, the prospect of doing a deal with the Liberal Democrats, be it a pact or in coalition, therefore held out the potential for Labour remaining in office.

The three remaining viable options all involved the Conservatives. Two of these were almost the equivalent of options involving Labour: *a Conservative–Liberal Democrat pact* and *a Conservative–Liberal Democrat coalition*. The difference was that the Liberal Democrats could now help deliver a majority. As Michael Laver and Norman Schofield have noted, coalition theory tends to presume that non-minimal winning governments are less stable than those that are. Minority governments are assumed to be more susceptible to defeat than majority governments.[12] Empirical evidence supports this intuition. Single-party majority governments tend to be the most durable, followed by minimal winning coalitions.[13] A Conservative–Liberal Democrat coalition would create a minimal winning majority. The support of third parties would not be necessary. (Evidence from around the world would also suggest that adding other parties, creating a surplus-majority coalition, would not necessarily reinforce stability.)[14] An agreement between the two parties thus offered a firmer basis for stable government than a single-party minority government; a coalition in particular offered the prospect of a consistent government majority, able to deliver legislation agreed by the two parties.

The other viable option was a *minority Conservative government*. Without the support of a minor party, it would be vulnerable to defeat by a combination of Labour and the Liberal Democrats (with or without the support of minor parties). With the support of the Democratic Unionists, it would be vulnerable to defeat by a combination of Labour, the Liberal Democrats and minor parties. However, it would be feasible given that there would be little political incentive for Labour and the Liberal Democrats to favour an early general election. Forcing an election at a time when the government was tackling major economic problems could prove counter-productive. Moreover, assuming Gordon Brown stood down as Labour leader, the party's new leader would need time to establish himself both in parliament and the country. There would be a financial disincentive too: neither party could afford to fight another general election so soon after the last one. Also, as Philip Cowley and Mark Stuart have shown (and as noted in Chapter 3), in the previous Parliament the Liberal Democrats and Conservatives had voted together, more frequently than before, in opposition to certain government policies. On some issues, the Conservatives could expect the Liberal Democrats to support them or at least abstain in House of Commons votes. If the government did encounter crippling obstruction by other parties in the Commons, it would be open to the prime minister to request a dissolution in order to seek a clear mandate from the people. A minority Conservative government was therefore an option. Indeed, Brown and his advisors apparently thought Cameron would form such an administration and then call a second election a few months later.[15] Many within the Conservative party regarded it as the preferable option. It may have led to a minority government, but it would at least be a *Conservative* government.

## The negotiations

The moment the election results were known, both Brown and Cameron decided on an approach to the Liberal Democrats to explore their respective options. Brown recognised that the only hope of him remaining in Number 10 for any length of time was to find some accommodation. He began telephoning leading Liberal Democrats 'to try to rally them behind the idea of some form of Lab–Lib Dem arrangement.'[16] Transport secretary Lord Adonis, who was working closely with him, had already been in contact with Nick Clegg's chief of staff, Danny Alexander. Adonis had been a Liberal Democrat local councillor before joining the Labour party, and his connections made him the obvious go-between.

Meanwhile, parallel discussions were taking place between the Conservatives and the Liberal Democrats. Cameron, having realised in the early hours of the morning that he would not be leading a single-party majority government, had also opted for trying to reach an accommodation. This decision was not wholly popular: 'by not appearing bumptious or cocksure about the Tory result, he disappointed some in his own ranks like John Redwood and the new 1922 committee leader, Graham Brady, who urged him to go for a minority government.'[17] However, a coalition was attractive in that it would negate the need for an early election. There was also a perceived advantage in relation to his own party. 'A full coalition would protect him not only from the electorate, but from his own mutinous backbenchers, a lot of whom are furious about the way the campaign was handled.'[18] Though he had warned voters against a hung parliament ahead of the election and had not made formal approaches, Cameron had actually given some thought to the possibility of co-operating with the Liberal Democrats and so had some idea of where there were areas of agreement between the two parties.[19]

At 1.30 pm on Friday 7 May, Brown made his announcement outside Number 10, and the civil service then provided the support mechanisms for the ensuing talks. The official support included providing neutral space for negotiations and, as appropriate, making a record of proceedings, though some meetings took place without officials present. The work of the civil service was essentially limited and, according to one former senior mandarin, not as great as it may have liked to think.[20] The only civil service involvement of significance was Sir Gus O'Donnell's insistence that agreement be reached in order to reassure the financial markets that there would be a robust plan to deal with the country's deficit.

Brown's announcement was followed by a televised statement by David Cameron expressing his willingness to engage in discussions with the Liberal Democrats and making what he termed a 'big, open and comprehensive offer'.[21] Both his willingness to be so public and the extent of the concessions he was offering took other politicians, including the Liberal Democrats, by surprise. Cameron telephoned Clegg and two teams of negotiators (George Osborne, William Hague, Oliver Letwin and Ed Llewellyn for the Tories; David Laws, Danny Alexander, Chris Huhne and Andrew Stunnell for the Liberal Democrats) met at the Cabinet Office to open negotiations. They made progress, but an apparent sticking point was electoral reform. The Liberal Democrats had a longstanding commitment to replacing the existing 'first-past-the-post' system of parliamentary elections with a system of proportional representation. It was a totemic issue for the party, seen as fundamental to any negotiations. The Conservatives, however, were supporters of the existing electoral system and were reluctant to go beyond offering to establish a committee of inquiry.

On the following day, Saturday 8 May, Clegg met with his MPs and in the evening with the party's federal executive. He then met with Cameron in Admiralty House, a building close to Downing Street, for more than an hour. Clegg later spoke to Brown on the telephone and agreed that the following day talks should begin between the Liberal Democrats and Labour. Though the conversation had been at Brown's request, Clegg was content to pursue talks with both parties simultaneously. As one Sunday newspaper noted shortly afterwards, 'Wooed by both the Tories and Labour, the Lib Dems felt there was all to play for.'[22]

The next morning, Sunday 9 May, the Liberal Democrats met the Labour team of Peter Mandelson, Andrew Adonis, Ed Balls and Harriet Harman. Brown also met Clegg for over an hour in the Foreign Office, another neutral negotiating space. Whereas the sticking point in the Conservative–Liberal Democrat talks appeared to be electoral reform, in the Labour–Liberal Democrat talks it appeared to be the future of Gordon Brown. The same day, the Conservative and Liberal Democrat negotiating teams met again in the Cabinet Office for an extended session. In the evening, Clegg saw Brown in the Commons.[23] Although one account insists that Brown already knew 'that he would have to make the ultimate sacrifice' if any deal was to be struck, he vacillated as to when he would actually go, saying he would need to be in place to ensure, among other things, that economic recovery was in place.[24] Mandelson describes how 'They went back and forth for some time, Nick explaining the "massive political risk" of being seen to legitimise Gordon as Prime Minister after the election result, and Gordon saying that he would announce he was leaving, but that he felt he could not go until he had successfully dealt with "the tasks in hand".'[25] Brown then came under pressure from some on his own side, including Mandelson, to signal unequivocally that he would resign.

On Monday 10 May, Clegg met again with his MPs. Most preferred a Labour–Liberal Democrat deal. Early that evening, Brown made a state-ment outside Number 10 announcing the opening of formal discussions with the Liberal Democrats and also saying that he had asked his party to begin the process of electing a new Labour leader by the autumn. He thus removed a major impediment to any deal. On hearing the news, Cameron rang Clegg to query why he was now talking officially to Labour. He also sought to regain the initiative by offering a referendum on the alternative vote (AV). 'It was a huge risk on the Tory leader's part, threatening uproar in his own party.'[26] The offer was then made public by William Hague, who said that they were willing to go 'the extra mile' and were now making a 'final offer' of the referendum.[27]

Labour's negotiating team met with the Liberal Democrats that evening. The talks, however, did not go well, either in terms of policy concessions or personal relations. Some of the Labour team were unwilling to move on key issues and there was little goodwill between Ed Balls on the Labour side and Chris Huhne on the other. Cameron called a meeting of Conservative MPs to brief them on what was happening. Clegg met with his MPs and reported on the negative outcome of the negotiations with the Labour party. They agreed to a further meeting with the Labour team, but apparently with-out any great anticipation of a successful outcome. However, many still favoured a Labour–Liberal Democrat deal, and there was also perceived mileage in maintaining the twin-track approach. It was thought that the Conservatives would be more likely to make concessions if they thought a Labour–Liberal Democrat coalition was a serious possibility.

Many on the Labour side had a different view. The cabinet was reported to be split and the next morning, Tuesday 11 May, various senior Labour MPs – former cabinet ministers David Blunkett and John Reid among them – made public their opposition to a deal.[28] They recognised that Labour had been rejected by the electorate and felt that any agreement to keep them in power would lack legitimacy. The Labour and Liberal Democrat teams met but appeared to be exchanging insults rather than engaging in serious negotiations. As Mandelson later observed, 'What was most striking… was a new attitude of prickliness, even truculence, from the Lib Dems.'[29] The

Conservative–Liberal Democrat negotiations, on the other hand, made further progress and resolved outstanding differences, including on income tax and national insurance. Realising that the Conservatives and the Liberal Democrats were going to do a deal, Brown telephoned Clegg that afternoon. Brown told him he was resigning, but Clegg asked him for more time while he consulted his party. 'Nick, Nick, I can't hold on any longer', Brown responded. Clegg reminded him of his obligation to remain until he was sure a new government could be formed. Brown responded that he had lost patience and so had the people and that he was going to the Palace.

Brown made a brief statement to the press in Downing Street and left with his family to resign. David Cameron was summoned to kiss hands as prime minister. At this point, he was a prime minister who could not yet command the confidence of a majority of MPs in the House of Commons. A coalition deal, though, was soon concluded. An outline agreement was published the following day, Wednesday 12 May, and a cabinet was formed comprising eighteen Conservatives and five Liberal Democrats. Nick Clegg became the new deputy prime minister. On 20 May, the government's full coalition agreement, *The Coalition: our programme for government,* was published.[30] The United Kingdom thus acquired a new form of government. The country normally had a single-party government, elected on the basis of a manifesto placed before electors at the start of the election campaign. Now it had a coalition government with what amounted to a post-election manifesto, one that nobody had actually voted for. It was an era of new politics.

### The key variables

What, then, explains the outcome? As seen, there were various viable options. Earlier in the year, when it looked as if there could well be a hung parliament, civil servants had engaged in some 'war games' to see what might result from party negotiations. One scenario was that of Conservative–Liberal Democrat negotiations, but the officials came up with a very different result to that which occurred. Under their gaming, no stable government emerged.[31] There was no certainty that the UK would end up with a coalition and certainly not a Conservative–Liberal Democrat coalition.

In terms of the key variables, one often identified in the literature on coalition formation is that of *timing*. Britain is one of the countries with a very short duration for government formation and, as seen, the parties were operating within a tight (though not certain) time constraint.[32] If necessary, the Queen's Speech could have been delayed, but the economic situation, reinforced by media coverage, was creating a timeline of its own. The Bank of England and the Treasury were fearful of the state of the markets if a new government had not been formed over the weekend. In the first meeting between Conservative and Liberal Democrat negotiators, the politicians were told by the cabinet secretary of the situation. Sir Gus O'Donnell later said that if things had gone wrong, 'the markets would really have made us pay a price on the Monday morning by selling our debt and that would have been a real problem for the country.'[33] In all likelihood, though the negotiators would not have known, the public too desired a speedy resolution. [34]

The other key variables that came into play in these negotiations were those of the three p's – *policy, politics,* and *personality*. These can be examined in relation to two key dimensions: whether to agree a deal, and with whom to agree a deal. There is also one other variable that needs to be considered, that of *opportunism*, which arises when one party to negotiations uses uncertainty to benefit its own position at the expense of another party.[35] As Lieven De Winter and Patrick Dumont record, bargaining may be affected by incomplete information: 'Even if government formation can be fruitfully understood as a relatively high-stakes game played by a small number of well-informed and experienced party leaders... these negotiators usually do not possess complete information'.[36] For the two major parties in May 2010, the incomplete information was principally a lack of knowledge of what was being offered by the other.

*Policy*. Some theorists see coalition formation as a means primarily or even exclusively of influencing public policy.[37] However, there are problems with this view in explaining the outcome in 2010. The Liberal Democrats did not have to enter into a coalition and take posts in the government in order to influence public policy. They held the balance of power in the House of Commons. They could influence policy outcomes as an opposition party, as indeed they had previously done in the House of Lords.[38] There were, however, political considerations that weighed heavily in reaching the decision they did. Insofar as a coalition was driven by policy considerations, then the more obvious deal was to be done with Labour. As Thomas Quinn and Ben Clements show in Chapter 3 (see Figure 3.2), over 70 per cent of Liberal Democrats classed themselves as being on the left. And, as John Bartle, Sebastian Dellepiane and Jim Stimson's discussion of policy positions in Chapter 6 demonstrates (see Figure 6.1), Labour and the Liberal Democrats were (as they have been for some years) closer to one another than were the Conservatives and the Liberal Democrats. The policy stances thus favoured a 'progressive coalition' of Labour and the Liberal Democrats. Such a coalition, as seen, was the preferred option of most Liberal Democrat MPs. It was also favoured by some of Gordon Brown's key advisers, such as Lords Adonis and Mandelson.

Nor did the Conservatives have to be part of a coalition. Given the policy space between them and the Liberal Democrats, a minority administration offered the prospect of pursuing a Conservative programme, albeit one that may need to be modified in the light of anticipated parliamentary reaction, but a Conservative programme nonetheless. It was also one that could be proceeded with relatively quickly. The civil service had in place proposals for acting on the Conservative manifesto. Meetings between senior civil servants and members of the shadow cabinet are now usually authorised to take place before a general election and such talks had been taking place for over a year by the time the election was called. Drawing on those meetings, the outcomes of policy groups, party pronouncements and the manifesto, the civil service had briefings ready for implementing the proposals of an incoming Conservative government.[39]

Viewed, then, from the perspective of influencing public policy, it was not axiomatic that the Liberal Democrats would agree to join a coalition and, if they did, the most logical partner, in terms of proximity on the policy spectrum, was Labour. Other variables need to be factored in to explain why they decided to become part of a coalition and why their partner was the Conservative party, and why the Conservatives – or at least the leadership – was a party to this arrangement.

*Politics*. There were particular political factors that pushed the Liberal Democrats towards forming a coalition and forming it with the Conservatives. Coalition theorists have posited that the thirst for office is sufficient to explain coalition formation.[40] The last time Liberals had held office in peacetime was 1922. Most members realised they were unlikely to win office on their own and would therefore need to join with another party. The prospect of office was a powerful attraction. Paddy Ashdown had pursued with Tony Blair the possibility of an alliance. Ashdown was the keen suitor. He told his parliamentary party in January 1998: 'I see very little chance of a coalition. But I do want you all to know that I am trailing my skirt like mad. I am tempting Blair to make an offer.'[41] The Liberal Democrats had been enthusiastic participants in the joint cabinet committee formed in 1997 to discuss constitutional reform. Meeting in the Cabinet Room was reputedly a particular attraction. Some members in 2010 undoubtedly wished to retain the party's ideological purity, but the potential to influence public policy from within government proved too great. The lure of office was also a powerful one for those MPs who were career politicians, people for whom 'politics is the sole focus and outside standing is largely irrelevant'.[42] Though some career politicians are content solely with being parliamentarians, others wish to be ministers and hence be in a position to be decision takers. There was now an unprecedented opportunity to be on the inside of government. As seen, the ideological inclination was to favour a coalition with Labour, but the parliamentary arithmetic – and the perception of Labour as being a losing party – precipitated a deal with the Conservatives.

If ambition and thirst for office pulled the Liberal Democrats into a formal coalition, there was also external pressure pushing the party into government. For a start, the state of the public finances made it difficult for the party to avoid the responsibility of government. With large numbers of voices calling for a stable government to deal with the deficit, and with the Liberal Democrats the obvious key to forming such a government, the party would have been seen as shirking its responsibilities if it had not entered into government. Such a decision would also have called into question the party's ability to deal with the consequences of its own preferred voting system, the single transferable vote, which would almost inevitably produce permanent hung parliaments. If the Liberal Democrats could not form a coalition now, how would they cope in a world where coalition government was the norm?

For the Conservatives, the length of time in opposition and the economic situation were also important considerations in explaining their willingness to enter into coalition. Conservatives are not used to being in opposition.[43] After thirteen years out of government, they had regained the thirst for power. One new Tory MP was struck by the fact that, whereas the newly-elected MPs were not desperate for the party to be in office, the desire to be in government, almost at any price, was a marked feature of returning MPs.[44]

A coalition offered the prospect of office *and* the potential to deliver the party's economic programme. If they were to carry through the tough aus-terity measures they were advocating, they needed to lock in the Liberal Democrats to supporting them. Although leading Conservative MP Peter Lilley was wary of a coalition, he conceded some months later that it was difficult to believe that a minority Conservative government 'could have announced the [emergency deficit-cutting] budget that we have had without it being subject to enormous vilification'.[45] The other key element was the leader. David Cameron adhered to much of the philosophy of his predeces-sors, but he sought to distinguish the new Conservative party from the old.[46] He carved out a distinctive approach and recognised the value of an alliance as part of the new politics.

It has also been argued that creating a coalition enabled Cameron to avoid a Tory government 'held hostage by its own right wing'.[47] If this was a con-sideration, it was a misplaced one. James Callaghan's Labour government (1976–79) faced consistent and substantial opposition from the party's left wing, but the left rarely threatened the government's position since it was usually unwilling to vote with the Tories. The real threat came from mem-bers of different wings of the party combining to vote with the opposition.[48] Similarly, in the 2010 parliament, the Tory right was unlikely to make com-mon cause on a regular basis with Labour and the Liberal Democrats. Even so, the perception of such a threat appeared to influence the thinking of some of Cameron's principal advisers, such as Steve Hilton.[49]

For Labour it was a case of the lure of remaining in office versus the purity and integrity of the Labour party. Though the policy distance between the Labour and Liberal Democrats may have been narrower than that between the Conservatives and the Liberal Democrats, the tribalism of some Labour MPs – and party heavyweights such as John Reid – meant that there was considerable animosity toward any deal. Some Labour MPs also recognised that the party was seen as a loser and that there would be a negative electoral reaction to what might be quickly labelled 'a government of the losers'. Their public declarations effectively undermined the talks between the two parties.

*Personality*. Personality is important, as it has been in previous periods of coalition.[50] Individuals have made a difference. In 2010, there were two elements that were crucial: personal chemistry and individual beliefs. In terms of personal relations, the position of the leaders was the reverse of the parties' policy positions. Nick Clegg and David Cameron, even though they did not know one another particularly well, had an amicable relationship. They had had a chance 45-minute meeting at the opening of the new Supreme Court in October 2009 and had got on well.[51] They shared similar backgrounds and were comfortable in one another's company. There was also the policy dimension. The gap between them in terms of their political beliefs was narrower than it was between their two parties. It was a case of '*Orange Book* Liberal' meets the self-declared 'heir to Blair'. Had the Liberal Democrats been led by one of Clegg's three predecessors, and the Tories by David Davis (Cameron's more right-wing opponent in the party's 2005 leadership contest), the outcome might have been notably different.

The outcome might also have been different had Tony Blair still been in office or had he been succeeded by someone other than Gordon Brown. The relationship between Nick Clegg and Gordon Brown was poor. This was apparent in their exchanges at prime minister's question time. When the election results were known, Brown preferred to deal with other senior Liberal Democrats. Clegg signalled that in his contacts with Brown he found him 'lecturing, uncongenial, bullying'.[52] Brown 'ignored the advice of [Vince] Cable and all his Lib Dem friends to find a way to get on with Clegg', recorded BBC political editor Nick Robinson. 'When I put it to Peter Mandelson that Clegg found Brown impossible, the Prince of Darkness replied with a wry grin that "No ... he found him Gordon-ish".'[53] Whatever the case, there was clearly little love lost between them.

The relationships between the leaders also appeared to be replicated in the relationships between the negotiating teams. The Conservative and Liberal Democrat teams appeared to get on well personally, assisted by the fact that the Tories' Ed Llewellyn had previously worked with Paddy Ashdown, while Danny Alexander was seen as non-tribal. By contrast, some of the Labour team were seen as notably tribal and never achieved a rapport with the Liberal Democrats. Facilitating progress was also the attitude taken to the negotiations, with the Conservatives following the leader in being open to compromise.

Political considerations were fundamental to the successful negotiation of a coalition. The economic situation was a necessary condition for creating a coalition in place of a minority government. However, it is not clear that it was sufficient. As noted already, gaming by civil servants, in circumstances where the economic imperatives were known, failed to produce agreement between the parties. The actors in the negotiations, especially the party leaders, were crucial to delivering a successful outcome, both in terms of a coalition as such and its party composition.

*Opportunism*. Having recognised that they could engage in a twin-track approach, the Liberal Democrats used the negotiations to extract as many policy concessions as they could. Their manifesto had committed them to four key priorities: 'fair, clean and local politics', 'fair taxes', 'a fair, green economy with jobs that last' and 'a fair start for every child'. The Tories would have to move towards them. To exert leverage, Nick Clegg left open the possibility of continuing talks with Labour even when it appeared clear that a Conservative-Liberal Democrat agreement was virtually sealed. Moreover, the Liberal Democrats are claimed to have persuaded the Conservatives to agree to a referendum on the alternative vote by leading the Conservatives to believe that Labour had offered them the introduction of this voting system *without* a referendum. David Cameron told his MPs, he believed on good evidence, that Labour had made such an offer. Nick Clegg said that no such offer was ever formally made. 'He said that MPs' perceptions was that such an offer might be on the table'.[54] The Liberal Democrats played their hand effectively in order to maximise policy outcomes closest to their position.

The referendum was their principal but by no means only achievement. According to one commentator's calculations, of the 397 pledges in the coalition agreement, 164 derived from the Liberal Democrat manifesto or both parties' manifestos.[55] At the same time, the jobs the party secured in government accorded, more or less, with its four manifesto priorities. Nick Clegg, as deputy prime minister, took overall responsibility for political reform. David Laws, briefly, then Danny Alexander became chief secretary to the Treasury, from where he could influence the fairness of taxes. Chris Huhne became secretary of state for energy and climate change. And Sarah Teather, though not in the cabinet, became the new minister for children and families.

It must be stressed, however, that the Conservatives were able to protect their own 'red lines', in particular maintaining a strong national defence, imposing limits on immigration and refusing to extend further powers to the European Union. Above all, the negotiation team were able to extract from the Liberal Democrats a commitment to reducing the deficit almost immediately. Indeed, the coalition agreement contained a clause that potentially trumped all others: 'The deficit reduction programme takes precedence over any of the other measures in this agreement, and the speed of implementation of any measures that have a cost to the public finances will depend on decisions to be made in the Comprehensive Spending Review.'[56]

## In government

The events surrounding and leading up to the formation of the new coalition were in combination unprecedented. They also contributed to and took place in the context of a distinctive parliamentary environment. Some Liberal

Democrat peers had been involved in negotiating the Lib–Lab Pact in 1977 and some had served in government when in other parties, but the party as such had no experience of office. Some Conservative MPs had experience of government but none of coalition. Most Labour MPs – 189 out of 258 – had no experience of being in opposition. Also, more than one third of the MPs elected in 2010 – 227 out of 650 – were new. They were an unknown quantity. The creation of the coalition would also affect the promotion prospects for Conservative MPs. There were former Conservative front-benchers who were not brought into government and some back-benchers who thought they might have been. The seeds of potential discontent were sewn from the start.

The House of Commons was also experiencing change. The implementation of the recommendations of the select committee on reform of the House of Commons (the Wright Committee) at the opening of the parliament meant that MPs for the first time elected chairs of select committees and the parliamentary parties each agreed rules under which their members elected the party members on the committees.[57] These changes gave select committees a new visibility and potentially an enhanced independence of the party leaderships. There was also a new backbench business committee, set up to determine business on the thirty-five days allocated for backbench business. Though the committee could not interfere with government business, it could always schedule business that the government may not have wished to be considered. The first substantive motion brought forward by the committee was one that enabled MPs, for the first time, to vote on the war with Afghanistan.

There were also some changes at the party level. Of particular note, David Cameron tried to ensure that ministers could attend meetings of the 1922 Committee (the body that represents backbench Conservative MPs when the party is in government) as voting members and not simply observers.[58] This initiative caused notable tensions within the parliamentary party. The prime minister eventually backed down and agreed that ministers could simply attend. Cameron's move was interpreted as an attempt to prevent right-winger Graham Brady – a former frontbencher who had fallen out with the leadership over education policy – being elected as chairman. Brady was duly elected, the manner of his success giving him a degree of leverage within the party.

Together these changes created a new and uncertain situation. The post-election coalition agreement also meant a relatively light legislative load at the start of the session. What measures were introduced created some tension. Abstentions by some Liberal Democrat peers contributed to the government being defeated in the Lords on an amendment to the Academies Bill, a law designed to give state schools greater freedom and autonomy within the education system. In the House of Commons, some Conservative MPs were opposed to the provisions of the bills providing for a referendum on the alternative vote and to fixed-term parliaments, forcing the Fixed-term Parliaments Bill to a vote on second reading.[59] Some commentators saw such dissension as indicating that the coalition would not last. Nick Clegg authorised the appointment of backbench party committees, with the chairs 'to speak up for the party's interests', leading to similar observations.[60] However, backbench dissent was a feature of previous parliaments – reaching unprecedented levels under the preceding Labour governments, as Nicholas Allen notes in Chapter 1 – and the development of a party infrastructure can help absorb backbench disquiet.[61] Meanwhile, the advent of the coalition was expected to have a different effect in the Lords. There the Blair and Brown governments had been defeated on many occasions because the government lacked a majority and could be outvoted by a combination of the Conservatives and Liberal Democrats. In the new coalition, the combination of Conservatives and Liberal Democrats outnumbered Labour's ranks, but the presence of a large body of independent members (known as crossbenchers) meant that the coalition lacked an overall majority. However, it was anticipated that the government would be in a strong position to avoid frequent defeats, given that crossbench peers were less assiduous in voting than those taking a party whip. The defeat on the Academies Bill was expected to be very much the exception, to the detriment of the House in exerting influence on government.

The leader of the House of Commons, Sir George Young, further complicated matters by announcing in September that in future the parliamentary sessions would begin in May rather than November, and that therefore the first session of the new parliament would run until May 2012 rather than November 2011. MPs were thus in for a long haul but with little idea of what this would entail.

## The opposition

If the Conservatives and Liberal Democrats had to learn to govern together as a coalition, Labour had to re-learn the ropes of opposition after thirteen years in power. There were two elements to this, one tactical and the other ideological. In parliament, it needed to determine the extent to which it was prepared to oppose coalition measures. Though an opposition sometimes supports a measure in principle, it nonetheless finds reasons to oppose it on practical grounds. For Labour, the potential to oppose measures that constitute compromises between the coalition partners (and were not contained in either partner's manifesto) may prove especially tempting. More generally, the party also had to determine where it stands on the ideological spectrum. Was it to be a continuation of New Labour or to be a distinct successor to it?

The answers to these questions were largely dependent on the choice of the new party leader. Gordon Brown's resignation as Labour leader, which preceded his resignation as prime minister by a day, triggered a four-month leadership contest. Five candidates secured sufficient nominations from Labour MPs to stand. Four had cabinet experience: Ed Miliband, a former environment secretary and adviser to Gordon Brown; David Miliband, Ed's elder brother and, as a former foreign secretary, the most senior of the contestants; Ed Balls, a former education secretary and, like Ed Miliband, a former adviser to Brown; and Andy Burnham, a former health secretary. The fifth candidate was a long-serving left-wing backbencher, Diane Abbott, the first black woman to be elected to the House of Commons and someone who enjoyed a high media profile. She had managed to get enough nominations to be a candidate, thanks to some Labour MPs who were prepared to nominate her even though they did not intend to vote for her. They wanted to ensure the choice available to the party was not confined to white male ex-ministers. In the event, the election was a two-horse race between the Miliband brothers. For much of the contest, David was considered the favourite, though his association with New Labour and Tony Blair was thought to count against him. Ed was perceived to be more left-wing and courted the trade union vote.

Voting for the leader took place through Labour's electoral-college system. Under the rules, the party was effectively divided into three equal sections: Labour MPs and Members of the European Parliament; individual members of the party who paid an individual membership fee; and members of trade unions and other organisations formally affiliated to the Labour party.[62] Members in each section could cast one vote in an alternative-vote system: the ballot enabled people to rank the candidates in their preferred order. Votes would then be aggregated by section, and each section would count towards one-third of the final result. The outcome was announced at the party's annual conference in late September. After successive rounds of counting preferences, with Abbott, Burnham and Balls eliminated, David won the most votes in the MP and membership sections, and Ed won the most votes in the affiliate section. Crucially, however, Ed won marginally more votes overall, 50.65 per cent to David's 49.35 per cent. Speaking to his party two days later, the new leader made an immediate rhetorical break with Tony Blair and Gordon Brown by promising to lead the 'new generation now leading Labour'. The defeated brother, David, chose to quit front-line politics.

To a large extent, of course, Labour's immediate political fortunes will be determined by events beyond its control, not least the state of the economy and the success or otherwise – and the popularity or otherwise – of the coalition's austerity measures. The challenge for Labour is to develop a coherent critique of the government's policies and advance a credible alternative. In addition to challenging the coalition, Labour must also confront the inter-related questions of why it lost the election and what it stands for now. Tony Blair's creation of New Labour was at least in part about creating a programme and electoral strategy for a centre-left party that was relevant to the post-Thatcher pro-market world. For Labour, the challenge is resolving the tension between finding the centre ground of British politics, deemed crucial for electoral success, and defining itself ideologically under a leader who is keen to signal a break from the Blair and Brown era and create a divide between the party and a coalition that is very much in or near to that centre ground.

## Coalition durability

The coalition was created in an uncertain environment. No sooner had it been created than speculation began as to its capacity to stay together for the duration of the parliament. Amidst the uncertainty, it is possible to identify conditions conducive to the coalition staying in office as well as those that could rent it asunder.

Research shows that minimal winning coalitions can endure, more so than other types of coalition and, as already mentioned, are second only to single-party majority governments in their durability. Research on coalitions also suggests that those where portfolio allocation is in proportion to party strength in the legislature tend to be more stable than those where there is an imbalance in such allocation. In the coalition government, there is (quantitatively) a minor imbalance in favour of the Liberal Democrats, whose ministerial posts also addressed their four manifesto priorities, though this imbalance is arguably balanced by the fact that (qualitatively) none of the five in cabinet was appointed to head a major department of state or a key economic ministry.[63] There is also the assumption in coalition studies that policy diversity affects stability, the inclusion of a centrist party acting as a stabilising force.[64]

Durability should not be confused with harmony. Comparative studies show that coalitions can absorb inter-party tensions.[65] After the May election, the parties moved quickly to agree a framework for consultation and dispute resolution. A *Coalition Agreement for Stability and Reform* was published on 21 May detailing the arrangements for sharing information and consultation. A cabinet committee was established, co-chaired by the prime minister and deputy prime minister, to discuss and resolve issues. Any unresolved issues could be referred to it by the chair or deputy chair of any cabinet committee, though day-to-day difficulties would be the responsibility of a four-member Coalition Operation and Strategic Planning Group. Though somewhat alien to the British conception of opposition, in which Her Majesty's Opposition is charged with challenging Her Majesty's Government, it is not unknown for coalitions to encounter internal opposition from one of its constituent partners: it is another type of opposition that a government may face.[66]

The Labour party's immediate attacks against the coalition, and particularly against the Liberal Democrats, constituted an incentive for the coalition partners to stick together. The early post-election opinion polls also suggested that there was nowhere else for the Liberal Democrats to go. The coalition was popular, but the Liberal Democrat party was not.[67] If the party broke away from the coalition, it risked the prospect of an early election and the loss of a large number of seats. If it stayed with the coalition, it risked losing its identify. It also risked sharing blame for painful economic measures but not necessarily getting the credit if they proved successful.[68] Previous periods of coalition with the Conservatives were not encouraging, with parts of the Liberal Party falling away and becoming absorbed within the Conservatives' ranks. For the party, it was in many respects between a rock and a hard place.

What are the conditions that could bring the coalition to an end? Experience suggests that it could be derailed by critical events that precipitate splits between the parties, intra-party conflict or parliamentary defeats.[69] As seen, tensions within the coalition partners' parliamentary ranks were soon realised. However, such tensions are not unusual, either in coalitions or in single-party governments. The biggest threat is from policy splits between the two parties rather than parliamentary defeat. As Akash Paun notes, 'When policy conflict does bring down a coalition, finance (including tax policy) and economic policy are by far the most common triggers.'[70]

Recognition of this fault line also underpins calls made by some Tory MPs for an electoral pact with the Liberal Democrats. The coalition is a parliamentary or executive coalition, not an electoral coalition. Conservative MP Nick Boles argued in September 2010 for an electoral pact, with both parties to the coalition fighting the 2015 election as partners.[71] He was echoing similar calls made earlier by another Tory MP Mark Field.[72] Such a pact, Boles argued, was necessary to deliver 'a radical programme for a two-term Liberal Democrat–Conservative coalition government'.[73] That programme would encompasse major economic and political reforms designed to push power down to the people.

There were historical precedents for such an arrangement, but the proposal was disavowed by new 1922 Committee chairman, Graham Brady, as well as by Nick Clegg and his new deputy leader, Simon Hughes.[74] It was not clear that the Liberal Democrats would benefit from such an arrangement. They would be locked into the coalition but with little prospect of significantly enhancing their parliamentary strength or their distinct identity. However, without such a pact both parties were committed to a parliamentary marriage and an electoral separation. It is not a recipe for stability, but, on the basis of comparative experience, nor is it necessarily a recipe for coalition collapse either. The coalition could last five years, but whether it does so, and in what shape, is uncertain. Comparative analysis suggests it could. British history is less helpful.

# Endnotes

1   A minimal winning coalition technically describes any coalition involving two or more parties that would change from a majority coalition to a minority coalition on the defection of any of its constituent parties. For the classic account of coalition theory, see William H. Riker, *The Theory of Political Coalitions* (New Haven, CT: Yale University Press, 1962).

2   See Philip Ziegler, *Edward Heath: The Authorised Biography* (London: HarperPress, 2010), pp. 436–42.

3   Alistair Michie and Simon Hoggart, *The Pact* (London: Quartet, 1978); Catherine Haddon, 'A brief history of the Lib–Lab Pact, 1977–78', in Robert Hazell and Akash Paun, eds, *Making Minority Government Work: Hung Parliaments and the Challenges for Westminster and Whitehall* (London: Institute for Government, 2009), pp. 20–24.

4   Philip Norton, 'David Cameron and Tory success: architect or by-stander?', in Simon Lee and Matt Beech, eds, *The Conservatives Under David Cameron: Built to Last?* (Basingstoke, Hants: Palgrave Macmillan, 2009), pp. 31–43. See also Tim Bale, *The Conservative Party from Thatcher to Cameron* (Cambridge: Polity, 2010), chaps. 7–8.

5   Nick Clegg, 'The Liberal Democrats are not for sale', *The Times*, 5 January 2010.

6   Mark Oaten, *Coalition: The Politics and Personalities of Coalition Government from 1850* (Petersfield, Hants.: Harriman House, 2007), p. 299.

7   Tom Newton Dunn, 'Squatter 59, holed up in No. 10', *The Sun*, 8 May 2010.

8   Chris Mullin, *Decline & Fall: Diaries 2005–2010* (London: Profile Books, 2010), p. 370.

9   Roland Watson, 'An ordinary beginning to an extraordinary campaign', *The Times Guide to the House of Commons 2010* (London: Times Books, 2010), p. 18.

10  Lady Hermon had sat previously as an Ulster Unionist, but was known to dislike the Conservative party and left the Ulster Unionists when it entered into electoral alliance with the Conservatives.

11  The Labour Government of 1974–79 was able to act on a majority of its manifesto pledges. See Richard Rose, *Do Parties Make a Difference?*, 2nd edn (London: Macmillan Press, 1984), p. 65.

12  Michael Laver and Norman Schofield, *Multiparty Government: The Politics of Coalition in Europe* (Ann Arbor: University of Michigan Press, 1998), p. 151.

13  Laver and Schofield, *Multiparty Government*, pp. 150–55.

14  See, for example, Thomas Saalfeld, 'Institutions, Chance, and Choices: The Dynamics of Cabinet Survival', in Kaare Strøm, Wolfgang C. Müller and Torbjörn Bergman, eds, *Cabinets and Coalition Bargaining: The Democratic Life Cycle in Western Europe* (Oxford: Oxford University Press, 2008), Table 10.4 and p. 346.

15  Nick Robinson, 'How the coalition government was formed', *Daily Telegraph,* 29 July 2010.

16  Peter Mandelson, *The Third Man: Life at the Heart of New Labour* (London: HarperPress, 2010), p. 543.

17  Anne McElvoy, 'The box that changed Britain', *Sunday Times Magazine,* 13 June 2010. At the time, Brady was not chairman of the 1922 Committee.

18  Isabel Oakeshott, Marie Woolf and Jonathan Oliver, 'Against the wall', *The Sunday Times, News Review,* 16 May 2010.

19  Robinson, 'How the coalition government was formed'.

20  Former permanent secretary to author, 26 July 2010.

21  The full transcript of Cameron's offer is available at http://www.conservatives.com/News/Speeches/2010/05/David_Cameron_National_interest_first.aspx. Last accessed 29 September 2010.

22  Oakeshott et al., 'Against the wall', p. 2.

23  See Mandelson, *The Third Man,* pp. 548–9.

24  Anthony Seldon, 'How Brown and Clegg let it slip', *Independent*, 29 July 2010.

25  Mandelson, *The Third Man,* pp. 548–9.

26  Oakeshott et al., 'Against the wall', p. 3.

27  'Hung parliament: Tories' "final offer" on vote reform', *BBC News website*, 10 May 2010, available at http://news.bbc.co.uk/1/hi/uk_politics/election_2010/8673807.stm (last accessed 29 September 2010).

28  Rosa Prince, 'Cabinet split that doomed talks from the start', *Daily Telegraph,* 12 May 2010.

29  Mandelson, *The Third Man,* p. 552.

30  HM Government, *The Coalition: our programme for government* (London: Cabinet Office, 2010).

31  Nick Robinson, 'Sir Humphrey praises politicians shock', *Nick Robinson's Newslog,* 14 July 2010. Available at http://www.bbc.co.uk/blogs/nickrobinson/ (last accessed 29 September 2010).

32  Lieven De Winter and Patrick Dumont, 'Uncertainty and complexity in Cabinet Formation', in Strøm et al., eds, *Cabinets and Coalition Bargaining*, pp. 123–57, at pp. 148–53.

33  Robinson, 'How the coalition government was formed'.

34  A focus group response suggested that the desire for a speedy resolution was not confined to politicians and the markets. See Deborah Mattinson, *Talking to a Brick Wall: How New Labour Stopped Listening to the Voter and Why We Need a New Politics* (London: Biteback, 2010), p. 304.

35  Arthur Lupia and Kaare Strøm, 'Bargaining, transaction costs, and coalition governance', in Strøm et al., eds, *Cabinets and Coalition Bargaining*, pp. 51–83, at p. 69.

36  De Winter and Dumont, 'Uncertainty and Complexity in Cabinet Formation', p. 134.

37  See the comments of Laver and Schofield, *Multiparty Government*, p. 38; and Wolfgang C. Müller, Torbjorn Bergman and Kaare Strøm, 'Coalition Theory and Cabinet Governance: An Introduction', in Strøm et al., eds, *Cabinets and Coalition Bargaining*, pp. 1–50, at p. 22.

38  Meg Russell and Maria Scalia, 'Why does the government get defeated in the House of Lords?', *British Politics*, 2 (2007), 299–322.

39  See Peter Riddell and Catherine Haddon, *Transitions: Preparing for Changes of Government* (London: Institute for Government, 2009).

40  Luca Verzichelli, 'Portfolio allocation', in Strøm et al., eds, *Cabinets and Coalition Bargaining*, pp. 237–67, at p. 237.

41  Paddy Ashdown, *The Ashdown Diaries, Volume Two 1997–1999* (London: Penguin Books, 2002), p. 152.

42  Peter Riddell, *Honest Opportunism: The Rise of the Career Politician* (London: Hamish Hamilton, 1993), p. 2.

43  See Stuart Ball and Anthony Seldon, eds, *Conservative Century* (Oxford: Oxford University Press, 1994).

44　Conservative MP to author, 21 September 2010.

45　Laura Kuenssberg, 'The first 10 days – in a parallel universe', *BBC News website,* 18 August 2010, available at http://www.bbc.co.uk/news/uk-politics-11009623 (last accessed 29 September 2010).

46　On Cameron's philosophy, see, for example, Simon Lee, 'David Cameron and the renewal of policy', in Lee and Beech, eds, *The Conservatives under David Cameron,* pp. 44–59, and Stephen Evans, '"Mother's Boy: David Cameron and Margaret Thatcher', *The British Journal of Politics and International Relations,* 12 (2010), 325–43. On Cameron's attempts to break with the past, see Norton, 'David Cameron and Tory success: architect or by-stander?', and Matt Beech, 'Cameron and Conservative ideology', in Lee and Beech, eds, *The Conservatives under David Cameron,* pp. 18–30.

47　McElvoy, 'The box that changed Britain'.

48　Philip Norton, 'Parliament', in Anthony Seldon and Kevin Hickson, eds, *New Labour, Old Labour* (London: Routledge, 2004), pp. 93–122.

49　McElvoy, 'The box that changed Britain'.

50　Stuart Ball, David Dutton and Martin Pugh, History of Parliament/House of Commons Library Seminar on Past Coalitions in Britain, Portcullis House, Palace of Westminster, 21 June 2010.

51　Hélène Mulholland and Patrick Wintour, 'Nick Clegg: I changed my mind on spending cuts before general election', *Guardian,* 29 July 2010.

52　Mandelson, *The Third Man,* p. 550.

53　Nick Robinson, 'A leap in the dark', *Nick Robinson's Newslog,* 28 July 2010. Available at http://www.bbc.co.uk/blogs/nickrobinson/ (last accessed 29 September 2010).

54　'Labour's Ed Miliband says coalition "built on untruths"', *BBC News website*, 30 July 2010, available at http://www.bbc.co.uk/news/uk-politics-10814972 (last accessed 29 September 2010).

55　Martin Ivens, 'What have the Romans ever done for us, Nick?', *Sunday Times*, 19 September 2010.

56　HM Government, *The Coalition,* p. 35.

57　House of Commons Reform Committee, *Rebuilding the House, First Report of Session 2008–09*, HC 1117 (London: TSO, 2009); and *Rebuilding the House: Implementation, First Report of Session 2009–10*, HC 372 (London: TSO, 2010).

58　The committee comprises formally Conservative private Members, which means backbench MPs when the party is in office and all Conservative MPs except the leader when in opposition. See Philip Norton, 'The Parliamentary Party and Party Committees', in Seldon and Ball, eds, *Conservative Century*, pp. 105–13.

59　The second reading was carried by 311 votes to 23. See *House of Commons Debates*, Vol. 515, Part 44, 13 September 2010, columns 704–6.

60　Sam Coates and Frances Elliott, 'Lib Dem moves to give MPs policy roles could be start of public split, Tories fear', *The Times,* 17 June 2010.

61　See Philip Cowley, *The Rebels* (London: Politico's 2005), Philip Cowley and Mark Stuart, *A Data Handbook* and *Browned off? Dissension amongst the Parliamentary Labour Party, 2007–2008,* and *Dissension Amongst the Parliamentary Labour Party, 2008–2009*, available at http://www.revolts.co.uk. (last accessed 29 September 2010).

62  Thomas Quinn, 'Leasehold or freehold? Leader-eviction rules in the British Conservative and Labour Parties', *Political Studies*, 53 (2005), 793–815.

63  Robert Hazell, *The Conservative–Liberal Democrat Agenda for Constitutional and Political Reform* (London: The Constitution Unit, 2010), p. 7. See also Verzichelli, 'Portfolio allocation', pp. 237–67.

64  Müller et al., 'Coalition theory and Cabinet governance', p. 22.

65  Rudy B. Andeweg and Arco Timmermans, 'Conflict management in coalition government', in Strøm et al., eds, *Cabinets and Coalition Bargaining*, pp. 269–300.

66  Philip Norton, 'Making sense of opposition', *The Journal of Legislative Studies*, 14 (2008), 236–50.

67  See Sam Coates, 'Too soon, too deep, says voters as coalition faces backlash on cuts', *The Times,* 14 September 2010.

68  Andrew Hough, 'Four in 10 Lib Dem voters "feel cheated by coalition", new poll claims', *Daily Telegraph,* 27 July 2010.

69  Müller et al., 'Coalition theory and Cabinet governance', pp. 28–9. See also Erik Damgaard, 'Cabinet Termination', in Strøm et al., eds, *Cabinets and Coalition Bargaining*, pp. 301–26.

70  Akash Paun, '*United We Stand? Coalition Government in the UK* (London: Institute for Government, 2010), p. 18.

71  Nick Boles, *Which Way's Up? The Future for Coalition Britain and How to Get There* (London: Biteback, 2010).

72  Jonathan Freedland, '100 days of the coalition government', *Guardian,* G2, 18 August 2010.

73  Boles, *Which Way's Up?,* p. xv.

74  Simon Hughes was elected deputy leader by Liberal Democrat MPs in June 2010. He replaced Vince Cable, who stepped down from the post to concentrate on his new role as business secretary in the coalition government.

# APPENDIX: GENERAL ELECTIONS SINCE 1945

Appendix  *Results of British General Elections, 1945–2010*

| Year | Turnout | Percentage of popular vote | | | | | | Seats in House of Commons | | | | | |
|---|---|---|---|---|---|---|---|---|---|---|---|---|---|
| | | Con | Lab | Lib | Nats | Other | Swing | Con | Lab | Lib | Nats | Others | Government majority |
| 1945 | 72.8 | 39.7 | 47.7 | 9.0 | 0.2 | 3.4 | -12.2 | 210 | 393 | 12 | 0 | 25 | 147 |
| 1950 | 83.9 | 43.3 | 46.1 | 9.1 | 0.1 | 1.4 | 2.6 | 297 | 315 | 9 | 0 | 4 | 6 |
| 1951 | 82.6 | 48.0 | 48.8 | 2.6 | 0.1 | 0.6 | 1.0 | 321 | 295 | 6 | 0 | 3 | 16 |
| 1955 | 76.8 | 49.6 | 46.4 | 2.7 | 0.2 | 1.1 | 2.0 | 344 | 277 | 6 | 0 | 3 | 59 |
| 1959 | 78.7 | 49.4 | 43.8 | 5.9 | 0.4 | 0.6 | 1.2 | 365 | 258 | 6 | 0 | 1 | 99 |
| 1964 | 77.1 | 43.3 | 44.1 | 11.2 | 0.5 | 0.9 | -3.2 | 303 | 317 | 9 | 0 | 1 | 5 |
| 1966 | 75.8 | 41.9 | 47.9 | 8.5 | 0.7 | 1.0 | -2.6 | 253 | 363 | 12 | 0 | 2 | 97 |
| 1970 | 72.0 | 46.4 | 43.0 | 7.5 | 1.7 | 1.5 | 4.7 | 330 | 287 | 6 | 1 | 6 | 31 |
| 1974 Feb | 78.8 | 37.8 | 37.2 | 19.3 | 2.6 | 3.2 | -1.4 | 297 | 301 | 14 | 9 | 14 | None |
| 1974 Oct | 72.8 | 35.7 | 39.3 | 18.3 | 3.4 | 3.3 | -2.1 | 276 | 319 | 13 | 14 | 13 | 4 |
| 1979 | 76.0 | 43.9 | 36.9 | 13.8 | 2.0 | 3.4 | 5.3 | 339 | 268 | 11 | 4 | 13 | 44 |
| 1983 | 72.7 | 42.4 | 27.6 | 25.4 | 1.5 | 3.1 | 3.9 | 397 | 209 | 23 | 4 | 17 | 144 |
| 1987 | 75.3 | 42.2 | 30.8 | 22.6 | 1.7 | 2.7 | -1.7 | 375 | 229 | 22 | 6 | 18 | 101 |
| 1992 | 77.7 | 41.9 | 34.4 | 17.8 | 2.3 | 3.5 | -2.0 | 336 | 271 | 20 | 7 | 17 | 21 |
| 1997 | 71.4 | 30.7 | 43.2 | 16.8 | 2.5 | 6.8 | -10.0 | 165 | 418 | 46 | 10 | 20 | 178 |
| 2001 | 59.4 | 31.7 | 40.7 | 18.3 | 2.5 | 6.9 | 1.8 | 166 | 412 | 52 | 9 | 20 | 166 |
| 2005 | 61.5 | 32.4 | 35.2 | 22.0 | 2.2 | 8.2 | 3.1 | 198 | 355 | 62 | 9 | 22 | 65 |
| 2010 | 65.1 | 36.1 | 29.0 | 23.0 | 2.2 | 9.7 | 5.0 | 306 | 258 | 57 | 9 | 20 | 77 |

*Sources:* For election results, see House of Commons Research Papers 08/12, *Election Statistics: UK 1918–2007*, and 10/36, *General Election 2010*. Both available from http://www.parliament.uk/business/publications/research/research-papers. For government majorities, see House of Commons Standard Note SN/PC/05650, *Twentieth Century Prime Ministers and their Governments*, available at http://www.parliament.uk/documents/commons/lib/research/briefings/snpc-05650.pdf. Last accessed 26 August 2010.

*Note:* Lib refers to the Liberal party (1945–79), the Social Democratic Party-Liberal Alliance (1983–87) and the Liberal Democrats (1992–2010). Nats refers to the combined voteshares and MPs of the Scottish National Party and Plaid Cymru. Swing refers to the Butler swing and compares the results of each election with the results of the previous election. It is calculated as the average of the Conservative's percentage gain and Labour's percentage loss compared to the previous election. A positive sign denotes a swing to the Conservatives, a negative sign denotes a swing to Labour. The Labour party formed a minority government after the February 1974 election. The Conservatives and the Liberal Democrats formed a coalition government after the 2010 election. The Speaker is excluded when calculating the size of the government majority.

# INDEX

comprehensive spending review
  2000, 7, 98
  2007, 9, 17
  2010, 256
'confidence and supply', 58, 246
Conservative Central Office, 217, 218, 221,
  222, 223, 235, 236, 240, 241
ConservativeHome, 40, 61
Conservative party, 37–9
  brand image of, 38–9, 44, 46, 49, 58
  economic policy, 51–2, 119
  electoral challenges, 37–9, 208–9, 212–5
  financial crisis and, 51–2, 116
  leadership elections, 39–43
  local associations, 40, 217, 219
  marginal-seats strategy, 54, 217–8,
    235, 240
  media and, 48–9, 50, 53
  MPs, 37, 42–3, 48, 250, 261
  party income, 219–20, 221, 229
  reputation for economic mismanagement,
    38, 45, 114, 165, 204
  surveys of members, 43, 51
  target seats, 54, 217, 221, 222,
    228, 235–7
  tax cuts and, 45, 53, 156
constituencies, 134, 206, 208
  boundaries, 215
  variations in size, 213–4
constructive opposition, 67
Cook-Mclennan agreement, 67
Cook, Robin, 27, 67
Corfu, 142
Cornwall, 66, 209
corporation tax, 152
'cost of ruling', 34, 169
Coulson, Andy, 44, 54
Cowley, Philip, 29, 248
'creative industries', 104
'credit crunch', 14, 89, 142, 203
  See also financial crisis
Crewe, Ivor, 163, 202
Crewe and Nantwich, 26, 27, 51
crime, 16, 18–19
Cripps, Sir Stafford, 7, 33, 94
Crosland, Tony, 93
Curtice, John, 163, 173
Cruddas, Jon, 8

Dacre, Paul, 53
Dagenham and Rainham, 135
Daily Mail, 6, 18, 48, 53

Daily Politics, 181, 182
Daily Telegraph, 24, 48, 127, 130, 164,
  192, 204
Daly, Janet, 48
Dannatt, Sir Richard, 21
Darling, Alistair, 13, 14, 109, 114, 152,
  182, 199
Darzi, Sir Ara, 8
data disks, loss of, 10, 133
Davey, Ed, 69, 75, 88
Davies, Dai, 135
Davies, Mervyn, 110
Davies, Quentin, 8
Davis, David, 27, 40, 41–2, 43, 184
debates. See prime ministerial debates
decontamination, 44–7
deficit, 14, 17, 52, 54, 55–6, 58, 78, 79,
  91, 104, 115, 116, 134, 148–9, 151,
  152, 156–8, 160, 171, 187, 188, 193,
  195, 198
  reduction of, 116, 249, 253, 254, 256
Dellepiane Avellaneda, Sebastian, 252
de Menezes, Jean Charles, 19
democracy in Britain, 126, 130, 143
  satisfaction with, 124, 131–3
Democratic Unionist Party (DUP),
  246, 247
Department of Economic Affairs, 93
Deripaska, Oleg, 142
detention of terror suspects, 4
Devine, Jim, 25, 36
De Winter, Lieven, 252
diffuse support, 130
'dinner-party test', 46
double-dip recession, 112, 157, 186,
  195, 198
'double whammy', 45, 156
Downing Street, 33, 53, 63, 243, 245,
  249, 251
Downs, Anthony, 165
drugs. See illegal drugs
Dublin, 108
duck houses, 24
Duffy, Gillian, 148, 194
Dumont, Patrick, 252
Duncan Smith, Iain, 26, 37, 40, 42, 46, 149
Dunfermline West, 27
Dunn, Anita, 184
Dunwoody, Gwyneth, 27

Ealing Southall, 27, 49
economic decline, 90, 102, 104